WHAT ABOUT MURDER?
1981-1991

A Guide to Books About Mystery and Detective Fiction

by

Jon L. Breen

The Scarecrow Press, Inc.
Metuchen, N.J., & London
1993

British Library Cataloguing-in-Publication data available

Library of Congress Cataloging-in-Publication Data

Breen, Jon L., 1943-
   What about murder?. 1981-1991 : a guide to books about mystery and detective fiction / by Jon L. Breen.
      p.   cm.
   Supplement to: What about murder?. 1981.
   Includes index.
   ISBN 0-8108-2609-7 (acid-free paper)
   1. Detective and mystery stories—History and criticism—Bibliography. 2. Detective and mystery stories—Technique—Bibliography. I. Title.
Z5917.D5B73 1993
[PN3448.D4]
016.813'087209—dc20   92-34547

In memory of Howard Haycraft

TABLE OF CONTENTS

INTRODUCTION

The original *What About Murder?* (1981) was compiled in response to the increasing number of books being published about the field of crime, mystery, and detective fiction. Slightly more than a decade later, the flow of new secondary sources in the field has increased to such an extent that this supplement, primarily covering material published since 1980, is significantly larger than the parent volume, which covered the whole century to that date.

What About Murder? considered 239 entries in 157 pages, including a 19-page index. The volume in your hands has 565 entries, totals 640 pages, and includes a 115-page index. Some of the difference is attributable to the addition of a category not covered in the original volume (anthologies with reference value), a format that has slightly fewer words to a page, and conceivably an increased verbosity on the part of the compiler, but most of it is a reflection of the explosion of publications about mystery and detective fiction in the past decade.

The categories in the parent volume have been retained except for the omission of Coffee-Table Books, a somewhat amorphous and artificial category to begin with and one to which few if any of the new entries would properly belong.

The sections are as follows:

1. GENERAL HISTORIES. Works devoted to a historical overview of the mystery genre, usually concentrating on the detective story.

2. REFERENCE BOOKS. Encyclopedias, dictionaries, bibliographies, and other items that by their format and content seem likelier candidates for the reference shelves of most libraries than the circulating shelves. (Reference books on individual authors are included in Part 6.)

3. SPECIAL SUBJECTS. Works concerning particular aspects, theories, or subgroupings of the crime-mystery-detective genre.

4. COLLECTED ESSAYS AND REVIEWS. Compilations of individual pieces by single authors or various authors. Collections of interviews have also been included.

5. TECHNICAL MANUALS. Devoted to instructing the prospective writer in the genre.

6. WORKS ON INDIVIDUAL AUTHORS. Biographical, autobiographical, critical, and bibliographic works on writers primarily known for mystery and detective fiction.

7. ANTHOLOGIES. Collections of stories by various authors that, through the editorial matter included, have some reference value. (Note that many fine anthologies, e.g. the British *Winter's Crimes* series and most of the compilations attributed to Alfred Hitchcock, lack secondary matter of interest and thus are not included.)

8. NEW EDITIONS AND SUPPLEMENTS. Volumes following up on works included in the parent volume of *What About Murder?*

9. ADDENDUM. Works in all the categories that came to my attention after the initial numbering of entries.

The length of the annotation does not necessarily reflect the value or importance of the book. It merely reflects how much I have to say about it that I find necessary or interesting. Some books need more space to describe than others. Some are of an excellence than can be expressed concisely, while others require more room to sort out just how wrong they have gotten things.

As before, the annotations don't hesitate to point out mistakes, whether born of carelessness or ignorance, when spotted, and I occasionally may appear somewhat testy on the subject. Intolerance of human error should not be inferred. Most of the works listed here were compiled out of love for the mystery genre, with little or no hope of monetary gain. Error is inevitable, especially in a book with a high quotient of names, dates, and titles. (I don't doubt the present volume has its share of errors, however many times I read it through to try to weed them out. Certainly the parent volume of *What About Murder?* was anything but free of them. Shortly after publication, Art Scott pointed out to me that the celebrator of bad movies is named Harry Medved, not "Harvey." I discovered on my own and to my horror that I had misspelled Dilys Winn's last name as "Wynn" throughout. And only when preparing the Raymond Chandler entries for this supplement did I discover I had miscalled the Chandler biographer Frank "McShane," instead of the correct MacShane. So any author of a book listed here who was especially burned by my finger-pointing is invited to have a fine time pointing out my own errors.)

Cross-references within the annotations are to entry numbers. If these are references to the parent volume they are preceded by WAM #, if to the present volume simply by #.

A word about selections: as before, some works have been included that are not strictly about mystery and detective fiction but include a substantial amount of material on the subject. Where the dividing line falls on these borderline sources is sometimes hard to decide. For example, works on mass-market paperbacks inevitably include a great deal of genre-related material, since crime fiction has always loomed so large in paperback publishing. Generally, histories of this area have been included where there is considerable genre content, but items like catalogs, indexes, and price guides have not. A similar approach has been taken to sources on pulp magazines. The gothic novel is a problematical area. Generally, writings on the early gothics of Radcliffe, Lewis, and Walpole have been ruled out of bounds, but books specifically relating to twentieth-century romantic suspense, which claimed the term "gothic" during its boom in the sixties and seventies, have been included.As with the parent volume, the following categories of materials have been excluded: Sherlockiana, dealer and exhibition catalogs, most publicity materials, works on most authors who have made a notable contribution to literature outside the mystery genre, and foreign-language works.

Aside from the anthology section, most of the works annotated here were published in the years from 1981 to 1991. Some 1992 items have been included, however, along with some pre-1981 titles that should have been in the first volume but were missed. Most, but not all of these, are in the section on individual authors.

Each entry lists first English-language edition, first American edition if different, and significantly revised editions. Reprints are not included. The heading includes the following information: author, title, others named on the title page (e.g., illustrator, translator, editor, introduction-writer), place, publisher, date, pagination, and the presence of any of the following special features: illustrations (abbreviated illus.), bibliography (bibl.), and index. In cases where the whole book is clearly by its title a bibliography or an index, these designations have been omitted as redundant. The term "bibliography" is generally used in the loose sense of any listing of books and other printed sources. Fully descriptive bibliographies are indicated as such in the annotation. In the case of most recent books published both in Great Britain and the United States, the pagination and content are identical. Where only one indication of pagination and special features is given, it may be taken to apply to both editions.

About fifty titles I was unable to examine. In most cases, I was able to include the above information on these titles, but in a few I was not and have given what partial information was available to me. Annotations on unexamined titles were drawn from reviews and other reference sources, of which the following were the most frequently valuable: Walter Albert's *Detective and Mystery Fiction: An International Bibliography of Secondary Sources* (see #6), Edward D. Hoch's annual *Year's Best Mystery and Suspense Stories* (see #369), and William G. Contento's *Index to Crime and Mystery Anthologies* (see #14).

Within the headings, I have adopted the new bibliographic fashion of abbreviating the names of publishers—university presses become U.P.; Random House becomes Random; the prolific and admirable Bowling Green State University Popular Press becomes simply Popular. However, I could not bring myself to separate Simon from Schuster, Hodder from Stoughton, or Harcourt from Brace from Jovanovich.

In the introduction to the original volume, I listed some of the topics that still needed to be covered in book form, and the present volume shows most of those gaps have been filled to a greater or lesser degree. The Christie, Sayers, Chandler, and Hammett industries continued unabated, but other subjects have received their due. There are now several monographs on John Le Carré; critical studies on John Dickson Carr, Mickey Spillane, and Eric Ambler; a major biographical/critical study of Cornell Woolrich; two secondary sources on Len Deighton; and wide-ranging studies of the police procedural and the private eye. But there are still numerous contemporary authors worthy of book-length studies (Ruth Rendell, say) as well as historically important figures (e.g., Earl Derr Biggers). I don't expect the flow of new studies to stop and look forward to a third volume in another decade or so.

ACKNOWLEDGMENTS

Some of the material in this volume first appeared in my quarterly "What About Murder?" column in *The Armchair Detective*, or in the "Murder in Print" column in *Wilson Library Bulletin*, which I contributed through June 1983.

Many individuals offered information or other help in the preparation of this volume. At the risk of missing some, I extend thanks to Sheldon MacArthur, Ellen Nehr, William F. Deeck, Clifford McCarty, Ed and Pat Thomas, Art Scott, Edward D. Hoch, Max Allan Collins, Enola Stewart (whose Gravesend Books catalogs are invaluable), and that circle of friends and co-enthusiasts who pioneered mystery fandom, including (but, as the lawyers say, not limited to) Francis M. Nevins, Jr., Marvin Lachman, Charles Shibuk, Robert E. Briney, J. Randolph Cox, Len and June Moffatt, and Allen J. Hubin.

Access to excellent library collections is indispensable to this kind of bibliographic project. I especially thank the staffs of the Orange County, Santa Ana, and Huntington Beach Public Libraries, the University of California, Irvine and Riverside campuses, the University of Texas, and my "home" library at Rio Hondo College.

I also owe special thanks to the faculty, administration, and board of trustees of Rio Hondo College for the sabbatical leave that permitted completion of this volume.

Finally, I thank Rita Breen, my wife, best friend, and constant collaborator, who did most of the work on the hand-compiled index and continued to cheer on the project as it grew and grew and grew.

Jon L. Breen
Professor/Librarian
Rio Hondo College
Whittier, California

1
HISTORIES

1. Benvenuti, Stefano, and Gianni Rizzoni. *The Whodunit: An Informal History of Detective Fiction.* Translated from the Italian by Anthony Eyre. Additional chapter by Edward D. Hoch. London: Collier Macmillan, 1980. New York: Macmillan, 1981. 216p. Illus., index. (Italian title: *Il romanzo giallo: Storia, autori i personaggi.*)

This well-illustrated but not particularly distinguished history is damaged by a frankly clumsy translation. The word "boring" is overused, I suspect in lieu of a more interesting Italian word, and a "criminal fiction writer" (page 99) sounds like one who cheats his or her agent.

The authors cover the usual pioneers in their early chapters. They love lists, drawing sets of rules from Poe, Chandler, Van Dine, Knox, and Carr (on locked rooms), and reprinting Watson's catalogue of Holmes' knowledge from *A Study in Scarlet.* As usual in a foreign source, it is interesting to note which British and American authors are given a greater-than-usual prominence—in this case, Stuart Palmer (hailed as the greatest of humorous mystery writers), Rufus King (seen in a rare photograph!), Helen Reilly, and James Hadley Chase—and which European writers turn up who usually escape notice in English-language histories. The coverage of the French is one of the major attributes of the book, discussing such writers as Marcel Allain and Pierre Souvestre (creators of Fantomas), Pierre Very, Claude Aveline, Boileau-Narcejac, Le Breton, Frederic Dard (Sanantonio), Hubert Monteilhet, and others even less well known to British and American readers.

Errors and questionable judgments abound. Gaston Leroux's Rouletabille (page 18) is declared "the youngest detective in the history of criminal fiction" (page 46). How about the Hardy Boys, to name only two? Ormond Sacker, an early name for Dr. Watson, is wrongly called an early name for Holmes. It is mistakenly implied that Perry Mason was a *Black Mask* character, J.G. Reeder a "private investigator," Earl Derr

Biggers a "thriller writer." Modern detectives are unfairly denigrated in the course of a deserved celebration of Sgt. Cuff. The Nero Wolfe novels are bizarrely credited with "the humor and style of P.G. Wodehouse" (page 128)—maybe they read that way in Italian translation. In a fascinating but unsubstantiated throwaway speculation, the authors suggest that Anthony Berkeley Cox wrote with a collaborator when using the name Francis Iles.

Edward D. Hoch has the thankless task of trying to squeeze into one chapter every important contemporary the Italians have missed, to name a few: Mickey Spillane, Josephine Tey, Ross Macdonald, John D. MacDonald, Donald E. Westlake, Dick Francis, Stanley Ellin, and virtually all the writers of spy fiction.

A "who's who" chapter, including both authors and character names, is of limited reference value.

2. **Binyon, T.J.** *Murder Will Out: The Detective in Fiction.* Oxford: Oxford U.P., 1989. viii, 166p. Bibl., index.

Binyon's book is a history of the detective character rather than of the detective story. An introductory chapter on Dupin and Lecoq is followed by topical treatments in three categories: The Professional Amateur (non-police detectives who encounter crime as a result of their professions: private detectives, lawyers, doctors, journalists, etc.); The Amateur Amateur; and The Police (the latter including a sub-group called The Amateur Professional, made up of characters like Ngaio Marsh's Roderick Alleyn who are official police but operate in a manner similar to gentleman sleuths like Lord Peter Wimsey and Philo Vance). A catch-all chapter considers humorous detectives, historical sleuths, Crooks and Villains, and Gentleman-burglars and Robin Hoods. In his Pro/Am section, Binyon differentiates between the Private Detective (e.g. Sherlock Holmes, Hercule Poirot, Nigel Strangeways, Nero Wolfe) and the Private Eye (e.g. Race Williams, the Continental Op, Philip Marlowe).

Binyon, a novelist, long-time detective fiction reviewer for the *Times Literary Supplement,* and Oxford Lecturer in Russian and Research Fellow, covers a very large number of authors, most in no more than a sentence or two, sometimes giving the book the feel of an elongated encyclopedia article. Nearly all of the famous names are at least mentioned along with some obscure figures, mostly British (e.g., W. Stanley Sykes, Frank Arthur, Victor MacClure, Katharine Farrer, and David Serafin).

The book's greatest asset is the range and freshness of Binyon's opinions. He awards Victor L. Whitechurch's Thorpe Hazell the edge over Arthur Morrison's better known Martin Hewitt, and gives a very favorable notice to Hesketh Prichard's *November Joe*. He finds Dr. Thorndyke "the most impressive and the most intellectually powerful of fictional detectives" (page 15), very much the superior of Holmes, though he ultimately admits Doyle was a better writer than Freeman. He is kind to Arthur B. Reeve's early Craig Kennedy stories, finding Jacques Futrelle's Thinking Machine tales "very similar to, though less convincing than" the Kennedys (page 50). He prefers P.D. James's Cordelia Gray to Adam Dalgliesh and finds J.J. Connington's Sir Clinton Driffield "among the outstanding detectives of the inter-war years" (page 97). Among amateurs of the Philip Trent school, he is surprisingly kind to Lee Thayer's Peter Clancy (really a private detective but ranked with gentleman sleuths for reasons that are explained). He gives Hammett's *The Thin Man* an extremely good notice but low marks to the Lockridges' Mr. and Mrs. North. In one of his most provocative maverick opinions, he ranks Georgette Heyer ahead of Margery Allingham and Ngaio Marsh. In my view, he seriously maligns Ellery Queen, overstating the lack of "novelistic qualities" in the early novels and giving no credit for the development of author and character in later novels.

Generally, Binyon is more reliable on traditional mystery fiction than on hardboiled. His comment that Harry Carmichael tries to "transpose the American private eye novel to an English setting" (page 30) seems off the mark to me. He believes with H.R.F. Keating (and probably with few American readers) that British private-eye pasticher Basil Copper depicts Los Angeles "convincingly" (page 45). Unimpressed with most of the private-eye writers of the past couple of decades, he writes, "Paradoxically, the genre that had begun as the most realistic, the closest to life, became the most artificial, the furthest removed from life" (page 45). (Binyon has disappointingly little to say about the female American private eyes who came into prominence in the 1980s.)

In a book with so many names, dates, and titles, errors are not overwhelmingly numerous. Some names are misspelled: "Earle" Stanley Gardner, Harry "Kurnits." At one point, the Q. Patrick books are credited to Hugh Wheeler alone, though only collaborator Richard Webb was involved in all of them. Antony Maitland is given a bad leg rather than a bad shoulder. And it is not true to say that "most" of the Continental Op short stories are collected in *The Big Knockover*.

Appended are a ten-page-plus list of recommended reading by some of the authors discussed in the text, a secondary bibliography of a little over a page, and a thorough 19-page index.

3. **Mandel, Ernest.** *Delightful Murder: A Social History of the Crime Story.* London: Pluto, 1984. viii, 152p. Bibl., index.

The idea of a Marxist history of crime fiction may be off-putting to some readers, but the author makes it clear in his apologetic preface and confirms in his enthusiastic text that he is not writing just to make ideological points at the expense of a popular form of entertainment. He really likes the genre, running the risk of being considered "a victim of bourgeois ideology being sucked into the vortex along with millions of other unfortunates, constructing an elaborate rationalization for a simple idiosyncratic vice," but refusing to "feel guilt for indulging in a pleasure proscribed by the Pharisees (for revolution, like religion, has its Tartuffes)" (page vii).

Among detective story commentators, Mandel's approach is unique. To over-simplify, he traces the detective story to tales of "good bandits" like Robin Hood, quite rightly admired as early proponents of Communism. Early in the 19th century, hostility to the police on the part of the lower classes was both pervasive and appropriate. But by mid-century, as crime became more capitalist, the natural roles reversed: the thief became bad, and the police, as protectors of social order, became good. Moving toward the present, Mandel consistently ties his discussion to social, economic, and political conditions. Addressing Agatha Christie's success in carrying out the "fair play" demands of Golden Age detective fiction, Mandel notes, "And indeed, to practice the art of deception while 'playing fair' is the very quintessence of the ideology of the British upper class" (page 16). Generally, Mandel discusses the works rather than the personalities and lives of the authors, but he makes some interesting points about the contrast between some authors and their characters (conventional Doyle vs. unconventional Holmes, unconventional Simenon vs. conventional Maigret), and he discusses the real-life political views of Hammett, Stout, Simenon, Chandler, and Graham Greene. His political interests lead him to discuss such relatively obscure books as Manuel Vazquez Montalban's *Murder in the Central Committee,* Alexis Lecage's *Marx et Sherlock Holmes,* and Sam Greenlee's *The Spook Who Sat by the Door.* Primarily concerned with the detective story, he believes spy stories do not constitute a separate genre. ("The thriller [including the spy thriller] is to the detective story what monopoly capitalism is to the capitalism of free competition. To enter its characteristic plots armed only with one's wits [even those of the formidable Nero Wolfe] is like challenging a multinational corporation with only five thousand pounds sterling in one's bank account" [page 85].)

Strong as Mandel's grasp may be of Marxian dialectic, his account of crime fiction history is both sketchy and error-prone. Holmes's model becomes "John" rather than Joseph Bell, and many bylines are abbreviated or mangled: Dorothy (No L.) Sayers, Earl "D." Biggers, "J." Dickson Carr, Manfred "D." Lee, "Nicholas" Freeling, Michael "Crighton," and more seriously Mignon "B. Eberhard," Ruth "Bendell," and "R.L. Fisk" (i.e., Robert L. Fish). Carr's *The Emperor's Snuff Box* is misidentified as a Dr. Fell novel. This distracting tendency to error is especially unfortunate, since Mandel (agree or not) has many interesting and stimulating things to say.

4. **Panek, LeRoy Lad.** *An Introduction to the Detective Story.* Bowling Green, OH: Popular, 1987. vii, 214p. Bibl., index.

The author of two earlier collections of essays on British detective novelists, *Watteau's Shepherds* (1979; see WAM #80), and spy writers, *The Special Branch* (1981; see #159), here presents a general history of the detective story, designed to identify its necessary elements and differentiate it from related genres. Early chapters discuss the form's alleged "pre-history," debunking most of it, and the work of William Godwin and Edward Bulwer Lytton, calling them the writers Poe and Collins "reacted against when they wrote real detective stories" (page 12). Poe's primacy is re-emphasized convincingly. The treatment of Dickens gives attention to *Barnaby Rudge* and *Martin Chuzzlewit* along with the expected *Bleak House* and *Edwin Drood*. Collins is contrasted with fellow sensation novelists Mrs. Henry Wood, Mary Braddon, and Sheridan Le Fanu, whose alleged contributions to detective fiction are essentially denied. Following an interesting discussion of Gaboriau and the French pioneers, the chapter on Doyle and Sherlock Holmes is more frankly critical than most. There follow chapters on turn-of-the-century writers, the Golden Age (undervaluing the Americans, in my opinion), the hardboiled story (tracing its roots to the 19th-century dime novel), the police procedural (crediting radio police shows more than early novels in the form), and a catch-all chapter on other post-World War II writers.

There are a few problems and errors. Book and story titles are frequently cited without dates or other publication information, necessitating the reader's having other secondary references at hand to track them down. The index is rather hit-and-miss: for example, there is a page reference to Dennis Wheatley but none to his "crime file" collaborator J.G. Links. Clemence Dane is credited with *Enter Sir John* without reference to co-author Helen Simpson. *Six Against Scotland Yard* (see #517), a short-story collection, is misidentified as a collaborative novel. Panek implies Horace McCoy's *They Shoot Horses, Don't They?*, really not a mystery at all, is a private eye novel. And finally, Sydney Horler is still getting his first name misspelled "Sidney," as in *The Special Branch*.

Quibbles aside, Panek is one of the best contemporary commentators on the form, and no fan or scholar will want to miss reading this book, which won the Edgar award for best biographical or critical volume of its year.

5. Woeller, Waltraud, and Bruce Cassiday. *The Literature of Crime and Detection: An Illustrated History from Antiquity to the Present.* New York: Ungar, 1988. 215p. Illus., bibl., index.

Based on a 1984 German work by Woeller, translated by Ruth Michaelis-Jena and Willy Merson and adapted for its American publication by Cassiday, this handsome volume has the usual advantage of foreign detective-fiction histories: an international scope. Among the authors covered are Swiss, Japanese, Russian, Polish, and Scandinavian practitioners, including many never translated into English. The German subjects especially have seldom if ever been mentioned in other histories published in English, even those from continental sources.

The book is strong on the "pre-history" of the genre, not reaching Poe until page 55 while discussing such figures as Cicero, Voltaire, Shakespeare, Diderot, and Schiller. The contribution of E.T.A. Hoffmann is especially strongly advanced. This early section and the last few chapters on the contemporary scene are the strongest, with the coverage of the early twentieth century the weakest. The authors have more interest and enthusiasm for the American hardboiled school than the British classical. Despite a somewhat ragged organization and occasional awkwardness in the translation, there are some interesting points made. Especially good is the coverage of contemporary women writers like Amanda Cross, P.D. James, Ruth Rendell, Phyllis A. Whitney, June Thomson, and Mary Higgins Clark. The well-selected and reproduced pictorial matter includes woodcuts, motion picture stills, book and magazine illustrations, book jackets and covers, and photos of authors. The Index of Crime Writers includes brief identifications as well as page references.

Unfortunately, the book is like too many sources in the field in its proneness to error. Fergus Hume's *Mystery of the (sic) Hansom Cab* is placed in London rather than Melbourne. Doyle's *The Valley of Fear* is discussed without reference to its title. The authors believe Rinehart's Letitia Carberry and Hilda Adams (Miss Pinkerton), characters who appear in separate works, were collaborators in detection and that Susan Dare appeared in Mignon G. Eberhart's novels as a recurring character rather than in short stories. Hornung's Raffles is made to sound like a Robin Hood figure, a characteristic the Amateur Cracksman did not take on until revived by Barry Perowne. Frances Noyes Hart is called "he"; R. Austin Freeman's main sleuth becomes Mr. (rather than Dr.) Thorndyke; Hugh Pentecost is identified with "spy thrillers"; Henry Slesar's *Enter Murderers* is miscalled by implication a short story collection; and the English title of *Maigret chez le Coroner* is given as *Maigret at the Coroner's Strange Case!* Finally, the authors commit an increasingly frequent and irritating solecism that must be stamped out before it is too late: saying "locked room" when they mean "closed circle."

2
REFERENCE BOOKS

6. **Albert, Walter.** *Detective and Mystery Fiction: An International Bibliography of Secondary Sources.* Madison, IN: Brownstone, 1985. xii, 781p. Index.

Though covering roughly the same ground as earlier efforts by David and Ann Skene Melvin (see #54) and Timothy and Julia Johnson (see #33), this volume is the first truly successful comprehensive secondary bibliography in the crime and mystery fiction field, an extraordinary achievement that puts all previous attempts in the shade. Total entries numbering more than 5000 (compared with the Johnsons' 1810 and the Skene Melvins' 1628) are divided into four sections: Bibliographies, Dictionaries, etc. (182 entries); General Reference (451 books and 886 articles); Dime Novels, Juveniles, and Pulps (503); and Authors (by far the largest section with 3167 items). Excluded, as usual in general sources, is the already well-covered body of Sherlock Holmes material. Albert also excludes material specifically on films, TV, radio, and stage adaptations.

The full range of possible sources has been consulted, from books to popular magazines to scholarly journals to fanzines to dealer catalogs. Entries on individual authors cite representation in other biographical and bibliographic references, including *Encyclopedia of Mystery and Detection* (see WAM #31), *A Catalogue of Crime* (see WAM #10 and present volume #544), the Hubin bibliographies (see WAM #18 and present volume #548), and the *Author Biographies Master Index* among others. Names of authors and characters, titles, and subjects are cited in the index, with reference to entry number rather than page for easy locating.

All entries are annotated, some extensively. Many are signed by distinguished contributors, including such familiar names as Robert E. Briney, Robert C.S. Adey, Greg Goode, Kathleen L. Maio, Everett F. Bleiler, J. Randolph Cox, Will Murray, John Nieminski, Robert Sampson,

John L. Apostolou, Iwan Hedman, Jiro Kimura, and Steven A. Stilwell. Annotations are occasionally critical, usually purely descriptive.

The book is especially commendable for its extensive coverage of non-Englishlanguage material. Annotations originally written in French, Italian, and Japanese are translated into English. The section on Edogawa Rampo made me wish at least a selection from his several volumes of criticism were available in English. Another most valuable feature is the strong coverage of juvenile and dime novel fiction, often ignored in general studies.

Though errors are inevitable in a work of this magnitude, the editor's meticulousness has kept the number down. Some titles are duplicated in different entries (for example, entries #A128 and D401 are the same item). Hugh Wiley is miscalled John at one point. There are undoubtedly others but quite likely fewer than in any of the handful of mystery references of similar comprehensiveness.

Albert's volume and its supplements in *The Armchair Detective* are frequently drawn on for information on *What About Murder?* titles I have been unable to examine.

7. **Benstock, Bernard, and Thomas F. Staley, eds.** *British Mystery Writers, 1860-1919.* (Dictionary of Literary Biography, volume 70.) Detroit: Gale, 1988. xi, 389p. Illus., bibl., index.

Dictionary of Literary Biography is a large and ambitious set of topical reference books on literary figures of various genres, nationalities, schools, and periods. Each entry includes a bibliography of the subject's major works, a signed critical essay, illustrations (e.g. portraits, book jackets and covers, interior illustrations from books and periodicals, title page reproductions, movie stills, and examples of manuscript pages), and a list of scholarly references. Several volumes on mystery fiction have been in the works for years, but this is the first to appear.

Thirty-five writers are covered at varying length. Doyle gets 23 pages, Chesterton 18, and Wilkie Collins 17, while comparatively obscure figures like M. McDonnell Bodkin (four pages) and William Hope Hodgson (three) are dealt with less extensively. Most but not all of the contributors are academics, many of them familiar names to mystery fans, including Jeanne F. Bedell (on Collins), Albert Borowitz (on Dickens and Hodgson), J. Randolph Cox (on Buchan, Doyle, Mason, and Wallace), John McAleer (on Freeman), and Will Murray (on Oppenheim and Rohmer). Though most of the subjects are primarily known for mystery fiction, a few borderline authors from other areas of writing are included: H. Rider Haggard, Bram Stoker, and H.G. Wells. The only important omission noted was L.T. Meade. As would be expected from the series, essays are of a high caliber: readable, scholarly, and reliable. There is a useful four-page secondary bibliography. Pages 331 and following consist of an index to all the volumes of DLB through volume 70 plus its yearbooks through 1987 and its Documentary Series through volume 4.

8. Benstock, Bernard, and Thomas F. Staley, eds. *British Mystery Writers, 1920-1939.* (Dictionary of Literary Biography, volume 77.) Detroit: Gale, 1989. xi, 414p. Illus., bibl., index.

The second DLB volume on British mystery writers covers the great names of the Golden Age. Longest entries are devoted to Sayers (19 pages), Graham Greene (19), Creasey (18, mostly bibliography), Ngaio Marsh (16), and Christie (15). Contributors include even more familiar names than the previous volume: B.A. Pike (on Allingham), Charles Shibuk (on Berkeley/Iles and Rhode), Earl F. Bargainnier (on Blake and Heyer), H.R.F. Keating (on Christie), Marvin Lachman (on John Collier, Creasey, Hilton, and Marsh), LeRoy Panek (on Milne), and Mary Helen Becker (on Anthony Gilbert). J. Randolph Cox is again a prolific contributor, writing on Wheatley, Valentine Williams, and Dornford Yates. The same secondary bibliography concludes the volume, and again a large concluding section (almost sixty pages) is devoted to an index of the whole DLB set.

While the cost will put DLB out of bounds for most private collectors, it is a useful and very handsomely produced resource that large public and all college and university libraries should have.

9. Bourgeau, Art. *The Mystery Lover's Companion.* New York: Crown, 1986. 311p.

The proprietor of the Whodunit? Bookstore in Philadelphia and the author of several novels in the field, Bourgeau here offers a one-man reader's guide divided into four categories his customers seem to prefer: American Mystery, English Mystery, Thriller, and Police Procedural. Besides a general introduction, there are introductions to each category, entertainingly written though sometimes overly generalized. Entries within each category are alphabetical by author and include date of publication, a mostly descriptive, sometimes critical annotation of a few lines, and a quality rating of one to five daggers. Readers looking for further bibliographic information must consult other sources. Pseudonym information is usually not included (and sometimes carelessly when it is), and alternate titles virtually never appear. The lack of an index is unfortunate, since some authors are covered in more than one section and there are no cross-references.

What makes Bourgeau a good guide is the wide extent of his reading and the breadth of his taste. Anyone who can be enthusiastic about both Mickey Spillane and Charlotte MacLeod need take a back seat to no one in catholicity of appreciation. The five-dagger books, touted by Bourgeau as classics, take in a wide range and include some surprising or little-known selections: David Anthony's *Blood on a Harvest Moon,* Roy Huggins's *The Double Take,* Jane Langton's *The Minuteman Murder,* Frances and Richard Lockridge's *A Pinch of Poison,* Hilda Lawrence's *The Pavilion,* Edna Sherry's *Sudden Fear,* Raymond Paul's *Tragedy at Tiverton,* Douglas G. Browne's *Too Many Cousins,* L.P. Davies's *Who is Lewis Pinder?,* George Hart's (not Carter Dickson's) *The Punch and Judy Murders,* and Dick Francis's *Twice Shy.* Among the writers getting high marks from Bourgeau are Earl Derr Biggers, Leslie Egan, Jim Thompson, Edmund Crispin, R. Austin Freeman, Clayton Rawson (better, he says, than Carr!), Rex Stout, Ellery Queen, Milton Propper, and Erle Stanley Gardner writing as A.A. Fair. Comparatively poorly received are Charlotte Armstrong, Loren D. Estleman, the Gordons, H.C. Bailey, Charles Dickens, Nicholas Meyer, and Erle Stanley Gardner as himself.

Any book like this is bound to provoke disagreement from any reader. Remarks that brought this one out of his chair with indignation were the characterization of Bertha Cool as "Nero Wolfe in drag" and the description of Ron Rosenbaum's appallingly bad *Murder at Elaine's* as "in the tradition of Ellery Queen." Some of the categorizations are surprising: Hillary Waugh in the American mystery instead of police procedural section, Ethel Lina White with the mystery writers rather than the thriller writers. In one extreme case, two books from the same series (about L.A. Taylor's UFO investigator J.J. Jamison) are covered in different sections. The police procedural category becomes a catch-all including some true crime and trial novels.

Like so many references in the field, this one has too many careless errors. *The Mousetrap* is misdated 1925. The author of *Before the Fact* is called Francis "Isles"—and the fact he is also Anthony Berkeley is not pointed out. Ethel Lina White's *The Wheel Spins* is listed only under its movie title, *The Lady Vanishes*. Sara Woods is credited with a novel called *Let's Choose Executioners* (should be *Executors*). Vincent Bugliosi and Ken Hurwitz's *Shadow of Cain*, a work of fiction, is mistakenly called "a true story." In fact, the whole book has an unfinished feel, as if it needed one last run-through to clean up errors and avoid, for example, two consecutive entries beginning, "A promising debut in which . . ." (page 58).

10. **Breen, Jon L.** *Novel Verdicts: A Guide to Courtroom Fiction.* Metuchen, NJ: Scarecrow, 1984. xiii, 266p. Bibl., index.

The main section consists of 421 annotated entries of novels and short story collections that include significant courtroom action. Coverage is limited to American and British courts and other courts in English-speaking jurisdictions. Though mainstream books have been included, the majority of the titles are from the crime/mystery genre, including complete coverage of the courtroom novels of Erle Stanley Gardner and nearly complete coverage of Sara Woods, Roderic Jeffries/Jeffrey Ashford, Henry Cecil, Arthur Train, Michael Underwood, and other specialists. Annotations include both plot summary and critical comment, with a symbol identifying the proportion of the book devoted to trial scenes. An unannotated supplementary list identifies more than 200 additional titles. Included are a general index (authors, titles, and names of actual persons mentioned in the annotations), a cause-of-action index, and a jurisdiction index (by state or country). In the kind of error he so gleefully pounces on in other writers' works, Breen mistitles Henry Wade's *The Verdict of You All* as *The Evidence of You All*.

The volume won the Edgar award for best biographical or critical work of its year.

11. **Bruccoli, Matthew J., and Richard Layman, eds.** *Hardboiled Mystery Writers: Raymond Chandler, Dashiell Hammett, Ross Macdonald.* (Dictionary of Literary Biography Documentary Series, volume 6.) Detroit: Gale, 1989. xi, 383p. Illus., bibl., index.

The intent according to the preface is to provide scholars with a "portable archive," consisting of "letters, notebooks and diary entries, interviews, and book reviews . . . " (page ix). Obviously, the amount of material included depends on availability. The Hammett section is the largest (158 pages) and most interesting, mainly for its documents of his political troubles, including correspondence, ads, court and congressional committee testimony, and red-baiting articles against him. Other Hammett items include his school record and marriage license, examples of his mystery book reviews, editorials from the *Adakian* (the service paper he edited in the Aleutians during World War II), and an affidavit from his lawsuit with Warner Bros. over the use of the character Sam Spade. The Chandler section (81 pages) draws heavily on his previously-published letters but includes a 1946 *Pageant* article on him by Irving Wallace, plus other articles and reviews not readily available. The briefest section on Macdonald (76 pages) includes relatively obscure interviews from *Concept* (the Santa Barbara City College literary magazine) and *Tamarack Review*. All sections are handsomely illustrated with photographs, book jackets and covers, ads, and manuscript pages. This is an invaluable volume for students of the hardboiled detective novel's big three. Beginning on page 321 is a complete index to DLB through volume 79, its yearbooks through 1987, and the Documentary Series through volume 6.

12. **Burgess, Michael.** *Mystery and Detective Fiction in the Library of Congress Classification Scheme.* (Borgo Cataloging Guides, Number Two.) San Bernardino: Borgo, 1987. 184p. Index.

This specialized cataloging manual will be of most value to public, academic, and research librarians, though owners of very large private collections may find it useful as well. Contents include Library of Congress subject headings related to mysteries, LC classification numbers for topics related to mystery fiction (with index by subject), author main entries and literature numbers (the largest section), and main entries and class numbers for individual motion pictures, television programs, and comic strips.

In the author listing, there are sometimes but not always cross references between real names and pseudonyms. Frederic Dard and his pseudonym San-Antonio have the same literature number (PQ2607. A558), but there is no cross-reference, and the same is true for Aaron Marc Stein, Hampton Stone, and George Bagby. There are sometimes separate literature numbers for a single author when the pseudonym is not known to the Library of Congress—for example, William L. DeAndrea (PS3554.E174) and Philip DeGrave (PS3554.E416). Some of the authors listed have never been assigned literature numbers by LC, usually paperback original specialists or writers who have not published new works in the past twenty years (e.g. Herbert Brean, Clyde B. Clason, Thomas W. Hanshew, Kenn Davis, Robert Colby).

13. Conquest, John. *Trouble is Their Business: Private Eyes in Fiction, Film, and Television, 1927-1988.* (Garland Reference Library of the Humanities, vol. 1151.) New York: Garland, 1990. liii, 497p. Bibl., index.

This massive and detailed reference replaces Baker and Nietzel's *Private Eyes* (see #61) as the most complete volume on private eye fiction. An Edgar winner in the biographical-critical category, it belongs on the small shelf of the dozen-or-so best mystery reference books.

The substantial introduction defines the private eye, including quotes from some major practitioners; discusses various sub-categories (women, ethnic, gay, period, future); touches on movie, radio, and TV eyes; excerpts some how-to advice; and finishes with a short bibliography of research materials on real-life private eyes and a more extensive annotated listing of secondary sources on literary detection.

The main listing is alphabetical by author with cross-references from character names. The entries, succinct and critical, typically give a brief description of the private eye with evaluative comments, sometimes Conquest's own and sometimes quoted from reviews or reference sources. Books are listed by series, in chronological order with dates of U.S. and British publication but no publisher information.

Coverage is wide-ranging and not strictly limited to the hardboiled: for example, the one novel in which Ellery Queen functions as a professional private detective, *The Dragon's Teeth* (1939) is listed, and sleuths as cozy as Patricia Wentworth's Miss Silver and R.A.J. Walling's Philip Tolefree find a place, though Christopher Bush's Ludovic Travers is one of the rare omissions of qualified candidates. (Conquest states in his introduction that one of the advantages of his 1927 beginning date was that it permitted him to leave out Carolyn Wells's Fleming Stone and Lee Thayer's Peter Clancy). As in Baker and Nietzel, some characters who act like private eyes but technically belong to other professions—e.g. George Harmon Coxe's Kent Murdock, Frank Gruber's Johnny Fletcher, Jonathan

Kellerman's Alex Delaware, and Harold Q. Masur's Scott Jordan—are included, but Erle Stanley Gardner's Perry Mason apparently spends too much time in court to qualify. One-book private eyes have been included, but those who appear only in short stories usually have not. There is, however, a useful list of private eye anthologies, and stories from these are referred to in the individual author entries.

Following the author listing are sections on TV series, including references to authors of novelizations and prominent scriptwriters (e.g. Steve Fisher on *Barnaby Jones* and Leigh Brackett on *Checkmate*), films, and radio series; a "Yellow Pages" geographical index; a checklist by author; and a title index. A 13-page "Stop Press" updates the book's various sections, mostly with 1989 items.

14. Contento, William G., with Martin H. Greenberg. *Index to Crime and Mystery Anthologies.* Introduction by Edward D. Hoch. Boston: G.K. Hall, 1990. xiv, 736p.

Here is an extraordinarily valuable reference for mystery collectors and potential anthologists. The contents of more than 1,000 anthologies of crime and mystery fiction published between 1875 and 1990 are indexed by author and title with full listings of their contents. Only previous source for this kind of information was the general *Short Story Index*, published by H.W. Wilson, and that set includes mystery anthologies selectively, with earlier compilations and paperback originals not covered. Alternate-title and pseudonym information is plentiful. The coverage appears remarkably complete and, best of all for such an ambitious project, obvious errors are not rampant.

This source was of great help in determining what should be listed in the anthology section of the present work.

15. Cook, Michael L. *Monthly Murders: A Checklist and Chronological Listing of Fiction in the Digest-Size Mystery Magazines in the United States and England.* Westport, CT: Greenwood, 1982. xv, 1147p. Index.

The title pretty well describes this massive undertaking, a very welcome one to serious collectors of mystery fiction. Cook has listed, issue by issue, the fictional contents of more than a hundred periodicals published between 1941 (the year *Ellery Queen's Mystery Magazine*, the first and still greatest of the digests, debuted) and the end of 1980. The other long-running survivor, *Alfred Hitchcock's Mystery Magazine*, a newsstand staple since 1956, is here, as well as *Mike Shayne Mystery Magazine*, still extant at the time of publication but since deceased, and such celebrated but departed competitors as *Manhunt* and *The Saint Magazine* (which would be revived for three issues in 1984 under new management). Indexing of these giants is undoubtedly the most useful feature of the volume, but for the nostalgic collector, the attention given to obscure and short-running magazines (*The Girl from UNCLE, Keyhole, MacKill's, Private Eye, Malcolm's, The Mysterious Traveler, Verdict*) does much to add to the fascination. Cook also includes an index by author, allowing the reader to trace all the digest appearances of such prolific short story writers as Edward D. Hoch (almost eight pages in the index!), Jack Ritchie, Fletcher Flora, and Robert Turner.

There are numerous errors, and indeed some unlocated issues, but no more than would be expected in a project of this magnitude. Cook has included quite a bit of pseudonym information, but mystery fans (obsessed as they are with who done it) would like more still. The most notable defect is the lack of alternate title information. For example, Craig Rice's "Hanged Him in the Mornin'" is the same story as her oft-reprinted "His Heart Could Break," but that information is not here, nor is the fact that Joseph Commings recycled the same short story under several different titles in *Mystery Digest*. Admittedly, trying to include this information would have added immeasurably to an already vast project.

16. **Cook, Michael L., and Stephen T. Miller.** *Mystery, Detective, and Espionage Fiction: A Checklist of Fiction in U.S. Pulp Magazines, 1915-1974.* (Garland Reference Library of the Humanities, Vol. 838; Fiction in the Pulp Magazines, Vol. 1.) New York: Garland, 1988. 2 volumes. xvi, 1183p. Index.

Indexing the pulps, given their rarity, fragility, and sheer volume, is one of the most daunting and seemingly impossible tasks ever attempted in mystery scholarship. But here it is, an awe-inspiring achievement, despite such small print many readers will need recourse to a magnifying glass. The first volume is arranged by magazine title, giving an abbreviation (for indexing purposes), the name and address of the publisher, and issue-by-issue contents. Appendices include a summary of publication data for each title (number of issues plus volume, number, and date of first and last issues) and a chronology of beginning dates from *Detective Story Magazine* (1915) to *Black Mask* (Second Series) (1974). The second volume is an author index. There is no pseudonym or alternate-title information.

17. **Cook, Michael L.** *Mystery Detective, and Espionage Magazines.* (Historical Guides to the World's Periodicals and Newspapers.) Westport, CT: Greenwood, 1983. xxiv, 795p. Bibl., index.

In a worthy companion volume to the two projects described above, Cook and a large group of expert consultants identify and describe nearly a thousand periodicals devoted to mystery and detective fiction, including pulps, digests, and fanzines. The contributors form (to borrow a cliché that appears all too often and usually inappropriately in the volume's annotations) "a veritable who's who" of fans and scholars, among them Robert C.S. Adey (specializing in British periodicals), Michael Avallone, Jane S. Bakerman, J. Randolph Cox (specializing in dime novel series), Robert Kenneth Jones (specializing in weird-menace pulps), Robert A.W. Lowndes (himself one of the most prolific of pulp editors), John J. McAleer, Frank D. McSherry, Jr., Will Murray, Francis M. Nevins, Jr., and the most frequent and entertaining commentator of all, Robert Sampson (specializing in the hero pulps).

Each entry includes the following data (or as much of it as is known): index and location sources, title changes, inclusive volumes and dates with number of issues, publisher's name and address, editors' names, price per issue, size and pagination, and current status (usually "discontinued," but occasionally "active"). There are cross references from variant titles. Following the main alphabetical section is a group of "Overviews of Foreign Magazines," including coverage of Australia, Denmark, France, Norway, and Sweden. (Some major markets have been omitted here, notably Japan.) Another section is titled "Book Clubs in Profile." Appendices classify magazines by category (e.g., Dime Novels, Pulps, Digests, Non-fiction) in the U.S. and Great Britain; identify "Key Writers of the Golden Age" (i.e., pulp writers of the twenties through fifties) with magazines contributed to and pseudonyms used; a chronology by year of debut of magazines covered; lists of American and Canadian true-detective magazines (otherwise outside the scope of the volume); and lists of Sherlock Holmes scion societies and other periodicals of interest to collectors. The volume concludes with a two-page bibliography of monographic sources; an exhaustive index of names and titles; and a directory of contributors.

Anyone who loves the old magazines will have a wonderful time with this book. Longest entry (ten pages) is justly accorded *Ellery Queen's Mystery Magazine*. *Black Mask* is covered in seven pages, and four of the hero pulps (*Doc Savage, The Phantom Detective, The Shadow*, and *The Spider*) rate six pages each. Most entries are much shorter, a couple of sentences in cases where little information but the title's existence is known. While coverage of major publications is most valuable (and usually excellent), the description of lesser-known journals is equally entertaining. The description of at least one fanzine, *The Holmesian Federation* (devoted to crossing Sherlock Holmes with *Star Trek*), sounds like a hoax, but I'm confident it isn't.

As with Cook's *Monthly Murders* (see #13), one approaches this volume torn between nit-picking errors and imbalances of coverage and celebrating the unlikely fact it exists at all. Emphasis was apparently left up to the contributors, making the coverage highly uneven in approach as well as length. In a few cases (notably *Manhunt*'s two pages), the coverage is disappointingly slight. Herbert Harris, writing on the Crime Writers Association's *Red Herrings,* contributes a history of the organization but relatively little about the contents of their newsletter. Faith Clare-Joynt's account of *London Mystery Magazine* seems more a valentine to publisher Norman Kark than an objective description of the periodical's contents. The incestuous liaisons of some contributors with their own publications somewhat damages objectivity, of course—contributor Joseph Lewandowski pronounces his own periodical *Cloak and Pistol* "distinguished."

Though there is plenty of room for argument about emphasis and extensiveness of coverage of particular titles, factual errors (at least those obvious to the present reader) are relatively few. George Harmon Coxe is mistakenly credited with Richard Sale's Daffy Dill stories. There is a reference to "Frederick" Brown, whose first name (Fredric) was constantly misspelled by the various periodicals he contributed to. (Talmage Powell has had the same problem.)

18. Cook, Michael L. *Mystery Fanfare: A Composite Annotated Index to Mystery and Related Fanzines 1963-1981.* Bowling Green, OH: Popular, 1983. 441p.

Since most of the fanzines indexed here were distributed to a very limited group of readers and are not easily available to researchers, this volume is of even more specialized interest than Cook's other indexes, and as such even more to be treasured by those who can use it. Following an introduction and guide to the use of the index are an alphabetical list of the codes used to identify the near-fifty titles indexed and a subject directory in four categories: Mystery and Detective, Boy's Book Collecting, Paperback Collecting, and Pulp Magazines. A guide and chronology lists the fanzines indexed alphabetically, giving a general description, a listing of issues indexed, size, current status, editors and publishers (with addresses), frequency, and subscription information if active. The main index is by author and subject, and there is a separate index of book reviews. Of special value in a fanzine index is the inclusion of letters of comment by author, though these have usually not been indexed by subject. This is an index in need of a supplement or expanded edition—but with the passing of the tireless Cook, who will attempt it?

Again, some errors are inevitable. I was surprised to be credited with an interview with Mary Roberts Rinehart. How I wish it were so.

19. **Cooper, John, and Barry A. Pike.** *Detective Fiction: The Collector's Guide.* Lydeard St. Lawrence, Somerset, England: Barn Owl, 1989.

Not examined. According to Edward D. Hoch (*The Year's Best Mystery and Suspense Stories 1990* #369), it includes "checklists of 105 of the most collected mystery writers, with details of first editions, series characters, uncollected short stories, etc."

20. **Cox, J. Randolph.** *Magnet Detective Library.* (*Dime Novel Review* supplement no. 51.) 1985. 48p.

Not examined. According to Walter Albert (*The Armchair Detective*, v. 20, n. 4, p. 386-387), Cox provides a "chronological listing of issues of the Magnet and New Magnet Library . . . with an author index." Less than half the issues dealt with the famous Nick Carter. "In his introduction, Cox traces the debt of the dime novel detective to writers such as Gaboriau and Fortune du Boisgobey and surveys the contents of the magazine. The Street and Smith publication is a rich source of nineteenth- and early twentieth-century detective fiction, and Cox's bibliography is an exemplary record of it."

21. Cox, J. Randolph. *Masters of Mystery and Detective Fiction: An Annotated Bibliography.* (The Magill Bibliographies.) Pasadena, CA: Salem, 1989. xii, 281p. Index.

Secondary sources on 74 significant writers are divided into biography and commentary and annotated by a Saint Olaf College librarian and formidable mystery scholar. Meticulous and informative, the annotations are consistently descriptive rather than critical. The volume is valuable enough on figures like Chandler, Chesterton, Christie, Dickens, Doyle, Hammett, Poe, and Sayers but even more so on writers who have not been subject to book-length biographical, critical, or bibliographic treatment, e.g. Robert Barnard, Anthony Berkeley, Edmund Crispin, Amanda Cross, Michael Gilbert, Cyril Hare, Emma Lathen, Richard and Frances Lockridge, Peter Lovesey, Margaret Millar, Ruth Rendell, Craig Rice, and Donald E. Westlake. One can always carp about selection of subjects (Fleming and not Deighton? Rohmer and not Biggers?), but Cox's list is hard to fault.

First choice for sources has been books, with periodical entries included when little is available in book form. In the interest of accessibility, Cox has usually not included fanzine materials, though *The Armchair Detective* and Bowling Green's scholarly journal *Clues* have been combed. The sparseness of entries on some excellent writers—a mere page each on Peter Dickinson and Nicolas Freeling—points up how much fertile ground remains for critical plowing. An annotated list of general studies follows the introduction, including eight standard works on mystery fiction and the non-specialized sources *Twentieth Century Authors* and *Current Biography.*

22. Crider, Allen Billy, ed. *Mass Market Publishing in America.* Boston: Hall, 1982. xii, 294p. Illus., index.

This encyclopedia of American paperback publishers from 1939 to 1979 includes signed articles on almost seventy firms, alphabetically arranged, including both the long-running successful houses (Pocket Books, Avon, Bantam, Dell) and the short-lived and obscure firms (Chi-

cago Paperback House, HandiBooks, Regency). Black-and-white reproductions of paperback covers illustrate the articles. Among the better-
known contributors are Bill Pronzini, Guy M. Townsend, Ellen Nehr,
Stephen Mertz, and editor Bill Crider. Though the essays cover mass-market paperbacks in all fields, mysteries loom largest here as they have in
most paperback publishing lists, especially in the forties and fifties.

23. **Drew, Bernard A.** *Action Series and Sequels: A Bibliography of
Espionage, Vigilante, and Soldier-of-Fortune Novels.* (Garland Reference Library of the Humanities, Vol. 842.) New York: Garland, 1988.
328p. Index, illus.

In a very valuable compendium of information not brought together
anywhere else, Drew covers 750 series, including "secret agent novels,
leading to, spawned by, and reacting to the James Bond phenomenon of
the 1960s; the vigilante and anti-Mafia novels of the 1970s; and the
soldiers-of-fortune, Vietnam War, and adjunct apocalyptic freedom
fighter novels of the 1980s" (page 4). The coverage is even wider than the
above suggests, taking in boys' books, thieves and rogues, and costumed
crimefighters and sometimes extending to private eyes, cowboys, and
science fiction characters. The main listing is by series title, preceded by
an index by author. Such an arrangement is logical here since many of the
series are signed by house names and/or varying bylines. Each entry
includes series title, byline, a brief description, and a chronological list
(numbered if appropriate) giving title, actual author (when known, in the
case of ghosted works or house names), American and British publishers
and dates. Coverage ranges from upscale stuff like Kenneth Roberts'
Arundel, Hans Hellmut Kirst's Gunner Asch, C.S. Forester's Hornblower,
Nordhoff and Hall's Bounty trilogy, Upton Sinclair's Lanny Budd, and
Evelyn Waugh's Guy Crouchback to many obscure paperback action and
boys'-book series and some porn or semi-porn series (e.g. Ted Mark's
Man from ORGY and Troy Conway's Coxeman) denied entry into
Hubin's crime fiction bibliographies (see WAM #18 and present volume
#548). It would take a real specialist to catch Drew in many omissions,
though George C. Chesbro's Mongo Frederickson certainly would seem
to qualify. (Chesbro's paperback Chant series, written as David Cross,
does get listed, though Chesbro is omitted from the author index.)
  In an appendix, Drew classifies the series listed into 18 categories
(e.g. Rogues, Criminals, Hitmen & Mobsters, Sea Adventure, Aviation,

Super-Villains, Martial Artists). There are also separate lists of juvenile series, movie tie-ins, TV tie-ins, heroines, and ethnic heroes, plus a good eight-page secondary bibliography and a title index. Some black-and-white illustrations and book covers are included.

Most of the errors noted were index omissions. Though there are numerous cross-references in the main list, there is none from Mack Bolan to the Executioner. The entry on Michael Avallone's Ed Noon omits *The Case of the Violent Virgin* (part of an Ace Double with *The Case of the Bouncing Betty*, which is listed). Van Wyck Mason's *The Castle Island Case* (1937) was not about Hugh North in its original illustrated form, though North was added in a subsequent paperback revision, *The Multi-Million-Dollar Murders* (1960).

24. Drew, Bernard A. *Lawmen in Scarlet: An Annotated Guide to Royal Canadian Mounted Police in Print and Performance.* Metuchen, NJ: Scarecrow, 1990. xx, 276p. Illus., index.

Much of the material in this bibliography/filmography is ancillary to mystery and detective fiction, but it is included because of its police focus. About 500 works of fiction and 200+ films are admitted under Drew's elastic inclusion guidelines: a Mountie need have only a small role. Entries on fictional works are keyed to a five-page list of reference sources in which they are discussed. There are synopses of selected titles, though many unexamined titles are listed. The biographical information on the authors is valuable, because many are obscure (e.g. Harold Bindloss, Ridgewell Cullum, Louis Charles Douthwaite, Joe Holliday, T. Morris Longstreth, William Byron Mowery, Harwood E. Steele). Among the major subject authors are James Oliver Curwood, Laurie York Erskine, and James B. Hendryx. Mystery writers included with several titles range from old-timer Hulbert Footner to contemporaries Alisa Craig (Charlotte MacLeod), Jim Lotz, L.R. Wright, and (in the addendum) James Powell. Among others touched on are Dick Francis, Dorothy Cameron Disney, Howard Engel, Jack Barnao (Ted Wood), Tim Heald, Bill Pronzini, Helen Reilly, Lee Thayer, and Eric Wright. In a prose section that comprises well over half the book, Drew also lists magazines (slick and pulp) that published Mountie fiction and ventures into comic books, newspaper comic strips, and Big Little Books. The film listings, also keyed to a bibliography of critical sources, include serials and animated cartoons along with features. There are separate listings of TV and radio series, musical and dramatic theatre, and opera.

25. *The Drood Review's Mystery Yearbook.* **Ed. Jim Huang.** Boston: Crum Creek, annual, 1989- .

Not examined. According to Edward D. Hoch (in *The Year's Best Mystery and Suspense Stories, 1991* #369), it is "an annual listing books published during the previous year, together with awards, periodicals, mystery bookshops, organizations, and conventions."

26. East, Andy. *The Cold War File.* Metuchen, NJ: Scarecrow, 1983. xiv, 362p. Bibl., index.

East presents dossier-style accounts of over seventy spy-novel series that debuted before 1969. Most entries are under authors' names, but a few entries for publishers are included, e.g., the Fawcett and N.A.L./Signet "Intelligence Groups." Though some readers may find the mock-official jargon a little too cute (a film adaptation, for example, is always referred to as a "visual project"), there is considerable critical content and much solid biographical information both on the authors and their fictional creations. The big names are here (James Bond, Matt Helm, George Smiley, Nick Carter, Quiller), plus lesser-known figures little covered in other reference sources, such as Norman Daniels's John Keith, Peter Rabe's Manny deWitt, Don Smith's Phil Sherman, and Don Von Elsner's Jake Winkman. East does not disparage TV novelizations, and there is considerable information on the various *Man from U.N.C.L.E.* paperbacks and their perpetrators.

Arrangement is by author, including a "Field Bibliography" (series checklist), giving both hardback and paperback reprint publishers. Appended are additional titles in series that continued past the 1969 cut-off date and information on series that changed paperback publishers after that date. There is a two-page bibliography of secondary sources, plus a name index to the secret agents covered. This is the most valuable reference source to date on series espionage fiction.

27. **Foord, Peter, and Richard Williams.** *Collins Crime Club: A Checklist of the First Editions.* "With a Guide to Their Value" by Ralph Spurrier. (The Dragonby Bibliographies, Number 1.) Scunthorpe, England: Dragonby, 1987.

Not examined. According to Robert E. Briney (*The Armchair Detective*, v. 24, n. 2, p. 208), "The approximately 1,700 books published by Collins Crime Club since May 1930 are listed alphabetically by author and chronologically by publication date. Number of pages, cover price, ISBN (where applicable), and approximate current market value are given for each title."

28. **Granovetter, Pamela, and Karen Thomas McCallum, eds.** *The Copperfield Checklist of Mystery Authors: The Complete Crime Works of 100 Distinguished Writers of Mystery and Detective Fiction.* New York: Copperfield, 1987. 128p. Second edition. New York: Copperfield, 1990. 160p.

Designed strictly as a personal rather than a library reference, this guide consists of chronological lists of the books of 100 writers, giving year of publication and alternate titles, with three boxes for the user to check: one for books read, one for books owned, and the middle one for whatever use the collector chooses. Especially good or important volumes are asterisked. There are ten blank pages the user can fill in with other books. Appendices include the most extensive list I've seen (twelve pages, increasing to seventeen in the second edition) of specialist dealers in mystery fiction, geographically arranged by state, province, or country. A six-item secondary bibliography headed "Recognitions," increasing to eight in the second edition, is regrettably sparse.

The information is generally reliable, and the format will undoubtedly be useful to individual collectors who can't afford the more expensive (and unwieldy) references of Hubin (see WAM #18 and present volume #548) and Reilly (see WAM #29 and present volume #556). I noted two problems: when a writer published more than one book in a year, the listing becomes alphabetical rather than chronological (e.g., Gardner's *The Case of the Velvet Claws*, published first, here is listed after *The Case of the Sulky Girl*, published in the same year); and in the Ellery Queen entry, a couple of the ghost-written paperback originals (*Where is Bianca?* and *How Goes the Murder?*) have snuck in among the real EQ novels.

(The second edition corrects the latter defect by adding more ersatz Queen but clearly indicating which books are ghost-written and when known identifying the ghost involved.)

The 1992 printing of the second edition further updates the listings through the end of 1991.

29. Granovetter, Pamela, and Karen Thomas McCallum, eds. *A Shopping List of Mystery Classics.* New York: Copperfield Press, 1986. 95p.

Listing selected titles by a larger number of authors, with boxes to be checked for books read, wanted, and owned, this predecessor to *The Copperfield Checklist* (see above) is somewhat less valuable to collectors of individual authors but no doubt useful to someone trying to build a broad general collection in the genre. Included is a fifteen-page list of specialist bookstores in a straight alphabetical arrangement, somewhat shorter and less helpfully arranged than its successor. A second appendix lists "25 Easy-to-Find Favorites," and a third gives an eight-page preview of the forthcoming *Copperfield Checklist.*

Another entry in this series, *The Copperfield Want-List* (1990) is mostly blank pages for the reader's use, with the only reference feature the same list of mystery book dealers included in the other volumes.

30. Hagemann, E.R. *A Comprehensive Index to Black Mask, 1920-1951.* Bowling Green, OH: Popular, 1982. 236p. Bibl.

Black Mask, famed for introducing such major writers of crime fiction as Dashiell Hammett, Raymond Chandler, and Erle Stanley Gardner, has long been recognized as the greatest of the mystery pulp magazines. But until Hagemann's effort, there had been no published index to its contents. Hagemann indexes all fiction, with selective inclusion of letters and features. The listing includes 2509 items, arranged alphabetically by author, Cleve F. Adams to Erika Zastrow (a rare female contributor). Brief annotations identify detectives and backgrounds. A separate list enumerates editors and writers chronologically by date of debut, listing series characters and total number of appearances. In an informative preface, Hagemann discusses the history of his project, as well as other supposed indexes of *Black Mask*, including one by the late William J. Clark which specialists swear exists but which cannot be located.

Gardner was the *Black Mask* champ in terms of volume, making 103 appearances under his own name between 1924 and 1943. He also made three early appearances as Charles M. Green (a name missing from the chronology in a rare Hagemann lapse). Other prolific bylines: Carroll John Daly (60), Hammett (45), Raoul F. Whitfield (66 plus 24 as Ramon Decolta), Frederick L. Nebel (67), Roger Torrey (50), W.T. Ballard (43), George Harmon Coxe (27), and Cornell Woolrich (24). Chandler's appearances numbered only 11. Notable less frequent contributors included John D. MacDonald, William Campbell Gault, Lester Dent, Frank Gruber, Steve Fisher, Baynard H. Kendrick, Thomas Walsh, Murray Leinster, Frederick C. Davis, and (most surprisingly) J.S. Fletcher. The almost complete absence of women authors is notable (though probably not too surprising), even though a woman, Fanny Ellsworth, edited the magazine for a few years in the late thirties, following the legendary Captain Joseph T. Shaw.

31. **Horning, Jane.** *The Mystery Lover's Book of Quotations.* New York: Mysterious, 1988. ix, 277p. Index.

A book like this was bound to come eventually, and I'm glad a compiler as meticulous and wide-ranging as Horning did the job. The 1602 numbered entries are arranged alphabetically by author, giving the author's dates and a brief identification. Most of the quotations are from works of mystery fiction, some from secondary sources about mystery fiction, and some about criminous subjects from general literary sources (including Aristotle, Chaucer, Shakespeare, Thoreau, and Voltaire among others). There are indexes by title and subject (including key-words).
    Most of the best and/or most famous writers of mystery fiction are represented, along with a good selection of lesser-known names. Numerical leaders include Doyle (48 quotes), Christie (23), Stout (21), Wilkie Collins (20), Poe (16), Hammett and Ambler (15 each), Chandler (14), and Sayers and John D. MacDonald (13 each). No reader will deem all the quotes gems, but that is true of Bartlett's and every other quotation book. Reading some of the quotes could turn more readers on to some unfamiliar writers than other secondary sources. To quote some of my favorites: #99, "Don't you think moderation in all things might in itself be a sort of excess?" (from Robert Barnard); #302, "The criminal is the creative artist; the detective only the critic" (from G.K. Chesterton); #485, "The Lord give, and then He robe you blind with his free hand" (from

Peter Dickinson); and #1070, "Most conversations are simply mono-
logues delivered in the presence of a witness" (from Margaret Millar).
(Note that in all these cases, a character is speaking, and thus the opinion
is not necessarily the author's!)

Only major complaint I have is the handling of alternate titles. The
Barnard line quoted above is attributed to a book called *Disposal of the
Living,* published in 1985. Not recognizing the title, I knew it must be a
British one changed for the American edition. The American title, *Fête
Fatale,* appears in the title index with the cross reference to *Disposal of
the Living,* but there is no easy way to figure out the American title without
scanning through the index. Including alternate titles in the main entry
would have made things easier, especially when the British title is usually
used for books published there first.

32. Husband, Janet. Sequels: *An Annotated Guide to Novels in Series.*
Chicago: American Library Association, 1982. vii, 361p. Index.

This painstaking work covers fictional series generally, but since the
crime and mystery genre probably has more such than any other category,
it's not surprising what a large percentage—I'd estimate between a quarter
and a third—is devoted to detective and spy series. The source is not
intended to be all-inclusive, attempting to include "the best, the most
enduring, the most popular novels in series that might appeal to today's
readers" (page vi). Though relatively recent series predominate, the more
significant older ones are covered as well. Short stories and children's
series are generally excluded. Arrangement is alphabetical by author with
a paragraph describing the series, followed by a numbered list of entries,
usually with a line or two of plot summary for each. The titles are listed
in the preferred order for reading, not necessarily the order in which they
were published—for example, Ellery Queen's *The Greek Coffin Mystery*
(1932) is listed before *The Roman Hat Mystery* (1929), because its action
occurred earlier in Ellery's career. In the case of some very prolific
writers—Erle Stanley Gardner, John Creasey, Ed McBain—there are no
individual annotations, though Husband does annotate the Maigret novels
of Georges Simenon.

Though there are occasional minor errors (Emma Lathen becomes
"Lathan" and Ross Macdonald "MacDonald," and Lawrence Sanders'
The Anderson Tapes really should be listed with the Edward X. Delaney
series, though admittedly Hubin [WAM #18] doesn't have it there either),
this is a well-written, attractively presented, and responsible compilation,

with a method of approach to series not provided in any other single reference source.

33. Johnson, Timothy W., and Julia Johnson, eds. *Crime Fiction Criticism: An Annotated Bibliography.* (Garland Reference Library of the Humanities, Vol. 233.) New York: Garland, 1981. xii, 423p. Index.

The Johnsons include 1810 numbered items, with brief descriptive annotations. "Section One: General Works" is divided into reference works, books, dissertations, and articles, while "Section Two: Individual Authors," comprising most of the volume, is arranged alphabetically by subject. Some foreign language items have been included. The annotations are generally informative, though some seem to belabor the obvious. The selection is limited to items of criticism, with purely biographical and technical items excluded. There is an index to critics but none to titles, and the arrangement obviates a subject index.

Though articles from *The Armchair Detective* are included, other fanzines are ignored on grounds of unavailability in libraries. There were some errors and omissions noted but probably fewer than average in mystery fiction reference sources. One of the stated purposes of the volume—to encourage research on under-represented authors—is furthered by the surprising sparsity of entries on some very major writers: Stanley Ellin (one entry), Andrew Garve (one), Geoffrey Household (one), Ed McBain (one), Julian Symons (three), and Phoebe Atwood Taylor (one). It should be pointed out that mere book reviews usually do not qualify for inclusion.

The Johnsons have a distinct edge over the competing Skene Melvins (see #54) in at least three areas: number of entries, convenience of arrangement, and inclusion of annotations. However, their volume is decisively superseded by Albert (see #6).

34. Keating, H.R.F. *Crime and Mystery: The 100 Best Books.* Foreword by Patricia Highsmith. London: Xanadu; New York: Carroll & Graf, 1987. 219p. Bibl., index.

Keating may be the ideal writer for a book like this, not because everyone will agree with his selections but because he is so good at celebrating the field's classics and explaining why they are classics. He has an appreciation of style, and his choice of quotes gives writers like Marsh, Queen, and Allingham their due as prose artists. Keating accepts Julian Symons's idea of the detective story's evolution into the crime novel, but he recognizes that "crime novel" and "novel" are not quite the same thing. His selection of titles has a pronounced (though not outrageous) British bias, but he offers fine appreciations of American writers like Futrelle, Rinehart, Gardner, Eberhart, McBain, and Hillerman, and he is especially good at articulating the differing emphasis and appeal of British and American crime fiction.

Certainly the choices offer plenty of room for argument. He includes a few writers, mostly British, that some readers will be surprised to see making the first hundred: John Bingham, Guy Cullingford (with the remarkable fantasy *Post Mortem*), Shelley Smith (her *Young Man, I Think You're Dying* is an especially hard choice for him to explain), George Sims, and June Thomson. Other obvious inclusions he represents with surprising titles: Helen McCloy's *Mr. Splitfoot*, Raymond Chandler's *The High Window*, John D. MacDonald's *The Green Ripper*, P.D. James's *The Black Tower*. (With that last one at least, I heartily agree.)

The authors omitted completely are a stickier wicket. With Simenon and Christie each represented by three titles (both *Ackroyd* and *Orient Express* for the latter) and several others with two, it would seem some other important writers could have been let in. Some he explicitly rules out as being outside his definition of the crime or mystery novel: Dick Francis, Charles McCarry, Stephen King, Daphne DuMaurier, and Mary Higgins Clark. His banning of spy fiction is so complete that not even Eric Ambler and John le Carré, each with at least one foot in the detective story, qualify. Historically important Americans Anna Katharine Green and S.S. Van Dine are denied a place, as is s.f./detection hybridizer Isaac Asimov. Keating specifies he left out the following writers because of present unavailability of their works: R. Austin Freeman, Alice Tilton (widely available in the U.S. but apparently not in Britain), Freeman Wills Crofts, and Stuart Palmer. Of this group, Freeman seems to me the most unfortunate omission. Though Rinehart and Eberhart make it, latter-day romantic suspense specialists are universally snubbed.

Apart from questions of selection (half the fun in a work like this), there are a few outright factual errors. *Uncle Abner* is oddly described as a novel of linked stories. Some of Chester Himes's novels were undoubtedly first published in French, but he didn't write them in French. Carter Brown (a writer, I hasten to add, alluded to in passing, not included in the hundred) was Australian, not American. Lillian de la Torre's *Elizabeth is*

Missing is a true crime account rather than a novel. And Mignon G. Eberhart, referred to by Keating in the past tense, is still alive at this writing and has had a new book published since Keating's volume appeared.

Keating almost always avoids solution giveaways, and when he does feel obliged to reveal the secrets, as of Christie's *The Murder of Roger Ackroyd* or Dorothy B. Hughes's *The Expendable Man,* he gives ample warning.

35. Keating, H.R.F., ed. *Whodunit: A Guide to Crime, Suspense, and Spy Fiction.* New York: Van Nostrand Reinhold, 1982. 320p. Illus., bibl., index.

This is one of the most entertaining of reference volumes, including some beautifully-written and penetrating (albeit brief) essays on mystery fiction. Keating has chosen his collaborators well, and his quality control is usually impeccable. In his introduction, the editor discusses the differences between crime fiction and mainstream fiction. "Crime Fiction and its Categories" includes essays by Reginald Hill (on pre-history, concentrating on DeFoe and William Godwin), Keating (crediting Conan Doyle with establishing crime fiction as a separate category), Robert Barnard (on the classical British novel, especially Christie, Sayers, Allingham, and Marsh), Julian Symons (on the American hardboiled school), Hillary Waugh (on the American police procedural), Michael Gilbert (on its British counterpart), Eleanor Sullivan (on the short story), Jessica Mann (on the suspense novel), Jerry Palmer (on the thriller), Michele Slung (on the gothic, mostly the original rather than contemporary type), and John Gardner (with an excellent and controversial piece on the espionage novel, rating American Charles McCarry higher than John le Carré and claiming only James Bond will live on among crime fiction characters since Sherlock Holmes). These authors are obviously well-qualified and do an excellent job in a short space to capture the essence of their subjects.

The next section is called "How I Write My Books." Answering the question are Stanley Ellin, P.D. James, Desmond Bagley, Dorothy Eden, Patricia Highsmith, Gregory Mcdonald, Lionel Davidson, Len Deighton, Eric Ambler, and editor Keating. For all but Bagley (who used a word processor) and Davidson, actual samples of working copy are included. All these essays are interesting reading, Bagley's most of all.

Next comes "Writers and Their Books: A Consumer's Guide," a section based in part on material in *Novels and Novelists: A Guide to the*

World of Fiction (St. Martin's, 1980), edited by Martin Seymour Smith. Over 140 pages, a team composed of Keating, Hill, Dorothy B. Hughes, and Melvyn Barnes comment on some 500 crime fiction writers. Each entry includes a short biographical-critical paragraph followed by a listing of (usually) two or three major works, which are rated with between one and ten stars in four areas: characterization, plot, readability, and tension. The ratings present two problems: The groups of stars are difficult to count in such profusion (seven, eight, and nine are hard to tell apart easily) and would better have been represented by a numeral. And the ratings, especially when one writer is compared with another, give some odd messages. Sara Woods, for example, is rated more highly than her page-mate, Cornell Woolrich. Michael Avallone is given the nod over George Bagby (though not over the same author writing as Hampton Stone or Aaron Marc Stein). Ross Macdonald rates higher on readability (and in other areas, too) than John D. MacDonald, whom many believe at least his equal. Adding insult to injury, both Philip MacDonald and Gregory Mcdonald also rate higher than JDM! Robert B. Parker's *Promised Land,* an Edgar-winning novel with almost no plot at all, gets nine stars in that category. In an example of courtesy toward contributors often seen in references of this type, John Gardner's James Bond pastiche *License Renewed* is rated much more highly here than in most reviews I have seen. Despite its idiosyncracies and lapses, though, this consumer's guide is a useful one. Portraits of some of the authors have been included.

Keating is credited as sole author of "The People of Crime Fiction," an illustrated biographical section on 90 major characters, most covered two to a page. Here Keating's ability to summarize the appeal of a book, author, or character in a few witty sentences is seen at its best. The illustrations are drawn from movie and TV stills, magazine and book illustrations, postage stamps, and (in some cases) original portraits. (Hillary Waugh in his depiction of Chief of Police Fred Fellows reveals a professional-caliber cartooning talent.) Finally, psychiatrist Philip Graham takes up the age-old question, "Why People Read Crime Fiction."

Though the various illustrations add much to the interest and attractiveness of this volume, they are also responsible for some absurdities, such as a comic strip chart rating tough detectives on their hardboiledness quotient from one to ten. The author believes Archie Goodwin (a five) is more hardboiled than Mike Shayne (a four). True, Archie writes good tough prose and is a handy fellow to have around in an emergency, but he prefers milk to cognac and rarely gets into a fight with fists or gun. Shayne, bracketed with insurance investigator Dave Brandstetter in the boiling contest, has been sadly misjudged.

Given Keating's profound knowledge of the crime fiction field and his strong editorial abilities, it is surprising so many factual howlers found their way into this book. Symons claims *Red Harvest* was the only Continental Op novel. What about *The Dain Curse*? The editor himself inaccurately states that Ellery Queen was the narrator of most of the books in which he appeared. Chester Himes is said to have begun writing when almost fifty—that may have been when he started on detective fiction, but he was a well-established mainstream novelist for many years before that. Jerry Palmer is allowed to say Chandler and Hammett "decided to put murder back where it belonged" in the mid-thirties, by which time Hammett's creative life was virtually over.

36. Kramer, John E., Jr., and John E. Kramer, III. *College Mystery Novels: An Annotated Bibliography, Including a Guide to Professional Series-Character Sleuths.* (Garland Reference Library of the Humanities, Vol. 360.) New York: Garland, 1983. xvii, 356p. Index.

In one of the best specialized bibliographies in the mystery field, the authors, father and son, have identified 632 novels and single-author collections of special interest to academic readers, 324 involving professorial series characters and the rest "free-standing." In the first section, more than fifty sleuths are profiled in considerable detail and their book appearances listed with British and American publication data. The subjects are arranged by date of first appearance from Jacques Futrelle's Augustus S.F.X. Van Dusen, a.k.a. the Thinking Machine (1906), to S.F.X. Dean's Neil Kelly (1982). Among those discussed are characters as well-known as Amanda Cross's Kate Fansler, Edmund Crispin's Gervase Fen, John Rhode's Dr. Priestley, and Arthur B. Reeve's Craig Kennedy, alongside names as relatively obscure as Francis Grierson's Professor Wells, Gavin Holt's Luther Bastion, Charles J. Dutton's Harley Manners, and Milton K. Ozaki's Professor Caldwell. Most comments are descriptive rather than critical, but there is much humor in the descriptions. The larger section annotates individual non-series books, these also arranged chronologically. The famous and the obscure are given equally thorough attention with plot summary, author biography, identification of characters and scenes of special interest to the academic world, and some usually favorable critical comments. (The compilers are so kindly in their assessments that the rare mildly disparaging remark screams out from the page.) The volume's title is broadly applied, both sections including books that involve academics *away* from the academy as well as those with campus settings.

There are some errors, though not too many for so ambitious a work. Death dates are lacking for many surely-deceased authors. Entry #353 has lost its title—it's John Stephen Strange's *Murder on the Ten-Yard Line,* which does appear in the index. A few names appear in mangled form: "Octavius" Roy Cohen, "Frederic" Brown, Edgar "Allen" Poe, Lord Peter "Whimsey," and John Putnam "Thayer."

An appendix lists the outstanding titles in both categories, which are also designated by an asterisk in the main text. There are indexes to series characters, authors, and titles.

37. **Lindsay, Ethel.** *Here Be Mystery and Murder: Reference Books in the Mystery Genre Excluding Sherlockiana.* Carnoustie: privately printed, 1982. Unpaged.

Limited to an edition of only 100 copies, Lindsay's checklist identifies 748 titles of non-fiction books with crime fiction reference value. Her guidelines are superficially similar to those of the present work, with the greater number of titles explained primarily by the inclusion of true crime items. Main listing is by title with an index by author. Entries give American and British publishers, dates, and pagination. Many entries are briefly annotated. The listing is useful in turning up odd and little-known publications, though the listing by title and the lack of a subject index make use somewhat difficult.

38. **McCarty, John, and Brian Kelleher.** *Alfred Hitchcock Presents: An Illustrated Guide to the Ten-Year Television Career of the Master of Suspense.* Foreword by Robert Bloch. New York: St. Martin's, 1985. Illus., bibl., index.

In a valuable contribution to both mystery and TV scholarship, the authors present a chronological episode-by-episode account of the *Alfred Hitchcock Presents* and *Alfred Hitchcock Hour* programs plus the contributions of Hitchcock's production company to *Suspicion* and *Ford Startime.* Each entry includes title, director, writers (of teleplay and original story), a plot synopsis identifying major actors, and the program's airdate. A few of the entries are illustrated with wallet-size stills, and some include sidelights on the actors, writers, and directors involved. In a book more oriented toward celebrating writers and directors than actors, some film and TV buffs will regret fuller cast information is not included.

The book leads off with an introductory history of the series, especially notable for the deserved credit it gives James Allardice, the author of those wonderful tongue-in-cheek program introductions delivered by Hitchcock himself. Quotes from these are interspersed throughout the volume. Other features include a listing of major television awards and nominations the program received, a brief bibliography of books and periodicals, and an index to show titles. A name index would also have been helpful. As it is, a person trying to trace all Henry Slesar's contributions to the program as writer or all John Williams's acting appearances can only browse for them.

Viewers of the series' reruns, still available to television stations in syndication, should be warned that the synopses come complete with surprise twist.

Some errors were noted. The authors mistakenly believe *Alfred Hitchcock's Mystery Magazine* antedated the TV show. Actually, the first issue of *AHMM* was dated December 1956, while the show debuted a year earlier, October 2, 1955. Also, Ziff-Davis never published *AHMM* (though it was purchased by Davis Publications, its present proprietor, in 1976), and the magazine did not start life as a stablemate to *Ellery Queen's Mystery Magazine,* which was then published by Mercury Publications and in fact never carried the Ziff-Davis banner either. Once again, Fredric Brown and Talmage Powell get their names constantly misspelled, and at one point C.B. Gilford turns into C.B. "Guilford" for a couple of entries. In the individual show entries, there is no director credit for "Miss Paisley's Cat" (page 120) or "Night of the Executioner" (page 121) and no writing or directing credit for "Touché" (page 160). Stanley Ellin is not given original story credit for "The Orderly World of Mr. Appleby" (page 78).

39. McCormick, Donald, and Katy Fletcher. *Spy Fiction: A Connoisseur's Guide.* New York: Facts on File, 1990. 346p. Bibl., index.

The first and larger section consists of an alphabetical arrangement of 200+ authors, mostly British and American, providing pseudonyms if any, nationality, dates, titles, biography, and "critical analysis" (usually a misnomer). In some cases, information on media adaptations is included. There's plenty of useful information but plenty of disappointments as well, mainly in the failure of the book as a critical guide. Writers already well covered in other sources get critical comment, but for lesser known writers, too often there isn't a clue, with quotes from the authors and plot summaries taking the place of analysis. In the listings of works by prolific writers, even as major a figure as Donald Hamilton, the editors seem to give up in fatigue, arbitrarily cutting the list short on a chronological or (in the case of Nick Carter) alphabetical basis.

Other idiosyncracies: Allen Dulles gets an entry by virtue of having edited a spy anthology. Films about Bulldog Drummond are discussed in the entry for Gerard Fairlie rather than Drummond's creator, H.C. McNeile. The two books listed for R. Wright Campbell give only the paperback reprint editions. When authors have also written non-spy fiction, it is sometimes included (Warren Adler's *The War of the Roses,* Michael Avallone's non-spy Ed Noon novels) and sometimes not (Bill S. Ballinger, Graham Greene). The entry on Kingsley Amis fails to mention that *Colonel Sun* was a James Bond pastiche. John D. MacDonald's Travis McGee is an odd inclusion in a spy-fiction reference. The only cross-references from pseudonym to real name appear in the index.

Turning from general sloppiness to pure error, Michael Kurland's *A Plague of Spies* is mistakenly awarded an Edgar, and Tom Clancy's *Patriot Games* is not identified as being about Jack Ryan—an odd mistake to make on so recent and popular a book. Will B. Aarons, the byline on the later Sam Durell novels, is said to be the son of Edward S. Aarons. In fact, it was a house name.

The second section, eight topical chapters totalling 55 pages, holds the kernel of a much better book than the encyclopedic section. Topics include a history of American spy fiction (citing the contribution of Henry James!), real-life events in spy fiction (mainly discussing fictional uses of the Kennedy assassination), moles (discussing Rebecca West's *The Birds Fall Down,* a work not included in the alphabetical section), non-English-language spy writers (French, German, Soviet, Japanese), future directions (considering the impact of glasnost), real agents as writers of fiction (discussing Maugham, Childers, Compton MacKenzie, Greene, Fleming, le Carré), and film adaptations (claiming the "spy novel does not adapt well visually" among other doubtful statements and devoting some space to Ronald Reagan's Secret Service movie series as Brass Bancroft).

Other features include a ten-page glossary of espionage terms (including some most interesting and unfamiliar ones), a four-page bibliography of secondary sources, and a nine-page index.

40. Mackler, Tasha. *Murder by Category: A Subject Guide to Mystery Fiction.* Metuchen, NJ: Scarecrow, 1991. xiii, 470p. Index.

This useful subject guide lists fewer titles than the compilations of Menendez (see #44) and Olderr (see #48), but unlike them offers annotations (non-critical plot summaries) and sticks to currently available material. (The latter decision may lessen potential reader frustration but leads to some disturbing omissions: for example, there is not a single Ellery Queen title in the whole book!) The alphabetical listing of topics, an inviting selection, ranges from the expected (Academics, Antiques, Bookstores, Cats, Clergy, Horses and Horse Racing, Indians, Journalism, Lawyers, Locked Rooms, Music, Television and Radio, Theater) to the more surprising (Crossword Puzzles; Espionage, the Industrial Kind; Pornography, Richard III, Witness Protection Program). There are only a few headings by locale (Africa, Australia, Canada, Hollywood, Orient, including some Charlie Chan exploits that take place far from the Orient, and Russia). Each heading has a brief introduction. Titles which belong to more than one category are cross-referenced. Where the book involves a series character, the number of the book in series is provided at the end of the annotation.

Following the alphabetical section, bookdealer Mackler provides several listings that answer frequent customer questions: of British woman mystery writers, female detectives (listed by author's name), and awards, including winners and nominees for best novel, best first novel, and best paperback original in the Edgar and Anthony awards, 1985-1989, and the Shamus awards, 1985-1988. Grand Master Edgar winners for those years are also noted. There follow a two-page secondary bibliography and an author index.

The compiler has an odd way of dealing with pseudonyms: *Unholy Moses* is listed under "DeAndrea, William, w/a writing as Philip DeGrave." There is no cross-reference from DeGrave to DeAndrea, and the name DeGrave does not appear in the index. Thus, a reader who knew the DeGrave byline but didn't know it was an alter ego of DeAndrea would have no convenient way of locating it in the book. The same occurs with Erle Stanley Gardner as A.A. Fair and Charlotte MacLeod as Alisa Craig.

In other cases (e.g. Roderic Jeffries/Jeffrey Ashford, Elizabeth Peters/Barbara Michaels), the dual identity is not noted at all.

41. McLeish, Kenneth, and Valerie McLeish. *Bloomsbury Good Reading Guide to Murder, Crime Fiction & Thrillers.* London: Bloomsbury, 1990.

Not examined. According to Edward D. Hoch (in *The Year's Best Mystery and Suspense Stories, 1991* #369), it is an "alphabetical guide to leading mystery writers and subject areas."

42. Magill, Frank N., ed. *Critical Survey of Mystery and Detective Fiction.* Pasadena, CA: Salem, 1988. xii, 1748p. in 4 volumes + separately paged indexes. Bibl., index.

The editor celebrated and sometimes reviled for the student staple *Masterplots* presents a critical guide to more than 270 mystery writers, historical and contemporary. Coverage is somewhat broader than the title suggests, with authors of espionage fiction and straight crime fiction included. Along with subjects primarily known for their work in the mystery field, mainstream literary figures like Gore Vidal (as Edgar Box), Mark Twain, William Faulkner, Robert Louis Stevenson, Voltaire, and Fyodor Dostoevski are included. The international coverage extends to some European writers whose names few fans will recognize: Heimito von Doderer, Annette von Droste-Hülshoff, Leonid Maksimovich Leonov, and Adolf Müllner. Certainly most major writers are covered, with some notable omissions among living writers: Sue Grafton, Gerald Petievich, Max Allan Collins, K.C. Constantine, Howard Browne, Robert Campbell, and Marcia Muller. Among deceased figures, room should have been found for Thomas B. Dewey, Philip MacDonald, and Aaron Marc Stein. And while I'll admit Carolyn Wells's importance is mostly historical, if Arthur B. Reeve makes it, so should she.

The entries follow a consistent format. The author's name, date and place of birth and (if applicable) death, pseudonyms, type of plot (categories like amateur sleuth, espionage, inverted), and principal series are noted in brief form, followed by a narrative discussion in five categories: principal series characters (if any, often including secondary characters as well as main sleuths in short thumbnail descriptions), contribution (usually a paragraph or two), biography, and analysis (the longest section). Finally, there are lists (title and date only) of the author's principal mystery and detective fiction, other major works, and a secondary bibliography. Most of the critical summaries run about 2500 words. The critics are nearly all academics, only a few of whose names—e.g. Hal Charles, J. Randolph Cox, and Douglas G. Greene—will be familiar to most fans.

The critical essays, usually both readable and knowledgeable, prove the most valuable feature of the set. The biographies often give details, especially on contemporary writers, not available elsewhere. There is little of the patronizing, condescending tone thin-skinned mystery fans look for in academic treatments of the genre.

The essays are highly variable in extent of coverage, however. Greene's piece on Edward D. Hoch is outstanding, efficiently covering every aspect and category of his work in what should have been a model for other contributors. But too many of the critics choose to deal with only one portion of an author's output. If Barbara Mertz had never written a book under the name Elizabeth Peters, her romantic suspense novels as Barbara Michaels would still place her in the forefront of writers in that genre, but they are utterly ignored in Marilynn M. Larew's essay, which covers the Peters output only. Similarly, the entries on John D. MacD-onald, Bill Pronzini, and Michael Collins deal only with Travis McGee, Nameless, and Dan Fortune respectively, though these writers have made some of their most significant contributions outside these series.

Of course, in any multi-author set, differences of opinion are inevitable. But at least one contributor here disagrees with himself. Bill Delaney credits Lawrence Treat with originating the police procedural form in one essay, while in another describing Helen Reilly, who started writing about police detectives more than a decade before Treat, as a police procedural writer.

The bibliographic information is far less complete and useful than it might be. Especially annoying is the consistent failure to identify works written under pseudonyms. The beginning of the Dean R. Koontz entry, for example, tells us he has written as Brian Coffey, K.R. Dwyer, Leigh Nichols, etc., but the checklist of his novels lists them all in one undifferentiated group. If you want to know which ones bore which pseudonyms, you have to go to Hubin (see WAM #18 and present volume #548) or Reilly (see WAM #29 and present volume #556). Similarly, though the information that Phoebe Atwood Taylor used the Alice Tilton pseudonym when she wrote about Leonidas Witherall is there, you have to look carefully for it. The well-written entry on Ellery Queen by Janet E. Lorenz

unfortunately contributes to the blurring of the "real" EQ works (sometimes in latter days with uncredited collaborators) and the purely ghost-
written paperback originals that unfortunately appeared under the Queen
name. Any scholarly work on Queen should more clearly separate the
genuine from the phony.

The secondary bibliographies tend to be spotty and inconsistent,
sometimes listing minor sources while missing major ones. For example,
Clifton K. Yearley's entry on Mickey Spillane—a rare negative assessment—significantly ignores Max Allan Collins and James L. Traylor's
book-length study, *One Lonely Night* (1984; see #331), which argues in
Spillane's favor as an important writer of crime fiction.

The final volume includes a 14-page glossary of dubious value and
reliability. It attempts to define both terms used to describe the genre and
example of crook, cop, and spy slang. The definition of "whodunit" as
"the classic English mystery" is way off the mark. A whodunit is a book
where you don't know which of several suspects committed the crime,
and it can reside at the toughest or coziest end of the mystery-story
spectrum. Dashiell Hammett's *The Maltese Falcon,* one of the greatest
whodunits of them all, falls outside the description given here. And
speaking of the *Falcon,* the definition of "gunsel" is rather badly botched,
too.

Also in the final volume are separately paged indexes by type of plot
and character names, followed by a very limited general index to names,
titles, and terms. It would be helpful if one could trace through the index
every reference to Anthony Boucher, for example, but the index entry
guides the reader only to the essay on Boucher's own fiction, which
appears in alphabetical order anyway.

In summation, this is a handsomely produced set with some valuable
information and some annoying quirks. It would be a reasonable addition
to a complete collection of mystery fiction references, but a combination
of several less expensive sources would be far preferable.

43. **Malloy, William.** *The Mystery Book of Days.* New York: Mysterious,
1990. Unpaged. Illus., index.

Mysterious Press editor Malloy records notable events in crime
fiction and fact from January 1 (release of the Charlie Chan film *The
Chinese Parrot* in 1928, debut of Sam Spade on radio in 1946, marriage
of William L. DeAndrea and Orania Papazoglou in 1984) through Decem-

ber 31 (birth of Helen Eustis in 1916, release of *London After Midnight* in 1927, and end of *I Love a Mystery*'s radio run in 1952). The pages between turn up hundreds of entertaining facts, handsomely illustrated on every page with portraits, movie stills, book and magazine covers. The events cited are highly varied: the execution of Landru (February 25, 1922), the birth of Jack Webb (April 2, 1920), the comic-book debut of Batman (May 1, 1939), the deaths of Bonnie and Clyde (May 23, 1934), and the receipt of the "most apparently genuine" Jack the Ripper letter (October 16, 1888). On relatively few days (e.g. June 29, September 3, October 20, November 7) was the author unable to find anything of criminous interest.

Errors are relatively few and generally minor. Lieutenant Valcour does not appear in Rufus King's *Museum Piece No. 13* (January 3), and Miss Marple does not die in Agatha Christie's *Sleeping Murder* (January 12).

Over the years, several mystery calendars have been published, omitted here because of their ephemeral nature. Malloy's work is included because it is not tied to a specific year.

44. **Menendez, Albert.** *The Subject is Murder: A Selective Subject Guide to Mystery Fiction.* (Garland Reference Library of the Humanities, Vol. 627.) New York: Garland, 1986. x, 332p. Index.
Volume 2. New York: Garland, 1990. x, 216p. Index.

The parent volume of this very welcome subject guide consists of 3812 unannotated entries in 25 subject areas, including advertising, archaeology, art, circuses and carnivals, department stores, gardening, academia, the "high seas," religion, hotels and inns, "literary people," radio and TV, Christmas, music, politics, newspapers, bookshops and libraries, trains, medicine, sports, the supernatural, theatre, motion pictures, weddings and honeymoons, and amnesia. Each chapter has a brief introduction, citing outstanding examples, series specialists, and sometimes printed sources of further information. Entries give the American place, publisher, and date, except for those books published only in Britain. An addendum cites newly-published titles (through summer 1985) and older titles omitted in the main list. A valuable added feature is an eight-page list of mystery book dealers, most American but some British or Canadian. Finally, there is an author index.

Menendez knows the field well, and his book is for the most part both admirably up-to-date and thorough, including some wonderfully obscure titles bound to appeal to totally-immersed mystery buffs. Most readers will be too grateful that this book exists at all to spend much time looking for errors and omissions.

On the debit side, however, Menendez has a tendency to refer to titles without their authors in his chapter introductions, forcing the reader to browse through long lists to find the author's name. If the book had a title index (which would be very nice), this tendency would be merely irritating. Without a title index, it can be maddening. In introducing the chapter on ecclesiastical mysteries, he lists some series characters without reference to their authors—an even worse offense, since it is impossible for the reader to find in this book whose character is who. Also regrettable is the author's decision to ignore the existence of pseudonyms, especially since some authors (e.g., John Evans/Howard Browne, Anthony Boucher/H.H. Holmes) appear in the book under more than one name with no cross references to inform the reader of their identity. The author index consistently omits co-authors (e.g., Frank L. Tedeschi, who collaborated with Barbara Ninde Byfield on *Solemn High Murder,* and Val Gielgud's sometime co-author Holt Marvell).

As to the selections, it is, as always, possible to nitpick. I think calling *The Moonstone* a gardening mystery because Sgt. Cuff's hobby was growing roses is stretching things a bit. A more likely choice would be Anthony Matthews' *Death has Green Fingers* (Walker, 1971), published in England as by Lionel Black. William Peter Blatty's *Legion* is listed with the religious mysteries, but not its more famous predecessor, *The Exorcist.* Fletcher Knebel surely belongs enough to the mystery/detective genre for titles like *Vanished* and *Night of Camp David* to make the political list. Helen McCloy is mentioned in the introduction to the chapter on medical mysteries, but none of her novels about psychiatrist-detective Basil Willing are listed in the chapter. In the supernatural chapter, there should be many more titles by John Dickson Carr, whose books are full of a supernatural aura (usually explained away), and Dennis Wheatley, who regularly dealt with real black magic and is represented here by only one title.

Though none of the above points are addressed save adding a couple more Carr titles, the second volume adds 2093 more entries and has a title index as well as an author index. Existing categories are supplemented, mostly with books published since 1985, and several additional categories have been added: antiques, cooking, fashion, Halloween, and (as sub-topics in the sports chapter) bird watching, coin collecting, stamp collecting, and mountain climbing. This time, there are no introductions to the individual chapters, but there is an interesting appendix ranking the categories numerically and discussing trends since 1980. (In the decade of the '80s, religion has moved from third to first place, ahead of academia and sports.)

45. Moody, Susan. *The Hatchards Crime Companion: 100 Top Crime Novels Selected by the Crime Writers' Association.* London: Hatchards, 1990.

Not examined. According to Edward D. Hoch (in *The Year's Best Crime and Suspense Stories 1991*, #369), Moody presents the "results of a poll of CWA members, with a brief comment on each book."

46. Nash, Jay Robert. *Encyclopedia of World Crime.* Wilmette, IL: CrimeBooks, 1990. 6 volumes. Illus., bibl., index.

This massive encyclopedia, recipient of a special Edgar award, deals with true-crime cases and thus is outside the usual *What About Murder?* boundaries. But there is some fictional interest in the occasional entries for authors of crime and mystery fiction and the inclusion of fiction titles in some of the bibliographies.

What mystery fiction writers belong in a true-crime encyclopedia? Agatha Christie, of course, merits more than a page largely because of her 1926 disappearance, probably not a crime but surely a real-life mystery that precipitated an extensive police investigation. Arthur Conan Doyle gets over a page of text, and one of illustrations, because of the influence of Sherlock Holmes—included, too, are references to his real-life detective work (with cross references to separate articles on Oscar Slater and George Edalji) and a claim that Professor Moriarty was based on an American Napoleon of Crime named Adam Worth, who also has an article of his own. Edgar Allan Poe gets an entry by virtue of his invention of the detective story, as well as his fictionalized solution (in "The Mystery of Marie Roget") to the Mary Rogers case, which gets an entry to itself. Dashiell Hammett, himself a Pinkerton detective before taking up fiction writing, merits an even longer article than Christie or Doyle. Erle Stanley

Gardner, who tried to clear the wrongly accused through his Court of Last Resort, receives a surprisingly brief entry compared to these others.

Selection criteria for writers are sometimes puzzling. Why include fiction writers without close association to true crime, e.g. Raymond Chandler (covered almost as extensively as Hammett), Ellery Queen, and Rex Stout, and ignore mystery writers like Edgar Wallace, who (like Doyle) was occasionally cast (successfully or not) as real-life sleuth? Meanwhile, some of the most renowned writers of true crime books and essays (e.g. Edward D. Radin and William Roughead) surprisingly do not merit entries, though Edmund Lester Pearson does.

The inclusion of fictional, theatrical, and film adaptations in the bibliographies is often helpful. Under Lizzie Borden, for example, we have the ballet *Fall River Legend* by Agnes DeMille, the George S. Kaufman/Moss Hart play *The Man Who Came to Dinner* (which included a character based on Lizzie) and its subsequent film adaptation, and several somewhat obscure novels—but not Evan Hunter's relatively recent Borden novel, *Lizzie* (1984). Three fictionalizations of the Hall-Mills case are cited, including Anthony Abbot's *About the Murder of the Clergyman's Mistress* and J.J. Connington's *The Twenty-one Clues.* The extensive Jack the Ripper bibliography reveals the inconsistency of the listings—some books only vaguely connected to the Ripper case are included (e.g. David Alexander's *Terror on Broadway* and Philip MacDonald's *The Mystery of the Dead Police*), while close fictionalizations like Robert Bloch's *The Night of the Ripper* (1984) and Terrence Lore Smith's *Yours Truly, from Hell* (1987) are excluded. And it's unfortunate that books cited in the bibliographies at the ends of the articles (with author and title only) are not always included in the full-information bibliography in volume VI.

Of course, nit-picking this book on the basis of its fiction-related content is like judging a steakhouse on the quality of its swordfish. As a resource on the history of real-life crime, this set has no equal, and for that it is recommended most highly.

47. **Nichols, Victoria, and Susan Thompson.** *Silk Stalkings: When Women Write of Murder: A Survey of Series Characters Created by Women Authors in Crime and Mystery Fiction.* Berkeley: Black Lizard, 1988. xviii, 522p. Bibl., index.

The second sub-title sets the parameters, though a few male writers have snuck in by virtue of using a female pseudonym (e.g., Evelyn Bond [Morris Hershman], Evelyn Hervey [H.R.F. Keating]) or working in a mixed collaboration (e.g., John and Emery Bonett, the Gordons). The series characters included may be of either sex. In the narrative chapters of the book's first half, a selection of them are profiled, usually in a page or two, in several categories, mostly occupational (e.g. academics, professional police, clergy, actors, private eyes), but sometimes otherwise (aristocrats). Some of the categories include lists of books not from the series under discussion that use the background in question. The profiles are well-written in a chatty, friendly style and often include telling quotes that offer insights into author and/or character. Critical analysis is included, with most comments celebratory, demonstrating the authors' wide-ranging taste and enthusiasm. Rediscovery (and reprinting) of past authors like Anna Katharine Green, Helen McCloy, Helen Reilly, and even two often maligned favorites of mine, Carolyn Wells and Lee Thayer, is warmly urged. Lillian O'Donnell and Leslie Ford, scorched as anti-feminist by some other commentators, are favorably received here. The authors give mixed notices to E.X. Giroux, Sara Woods, Virginia Rich, and Sarah Caudwell and extend grudging respect to Joyce Porter and Sara Paretsky (though V.I. Warshawski is "one of the least attractive heroes we've recently encountered" age 216). Among those getting the rare bad notice are Tobias Wells (Stanton Forbes), Mignon G. Eberhart (on the Nurse Keate novels rather than the Susan Dare stories), Theodora M. DuBois, Evelyn Anthony, Gwen Moffatt, and (most damned of all) Marjorie Grove. (The latter was one of the authors of Zebra's illustrated mystery series of the late seventies, a line that produced at least some good work. Norma Schier's Kay Barth, listed in the chronological section but not profiled, might have served to balance Grove's Maxine Reynolds.) Among the characters profiled are some obscure ones that may not have been written about as extensively in any other source: e.g., Gwen Bristow and Bruce Manning's Wade, Nancy Barr Mavity's Peter Piper, Ann Bridge's Julia Probyn, John Stephen Strange's Barney Gantt, Harriette Campbell's Simon Brade, and (among more recent characters) Leela Cutter's Lettie Winterbottom and Barbara Ninde Byfield's Simon Bede and Helen Bullock. A chapter on "Wives and Other Significant Others" lists spouses, butlers, housekeepers, secretaries, and assistants of some of the profiled sleuths. While most of the really major characters have been profiled, it's surprising the authors omitted Mr. and Mrs. North—or, for that matter, any other Frances and Richard Lockridge characters.

Following the narrative section is an alphabetical listing by author's name with cross references from pseudonyms, listing each series character and the entries in the series chronologically. Short story collections have been noted as well as novels, and an occasional pure short story character (e.g. Phyllis Bentley's Marian Phipps) has been included. (These listings can be confusing, since there is nothing to differentiate individual short stories from short story collections—for an especially blatant example of this problem, see the Baroness Orczy entry.) There is also a series character chronology (from M.E. Braddon's Valentine Hawkehurst K to M.J. Adamson's Marten Balthazar and Carolyn G. Hart's Annie Laurence h 1987), a separate index of pseudonyms, and an index by series character.

Errors are commendably rare, though Lillian de la Torre's four books about Dr. Sam: Johnson have not been identified as collections; in one listing the character of Maggie Rome is credited to Lilian Jackson Braun rather than Lucille Kallen; and it is stated that Dorothy Dunnett's books about Johnson Johnson have the word "bird" in "all American titles" (page 199)—in fact, it was the British editions that had titles like Dolly and the Doctor Bird, while the American publisher went for more conventional titles like *Match for a Murderer.*

This is a valuable reference, well enough done to make one regret it is confined to authors of one sex.

48. Olderr, Steven. *Mystery Index: Subjects, Settings, and Sleuths of 10,000 Titles.* Chicago: American Library Association, 1987. xiv, 492p. Bibl., index.

At first glance, this looks like a less complete version of Allen J. Hubin's *Crime Fiction* bibliographies (see WAM #18 and present volume #548). The main section, arranged by author, is in a very similar format, giving both U.S. and British first edition information, and it is followed by title, subject, and character indexes. But the book does have some value to collections already having Hubin: the subject index is the most extensive ever published in book form, offering many more subjects than either Hubin or Albert Menendez in *The Subject is Murder* (see #44). Using Library of Congress subject headings, Olderr guides the reader to mysteries by locale, occupation of detective, type of crime, murder method, specialized background, and many other surprising means of access. Olderr is a bit less reliable than Hubin or Menendez, however, and a library or collector would need all three volumes (plus Tasha Mackler's *Murder by Category* #40) to approach full subject coverage of the field.

Emphasis is on detective fiction proper, with espionage excluded. Thus, Fleming, Deighton, and even le Carré are out, though Ritchie Perry, unaccountably, is in with some of his Philis novels.

There are some rather glaring errors in the assignment of subject headings. William Marshall's Yellowthread Street Precinct, located in Hong Kong, appears under the heading Yellowstone National Park. My own novel *The Gathering Place*, firmly set in Los Angeles, is designated as having a San Francisco locale. Charles Merrill Smith's Reverend Randollph is wrongly indexed as an Episcopal priest; his denomination is never specified, but I always thought he was a Methodist, like his creator.

Other headings, if not wholly wrong, are questionable. Under Trials, many possible titles are missed (see *Novel Verdicts* #10), but George Harmon Coxe's *Murder with Pictures*, which never gets into court, is listed. Under the same heading, only a few of Erle Stanley Gardner's later Perry Masons are listed, though almost all the books in the series had substantial courtroom action. Under Future, we have Isaac Asimov's *Caves of Steel* but not the same author's equally futuristic *The Naked Sun*. Dwight Steward's *The Acupuncture Murders*, though included in the main listing, is not indexed under the heading Deaf Detectives. Sometimes, instead of listing specific titles, the subject index gives the author's name and the number of books on the subject. If the main listing has more than that number under the author's name, the user is left to wonder which of the ones listed belong to the subject heading.

The index of character names reveals another unique feature of this book: in many case, non-series detectives are identified. Olivia Barchester, who shares detecting duties in my *Listen for the Click* with Jerry Brogan, is listed as the sleuth in the main listing and thus included in the character index. Jerry became a series sleuth and Olivia (outside of short stories) did not, but Olderr could not have been expected to anticipate that.

More information on the standards for inclusion would have been helpful, as would a cut-off date. Though the book was published late in 1987, citations don't seem to go beyond 1985.

Coverage of the important writers in the field is fairly complete, though some private-eye writers of note are unaccountably excluded: Richard S. Prather, Michael Avallone, Ed Lacy, and perhaps most surprisingly, Brett Halliday. Imagine having a list of Miami mystery novels with none of the Mike Shayne books listed!

49. **Oleksiw, Susan.** *A Reader's Guide to the Classic British Mystery.*
Boston: Hall, 1988. xiii, 585p. Bibl., index.

The author lists and annotates over 1400 titles by 121 authors,
generally British though at least one American who writes of a British
locale, Martha Grimes, has been included. Arrangement is alphabetical
by author, with titles listed chronologically and separated by series.
(Listings within series are chronological by occurrence, not necessarily
publication—see, for example, the entries in Sara Woods's Antony Maitland series.) British and American place and publisher information are
given, with reprint editions noted where there has been a title change. In
most cases, all the author's output up to 1985 is listed; partial listings are
indicated by an asterisk. (Some well-known and/or important oldtimers—
e.g., Anthony Berkeley, Gladys Mitchell, John Rhode, Patricia Wentworth—are only sparsely covered.) The annotations are brief plot
summaries, usually (and to me, regrettably) excluding any evaluation. It's
hard to imagine someone reading all these books and resisting making
some comment on their relative merits.

Despite the title, inclusions are not limited to the classical form, with
some thriller and procedural writers included. The entries include alternate title information, reprint as well as trans-Atlantic, but pseudonym
information is lacking. For example, Peter Alding, Jeffrey Ashford, and
Roderic Jeffries are listed separately, with no cross-reference to let the
reader know they are all the same writer. Also not helpful is listing the
Detection Club collaborative mysteries without providing even a partial
list of the authors involved. In another oddity, short-story collections are
excluded but novellas are included—thus, Chesterton's Father Brown is
out but his *Four Faultless Felons* is in.

Aside from the often valuable plot summaries, the most useful feature
is the section of indexes: by character name, occupation of series characters, period of the story, locations outside England, setting (e.g., Art
Gallery, Boardinghouse, Island, Zoo), and "miscellaneous information"
(technical knowledge, e.g., Botany, Bullfighting, Change-ringing).
Oleksiw also offers a list of "One Hundred Classics of the Genre" and a
charting of the British class system.

50. **Parish, James Robert.** *The Great Cop Pictures.* Metuchen, NJ:
Scarecrow, 1990. xii, 681p. Illus., bibl.

The author with Michael R. Pitts of *The Great Detective Pictures* (see #51) and two volumes of *The Great Spy Pictures* (see WAM #24 and the present volume #550) goes it alone in annotating about 330 features and TV movies about police. Films from the '20s to the present are included, with extensive credits, synopses, and critical comments from the author and contemporary reviewers. Some entries you would expect (*Dirty Harry, In the Heat of the Night, The Naked City, Detective Story, The French Connection, The Blue Knight, Bullitt*); others you might not (*It's a Mad, Mad, Mad, Mad World*); and still more you've never heard of, unless you're a more devoted film buff than I. Parish deserves special applause for celebrating one of my favorite films, the sadly underrated *True Confessions.* He is unfavorable to the 1954 film of Patrick Quentin's *Black Widow* (included here instead of in *The Great Detective Pictures,* giving lead detecting credit to George Raft's Lt. Trant rather than Van Heflin's amateur Peter Duluth). I thought *Black Widow* was a terrific picture—but I haven't seen it since I was eleven years old.

Appended are lists of radio and TV police series by Vincent Terrace, a chronology of films listed, and a bibliography of non-fiction books on police by T. Allan Taylor.

51. Parish, James Robert, and Michael R. Pitts. *The Great Detective Pictures.* Metuchen, NJ: Scarecrow, 1990. xiii, 616p. Illus.

In their introduction, the authors of *The Great Spy Pictures* (see WAM #24) and several similar volumes clear up one question: the word "great" in the title refers to the genre as a whole, not necessarily to the about-350 individual pictures covered, most far from great. The typical entry has extensive credits, a plot summary, and quotes from contemporary reviews and/or from later retrospective books and articles. The most famous films are well-covered elsewhere, making the considerable detail on many obscure B mysteries the book's most valuable feature. (It was nice to see a favorite B maybe C? film of my childhood, *Campus Sleuth*, given a good notice.)

Interesting tidbits of information abound. The Charlie Chan series with Roland Winters would have continued after 1949's *Sky Dragon*, with new entries to be shot in England, had not a devaluation of the pound lowered the value of Monogram's holdings in British banks. A list of the old films excerpted in the Steve Martin comedy *Dead Men Don't Wear Plaid* (1982) is provided in a footnote. The authors detail a surprising

number of early attempts at a female private eye on film—e.g. *Exposed*
(1947), *Private Detective* (1939), *Detective Kitty O'Day* (1944), and *The
Undercover Woman* (1946).

There are a few errors. Sayers's play about Lord Peter Wimsey is
mistitled *Busman's Holiday* (should be *Honeymoon*). In the essay on *The
Maltese Falcon*, Gladys Cooper is credited instead of Gladys George. And
the identification of Maurice Leblanc's *The Memoirs of Arsene Lupin*
(1925) as the last Lupin novel is mistaken.

52. Pronzini, Bill, and Marcia Muller. *1001 Midnights: The
Aficionado's Guide to Mystery and Detective Fiction.* New York: Arbor,
1986. 879p. Bibl.

Here is another hefty volume for the growing shelf of key mystery
reference books. The thorough reviews collected here touch on the work
of virtually every major writer in the genre, plus a judicious selection of
newcomers and interesting minor practitioners. Arrangement is alphabetical by author, Edward S. Aarons to Donald Zochert, giving place, publisher, and date of first American edition (or first British for books not
published in the United States), and a symbol for the category the book
belongs to—e.g., AD for Amateur Detective, CS for Classic Sleuth, W for
whodunit. The categories, undefined beyond a phrase, frequently overlap
and often more than one is assigned to a given book. (The symbols
occasionally give some questionable signals—for example, surely Leo
Bruce's classical satire *Case for Three Detectives* is not accurately described as a police procedural, even though Sgt. Beef is a professional
policeman.) Especially good or notable works are marked * and corner-
stone volumes are marked **. Most authors are covered via one representative volume, but for major authors several volumes are reviewed.
Other notable works by the authors are mentioned in the annotations.

For some entries, biographical information is provided. The reviews
emphasize plot summary, usually very effectively presented, and (as noted
in the introduction) most evaluative remarks are favorable. Unfavorable
reviews are included for authors who are very popular, collectible, or
historically important or who have produced what Pronzini labels "alternative classics"—e.g., the amazing Phoenix Press scriveners. Among the
writers received less than glowingly are contemporaries Robert B. Parker,
Margaret Truman, L.A. Morse, and Nathan Aldyne and old-timers Lee
Thayer, Carolyn Wells, John Franklin Bardin, H.C. Branson, and Margaret

Erskine. Receiving a fresh view, some vaunted classics are debunked, not as bad but as less than classic, notably Nicholas Blake's *The Beast Must Die*.

Besides Pronzini and Muller, an impressive group of other mystery writers, fans, and critics have contributed reviews, among them Robert E. Briney, Max Allan Collins, Edward D. Hoch, Marvin Lachman, John Lutz, Kathleen L. Maio, Francis M. Nevins, Jr., Art Scott, Charles Shibuk, and Julie Smith. Readers will note (and it is admitted up-front) that there are quite a few cases here of friends reviewing friends, and sometimes reviewing each other, but we are assured that objectivity did its best to triumph over cronyism.

Since the two principal authors and their consultants know the mystery field intimately, inaccuracies are rare. Somehow, though, Herbert Brean becomes "Robert" and Gore Vidal becomes "George."

One could go on for pages about the delights and surprises contained in this book. Pronzini describes Dolores Hitchens' *Sleep with Slander* as "the best hard-boiled private eye novel written by a woman—and one of the best written by anybody," preferring it to Leigh Brackett's better-known *No Good from a Corpse*. In a rapturous celebration of Agatha Christie's *The Murder of Roger Ackroyd*, Barry N. Malzberg theorizes that the novel must have influenced Vladimir Nabokov's *Pale Fire*. Robert J. Randisi speculates that the shadowy paperback writer Jeff Jacks might have been a pseudonym of Lawrence Block.

Is it possible to quibble about selection? Of course, though less about the authors chosen than the titles they are represented by. Why cover Robert Bloch's *Psycho II*, characterized as "a terrible letdown," rather than the original *Psycho?* Why represent Hillary Waugh by *The Con Game* rather than the acknowledged classic *Last Seen Wearing?* Is it fair to the memory of Brett Halliday to include as one of only two Michael Shayne novels covered the ghost-written (by Robert Terrall) *Nice Fillies Finish Last*, good though that book is? Why is George Bagby represented by an inferior later work rather than by an example from his best period? And why is the same author represented by two books under his real name Aaron Marc Stein but not at all under possibly his best byline, Hampton Stone? Why are Michael Innes' best-known early novels, *Lament for a Maker* and *Hamlet, Revenge,* not even mentioned in the Innes entry?

The most similar earlier reference is, of course, Barzun and Taylor's *A Catalogue of Crime* (WAM #10, revised edition covered in this volume, #544), an equally entertaining and provocative volume that is both more error-prone and narrower in its enthusiasms. At times, this book is a direct reply to B&T, as when their assessment of David Alexander's *Madhouse in Washington Square* ("Close to unreadable") is heartily disputed.

To sum up, this is one of the half-dozen-or-so indispensable titles in any mystery reference collection.

53. **Rosenberg, Betty.** *Genreflecting: A Guide to Reading Interests in Genre Fiction.* Littleton, CO: Libraries Unlimited, 1982. 254p. Bibl., index. Second edition. Littleton, CO: Libraries Unlimited, 1986. xxviii, 298p. Bibl., index.

The following description is based on the second edition.

Library school professor Rosenberg provides valuable bibliographic guides to several popular fiction genres here, but by far the largest section (nearly 90 pages) is devoted to the Thriller, taking in most of the crime-suspense-mystery-detective-espionage subgroups. Among the features are regional checklists of police and private eye series; occupational checklists of amateur detectives; lists of women detectives and "unusual" detectives (which usually means ethnic and/or handicapped); secondary bibliographies of Doyle, Christie, Sayers, and Stout; and examples of various settings and types. As might be expected in a source intended to aid librarians, the annotated lists of secondary sources are most valuable. Publisher and date are usually given for secondary sources, usually not for individual works of fiction. Rosenberg also touches on magazines and fanzines, associations and conventions, book clubs, and publishers. Books selected for both the Barzun-Taylor Classics of Crime Fiction reprint series, published by Garland, are listed, forming a valuable checklist for those without access to the sets.

The Romance section has several pages on romantic suspense and gothic novels, while the Science Fiction section has a list of s.f./detective crossovers. Also of related interest are many items in the Horror section.

Rosenberg's introduction discusses genre fiction generally, including a few paragraphs on review sources where she lauds one of the mystery field's best if most caustic reviewers, Henri C. Veit, who reviewed for *Library Journal* from 1972 to 1980.

54. **Skene Melvin, David, and Ann Skene Melvin.** *Crime, Detective, Espionage, Mystery, and Thriller Fiction and Film: A Comprehensive*

Bibliography of Critical Writings Through 1979. Westport, CT: Greenwood, 1980. xx, 367p. Index.

The Skene Melvins include 1628 unannotated entries, arranged alphabetically by author, followed by title and subject indexes. They include
material in both books and periodicals and do not limit themselves to
English language items. Although there was undoubted usefulness to
bringing all these citations together, there is a considerable problem in the
lack of annotations. Quite often, particularly with the foreign language
materials, what an article is about is not obvious from its title, and the
subject index (confined mostly to individual authors as subjects) is not
sufficient to bridge the gap. In addition, the compilers have left out some
very well-known and obvious sources of material: some *Journal of
Popular Culture* items have been missed, as have articles from *The New
Republic*'s annual mystery criticism sections. Articles from *The Armchair
Detective* have been included only if cited in some other source, an
eccentric decision indeed and one not adequately explained. As a general
bibliography, Skene Melvin proves far less valuable than Johnson's *Crime
Fiction Criticism* (see #33) and is completely eclipsed by Albert's *Detec-
tive and Mystery Fiction* (see #6).

55. **Skinner, Robert E.** *The Hard-Boiled Explicator.* Metuchen, NJ:
Scarecrow, 1985. x, 125p. Bibl., index.

This 626-item annotated bibliography cites secondary sources about
Dashiell Hammett, Raymond Chandler, and Ross Macdonald divided into
four chapters: articles and essays, monographs, fugitive material (eight
items cited wrongly or incompletely in other sources and not found by
Skinner), and book reviews. A 24-page introduction offers an adequate
summary of the three subjects.

The annotations, mostly descriptive but occasionally critical, are full
and helpful if sometimes awkwardly written—for example, James
Sandoe's hard-boiled checklist (see WAM #57) is characterized as "rare
and hard to find." The compiler aimed for comprehensive coverage and
is hard to fault on that score, though he has included Ellery Queen's
introduction to *A Man Called Spade* and omitted the introductions to the
other EQ-edited Hammett collections. Most of the material in the first two
chapters is duplicated in Walter Albert's *Detective and Mystery Fiction*
(see #6), leaving the book review guide as perhaps the most useful feature.

Skinner characterizes the reviews, usually as positive, negative, mixed, or noncommittal. (Could James Sandoe really have been noncommittal in his review of *Blue City*? Not his style at all.) Usually meticulous on names, Skinner twice cites someone called John "Dickenson" Carr.

Skinner provides a short subject index but, unfortunately, none to authors and critics.

56. Strosser, Edward, ed. *The Armchair Detective Book of Lists.* New York: Armchair Detective, 1989. 266p. Illus.

The title, which implies a whimsical, superficial non-reference book, led me to expect a list of books in which the butler did it. But actually this is a guide to quality in the mystery field, emphasizing award winners and specialists' selections of the good and/or important in the genre. The first 108 pages are devoted to the most complete listing of the Edgar awards extant, including all winners and nominees from the first awards in 1945 through 1988. There follow the 125 books of short stories enshrined by Ellery Queen in "Queen's Quorum" (see WAM #27); the favorite mystery writers as revealed in a 1950 Gallup poll; Julian Symons's 1959 *Sunday Times* list of the 100 best crime stories; James Sandoe's "The Hard-Boiled Dick: A Personal Checklist" (see WAM #57); H.R.F. Keating's 100 best (see #34); "The Haycraft-Queen Definitive Library of Detective-Crime-Mystery Fiction," ending in 1948, with Herbert Brean's suggested additions through 1952; the Crime Writers Association Dagger awards, 1955-1978; Otto Penzler's selection of the top 100 Sherlock Holmes books (with values attached); Robin W. Winks's 12-page list of personal favorites; the Private Eye Writers of America Favorite Private Eye/Author survey; the 1984 *TAD* reader's survey of favorite authors, characters, and books; the 1986 *USA Today* list of top mystery books, selected by Otto Penzler; and listings of the Bouchercon's Anthony awards, 1986-87; the Mystery Readers International Macavity awards, 1986-88; and the first year's Malice Domestic Agatha awards (1988). A four-page afterthought at the very end of the book adds the Wolfe Pack's Nero award winners, 1979-1987, and *Variety*'s 50 top-grossing mystery films through December 1988.

Virtually all of the above is previously published material, the great benefit being having it all brought together in one place for the first time. The balance of the book is a 53-page section of new material in which prominent mystery writers and book dealers list their favorite books and/or authors. The writers mostly stick to the classics, with some contemporary titles thrown in. Some of the more surprising inclusions and their champions include Herbert Brean's *Wilders Walk Away* (Isaac Asimov), Joyce Porter's *Dover One* (Robert Barnard), Leo Bruce's *Furious Old Woman* (Jacques Barzun), Dick Francis's *The Danger* (Simon Brett), Joseph Hansen's *Skinflick* (Dorothy Salisbury Davis), Barnard's *Death of a Mystery Writer* (Aaron Elkins), Edward Bunker's *No Beast So Fierce* (James Ellroy), David Ignatius' *Agents of Innocence* (John Gardner), Ruth Rendell's *Talking to Strange Men* (Sue Grafton), Daniel Defoe's *Roxana* (Reginald Hill), K. Arne Blom's *The Limits of Pain* (Tony Hillerman), James McClure's *The Artful Egg* (H.R.F. Keating), Stanley Ellin's *Stronghold* (Peter Lovesey), Evelyn Smith's *Miss Melville Regrets* (Charlotte MacLeod), Thomas Berger's *Who is Teddy Villanova?* (Michael Malone), MacLeod's *The Family Vault* (Barbara Mertz), Patricia Highsmith's *Ripley Underground* (Marcia Muller), Liza Cody's *Under Contract* (Sara Paretsky), Lawrence Block's *When the Sacred Ginmill Closes* (Peter Straub), Eric Ambler's *Doctor Frigo* (Julian Symons), Joe Gores's *Interface* (Donald E. Westlake), and William P. McGivern's *Night of the Juggler* (Phyllis A. Whitney). Of the authors providing lists, only Michael Gilbert and Robert B. Parker fail to come up with a really surprising title. Elmore Leonard provides a one-book list, George V. Higgins's *The Friends of Eddie Coyle,* while Patricia Highsmith and Ross Thomas decline to participate for contrasting reasons: Highsmith doesn't even like mystery novels, and Thomas finds his opinions fluctuate too much.

Most of the dealers list favorite writers rather than individual titles, and they understandably tend more toward contemporary rather than historical figures than the writers do. There are surprises here as well. Beth Caswell of Long Beach lists Dornford Yates, D.B. Olsen, and Rufus King on a list which has Sherlockian pasticher Michael Hardwick as its most contemporary member. Kate Mattes of Cambridge, Massachusetts, appreciates both Charlotte MacLeod and Andrew Vachss, bespeaking the most catholic possible tastes.

The editor does not compile these new lists into any kind of master consensus list, but there is no reason to think such a list would be all that interesting compared to the quirky individual ones. It's pretty clear which of the contemporaries are viewed as producing our present-day classics. Two individual titles that turn up more than once are Elizabeth Peters's *Crocodile on a Sandbank* and Gregory Mcdonald's *Fletch,* and writers who turn up repeatedly (not always with the same books) include George V. Higgins, Tony Hillerman, Sue Grafton, Peter Dickinson, Ruth Rendell,

Amanda Cross, Sara Paretsky, Elmore Leonard, and Dick Francis. Present but not named quite as frequently as one might expect is P.D. James.

One thing that jumped out (at me at least) from these newly-minted lists is the astonishing erosion of the reputation of Ellery Queen. The Queen name appears frequently (and deservedly) in the early part of the book, but among the writers and dealers, only Barbara Mertz, who lists *Calamity Town* on her list of ten favorites, and Providence, Rhode Island, dealer Kevin J. Barbero, who lists EQ at the bottom of his list of ten favorite writers, save the famous team from a shutout.

I could obviously go on all day about this book, and before I prove that definitively, I'll just recommend it to every fully-immersed fan.

57. Symons, Julian. *British Crime Fiction.* London: British Council and National Book League, 1974. 51p. Bibl.

Following a three-page essay on "British Crime Stories Now," important books are listed and annotated in four time periods: The Forerunners; Writers of the Golden Age; Writers of the Forties, Fifties, and Sixties; and New Writers. Annotations for the first three sections are drawn from the first edition of Symons's *Bloody Murder* (WAM #5), for the last section from favorable reviews in the *Sunday Times* and *Observer.* There is also a two-page listing of anthologies and histories and a list of publishers' addresses. All items listed were in print (with publisher and price given) at the time of the pamphlet's publication. A worthy endeavor at the time, it offers nothing not covered more extensively elsewhere.

58. Traylor, James. *Dime Detective Index.* New Carrollton, MD: Pulp Collector Press, 1986. v, 124p. Illus.

Not examined. According to Walter Albert (*The Armchair Detective,* v. 22, n. 1, p. 59), "In his introduction, Traylor writes of the publishing history of the magazine and points out that it depended on series characters for its continuing success. The index (pp. 1-51) is an issue-by-issue listing of all fiction contents, giving title of story, author, and series character (if any); cover artists are also identified." Author and character indexes and statistical rankings of authors and characters are among other features. "In short, a comprehensive, detailed guide . . . a model for similar projects."

3
SPECIAL SUBJECTS

59. **Atkins, John.** *The British Spy Novel: Styles in Treachery.* London: Calder; New York: Riverrun, 1984. 287p. Bibl., index.

This is a highly entertaining survey, comparable in its enthusiasm and readability to William Vivyan Butler's *The Durable Desperadoes* (WAM #36). The approach is primarily topical, but some writers are discussed in full chapters: Buchan, Fleming (three chapters), Maugham (accorded the seminal role in spy fiction played by H.G. Wells in science fiction and Zane Grey in westerns), le Carré (two), Greene, and Deighton. Among other authors covered at greater or lesser length are Frederick Forsyth, William Haggard, Brian Freemantle, Anthony Price, Trevanian, Warren Tute, Geoffrey Household, and Lionel Davidson. The most surprising omission is probably Adam Hall. Individual novels discussed include the expected (Erskine Childers' *Riddle of the Sands*) and several less so: Baroness Orczy's *A Spy of Napoleon*, Alan Williams's *Gentleman Traitor*, and what sounds like a brilliant parody of le Carré's *Tinker, Tailor, Soldier, Spy: Eeny, Meeny, Miny, Mole* by Marcel d'Agneau (Sam North).

Despite the title, Atkins gives extended coverage to R. Wright (Robert) Campbell's *The Spy Who Sat and Waited*, which he ranks with works of Greene and le Carré. Though the setting is British, Campbell is American. Other American writers, including Max Brand and Patricia McGerr, are occasionally mentioned.

One thing that makes the book so enjoyable is the author's blunt and forthright opinions. Some examples: "Oppenheim and Le Queux are jokes. It is fashionable to sneer at them but no sneer will eradicate them" (page 19). "It is often said, with God knows what authority, that Buchan had an attractive literary style. He hadn't" (page 36). "One of the great mysteries of popular literature is how Bulldog Drummond ever became a folk hero. Sapper is indisputably the worst of all the popular authors, in the literary sense, and also the most distasteful" (page 60). On the other hand, Atkins writes that "Valentine Williams was frequently absurd but there was always vitality in his writing" (page 60), and offers a spirited defense of the usually disparaged Dennis Wheatley: "It is to his credit that he never wrote a novel, whether historical or occult, without first doing his homework. But apart from accuracy, he was also relatively realistic. . . . Wheatley is credible where Fleming, and even Deighton, is not" (page 30).

Atkins describes N. St. Barbe Sladen's *The Real Le Queux* (WAM #187), which I was unable to locate, as "probably the least illuminating biography in literary history" (page 51). I'll stop looking.

60. Bailey, Frankie Y. *Out of the Woodpile: Black Characters in Crime and Detective Fiction.* (Contributions to the Study of Popular Culture, Number 27.) New York: Greenwood, 1991. xiii, 188p. Bibl., index.

In a remarkably thorough and far-reaching discussion, Bailey begins with the treatment of blacks in Poe and Twain and proceeds to discuss their incidence in the genre through the present day. The early record is as shameful and embarrassing as you might expect, but it's good to see that American Golden Age icons Van Dine, Stout, and (especially) Queen get fairly good marks for their depiction of black characters in a time of pernicious racism. A chapter on the hardboiled pulps includes an extended description of *Black Mask*'s special KKK issue of 1923. A chapter on Harlem discusses the earliest African-American mystery writers: W. Adolphe Roberts, who wrote almost entirely of white characters, and Rudolph Fisher, who did classical detective stories in a black milieu. Bailey's "Black Rage" chapter deals with Richard Wright and Chester Himes. The chapter on black detectives covers black playwright Hughes Allison's one-shot *EQMM* character Joe Hill as well as the expected figures, most created by white authors: John Ball's Virgil Tibbs, Ed Lacy's Touie Moore, Ernest Tidyman's Shaft, and Kenn Davis's Carver Bascombe, among others. (Two characters Bailey misses are J.F. Burke's Sam Kelly and B.B. Johnson's Richard Spade, the latter a paperback original character who was ostensibly created by a black writer, though the truth of this is not certain.) Among the contemporary sleuths cited are Clifford Mason's Joe Cinquez and Gar Anthony Haywood's Aaron Gunner, both created by black authors, and Dolores Komo's Clio Browne and Susan Moody's Penny Wanawaki, both the creation of white women. (Since Bailey's work appeared, at least three black female detectives created by black women writers have been introduced: Virginia Kelly in Nikki Baker's *In the Game* [Naiad, 1991], Blanche White in Barbara Neely's *Blanche on the Lam* and Mari MacAlister in Eleanor Taylor Bland's *Dead Time*, the latter two both published in 1992 by St. Martin's.)

Responding to a series of questions in a 21-page Symposium of "Writers' Views on Creating Black Characters" are Michael Avallone, Kenn Davis, Joseph Hansen, Gar Anthony Haywood, Michael Jahn (at greatest length), Dolores Komo, Margaret Maron, Susan Moody, Sara Paretsky, Percy Spurlark Parker, Robert B. Parker (most briefly), Nancy Pickard, Les Roberts, and Richard Martin Stern. Also appended are the results of a survey of MWA members on their favorite black characters and books and writers effective in portraying black themes; a directory of black characters in print, film, and TV crime; an index of black detectives; and an 11-page bibliography.

Both scholarly and readable, this is a model of a specialized mystery fiction study. Treating a subject that could easily lend itself to an angry and/or sarcastic treatment, Bailey's approach is notably measured and non-judgmental. For example, she writes, "In his Sherlock Holmes adventures, Doyle created two compassionate and civilized heroes, but they are also men of their age" (page 20).

61. Baker, Robert A., and Michael T. Nietzel. *Private Eyes: One Hundred and One Knights: A Survey of American Detective Fiction, 1922-1984*. Bowling Green, OH: Popular, 1985. 385p. Illus., index.

In the introduction to the parent volume of *What About Murder?*, I complained of the lack of "any book-length study of the private-eye novel that does not a) have a special thematic ax to grind or b) limit itself to a very small number of authors." Here is the first of two 1985 volumes to address that need. (The second was David Geherin's *The American Private Eye* [see #76]) Baker and Nietzel, two university professors who write here in a fannish rather than an academic mode, are certainly thorough. The goal seems to be to mention virtually every American private eye to appear in even one novel, and the authors very nearly achieve it. They also make many sound critical points about their subjects. The dyed-in-the-wool mystery fan can hardly help loving this book, both for what it tries to do and what it actually achieves, and even though partially superseded by Conquest's *Trouble is Their Business* (see #13), it remains worth seeking out.

In their opening chapter, the authors present the results of a poll of private eye writers and critics, who were asked to rate a long list of past and present writers and characters on literary value, overall entertainment value, character development, plot, writing style, and Final Grade. Highest ranked among the old-timers in both quality and familiarity were (unsurprisingly) Chandler's Marlowe, Hammett's Spade, Macdonald's Archer, and Hammett's Continental Op. (At the bottom end were John Jakes's Johnny Havoc and Michael Brett's Pete McGrath.) Among the present-day, Parker's Spenser was the most familiar but rated only twenty-second, with James Crumley's C.W. Sughrue, though known to only half the respondents, rating highest in quality.

Then the authors offer chapters on Hammett and Chandler (the "King" and "Royal Heir"); the trio of Ross Macdonald, John D. MacDon-ald, and Spillane (the "Princes of the Realm"); other old-timers; the best of the "moderns"; other present-day eyes; and finally individual chapters on female, humorous, and science-fictional private eyes. An appendix adds more names not covered in the main sections. There are omissions, to be sure, but not many—one that sprang to mind was Day Keene's Hawaiian shamus Johnny Aloha.

The selection criteria are sometimes questionable. Rex Stout's Nero Wolfe, Anthony Boucher's Fergus O'Breen, and Baynard Kendrick's Duncan Maclain are included, though they surely don't belong to the hard-boiled private eye tradition. Since Ellery Queen and Philo Vance are not covered, one must conclude Wolfe, O'Breen, and Maclain are here because they detect as professionals rather than amateurs, but so did Carolyn Wells's Fleming Stone and Lee Thayer's Peter Clancy, neither of whom is covered here. And how do Frank Gruber's book salesmen Johnny Fletcher and Sam Cragg, amateur detectives, and George Harmon Coxe's "Flashgun" Casey, a newspaper photographer, qualify when tough lawyers like Erle Stanley Gardner's Perry Mason and Harold Q. Masur's Scott Jordan do not?

Unfortunately, this book brings forth the question so often inspired by Popular Press products: does anybody read these things before they get into print? If a good copy editor had smoothed out the contradictions, repetitions, and stylistic infelicities, and if a knowledgeable mystery specialist had vetted the manuscript for errors (which approach the Hagen [see WAM #16] or Barzun/Taylor [see WAM #10] level), this book would be twice as good as it is. (The section on Brett Halliday offers a particularly egregious example of bad editing.) The authors are sometimes careless in crediting their sources. Beginning on page 33, they quote David Bazelon at length and give absolutely no hint of where his remarks appeared. In their Michael Avallone section, they seem to lean heavily on Francis M. Nevins, Jr., but give him no credit.

A few of the many out-and-out mistakes noted: the authors imply that Avallone's Ed Noon lives in a literal auditorium rather than a metaphorical "mouse auditorium"; they state that Howard Browne "learned his trade" writing TV and movies, when he actually entered these fields when most of his books and stories were already written; they seem to believe Thomas B. Dewey, Bill S. Ballinger, and Bill Miller (of the Wade Miller team) are still alive—would it were so!; they mistakenly award William Campbell Gault's *The CANA Diversion* an Edgar; they believe Brett Halliday (Davis Dresser) used the pseudonym Asa Baker after marrying Helen McCloy; they also believe Halliday personally edited *Mike Shayne Mystery Magazine,* which he never did; they suggest Talmage Powell has been a free-lance writer since age twelve—possible but unlikely; they repeatedly quote Art Scott but unaccountably leave him out of the index; they don't make it clear Marvin Albert's Tony Rome novels were published under the pseudonym Anthony Rome; their index has Lester Dent writing under the name "Paul" Robeson; they garble a famous Rex Stout title as *The Case of the Frightened Man;* they state Anthony Boucher "edited" the *New York Times Book Review'*s "Criminals at Large" column—in fact, he wrote it all himself; and finally they still think Englishman Miles Tripp wrote the private eye books signed by Michael Brett.

Some of the critical judgements, admittedly matters of opinion, are also worth questioning. There's a bit too much puffery at times, an "every-writer-in-the-bookshop-is-lovely" approach. Much as I admire Ron Goulart's writing, I can't believe his most devoted fan would claim Jake and Hildy Pace are "as crazy and as funny as the Marx Brothers at their zenith" (page 351).

One of the best things about this book is the good, appreciative comment on such notable writers as Loren D. Estleman, James Crumley, Joe Gores, Stephen Greenleaf, Joseph Hansen, Richard Hoyt, and Stuart Kaminsky. The section on Roger L. Simon's Moses Wine is one of the few that is unfavorable on balance.

Bill Pronzini contributes a two-page introduction. The book is illustrated with photos of some of the writers. There is no separate bibliography, though many titles and dates are listed in the body of the work. There are indexes to names of authors and private eyes.

62. Billman, Carol. *The Secret of the Stratemeyer Syndicate: Nancy Drew, the Hardy Boys, and the Million Dollar Fiction Factory.* New York: Ungar, 1986. xi, 187p. Illus., bibl., index.

Edward Stratemeyer (1862-1929) was responsible for creating some of the best-known and least "respectable" characters in juvenile fiction. Some of the books he wrote himself; others he outlined and farmed out to a number of anonymous writers who were hidden behind such house names as Victor Appleton, Arthur M. Winfield, Laura Lee Hope, Franklin W. Dixon, and Carolyn Keene. Nancy Drew novels under the latter name were usually the work of Harriet Stratemeyer Adams, who called the shots for the syndicate from her father's death to her own passing in 1982.

Though lacking the stylistic verve of Bobbie Ann Mason's *The Girl Sleuths* (see WAM #50), this is the fullest treatment of the syndicate to date. Its emphasis is on five detective series: the Rover Boys, Ruth Fielding (Billman's favorite, little remembered today), the Hardy Boys, Nancy Drew, and the Happy Hollisters. Billman synopsizes a representative title from each series: *The Rover Boys Down East, Ruth Fielding at Cameron Hall, The Mystery of the Chinese Junk* (Hardys), *The Clue in the Crumbling Wall* (Drew), and *The Happy Hollisters at Sea Gull Beach.* She puts Stratemeyer's output in perspective with nineteenth-century boys' and girls' fiction; offers details on exactly how the series-book assembly line worked; identifies some of the writers behind the house names (Howard Garis, St. George Rathbone, Walter Karig, Leslie Mac-Farlane, the last three of whom do not appear in the book's rather hit-and-miss index); finds the parallels between juvenile and adult mystery fiction (for example, the similarities of Nancy Drew's adventures and Mary Roberts Rinehart's novels); and provides a sound analysis of the style and plot formulae of the series books. A final chapter describes the syndicate's more recent history, including a discussion of movie and TV adaptations, and analyzes the reasons for its success.

Billman includes a three-page checklist of Stratemeyer mystery and adventure series (but no listing of titles in individual series), sixteen pages of notes, and a six-page secondary bibliography.

63. Bonn, Thomas L. *Under Cover: An Illustrated History of American Mass Market Paperbacks.* Foreword by John Tebbel. Harmondsworth, Middlesex, and New York: Penguin, 1982. 144p. Illus., bibl., index.

There are fewer genre references here than in some other paperback histories, but the reproduced covers, many in color, include a significant number from volumes of crime fiction. Bonn presents a general history of paperbacks, including their dime-novel roots; accounts of Pocket Books and other major publishers; considerable material on covers, including separate chapters on the work of the art editor and the artist; and a chapter on collecting. The interesting information on censorship of cover art is exemplified by the original and Bowdlerized versions of a Dell cover for A.A. Fair's *Fools Die on Friday.*

64. **Caillois, Roger.** *The Mystery Novel.* Translated from the French by Roberto Yahni and A.W. Sadler. Bronxville, NY: Laughing Buddha, 1984. 49p.

Not examined. According to Walter Albert (*The Armchair Detective,* v. 20, n. 3, p. 283), this limited edition (200 copies) is probably "the first complete translation into English" of the 1941 essay "Le Roman policier: evolution, jeu, drame." The middle segment of the essay appears in Most and Stowe's *The Poetics of Murder* (see #156).

65. **Cawelti, John G., and Bruce A. Rosenberg.** *The Spy Story.* Chicago: U. of Chicago P., 1987. x, 259p. Bibl., index.

In describing Cawelti's very influential *Adventure, Mystery, and Romance* (WAM #38), regarded in academic circles as a key text in the study of popular fiction, I criticized the "rather verbose writing style." The present volume is probably the best book-length work to date on espionage fiction, and it is more tightly written and "fan friendly." The only thing that keeps me from proclaiming it the *Murder for Pleasure* (WAM #1) of the spy novel is the relatively small number of authors given in-depth coverage.

The introduction reviews some earlier writers on the spy thriller genre, Bruce Merry (WAM #51), Jerry Palmer (WAM #53), Ralph Harper (WAM #46), Donald McCormick (whose *Who's Who in Spy Fiction* [WAM #20] is found "delightful"), and LeRoy Panek of *The Special Branch* (see #159). The opening chapter explores the cycle of "clandestinity" in fiction and fact with examples from Watergate and the Dreyfus case. A chapter of general history of the form follows, with much attention to James Fenimore Cooper's *The Spy*. A categorization of the spy story's forms and structures offers a detailed reading of Adam Hall's *The Quiller Memorandum* and its use of spy-novel formulae. Subsequent chapters focus on John Buchan, Eric Ambler and Graham Greene, Ian Fleming, John le Carré, and a survey of recent spy writers.

A concluding section labeled "A Guide to the Spy Story" contains many useful and/or enjoyable features: a sometimes-critically annotated secondary bibliography of writings on spy fiction; an annotated bibliography on real-life espionage; a chronology of spy-story landmarks; the authors' choices for the best 25 spy stories in ranked order (Greene's *The Human Factor* heads the list, which allots four spaces to Greene [actually representing six different novels], four to le Carré [representing seven novels], three to Ambler, and one each to Robert Littell, Len Deighton, John Buchan, and Frederick Forsyth); a list of major spy films from Leonard Rubenstein's *The Great Spy Films* (see #112), plus some others; a list of major series writers and their characters; a list of the twenty best spy writers; an annotated list of non-genre novels with spy themes (by authors like Conrad, Hemingway, Nabokov, Pynchon, and Mary McCarthy); a list of "public figures" as spy authors (e.g., William F. Buckley, Jr., John Ehrlichman, Jim Garrison, Pierre Salinger); and a list of TV spy series.

Some major writers have been omitted from consideration. Though not discussed in the text, William Haggard and Anthony Price at least make the author/character list. Ted Allbeury, Manning Coles, Brian Freemantle, and Charles McCarry are left out completely. Errors are relatively few, though at least a couple of names get misspelled—Michael "Avallon" and Bill S. Ballinger's Jaoquin "Hawke" (should be Hawks). In an amusing slip, Nayland Smith's associate in Sax Rohmer's Fu Manchu books is identified as "Dr. Flinders Petrie" (page 43).

66. Charney, Hanna. *The Detective Novel of Manners: Hedonism, Morality, and the Life of Reason*. Rutherford, NJ: Fairleigh Dickinson U.P.; London: Associated University Presses, 1981. xxv, 125p. Bibl., index.

Finding in detective fiction elements of Trollope, Austen, George Eliot, and Henry James, Charney aims to explore its effects in the manner of Ralph Harper's *The World of the Thriller* (see WAM #46) on espionage fiction. Though it's a little too stylistically wooly to stand the comparison with Harper, Charney's work says interesting things about the use of parody in classical detective fiction; its language and character psychology; and its film adaptations. Writers used as examples include some who have been comparatively little written-about—V.C. Clinton Baddeley, Patricia Moyes, Elizabeth Lemarchand, and Robert Bernard (not to be confused with Barnard)—along with more expected names like Christie, Sayers, Simenon, and Stout. Absent from the discussion are giants Ellery Queen and John Dickson Carr as well as notable classicists Christianna Brand and Helen McCloy. The primary bibliography lists only those titles quoted in the text.

Some oddities: Charney very unfairly states that Julian Symons "has an obvious distaste for detection" (page 19). She refers to William Irish with no indication he is better-known as Cornell Woolrich. And, significantly in a study that fails even to mention Carr, she seriously misunderstands the term "locked room" (page 97).

67. Collins, Max Allan, and John Javna. *The Best of Crime and Detective TV: Perry Mason to Hill Street Blues, The Rockford Files, and Murder, She Wrote.* New York: Harmony, 1989. 114p. Illus., bibl.

The results of a poll of fans, mystery writers, and critics as to their favorite TV mysteries are presented in a lively, extensively illustrated, magazine-style format. The shows are discussed in categories: private eye (with *The Rockford Files* a nearly unanimous choice, followed by *Harry O* and *Peter Gunn*), police procedurals (highest marks to *Hill Street Blues* and *Dragnet*), amateur sleuths (*Lord Peter Wimsey* edges out *Ellery Queen* and *Murder She Wrote*), and comedy crimefighters (with *Rumpole of the Bailey* followed by several American sitcoms). Of most interest for our purpose are those programs adapted from print media—aside from the Sayers and Queen characters mentioned above, the authors discuss at some length *Perry Mason* (in with the private eyes because of Paul Drake's presence), *77 Sunset Strip* (from Roy Huggins's two Stu Bailey books), and *Sherlock Holmes*, and refer to several others with literary origins more briefly. The discussions of the shows often include comments from participants, from TV critics, and from such writers as Michael Avallone, Mary Higgins Clark, William L. DeAndrea, Loren D. Estleman, Ed Gorman, Stuart M. Kaminsky, Stephen King, Otto Penzler, Mickey Spillane, and Donald E. Westlake. Adding to the book's entertainment value, the authors take some memorable swipes at bad mystery shows. Appended are a recommended reading list, addresses of fan publications, and photo and collectible sources. Presented for fun rather than as an in-depth scholarly reference, the book does its job admirably.

68. Corsaut, Anita; Muff Singer; and Robert Wagner. *The Mystery Reader's Quiz Book.* New York: Evans, 1981. 191p.

The quizzes, grouped under headings like "About the Good Guys," "Whodunit and Why," "Dicks of the Flicks," "Cops on the Box," and "Little-known Facts About the Authors," are mostly multiple choice or matching with occasional fill-in-the-blanks questions. There is also a crossword. For deeply-immersed buffs, most of the questions will not be very difficult, in contrast to single-author quiz books (e.g., on Doyle, Christie, and John D. MacDonald) that to fill their pages must concentrate on obscure plot details of a limited number of stories. "Postmortem—A Master Sleuth's Quiz" finishes the book and is somewhat tougher than the rest of the book's contents.

The authors don't make many mistakes in their quizzes, but there are a few: a reference to a mystery novel called *The Man in the Cue,* which sounds like a pool-playing fantasy (page 43); to another called *Harvard Has a Murder* (should be *Homicide*) (page 184); multiple references to an author called Edmond (should be Edmund) Crispin; and another to H.R. (without the F.) Keating (page 185). For a non-book of this kind, the miscue total isn't bad at all.

69. Craig, Patricia, and Mary Cadogan. *The Lady Investigates: Women Detectives and Spies in Fiction.* New York: St. Martin's, 1981. 252p. Illus., bibl., index.

Beginning with W.S. Hayward's Mrs. Paschal (in the 1861 volume *The Revelations of a Lady Detective*) and Andrew Forrester, Jr.'s *The Female Detective* (1864) and finishing with contemporary favorites like P.D. James's Cordelia Gray and Amanda Cross's Kate Fansler, the authors trace the history of women leading characters in crime and mystery fiction from a strongly feminist perspective. Though they "have tried to keep literary judgements to a minimum," there is ample indication of which authors and series are most worth seeking out, and the writing is intelligent and stylish. Most of the familiar characters are, of course, covered, but for the buff, the attention given relatively obscure names will be of greatest interest. For instance, the authors pronounces Hugh C. Weir's *Miss Madelyn Mack, Detective* (1914) superior to Anna Katharine Green's sleuth of the same period, Violet Strange. Among authors of girls' fiction, the British writers for Amalgamated Press are credited with a more effective use of atmosphere than the writers of the Nancy Drew series. Will Oursler and Margaret Scott's Gale Gallagher (whose adventures were also published under that name as author) is given a strong vote of confidence, while Leslie Ford is seen as anti-feminist.

Among the characters given interesting treatment are Nigel Morland's Mrs. Pym, G.D.H. and M.I. Cole's Mrs. Warrender, Nancy Spain's Miriam Birdseye, Mignon G. Eberhart's Nurse Keate (whose adventures do not "fill many volumes" as claimed here), and a special favorite of the authors, Gladys Mitchell's Mrs. Bradley. Female spies like Dorothy Gilman's Mrs. Pollifax and Peter O'Donnell's Modesty Blaise are covered. A separate chapter on the wives of famous detectives covers Sayers's Harriett Vane, with much emphasis on *Gaudy Night*, along with the wives of Nicholas Blake's Nigel Strangeways, Margery Allingham's Albert Campion, and Ngaio Marsh's Roderick Alleyn. Some of the husband-and-wife detecting teams are also covered, and there is room to celebrate a few notable secretaries, such as Erle Stanley Gardner's Della Street.

While it sometimes seems every notable female sleuth in fiction must be in here, there is no pretense of completeness. And it is surprising that Jenny Melville's Charmian Daniels is covered, but Lillian O'Donnell's Norah Mulcahaney is not. American female private eyes seem to have been slighted, though admittedly most of the current crop have come into their own since the book's publication date.

In summation, this is an outstanding treatment of its subject and a good choice for any basic library of detective fiction history.

70. **Dale, Alzina Stone, and Barbara Sloan Hendershott.** *Mystery Reader's Walking Guide: London.* Maps by John Babcock. Lincolnwood, IL: Passport, 1987. xx, 294p. Illus., bibl., index.

London is perfect for a mystery walking tour: compared to cities with a comparable range of landmarks and associations, it is more compact than Los Angeles and safer than either L.A. or New York. This admirable guidebook has eleven walks, arranged by neighborhood, e.g. The City,

Inns of Court/Fleet Street, Bloomsbury, Soho, Westminster. Each walk has a short introduction, including length, places of interest (general rather than criminous), and places to eat, and each has a clear and usable map. The description of the walk itself is loaded with detective-fiction references. A "Special Helps" section includes an index of authors, titles, and sleuths referred to in each walk. Among the authors that occur most frequently are ones you would expect: Margery Allingham, Arthur Conan Doyle, John Dickson Carr, Agatha Christie, Ngaio Marsh, G.K. Chesterton, and Dorothy L. Sayers. (Note that co-author Dale is the author of biographies of the last two named.) Most surprising recurrent subject is American Robert B. Parker—Spenser's wanderings in *The Judas Goat* are traced.

71. Dale, Alzina Stone, and Barbara Sloan Hendershott. *Mystery Reader's Walking Guide: England*. Interior maps by Alisa Mueller Burkey. Lincolnwood, IL: Passport, 1988. xv, 416p. Illus., bibl., index.

In the same format as the London guide described above, the authors widen their range, choosing English towns according to the following rules: "The towns must be accessible by British Rail (each walk starts and ends at the British Railway Station). The town must have some mystery associations and it must be a place about which we were enthusiastic" (page xiv). Chosen locales are Bath, Brighton, Cambridge, Canterbury, Dorchester/Charmouth, Ely, Greenwich/Blackheath, Newmarket, Oxford (two walks), Salisbury, Shrewsbury, Stratford-upon-Avon, Thames River, and Windsor/Eton. Allingham, Christie, Chesterton, and Sayers again loom large; Carr, Marsh, and Doyle appear less frequently; and extensive attention is paid Nicholas Blake, John Creasey, Charles Dickens, Dick Francis, Martha Grimes, Georgette Heyer, P.D. James, Peter Lovesey, Ellis Peters, and Josephine Tey. Non-genre names like Jane Austen, Thomas Hardy, and William Shakespeare also occur frequently.

72. Davis, Kenneth C. *Two-Bit Culture: The Paperbacking of America*. Boston: Houghton, Mifflin, 1984. xvi, 430p. Illus., bibl., index.

This in-depth history of American paperback publishing has less extensive mystery genre references than some such sources, but they are present throughout with special (and thoughtful) attention accorded softcover phenomena Erle Stanley Gardner and Mickey Spillane. Davis does not seem overfond of either writer but tries to figure out why they were as popular as they were. He sees the Perry Mason series as moving from the tough school of Hammett and *Black Mask* in its early entries to the purist (or deductive) school of Christie, Sayers, and Van Dine in later books.

Many of the paperback covers illustrated are from mysteries.

73. Denning, Michael. Cover Stories: Narrative and Ideology in the British Spy Thriller. (Popular Fiction Series.) London and New York: Routledge & Kegan Paul, 1987. x, 168p. Index.

The author sees the spy novel, primarily a British genre, as a reflection of twentieth-century British culture and politics. Offering a social history of the category, Denning pays more attention to publishing history than most authors of genre studies. (In discussing the rise of paperbacks, Denning is somewhat unfair to Pocket Books, which he unfavorably compares to Penguins. Early Pockets were not as dominated by pulp fiction as he believes.) Most extensive coverage is accorded Eric Ambler, Ian Fleming, Graham Greene, and John le Carré. Recounting the Kim Philby story, Denning looks at two novels based on the case, Alan Williams's *Gentleman Traitor* (1974) and Dorothea Bennett's *The Jigsaw Man* (1976), finding neither convincing. Other subjects include Frederick Forsyth, Ken Follett, and Julian Rathbone, whose *A Spy of the Old School* (1982) is described approvingly. Noting the right-wing perspective of most spy fiction, Denning finishes with a discussion of three relatively little-known socialist thrillers: Ivan Ruff's *The Dark Red Star* (1985), Chris Mullins's *A Very British Coup* (1982), and Raymond Williams's *The Volunteers* (1978). This is a readable and stimulating academic study with some well-observed critical tidbits: Oppenheim failed to invent convincing heroes, and "Fleming's greatest and not inconsiderable talent lies as a sports writer" (page 32). Though there is no bibliography, extensive notes are included.

74. Dove, George N. *The Police Procedural*. Bowling Green, OH: Popular, 1982. 274p. Bibl., index.

With this study, Dove has filled one of the gaps in the literature of mystery fiction history and criticism. In doing so, he passes the severest test of a work of literary analysis: he makes the reader want to discover (or rediscover) the great procedural writers. Dove's work is almost wholly descriptive rather than critical (though he does make occasional critical judgments, celebrating the excellence of Hillary Waugh's *Last Seen Wearing* and pointing out Ed McBain's rare failure in *Hail to the Chief*). He describes the elements and traditions of the procedural story in much the same fashion as Bruce Merry covers another branch of crime fiction in his *Anatomy of the Spy Thriller* (see WAM #51).

Dove begins with a historical summary of the procedural, dated from Lawrence Treat's *V as in Victim* (1945), then discusses the role of the police detective in classical and hardboiled mystery fiction. He devotes several chapters to the procedural's conventions, characters, and techniques; compares European and American procedural styles; discusses in individual chapters various police minorities (women, blacks, Jews, Hispanics); and gives full-chapter consideration to several of the most significant writers: John Creasey (whose name is spelled two different ways, in an untypical bit of carelessness), Maurice Procter, Hillary Waugh, Ed McBain, Bill Knox, Nicolas Freeling, Maj Sjöwall and Per Wahlöö, Collin Wilcox, and James McClure. In a concluding chapter, Dove states that the procedural mystery, unlike the hardboiled, does not represent a rebellion against the classical tradition, and he offers an extended discussion of two recent writers he believes are extending the boundaries of the procedural: Lawrence Sanders and Janwillem van de Wetering.

Dove discusses nearly all the major writers of the procedural, but there are a few notable omissions: Jeffrey Ashford, Jonathan Craig, John Wainwright, the latter-day Richard Lockridge, and Ben Benson. (Dove might well claim that the police detectives of the latter two writers belong in the Great Policeman category, along with Roderick Alleyn, Maigret, and Inspector French, rather than the procedural proper, where investigation is shared among several police.)

Excellent as this book is at attaining what it sets out to do, I frankly wish there were more critical assessment. Who are the best writers and which are their best novels? Dove offers a partial answer here for the careful reader. But which writers get better (or worse) as they go along? Which are most (or least) consistent? Given a choice among Dell Shannon, John Ball, and Maurice Procter, which should the discriminating reader pounce on first? Dove's stated reason for not including more criticism strikes me as distinctly odd: "The critical assumption in this study is that any work of art should be judged basically in terms of its purposes. If a story is written for the purpose of being popular, then the only basis for evaluation is the degree to which it achieves popularity. The task of the critic, then, is not to evaluate (the reading public does that) but to interpret" (page 6). Surely, the goal of a writer of detective fiction is to write a good detective story as well as to sell copies. Following Dove's statement to its logical conclusion, the artistic success of mystery writers would be gauged strictly by sales, and writers like Mickey Spillane and Don Pendleton would achieve a much higher ranking than some of us are willing to give them.

75. Dove, George N. *Suspense in the Formula Story.* Bowling Green, OH: Popular, 1989. 137p. Bibl., index.

This study is an example of "Process Criticism," which stresses the collaboration and interaction between author and reader that Dove believes is an essential focus of any critical consideration of popular fiction. (A similar approach is used in Thomas J. Roberts' *An Aesthetics of Junk Fiction* [see #111], whose title is no more intended to be pejorative than Dove's.) He defines suspense and analyses its use in individual chapters on works from various subgenres: Van Dine's *The Greene Murder Case,* Hammett's *The Maltese Falcon* (devoting much of his essay to explicating the Flitcraft story), Michael Gilbert's *The Black Seraphim* (one of the most extensive and thoughtful bits of criticism on an undervalued giant), Nelson DeMille's *Night of the Phoenix* (as an example of Process Criticism applied to a less-than-great text), Hillary Waugh's *Last Seen Wearing,* le Carré's *The Spy Who Came in From the Cold* and Fleming's *You Only Live Twice,* Peter Straub's *Ghost Story,* Tom Clancy's *The Hunt for Red October,* and Ross Macdonald's *The Chill.* Other works discussed at less than chapter length include Robert Ludlum's *The Bourne Identity,* Richard Martin Stern's *The Tower,* Peter Benchley's *Jaws,* William Peter Blatty's *The Exorcist,* William X. Kienzle's *The Rosary Murders,* and pairs of novels by Lillian O'Donnell, Josephine Tey, and Fletcher Knebel.

A couple of names get gratuitous double-consonants (author Harry "Kemmelman" and fictional sleuth Father "Koessler"), but general accuracy is high. Dove again shows himself one of the best and most readable of academic mystery critics.

76. Geherin, David. *The American Private Eye: The Image in Fiction.*
New York: Ungar, 1985. xi, 228p. Bibl., index.

Geherin offers a narrower focus than Baker and Nietzel in *Private Eyes: 101 Knights* (see #61) but is generally more accurate and critically acute. Following a chapter putting the private eye in context with the earlier history of detective fiction, he covers 27 writers, chosen on the basis of influence, popularity, and general contribution to "growth and vitality of the genre." Each writer is covered in a sketch of a few pages, long enough to whet the reader's appetite, capture the writer's appeal and the reason for his importance, without overburdening the account with too much detail or plot summary. The treatments are soundly critical rather than merely descriptive. Especially commendable are the accounts of writers and characters not widely covered elsewhere, e.g., Raoul Whitfield's Jo Gar, John K. Butler's Steve Midnight, Jonathan Latimer's Bill Crane, Bart Spicer's Carney Wilde, Thomas B. Dewey's Mac, and William Campbell Gault's Brock Callahan.

Inclusion of some characters who belong to the hardboiled tradition but are not private detectives by profession, e.g. George Harmon Coxe's photographer "Flashgun" Casey, leads one to ask if Perry Mason, whose early cases are solidly in the tradition of tough pulp stories, doesn't also belong. And if not Mason, why not Gardner's genuine private eyes, Bertha Cool and Donald Lam, whose cases he recorded as A.A. Fair? Also, some readers will question the lack of even one female private eye among Geherin's subjects. (He does manage to list a few in his concluding chapter.)

Generally, though, the list of selections is sound. Others discussed are Daly's Race Williams, Hammett's Continental Op, Nebel's Dick Donohue, Norbert Davis's Max Latin, Bellem's Dan Turner, Chandler's Philip Marlowe, Halliday's Mike Shayne (somewhat undervalued, I think), Howard Browne's Paul Pine, Wade Miller's Max Thursday, Prather's Shell Scott, Spillane's Mike Hammer (a very accurate assessment, in my opinion), Macdonald's Lew Archer, Michael Collins's Dan Fortune, Parker's Spenser (very briefly, since Geherin covered him at length in his earlier study, *Sons of Sam Spade* [see WAM #41]), Pronzini's "Nameless," Michael Z. Lewin's Albert Samson, Arthur Lyons's Jacob Asch, and Lawrence Block's Matt Scudder.

Usually meticulously accurate, Geherin occasionally refers to books by their paperback retitlings instead of the original title—and at least once, he uses both titles at different points.

77. **Goulart, Ron.** *The Dime Detectives.* New York: Mysterious, 1988. 248p. Illus., bibl., index.

The author of a general short history of the pulp magazines, *Cheap Thrills* (see WAM #43), now contributes a highly readable and efficient survey of the pulp detective story. With all the material in print on Hammett and Chandler, it is appropriate that Goulart devotes more attention here to writers like Carroll John Daly, Cleve F. Adams, Theodore Tinsley, Frederick Nebel, Merle Constiner, and Roger Torrey. After a generally chronological account of the field through the thirties, there are topical chapters on the Hollywood dicks (with extensive quotes from Fred MacIsaac, Norbert Davis, W.T. Ballard, and John K. Butler), Robert Leslie Bellem and the *Spicy* school, female detectives (rare in the pulps and always the work of male authors), reporter detectives, "phantom" detectives, and "Screwballs, Oddballs, Etc." The final chapters trace the field in the forties and account for its eventual demise in the fifties. There is a good 16-page black-and-white section of covers and interior illustrations.

Goulart is certainly convincing in his claim that there is much pulp fiction worthy of rediscovery. In fact, his book almost seems to be scouting additional subjects for the publisher's pulp reprint series, unfortunately now ended. Some who would have been likely candidates are Butler's Steve Midnight, Richard Sale's Daffy Dill, Lester Dent's Chick Rush, the Gadget Man, and any of a dozen Erle Stanley Gardner characters.

No obvious errors were spotted related to the pulps per se, but there are some on the mystery genre generally. Dickens's Inspector Bucket was surely not "the first detective to appear in British fiction" (page 6), and radio's Richard Diamond was a New York private eye, not an L.A. op as claimed on page 119. Goulart has an irritating tendency not to attribute all his quotes, especially disparaging ones, and (occasionally) to refer to books and articles in his text that do not appear in his bibliography. His well-chosen quotes from pulp stories usually come without identifying titles and dates.

78. **Green, Martin.** *Seven Types of Adventure Tale: An Etiology of a Major Genre.* University Park: Pennsylvania State U.P., 1991. 244p. Bibl., index.

Of the seven categories in Green's taxonomy, two (the "Robinson Crusoe Story" and the "Three Musketeers Story") have no references to the mystery genre and two more (the "Wanderer Story" and the "Sagaman Story") have very few. But the chapter on the "Avenger Story" includes discussion of the crime fiction of Eugene Sue, Bulwer-Lytton, Dickens, and Balzac, with brief reference to contemporaries like John D. MacDonald and Robert B. Parker; and the "Hunted Man Story" includes the thriller exemplified by John Buchan and Raymond Chandler, with reference to such varied writers as Christie, Sayers, Ross Macdonald, Geoffrey Household, Ambler, Charteris, Oppenheim, le Carré, and Leblanc. Green points out that George Smiley is to Richard Hannay as Father Brown to Sherlock Holmes: "an assertively dowdy figure [who] replaces a dazzler" (page 203). The presence of adventure is the element Green sees as differentiating contemporary American writers like Sue Grafton and Sara Paretsky from British writers like P.D. James and Ruth Rendell.

79. Hamilton, Cynthia S. *Western and Hard- Boiled Detective Fiction in America: From High Noon to Midnight*. London: Macmillan, 1987. xi, 200p. Bibl., index.

The "American adventure formula" is examined through two subgenres: the Western and the hard-boiled detective novel, which Hamilton persuasively argues is closer to the adventure tradition than to the classical detective story from which it also draws elements. Hamilton presents a ringing defense of popular fiction, writing that, "while high art is defined in terms of its most successful examples, popular culture is defined in terms of its lowest common denominator" (page 3). She flays the intellectual snobbery seen in critical approaches to popular culture and denies that popular or "formula" literature needs to be addressed differently from other literature. She finds Cawelti's view of formula (see WAM #38) too restrictive.

A general discussion of the formula is followed by individual chapters on its use in the works of Zane Grey, Frederick Faust (better known as Max Brand), Dashiell Hammett, and Raymond Chandler. These chapters also include considerable biographical information. The only other mystery writers referred to more than glancingly are Frank Gruber (whose mystery-plot formula is discussed as part of a chapter on "Formula and the Marketplace") and hardboiled pioneer Carroll John Daly. The twenty-page bibliography is impressive in its extensiveness, though it gives only the reprint editions used for its primary sources.

This is a stimulating scholarly study, both original and effectively executed.

80. **Hart, Patricia.** *The Spanish Sleuth: The Detective in Spanish Fiction.* Rutherford, NJ: Fairleigh Dickinson U.P., 1987. 252p. Bibl., index.

This is undoubtedly the most extensive study of a non-English-language national body of crime fiction to be published in English. The subject matter is fascinating, but a bilingual reader is assumed. There are many untranslated quotations and (even more exasperating to the non-reader of Spanish) the transcripts of Hart's interviews with some of her subjects have the questions in English but the responses in Spanish. The implied assumption that most readers of such a specialized book will be students of Spanish literature is probably justified, but that doesn't make the practice any less irritating to the non-linguist mystery fiction specialist.

Hart notes there were virtually no Spanish mystery writers of note before the death of Franco and finds in Spanish detective fiction a tradition of distrust of the police, lack of conventionally happy endings, and fallible sleuths. Her major subjects (none as far as I know published in English) are Mario Lacruz, Francisco García Pavón, Manuel de Pedrolo, Jaume Fuster, Manuel Vázquez Montalbán, Eduardo Mendoza, Andreu Martín, Jorge Martínez Reverte, Fernando Savater, Juan Madrid, and Lourdes Ortiz. All but Lacruz and Mendoza are interviewed; for all but Ortiz, the interview responses are given in Spanish, though an appendix gives a translation from Catalan to English of Pedrolo's replies. Other appendices include dossiers on the major sleuths and a slang dictionary.

81. **Hoppenstand, Gary.** *In Search of the Paper Tiger: A Sociological Perspective of Myth, Formula and the Mystery Genre in the Entertainment Print Mass Medium.* Bowling Green, OH: Popular, 1987. 134p. Bibl.

Even those readers who manage to get past the dauntingly pretentious sub-title may be ready to bail out during the jargon-filled introduction, which includes statements like this: "The first chapter of this study will present social construction of reality theory as a methodology upon which the structure of mass mediated popular fiction can be examined, with definitions of myth and formula postulated, and a new language of literary analysis advanced that acknowledges the socially defining, democratizing experience of popular fiction" (page 9). Hoppenstand argues against literary evaluation of mystery fiction, believing the field is worth studying for its social significance only. He provides a fairly interesting taxonomy of the field, proceeding from the least to the most rational formulae: the supernatural (Walpole, Lovecraft, Bloch); fiction noir (Woolrich, Cain), tales of gangsters bad (Packard's *The Big Shot*) and good (Puzo's *The Godfather*) and of thieves bad (Hornung's Raffles) and good (Hanshew's Cleek); thrillers concerning spies charismatic (Fleming's James Bond) and "dark" (characters from le Carré and LeQueux, here misspelled LeQuex); and finally detective stories classical (Poe), procedural (Vidocq), hardboiled (Daly), and vengeful (Nick Carter). The most obscure work discussed, Frank L. Packard's *The Big Shot*, unfortunately is omitted from the bibliography. Some scholars may find this work stimulating, but most fans can safely pass it by.

82. **Jones, Robert Kenneth.** *The Shudder Pulps: A History of the Weird Menace Magazines of the 1930s.* West Linn, OR: FAX Collector's Editions, 1975. xv, 238p. Illus., index.

The subject magazines (e.g. *Dime Mystery, Thrilling Mystery, Terror Tales*) were somewhere on the borderline between the mystery and horror genres, with a dollop of science fiction thrown in. Among the authors were well-known pulpsters (Wyatt Blassingame, Arthur J. Burks, Ray Cummings, Paul Ernst, G.T. Fleming-Roberts, Arthur Leo Zagat) and novelists who became well-known outside the pulps (Bruno Fischer, Steve Fisher, Frank Gruber, Richard Sale). Though sometimes carelessly and awkwardly written, this is an informative and often amusing piece of fannish history with many entertaining anecdotes about the old pulp writers. Jones has the annoying habit of quoting from stories without identifying the author.

83. **Kalikoff, Beth.** *Murder and Moral Decay in Victorian Popular Literature.* Ann Arbor, MI: UMI Research, 1986. ix, 193p. Illus., bibl., index.

The Victorian era once again proves fertile ground for the crime fiction scholar. The author considers murder in "street literature, newspapers, middle-class journals, melodrama, and fiction" (page 2), dividing her discussion into three time periods: 1830-1850, 1850-1870, 1870-1900. Works of mystery fiction discussed include Le Fanu's *Uncle Silas*, Collins's *The Moonstone*, Dickens's *Bleak House*, Marie and Robert Leighton's *Michael Dred, Detective*, Zangwill's *The Big Bow Mystery*, Hume's *The Mystery of a Hansom Cab*, Stevenson's *Dr. Jekyll and Mr. Hyde*, and Doyle's Sherlock Holmes saga. Among the plays covered is Tom Taylor's *The Ticket-of-Leave Man*, featuring Hawkshaw the Detective.

84. Kimura, Jiro. *The Second International Congress of Crime Writers Picture Book March 14-17 1978*. Sakai City, Osaka, Japan: Kikugoro, 1979. 48p.

Held in New York City in 1978, the Second International Congress drew crime writers from all over the world. Following introductions by Robert J. Randisi and Lucy Freeman, recounting their memories of the event, photographer Kimura presents 37 pages of images of writers and guests in attendance at the various activities, interspersed with pages from the event's official program. Identifying captions are bilingual. This is probably the best selection of candid shots of mystery writers ever to appear in one volume. The final three pages describe the Congress in Japanese—how well I am in no position to tell you.

85. Klein, Kathleen Gregory. *The Woman Detective: Gender & Genre*. Urbana: U. of Illinois P., 1988. x, 260p. Bibl., index.

In this well-written and stimulating scholarly study, Klein spells out her major thesis on the first page: "Since the 1864 appearance of the first professional woman detective, she and her professional competence have been consistently undercut despite overt claims for her abilities, successes, intelligence, and cunning. Although she is identified as the hero, her authors—whether male or female—seldom allow her to function like one; her failures can be found among all the major sub-genres."

Coverage is generally limited to private detectives, disqualifying both amateurs like Miss Marple and cops like Lillian O'Donnell's Norah

Mulcahaney. Beginning with chapters on 19th-century British police characters (who satisfy the guidelines because they commonly functioned independently and for bounty in contrast to 20th-century cops) and American dime novel detectives, and continuing to the present, Klein consistently puts her subject in context of both detective-story history and the changing status of women. Within her guidelines, she is wide-ranging, offering substantial discussion of characters little treated elsewhere, e.g. Andrew Forrester's Mrs. Gladden, M. McDonnell Bodkin's Dora Myrl, Reginald W. Kaufman's Frances Baird, E. Phillips Oppenheim's Lucie Mott, Rex Stout's Dol Bonner, Kay Cleaver Strahan's Lynn MacDonald, Gale Gallagher ("the first woman independent hard-boiled detective" [page 126], written about under that name by the team of Will Oursler and Margaret Scott), G.G. Fickling's Honey West, Henry Kane's Marla Trent, David Linzee's Sarah Saber, Phyllis Swan's Anna Jugedinski, and James D. Lawrence's Angela Harpe. Also discussed are such one-shot novels as Mrs. Sidney Groom's *Detective Sylvia Shale* (1923) and Hazel Campbell's *Olga Knaresbrook—Detective* (1933), two books by Marie Connor Leighton, *Joan Mar, Detective* (1910) and *Lucille Dare, Detective* (1919), Fran Huston's (Ron S. Miller's) *The Rich Get It All* (1973), Arthur Kaplan's *A Killing for Charity* (1976), and Lee McGraw's *Hatchett* (1976), the last three male writers' failed shots at a liberated female private eye.

Few characters even come close to escaping confirmation of Klein's theme, though Patricia Wentworth's Miss Silver and Zelda Popkin's Mary Carner are more favorably received than their '30s and '40s contemporaries. Even such recent characters as P.D. James's Cordelia Gray and Liza Cody's Anna Lee are seen as continuing to undercut the credibility of women as detectives. (I think Klein is too tough on A.A. Fair's [Erle Stanley Gardner's] Bertha Cool and overstates in calling Gardner's work "misogynistic" [page 193], but there are arguments to be made either way.)

The final chapter discusses five writers—the well-known Sue Grafton, Marcia Muller, and Sara Paretsky, and one-shots Susan Steiner and M.F. Beal—who "attempt to integrate gender awareness into the most resistant form, the hard-boiled novel" (page 202). Paretsky's V.I. Warshawski gets by far the best notices, but Klein finishes her study doubting real feminist detective fiction is possible.

Substantive notes follow each chapter. Klein includes a thorough 21-page primary and secondary bibliography, an index of women detectives, and a general subject index. In a work that is usually careful and

meticulous in its accuracy, the occasional error leaps out: Edmund Cleri-
hew Bentley becomes Eric at one point, and there is a reference to Ed
McBain's "96th" Precinct.

86. **Knight, Stephen.** *Form and Ideology in Crime Fiction.* Blooming-
ton, IN: Indiana U.P., 1981. viii, 202p. Bibl., index.

An Australian scholar discusses the *Newgate Calendar,* Godwin's
Caleb Williams, Vidocq, Poe, Doyle, Christie, Chandler, and McBain.
Though some fans may find the academic tone initially off-putting, the
volume is more readable than most such studies and genuinely adds to our
understanding of most of its subjects. The volume is self-described as a
work of literary sociology, mainly devoted to showing how the authors'
works reflected the attitudes of their times toward crime control. A
primary and secondary bibliography follows each chapter.

87. **Knudson, Richard L.** *The Whole Spy Catalogue: An Espionage
Lover's Guide.* New York: St. Martin's, 1986. 182p. Illus., bibl.

Not examined. According to Edward D. Hoch (*The Year's Best
Mystery and Suspense Stories 1987* [see #369]), it is "[a]n 'espionage
lover's guide,' containing bibliographies of leading spy novelists, descriptions of film and TV spies, and accounts of real spies and how they
operate." Reviewer Richard Meyers (in *The Armchair Detective,* v. 20, n.
3, page 302) finds the book disappointing, "suffer[ing] from an acute case
of the galloping shallows."

88. **Lehman, David.** *The Perfect Murder: A Study in Detection.* New
York: Free Press, 1989. xix, 242p. Bibl., index.

The poet and former *Newsweek* book critic covers little new ground
here, but his work is an intelligent, well-written aesthetic/philosophical
discussion of the detective story, both in its classical and hardboiled
varieties. As a pure intellectual celebration of fictional detection, it is
virtually unmatched, coming as it does from an enthusiast who is equally
knowledgeable about the genre and about literature generally, one who

can discuss Jim Thompson's *The Killer Inside Me* as convincingly as
Vladimir Nabokov's use of detective story conventions.

Most attention is paid to established icons: Poe, Doyle, Christie, Carr,
Stout, Chesterton, Hammett, Chandler, McBain, and Ross Macdonald.
Lehman especially admires *The Maltese Falcon* and provides an extended
discussion of the various theories advanced on the meaning of Sam
Spade's Flitcraft story. As interested in film as print detection, he offers a
fresh view of *The Big Sleep* in its novel and movie forms. Among newer
writers, he provides a good discussion of Sue Grafton and Sara Paretsky
and touches on Richard Rosen as an example of detective fiction reflecting
the headlines of its time. The penultimate chapter on escapism discusses
works of Greene, Ambler, and Kafka, while the final chapter focuses on
Jorge Luis Borges and Umberto Eco. Lehman is especially interesting on
Eco's debt to and surprising use of Borges in *The Name of the Rose*.
Lehman's Further Reading list is both primary and secondary and includes
a list of movies and poems. An annotated list of fifteen favorites consists
of well-established classic novels plus Dennis Potter's TV series *The
Singing Detective* (1986). There are ten pages of notes and an Index of
Concepts (e.g. Armchair detective, Damsel in distress, Locked room,
Puzzle, Simile) as well as a conventional name and title index.

Lehman gives early warning he will freely reveal solutions where
necessary to his argument. To prove it, he tips *Roger Ackroyd* on page 5.

89. Lovisi, Gary. *Science Fiction Detective Tales.* Brooklyn, NY:
Gryphon, 1986. 107p. Illus., bibl.

The cover carries the subtitle "A Brief Overview of Futuristic Detective Fiction in Paperback." Lovisi cites a large number of mystery/s.f.
hybrids, including many published in the last decade. Only books published in paperback, original or reprint, are covered, and there is considerable detailed information (stock numbers, descriptions and
reproductions of cover art) for the paperback collector. A dozen introductory pages make some sound general points about the combination of the
two genres. There follows an alphabetical list (Asimov to Zelazny) of
writers in the field with descriptive and sometimes critical comment. Ron
Goulart, who has mixed his categories more often than any other writer,
appropriately gets the most space. Though the coverage is remarkably
comprehensive, taking in such scarce items as David V. Reed's *Murder in
Space* (1954) and Leslie Charteris' misleadingly-titled s.f. anthology *The*

Saint's Choice of Impossible Crime (1945; see #384), Lovisi lists only the weakest of Edward D. Hoch's three Computer Cops novels, *The Fellowship the Hand,* first published in hardcover by Walker in 1973, not as a paperback original as Lovisi believes. The two unlisted Computer Cops titles are *The Transvection Machine* (Walker, 1971) and *The Frankenstein Factory* (Warner, 1975).

Lovisi is a prolific fanzine publisher, and his monograph is a proudly and insistently amateur effort both in writing and production. He is anything but a tough critic, his rare unfavorable comments presented almost apologetically, and his comments range from the perceptive to the obvious. The style is rambling, repetitious, and unedited. Clearly, getting the information to the reader is more important to Lovisi than making it pretty, and there is much valuable information here for any reader or collector of s.f. detective stories.

90. **Lyles, William H.** *Putting Dell on the Map: A History of the Dell Paperbacks.* (Contributions to the Study of Popular Culture, Number 5.) Westport, CT: Greenwood, 1983. xxiv, 178p. Illus., bibl., index.

As with most of the early mass-market paperback houses, a large proportion of Dell's output was mysteries. Among the mystery writers quoted or discussed in this entertaining history are Harold Q. Masur, Leslie Ford, Brett Halliday (with a comment from Robert Terrall on how the Mike Shayne series came to use ghost writers), James McKimmey, Fredric Brown (whose Dell novel *Madball* Ralph Ellison found to be in poor taste), Frank Kane, Matthew Head (John Canaday), Kelley Roos, and Richard Burke. In an especially interesting chapter on the famous Dell Map-Backs, several writers comment on the quality and accuracy of the maps used to illustrate their works, including Donald Hamilton, Aaron Marc Stein, C.W. Grafton, Lenore Glen Offord, Dorothy B. Hughes, Lawrence Treat, and Jack Iams. As usual with books on paperbacks, much attention is devoted to cover art, and illustrators like Robert Stanley and Robert McGinniss are discussed at length. Illustrations include photos, front and back covers, ads, and charts of the Western Publishing plant where Dell books were produced.

Lyles' companion volume *Dell Paperbacks, 1942 to Mid-1962: A Catalog-Index* (Greenwood, 1983) has less specific genre interest, though obviously many of the books indexed are mysteries.

91. McArdle, Phil and Karen. *Fatal Fascination: Where Fact Meets Fiction in Police Work.* Boston: Houghton Mifflin, 1988. x, 228p. Illus., bibl., index.

Though too compact in size to be designated a coffee-table book, this fact-vs.-fiction compilation is similar to Dilys Winn's *Murder Ink* (see WAM #107 and the present volume #558) and *Murderess Ink* (WAM #108) in its magazine format, with many illustrations, sidebars, quizzes, and puzzles scattered through the text. Based on the authors' articles on police procedure in *Lineup*, a journal of the Northern California chapter of Mystery Writers of America, the book is primarily a true crime source, but one of its main subjects is the difference between real life police investigation and its fictional equivalents in print and visual media. Thus, there are many fiction-related features, including a satirical half-page "Handy Guide to Who Done It in Mystery Fiction." The book is a great source for practitioners who wish to sprinkle bits of reality in their improbable fictions. Besides the procedural information, there are some fascinating factual tidbits: for example, that Mr. Spock of *Star Trek* was based on L.A. Chief of Police William Parker, for whom Gene Roddenberry once worked.

Most interesting section for our purposes concerns the fictional uses of real-life crimes, including Poe's cover letter offering "The Mystery of Marie Roget" to a Boston magazine; a comparison of Wilkie Collins's *The Moonstone* with the Constance Kent case; Agatha Christie's use of the Lindbergh kidnap case in *Murder on the Orient Express;* and S.S. Van Dine's adaptation of the mysterious death of Dot King in *The "Canary" Murder Case.* (Delightfully for fans of the much-maligned Van Dine, the McArdles champion *"Canary"* as a sound early example of the police procedural!)

Generally the authors are well-versed in crime fiction as well as fact, though their statement (in an article on "Chinatown, Fu Manchu, and Charlie Chan") that Sax Rohmer wrote thirty novels about Fu Manchu is way off—the actual number is more like half that, and some of those are more accurately short-story collections.

The book ends with two pages quoting detective-story wrap-ups, beginning with Lord Peter Wimsey's emotional breakdown at the end of Sayers's *Busman's Honeymoon,* followed by passages from Doyle, Queen, Freeman, Marsh, Lathen, Bramah, le Carré, Shannon, Simenon, and Tey.

92. McMillen, Jean M., and Ron McMillen, eds. *Cooking with Malice Domestic.* Foreword by Elizabeth Peters. Bethesda, MD: Mystery Bookshop, 1991. xiv, 177p. Index.

Prepared in connection with the "cozy" mystery convention held each spring in the Washington, D.C., area, this volume joins the small but distinguished shelf of mystery oriented cookbooks pioneered by Jeanine Larmoth's *Murder on the Menu* (see WAM #49). Following four pages of directions for "A Proper Tea," the arrangement is alphabetical by contributing author. Most contributors are mystery writers (including such luminaries as Marian Babson, Dorothy Cannell, Aaron Elkins, Carolyn G. Hart, Joan Hess, Faye Kellerman, Jonathan Kellerman, Charlotte MacLeod, Sharyn McCrumb, and Patricia Moyes), who often attribute the recipes to their continuing characters, with a few fans, critics, and the bookdealing editors joining in. Susan Dunlap wins the prize for entertainment value, Nicole St. James for (the editors apart) most recipes. There is a five-page index to the recipes. Not having tested them all, I can recommend only the two soups attributed to Rachel Hennings (via Rita Breen) with complete confidence.

93. Mann, Jessica. *Deadlier Than the Male: Why Are Respectable English Women So Good at Murder?* Newton Abbot: David and Charles; New York: Macmillan, 1981. 256p. Bibl., index.

In addressing the question of her subtitle, Mann devotes chapters to the history and development of detective fiction and detective characters, followed by individual treatments of Christie, Sayers, Allingham, Tey, and Marsh. If the author had done the latter three with the same thoroughness and depth she accords the first two, already well covered in many other sources by 1981, this would be a most valuable book. But Mann is a better novelist than a critic and this is a disappointing work, gracefully written but offering nothing new save a sneering dismissal of male Golden Age writers.

Also, this is another of those all-too-numerous books about mysteries that are full of careless errors. She has Anna Katharine Green (born 1846) dying at age 90 in 1935; she makes Collins's Sergeant Cuff an inspector; she dates Carolyn Wells's first mystery novel correctly as 1909, then states Wells did not "consider either reading or writing detective fiction" until 1910 (page 33); she miscredits Emma Lathen as sole author of *Agatha*

Christie, First Lady of Crime (see WAM #132); and she indicates *The Second Shot,* published as by Anthony Berkeley, carried the byline A.B. Cox. More a matter of opinion is her statement that with "very few exceptions," crime writers "have no personal experience at all of crime and detection" (page 54). Too many exceptions come readily to mind— Maurice Procter, Erle Stanley Gardner, John Wainwright, Dorothy Uhnak (whom Mann mentions), Sir Basil Thomson, Joseph Wambaugh, Dallas Barnes, Dashiell Hammett, Joe Gores, Donald MacKenzie, Al Nussbaum, E. Richard Johnson, Malcolm Braly, E. Howard Hunt, P.D. James—to make such a generalization acceptable.

94. **Margolies, Edward.** *Which Way Did He Go?: The Private Eye in Dashiell Hammett, Raymond Chandler, Chester Himes, and Ross Macdonald.* New York: Holmes & Meier, 1982. xii, 97p. Illus., bibl., index.

It's not surprising that Margolies provides his most interesting chapter on the author least extensively covered in earlier works: Chester Himes, who (paradoxically) really wrote about cops rather than private eyes. Margolies' study is concise, well-written, and well-organized, avoiding the usual over-dependence on plot summary. However, little new ground is covered.

95. **Melling, John Kennedy.** *Murder Done to Death: A Survey of Pastiche and Parody of the Detective Story.* N.p., privately printed, 1979. 8p. Bibl.

This self-published chapbook, limited to 500 copies, discusses both film and print pastiches and parodies, including Neil Simon's *The Cheap Detective* and *Murder by Death; The Laurel and Hardy Murder Case,* the various imitations of Sherlock Holmes, Agatha Christie's *Partners in Crime,* collaborative works like *The Floating Admiral* and *The President's Mystery Story,* and Marion Mainwaring's *Murder in Pastiche.*

Not everything that would qualify is covered—Corey Ford's Philo Vance parody *The John Riddell Murder Case* is a notable omission—and the line between parody and pastiche is somewhat confused. (Barry Perowne's Raffles stories, parodies to Melling, are more accurately called pastiches.) Authorial sloppiness credits Clinton H. Stagg's blind sleuth Thornley Colton to Austin Freeman and leads to the implication that *The*

Misadventures of Sherlock Holmes is by (rather than edited by) Ellery Queen. But Melling certainly gives a wealth of tips to the devotee of parody in a short essay. The bibliography lists eleven standard secondary sources on the detective genre.

96. Menendez, Albert. *Mistletoe Malice: The Life and Times of the Christmas Murder Mystery.* Silver Spring, MD: Holly Tree, 1982. 35p. Bibl.

Menendez identifies 89 mystery novels with Christmas backgrounds, divides them into categories (e.g., Country House Party Thriller, Police Procedural, Department Store Glitter, etc.), and provides tantalizing plot summaries for some. The selection seems remarkably complete and the summaries, usually descriptive rather than critical, are gracefully written. It's especially nice to see notice given such relatively obscure books as M.P. Rea's *Death of an Angel* (1943), Frederick C. Davis's *Drag the Dark* (1953), David William Meredith's *The Christmas Card Murders* (1951), and Stuart Palmer's *Omit Flowers* (1937). The authors to return most frequently to a yuletide setting are Nicholas Blake, Helen McCloy, and Ed McBain (three novels each).

The main section is followed by a checklist, arranged alphabetically by author and including publisher and date of the first edition as well as alternate titles. The one minor irritant of the pamphlet is that Menendez sometimes refers to titles without their authors in his text, and it is necessary to scan through the checklist to find out who done it.

97. Meyers, Ric(hard). *Murder on the Air: Television's Great Mystery Series.* New York: Mysterious, 1989. xiii, 290p. Illus., index.

Meyers's earlier work, the Edgar-nominated *TV Detectives* (see below) was an entertaining book, but this more detailed and thoughtful volume represents a great advance over its predecessor. Meyers does not deal with every major television mystery or detective series—among important shows mentioned only in passing are *Perry Mason, Cagney and Lacey,* and *The Untouchables*—but those he considers are covered in depth, with a thoughtful critical perspective and frequent inside details gleaned from interviews with actors, writers, and producers who worked on the shows. The first two chapters concern the pioneering series *Martin*

Kane (starring William Gargan and successors—the star was changed each time the sponsor wanted to feature a different tobacco product) and *Man Against Crime* (with anecdotes from star Ralph Bellamy). The third considers the various TV incarnations of Ellery Queen. There follow meaty and informative chapters on Jack Webb and *Dragnet, Peter Gunn, 77 Sunset Strip* and its various clones, *Mannix, Hawaii Five-0, Charlie's Angels* (viewed with appropriate feminist outrage), *Cannon, Barnaby Jones* (with the provocative assertion that "Barnaby was one of the best private eyes in the business, and . . . the program's plots were the most perverted in television history" [page 181]), *Harry O, The Rockford Files, Magnum P.I., Hill Street Blues,* and finally the Levinson-Link creations *Columbo* and *Murder, She Wrote.* The afterword makes some serious points about TV's tendency to blur fiction and reality. Meyers has interesting things to say about all his subjects, and this is certainly the best book to date on TV mysteries.

98. **Meyers, Richard.** *TV Detectives.* San Diego: Barnes, 1981. xii, 276p. Illus., index.

Meyers offers a year-by-year history, generously illustrated, of television detective series. Individual specials, movies, miniseries, and anthology entries are generally excluded. The author writes entertainingly, with much lively critical comment. He admits his selection criteria are not always consistently applied, and one distinct bias is toward comedy. He offers an evocative tribute to *Car 54, Where Are You?*, a great show about cops but surely not a mystery or detective program. *Get Smart* and *Barney Miller* also get extended treatment. Oddly, though, *Batman*, more nearly a detective show than any of these, is discussed only glancingly. Few will share all of Meyers' opinions as to shows' relative quality. For me, he seems overly kind to the William Conrad *Nero Wolfe* series.

Meyers sometimes fails to identify the literary sources of TV series characters. Lawrence G. Blochman is not credited with the creation of Dr. Coffee, nor is the G.G. Fickling team credited with Honey West. Some of the inferences he draws reveal a sketchy knowledge of some corners of printed detective fiction: Inspector Duff, a character in Earl Derr Biggers' Charlie Chan novels of the twenties and thirties, could hardly have been named in honor of actor Howard Duff. Meyers seems to believe that Dashiell Hammett wrote about the Continental Op and Sam Spade after he created Nick and Nora Charles in *The Thin Man* (see page 41). And for a purely television-oriented gaffe, it is surely mistaken to imply that Peter Falk's Columbo was virtually the same character he earlier played in *The Trials of O'Brien.*

99. Miller, D.A. *The Novel and the Police.* Berkeley: U. of California P., 1988. xv, 222p. Index.

In a narrower discussion than the title suggests, Miller considers the role of police as characters in Victorian novels. The most interesting chapter on *The Moonstone* concentrates on the reception of Sgt. Cuff in the upper-crust world of the story and that world's inclusion of a self-contained policing function that is able to solve the case without him. Collins's novel is seen in a fascinating relationship to later detective fiction: it goes beyond a formula not yet fully established. Other works accorded chapter-length treatment are Dickens's *Bleak House* (seen as the novel in which the necessity for a police force becomes clear, as it does not in the later *Moonstone,* though the police are not presented without reservation), Trollope's *Barchester Towers* (in which police are present only in metaphor), Collins's *The Woman in White,* and Dickens's *David Copperfield.* Other subjects either in or bordering on the detective story genre are Dickens's *Oliver Twist,* Trollope's *The Eustace Diamonds,* Braddon's *Lady Audley's Secret,* and several works of Balzac. Passing reference is made to Gaboriau, Doyle, Poe, and Christie.

This is a book with interesting points to make that erects barriers (notably a mannered, over-decorated writing style) to ward off at least part of its potential audience. The lack of a bibliography is unfortunate, though there are plenty of footnotes. At one point, reference is made to critic Ian Ousby with no easy way for the reader to identify the work referred to (*Bloodhounds of Heaven* [see WAM #52]).

100. O'Brien, Geoffrey. *Hardboiled America: The Lurid Years of Paperbacks.* New York: Van Nostrand, 1981. 144p. Illus., bibl., index.

The early stages of this thoughtful, serious, and very well-written study are concerned primarily with the sociological significance of paperback books, with more emphasis on the cover art and packaging than the contents. But the latter stages hold some excellent commentary on several authors prominent in paperback (sometimes as authors of originals, more often of reprinted material written before the post-war paperback boom): Hammett, Cain, Chandler, Horace McCoy, Kenneth Fearing, Latimer, Goodis, Dorothy B. Hughes, Woolrich, Spillane, John D. MacDonald, Jim Thompson, and Ross Macdonald. Among the subjects touched upon are the role played by women in detective fiction, the use of alcohol and narcotics in hardboiled mysteries, the rise of the juvenile delinquent novel in the fifties, and a comparison of paperback crime fiction and film noir. Appended are a six-page chronological list of books, "The Hardboiled Era: A Checklist, 1929-1958," and a page each of secondary bibliography and index (including personal names and publishers but not titles). There are sixteen pages of color reproductions of paperback covers and many more black-and-white covers throughout the text. Unfortunately, there is no easy way to find the reproduction of a cover when it comes up in the text, and sometimes back covers have been reproduced without disclosing the names of the books they go with.

O'Brien makes occasional errors: he throws Gruber's Johnny Fletcher and Prather's Shell Scott together in the "breezy shamus" category (Fletcher was a book salesman, not a private eye); thinks "The Whistler" of radio was a private eye, which he was not (though Robert Campbell's more recent Whistler is); and misdates the Brando film *The Wild One* 1951 (should be 1954). And though he gets the MacDonald/Macdonald spellings correctly sorted out, he makes a reference to Edgar "Allen" Poe. But given the genre average, the miscues are few, and this is one of the outstanding studies of the hardboiled school.

101. Panek, LeRoy Lad. *Probable Cause: Crime Fiction in America*. Bowling Green, OH: Popular, 1990. ii, 167p. Index.

Panek essays an "introductory survey" of American crime fiction between 1840 and 1940. Each of three period subdivisions (1840-1890, 1890-1917, and 1917-1940) begins with a historical survey chapter, chronicling events both in criminous history and literature, followed by a discussion of specific titles from the period. Always an informative and provocative critic, Panek takes some interesting positions. He does not think highly of the literary merits of the pioneers, including Anna Katharine Green, whose contributions are downplayed. He identifies Samuel Hopkins Adams's *Average Jones* (1911) as the key American progenitor of the Golden Age of Detection. He believes American writers before Daly and Hammett shunned writing about explicit violence mainly because they did not have the language to do it.

Among the specific books discussed by Panek that constitute fresh critical ground are Rodrigues Ottolengui's *A Conflict of Evidence* (1893), Josiah Flynt and Francis Walton's *The Powers That Prey* (1900), William J. Burns and Isabel Ostrander's *The Crevice* (1915), Jack Boyle's *Boston Blackie* (1919), and Edward Anderson's *Thieves Like Us* (1937). On the more familiar titles, Panek usually has something new and illuminating to say.

There is a three-page index but, regrettably, no notes or bibliography. As has often been true of the author's earlier books, there are too many careless errors. Authors' bylines are sometimes misspelled (Hugh "Green," Mignon "C." Eberhart) and sometimes given in incomplete form (Harry Keeler, George H. Coxe), and titles without initial articles have them added (Hammett's *"The" Red Harvest*, Paul Cain's *"The" Fast One*). Hitchcock's silent *The Lodger* was not an American film, and I don't believe *I Am a Fugitive from a Chain Gang* is accurately called a gangster film. The San Francisco earthquake is misdated 1905. Finally, the publisher's blurb mistakenly credits Panek with two Edgar awards. Though he has been nominated twice, he has won only once, for *An Introduction to the Detective Story* (see #4).

102. **Parker, Robert B.** *The Private Eye in Hammett and Chandler.* Northridge, CA: Lord John Press, 1984. 63p.

Not examined. This limited edition is adapted from Parker's unpublished 1971 doctoral dissertation, *The Violent Hero, Wilderness Heritage and Urban Reality: A Study of the Private Eye in the Novels of Dashiell Hammett, Raymond Chandler, and Ross Macdonald,* which I have examined. As would be expected from the author, it avoids the inherent dullness and tedium of the dissertation breed almost completely. Parker traces the private eye character to James Fenimore Cooper's novels, believing the private eye of the urban 20th century is Deerslayer the frontier hero with no frontier or wilderness to escape into. In tracing the hardboiled hero to the adventure tradition rather than to classical detective fiction, he agrees with Cynthia Hamilton (see #79).

103. **Paul, Robert S.** *Whatever Happened to Sherlock Holmes?: Detective Fiction, Popular Theology, and Society.* Carbondale: Southern Illinois U.P., 1991. 305p. Bibl., index.

Not examined. According to Edward D. Hoch in *Year's Best Mystery and Detective Stories 1992* (see #369), it explores "[t]he connections between theology and the popularity of detective fiction."

104. **Peterson, Audrey.** *Victorian Masters of Mystery.* New York: Ungar, 1984. vii, 235p. Illus., bibl., index.

A Professor of English at California State University, Long Beach, Peterson presents a readable and unexceptionable summary of the lives and works of several nineteenth century writers of detective fiction. Most of her material has been covered in depth in earlier works, particularly the chapters on Collins, Dickens, and Conan Doyle. Joseph Sheridan Le Fanu is also the subject of an individual chapter, while "Some Minor Voices" includes shorter accounts of Mary Elizabeth Braddon, James Payn (freshest subject treated in the book), and Anna Katharine Green, the only American discussed. The Dickens chapter is most notable for its summary of the various theories of how *The Mystery of Edwin Drood* would have been completed. Though a good introduction for someone new to the field, the book has little to offer the experienced reader.

105. **Pierce, Hazel Beasley.** *A Literary Symbiosis: Science Fiction/Fantasy Mystery.* (Contributions to the Study of Science Fiction and Fantasy, Number 6.) Westport, CT: Greenwood, 1983. viii, 255p. Bibl., index.

The first book-length work on this fertile topic identifies and describes science fiction and fantasy equivalents of the detective story, the crime story, the thriller, and the gothic. Following a discussion of some early creators of scientific detectives (L.T. Meade and her collaborators, R. Austin Freeman, Edwin Balmer and William MacHarg, Arthur B. Reeve, and T.S. Stribling), Pierce addresses the most famous pioneering s.f./detection hybrids: Hal Clement's *Needle,* Alfred Bester's *The Demolished Man,* and various works of Isaac Asimov: his two classic robot novels, *The Caves of Steel* and *The Naked Sun,* and his short stories about Dr. Wendell Urth. Among the other authors discussed are Mack Reynolds,

Dean R. Koontz (whose Sherlockian *A Werewolf Among Us* featured a robot sleuth), Jack Vance, Ron Goulart (most prolific cross-pollinator of them all), Avram Davidson, Robert Sheckley, Stanislaw Lem, Isidore Haiblum, Philip Jose Farmer, Arthur Byron Cover, Lloyd Biggle, Jr., Mike McQuay, William F. Nolan, Lee Killough, Per Wahlöö, L. Neil Smith, Harry Harrison, Michael Kurland, Frederik Pohl, and D.G. Compton. Most of these are more associated with the s.f. or fantasy genres than with mystery, but there is interesting discussion of John Dickson Carr's use of time travel in *Fire, Burn* and Len Deighton's alternate universe in *SS-GB*. Randall Garrett's impossible-crime detective stories about Lord Darcy are discussed last, offered as an example of a series that drew on the characteristics of each mystery sub-category, as well as combining elements of s.f. and fantasy. Following the main text is an excellent bibliographic essay of six pages, identifying anthologies and articles bearing on the subject.

106. **Porter, Dennis.** *The Pursuit of Crime: Art and Ideology in Crime Fiction.* New Haven, CT: Yale U.P., 1981. ix, 267p. Index.

This heavily academic work has some interesting points to make on the way to its conclusion that in its "reaffirmation of national mythical values and of fixed cultural quantities, as well as on the level of an asserted narrative order, the detective story functions as a literature of reassurance and conformism" (page 220), but it sometimes exemplifies the main complaint some readers bring against much academic criticism: the few nuggets of insight are not worth wading through the dense swamp of prose, where most points merely belabor the obvious in an unenteraining way. The chapter on "readability" of detective novels is a prime example.

Porter's principal subjects are Wilkie Collins, Chandler, Simenon (the one author with a chapter to himself), Fleming (viewed here as a detective fiction writer), Hammett, and (in a final chapter on "anti-detection") Henry James, Kafka, Robbé-Grillet, and Borges.

The section on ideology makes too much of the distinctive differences between British and American detective fiction. The excessive generalization tends to render irrelevant the work of any writer who crosses the line. A particularly insulting denigration of American classicists comes when Queen, Van Dine, and Stout (as Americans following the British pattern) are compared to two far inferior British writers of quasi-American mysteries, Peter Cheyney and James Hadley Chase.

There are a number of careless errors that seem especially serious in such a scholarly context: a reference to "Claude" Dupin; a statement that Doyle did five volumes of detective short stories before attempting a full-length novel (I assume this means *The Hound of the Baskervilles,* a book that was preceded by only two volumes of Sherlock Holmes short stories, *The Adventures* and *The Memoirs*); a claim that at the time of *Black Mask's* debut in 1920, S.S. Van Dine, whose first Philo Vance novel did not appear until 1926, was "the best-known detective story writer in the United States" (page 164); and a reference to editor "J.S." (should be Joseph T.) Shaw.

Though there is no bibliography, Porter includes many footnotes.

107. **Pronzini, Bill.** *Gun in Cheek.* Introduction by Ed McBain. New York: Coward, McCann, and Geoghegan, 1982. 264p. Bibl., index.

Pronzini believes the good writers of mystery, detective, and espionage fiction have received more than their share of attention in past studies and that the time has come to give some credit to the bad writers. Thus, he spends many pages quoting choice bits of wonderfully horrible writing, summarizing elaborately implausible plots, and otherwise celebrating crime fiction's "alternative classics." With the wrong touch, this kind of book could degenerate into rock-throwing and coffin-kicking—and indeed some of the few still-living targets have taken it in the wrong spirit—but Pronzini's approach is good-humored, even loving. He really enjoys these awful writers, in a way that possibly only another totally-immersed popular fiction buff can understand. There is no bile in his descriptions, except perhaps when he confronts the pernicious racism of a writer like Sydney Horler or the frightening social attitudes of Mickey Spillane.

The tone for the volume is set by Ed McBain's introduction. McBain (a.k.a. Evan Hunter) spends nearly all his space quoting embarrassing passages from his own (mostly early) work, and he expresses mock resentment at their not being included in the text. (One example: " . . . her voice sounded deep and throaty even when she spoke.") In his own preface, Pronzini cites a line from his first novel, *The Stalker* ("When would this phantasmagoria that was all too real reality end? he asked himself") and claims the author of such a bit of prose must be uniquely qualified to write an appreciation of bad writing.

Inevitably, some of the writers Pronzini implicitly labels bad—and in response to this observation, he has insisted he does not consider all his subjects bad writers—are ones others think are good: Gaston Leroux, Richard S. Prather, Gladys Mitchell, Ross H. Spencer (whose one-sentence-to-a-line-and-no-internal-punctuation style Pronzini parodies tellingly), and even Carter Brown (the staggeringly prolific Australian who got consistently good reviews from Anthony Boucher). One of the supposed "alternative classics," Gwen Bristow and Bruce Manning's *The Invisible Host* (1930), the novel that anticipated by several years the plot structure of Agatha Christie's *And Then There Were None*, is regarded as a real classic by some readers. And at least a few of the writers discussed (Robert Leslie Bellem, Michael Avallone, and Harry Stephen Keeler) are so unique and so entertaining in their outrageous excesses as to be beyond any judgment of good and bad.

Among the books Pronzini discusses at greatest length are Milton M. Raison's *Murder in a Lighter Vein* (1947), a mystery with a radio background in which the victim, comedian Artie Aragon, wants to insert his familiar tag-line "Wanna woo-woo?" into the script of a production of *Cyrano de Bergerac*; Eric Heath's *Murder of a Mystery Writer* (1955), of which Pronzini recommends two or three readings for full appreciation; Cortland Fitzsimmons's *70,000 Witnesses* (1931); A.E. Apple's *Mr. Chang's Crime Ray* (1928); Tom Roan's *The Dragon Strikes Back* (1936); and the book that may be awfulest of them all, Michael Morgan's *Decoy* (1953), the collaborative effort of Hollywood publicity men C.E. "Teet" Carle ("a poet laureate of the absurd") and Dean M. Dorn.

Other writers to receive substantial attention are Nick Carter (of the spy novels, not the dime novels), G.G. Fickling, William LeQueux, Carolyn Wells, Thomas W. Hanshew, Joseph Rosenberger, R.A.J. Walling (who "elevated dullness to a fine art"), and John B. West. An entire chapter is devoted to Phoenix Press, a rental-library publishing firm of the forties that paid rock-bottom rates to such memorable writers as Sidney E. Porcelain, Amelia Reynolds Long, Robert Portner Koehler, and James O'Hanlon.

The best way to capture the flavor of the enterprise, one of the funniest books ever written about mystery fiction, may be to quote a few of its examples. Avallone: "She . . . unearthed one of her fantastic breasts from the folds of her sheath skirt." Bellem: "Welch gasped like a leaky flue, hugged his punctured tripes, and slowly doubled over, fell flat on his smeller." O'Hanlon: "The moon, from which some heavenly force had taken a huge bite, and to which a faraway coyote was paying wailing tribute, hung over Horsethief."

108. **Pronzini, Bill.** *Son of Gun in Cheek.* New York: Mysterious Press, 1987. 229p. Bibl., index.

The author continues to get plenty of laughs from horrible quotes and outrageous plot summaries. His targets again are divided between those who really are worth reading—Keeler and Avallone certainly, Michael Morgan maybe—and those it's hard to imagine any reader wanting to peruse at length—Sydney Horler, F.M. Pettee, Anthony Rud. How grateful we should be not to have to read these writers when we have Pronzini to read them for us, picking out all the best bits. While the compilation of quotes is impressive, the author's own comments on the works under discussion are often just as amusing, e.g., his definition of Yellow Peril novels: "flights of fancy in which the villains are evil Orientals bent on taking over the world, enslaving the white races, and turning them into laundrymen, servants, and coolie labor" (page 45).

In addition to celebrating bad novels and pulp stories, Pronzini includes chapters on B movies (concentrating on the Charlie Chan series), blurb writers, and titles. He also institutes an Alternative Hall of Fame, in which such obscure opuses as Mary Gaunt's *The Mummy Moves,* Joseph Auslander's *Hell in Harness* (a gangster novel in verse!), Cromwell Gibbons's *The Bat Woman,* and Peter C. Herring's *The Murder Business* achieve unexpected immortality.

How bad can professionally published mystery fiction get? As a partial answer, Pronzini reprints in its entirety Florence M. Pettee's "Death Laughs at Walls," a locked-room short story about master detective Digby Gresham, from a 1930 issue of the Fiction House pulp magazine *Detective Classics.* Critics may argue forever whether the narrative style, the dialogue, or the plot achieves a more definitive ineptitude.

109. **Reddy, Maureen T.** *Sisters in Crime: Feminism and the Crime Novel.* New York: Continuum, 1988. viii, 172p. Bibl., index.

As the title suggests, this, along with Klein's *The Woman Detective* (see #85) is one of the most militantly feminist of detective fiction studies. It's well-written, effectively argued, and full of intriguing observations. (I believe the alleged male bias of detective fiction history and criticism is over-stated here, but that's easy to do in a study with such a specific focus.) Though she provides a historical context, tracing the female crime novel to Ann Radcliffe, Mrs. Henry Wood, and Mary Elizabeth Braddon, Reddy devotes most of her pages to contemporary writers, with an emphasis on creators of strong woman detective figures. She devotes chapters to amateurs, academicians, cops, private eyes, and (in a separate category partaking of the others) lesbians. Among the authors discussed, many more lengthily and deeply than in any other source, are Lucille Kallen, J.S. Borthwick, Marcia Muller (I share Reddy's enthusiasm for her Elena Olivarez), Susan Dunlap, Victoria Silver, Amanda Cross, Lillian O'Donnell (seen as anti-feminist), Barbara Paul, P.D. James, Sara Paretsky, Liza Cody, Sue Grafton, Barbara Wilson, Vicki McConnell, and Katherine V. Forrest. A primary and secondary bibliography is included.

110. **Reese, Kitty, and Regis Sinclair.** *The Mystery Trivia Quiz Book*. New York: Warner, 1985. xii, 180p.

In contrast to *The Mystery Reader's Quiz Book* (see #68), most of these quizzes are devoted to individual authors, with a few topical ones (e.g. on short stories, mysteries based on fact, and radio, TV, and movie mysteries). The questions are short-answer rather than multiple choice and much more difficult, running to plot details rather than names of authors, titles, and continuing characters. (Anyone who can get a decent percentage on these quizzes is a much sharper mystery fan than I.)

111. **Roberts, Thomas J.** *An Aesthetics of Junk Fiction*. Athens: U. of Georgia P., 1990. x, 284p. Bibl., index.

In his preface, the author falls all over himself apologizing for the inflammatory title, and truthfully this book is more friendly than not to popular fiction, here called paperback fiction and distinguished from serious (i.e. literary) fiction and plain (i.e. bestselling) fiction. Though the subject is popular fiction generally, a large proportion of the examples are drawn from the crime and mystery category, with slightly more from science fiction, less from western fiction, and hardly any from romance fiction. The latter suggests a male bias, continued by Roberts's crime fiction preference of thriller and hardboiled writers and his admitted aversion to the English country-house mystery. Among the crime writers discussed are John D. MacDonald, George V. Higgins, Ross Thomas, Brian Garfield, Jim Thompson, Ross Macdonald, William Marshall, Maj Sjöwall and Per Wahlöö, John le Carré, Frederick Forsyth, Dashiell Hammett, Adam Hall, and Anthony Berkeley. Roberts is well-read in their works and obviously admires them. He is not disparaging toward popular fiction, merely believes it is read differently from serious fiction—"reading in a genre is different from reading story by story" (page 185).

Roberts makes many points the genre buff should applaud. He bemoans academic scholars who base judgment of a genre on one writer or a few books ("Occasional readers just do not know enough" [page 86]), and he skewers the frequently and gratingly applied phrase "transcending the genre." He writes that "paperback fiction is no more an unsuccessful imitation of literary fiction than Dublin English . . . of Oxford English" (page 203).

The combination of readability, originality, and intelligence makes this one of the best academic treatises on popular fiction I've encountered. The title apart, this enormously stimulating book is in no way insulting to popular genres or their readers.

A couple of quibbles, though: It's not true that Barzun and Taylor don't consider spy stories in *A Catalogue of Crime* (WAM #10 and the present volume #544), though admittedly it's not one of their favorite categories, and it's surely not accurate to say they think the detective story includes the ghost story simply because they devoted a section to the latter in the first edition of their reference. Also, I believe Roberts is wrong in his claim there are no critics in the "paperback bookscape"—there are writers in fanzines and general publications who perform those tasks Roberts describes a critic as doing.

112. **Rubenstein, Leonard.** *The Great Spy Films.* Secaucus, NJ: Citadel, 1979. 223p. Illus.

Not examined. It is used as a source by Cawelti (see #65).

113. **Sampson, Robert.** *Spider.* Bowling Green, OH: Popular, 1987. 250p. Illus., bibl., index.

In the same evocative, enthusiastic, often hilarious style that characterizes *Yesterday's Faces* (see below), Sampson recounts the history both of the Spider (a.k.a. Richard Wentworth), one of the great costumed crimefighters of the pulps, and of the magazine that bore his name from 1933 to 1943. Preceding the exhaustive account of *The Spider* proper, there is an extensive chapter on R.T.M. Scott and his once-famous character Secret Service Smith, on whom Wentworth was based. With the advent of Norvell Page as author (under the house name Grant Stockbridge), considerable debt is owed Frank L. Packard's Jimmie Dale series as well as Page's own Ken Carter stories.

Black and white illustrations reproduce covers and interior art, and some of the artists receive biographical treatment along with the authors. Appendices include a checklist of all the Spider novels and their authors (Scott did only the first two, Page most of the others, with occasional contributions by Emile C. Tepperman, Wayne Rogers, and in the last adventures Prentice Winchell [best-known as Stewart Sterling] and Donald G. Cormack) and checklists of short fiction from the magazine arranged chronologically and by author (among them Wyatt Blassingame, G.T. Fleming-Roberts, Frank Gruber, and, most prolifically, Tepperman and Arthur Leo Zagat).

Sampson is the kind of stylist who cries out to be quoted. "[T]o most critics and all teachers . . . magazine fiction was an ephemeral nuisance, like sunburn" (page 11). In Norvell Page's Ken Carter stories, the "pace is so ferocious that the agency and its employees have only most tenuous existence, like soap bubbles at the furnace lip" (page 51). "Sex does not mean naked people jiggling together. The *Spider* was, after all, a family magazine devoted to justifiable homicide" (page 54). One pair of Spider novels are "about as realistic as Groucho Marx's mustache" (page 110).

114. **Sampson, Robert.** *Yesterday's Faces: A Study of Series Characters in the Early Pulp Magazines*/Volume 1: *Glory Figures*. Bowling Green, OH: Popular, 1983. 270p. Illus., bibl., index. Volume 2: *Strange Days*. Bowling Green, OH: Popular, 1984. 290p. Illus., bibl., index. Volume 3: *From the Dark Side*. Bowling Green, OH: Popular, 1987. xii, 266p. Illus., bibl., index. Vol 4: *The Solvers*. Bowling Green, OH: Popular, 1987. xi, 307p. Illus., bibl., index. Volume 5: *Dangerous Horizons*. Bowling Green, OH: Popular, 1991. 210p. Illus., bibl., index.

This beautifully written and wonderfully evocative study of dime novel and pulp characters constitutes one of the great works of "fannish" genre history. For an example of Sampson's style, see his description of the "Justice Figure": "Seeking neither personal gain nor revolution, he is an agent of stability, a free-lance law-enforcement agent, like a white corpuscle with a gun" (volume 1, page 100). Beginning with a description of the anticipation felt by a youth while watching the magazine distributor's truck delivering his merchandise in the early hours before school, Sampson tries not just to describe these works and convey their great appeal but to place them in the context of their times.

In the first volume, Sampson covers hero figures generally and includes a long chapter on Hopalong Cassidy, plus accounts of other western characters like Jesse James and Buffalo Bill, and schoolboy sports heroes like Frank and Dick Merriwell. Most of the coverage concerns detective or rogue characters, however. He gives the most extended coverage seen to date of Frank L. Packard's Jimmie Dale (the Gray Seal) and Louis Joseph Vance's Michael Lanyard (the Lone Wolf) and devotes considerable space to Nick Carter, E.W. Hornung's (and Barry Perowne's) Raffles, Edgar Wallace's Four Just Men, Thomas W. Hanshew's Cleek, Maurice Leblanc's Arsene Lupin, Grant Allen's Colonel Clay, and Clifford Ashdown's Romney Pringle.

The author's care renders volume one relatively error-free. He does make the mistaken statement, however, that *His Last Bow* was, as it sounds like it ought to have been, the last Sherlock Holmes collection. It was followed more than a decade later by *The Case Book of Sherlock Holmes.*

The second volume is equally rewarding. Sampson's style is long-winded, facetious, and self-indulgent, but it is also penetrating and evocative, capturing the flavor of the pulps and their time. He begins with the so-called scientific detectives, giving extended coverage to R. Austin Freeman's Dr. Thorndyke (who deserves the label more than most), Edwin Balmer and William MacHarg's Luther Trant, Arthur B. Reeve's Craig Kennedy, and Ernest M. Poate's Dr. Bentiron. By Sampson's account, Poate may be something of a lost giant—he is compared to John Dickson Carr! Even lesser-known figures are also covered, doubtless in more detail than they deserve. (But where if not here?) The author then turns to psychic/occult detectives: Algernon Blackwood's John Silence, William Hope Hodgson's Carnacki, J.U. Giesy and J.B. Smith's Semi-Dual (compared to whom Luther Trant and Dr. Bentiron are household names), Sax Rohmer's Moris Klaw, Seabury Quinn's Jules de Grandin, and others. Toward the end of the book, David H. Keller's nutty s.f. sleuth Taine of

San Francisco is discussed at length, but most of the intervening space is spent on non-mystery pulp figures, notably Edgar Rice Burroughs' Tarzan.

Volume three is devoted to criminals and seeming criminals. While some relatively well-known series are discussed—Sax Rohmer's Fu Manchu, Edgar Wallace's Four Square Jane and others, Bruce Graeme's Blackshirt—the proportion of lesser-known, indeed virtually forgotten figures, is greater than ever. Among them are several inventions of Zorro's creator, Johnston McCully: Black Star, The Spider (a '20s Spider, not to be confused with the '30s hero of that sobriquet), Thubway Tham, The Thunderbolt, The Amazing Twins, The Man in Purple, and The Crimson Clown. A sampling of other intriguing subjects includes A.E. Apple's Mr. Chang, Christopher B. Booth's Mr. Clackworthy, Charles W. Tyler's Big-Nose Charlie, Anna Alice Chapin's Boston Betty, Roland Krebs' Shiek Shannahan and Andy Simpson, a pair of Hugh Kahler characters (The White Rook and The Joker, the latter not to be confused with Batman's nemesis), and a couple of Herman Landon's (The Gray Phantom and The Picaroon).

Volume four discusses a fair number of well-known sleuths: Agatha Christie's various detectives, August Derleth's Solar Pons, T.S. Stribling's Poggioli, H.C. Bailey's Reggie Fortune, Anthony Wynne's Dr. Eustace Hailey, Baroness Orczy's Lady Molly of Scotland Yard, Hulbert Footner's Madame Rosika Storey, Vincent Starrett's Jimmie Lavender, Edgar Wallace's J.G. Reeder, Carroll John Daly's Race Williams, Dashiell Hammett's Continental Op, and Frederick Nebel's MacBride and Kennedy. But there are many more obscure characters, some of whom even the most fully-immersed fan is unlikely to recall: the various detectives of Florence Mae Pettee (Dr. Nancy Dayland, Digby Gresham, Beau Quicksilver), Charles Rodda's Derek Trent, Oscar Schisgall's Barron Ixell, David Fox's (Isabel Ostrander's) The Shadowers, Scott Campbell's Felix Boyd, Johnston McCully's Terry Trimble, George Allan England's T. Ashley, Ellis Parker Butler's Rev. Brace (an early clerical sleuth), John T. McIntyre's Ashton-Kirk, Lewen Hewitt's Balbane the Conjurer Detective (a Great Merlini precursor of whom Sampson thinks highly), Max Pemberton's Bernard Sutton, Arnold Fredericks' (Frederick Arnold Kummer's) Richard and Grace Duvall "The Honeymoon Detectives" (a pioneering husband-and-wife sleuthing team), William Almon Wolff's John Hudson, and a number of early female sleuths: Richard Marsh's Judith Lee, Arthur B. Reeve's Constance Dunlap, and Raymond Lester's Nan Russell.

The fifth volume, devoted to adventure fiction, is more tangential to our concerns, but it does discuss characters of mystery writers Joseph Louis Vance, Edgar Wallace (Sanders of the River), and Hesketh Prichard. A sixth volume, to be titled *Violent Lives,* is promised.

All volumes include notes, bibliography, and index. Volumes from two on also include listings of the magazine appearances of the series characters discussed.

115. Sauerberg, Lars Ole. *Secret Agents in Fiction: Ian Fleming, John le Carré, and Len Deighton.* (Macmillan Studies in Twentieth-Century Literature.) London: Macmillan; New York: St. Martin's, 1984. xvi, 260p. Bibl., index.

In a heavily academic study, most enlivened by the frequent quotes from its subjects' works, Sauerberg begins with a brief history of secret-agent fiction (a term he prefers to spy or espionage fiction), proceeds to a discussion of formula (with the requisite nod to John Cawelti), and considers the subtitle's trio, first in relation to various structural elements, then individually. As in several other sources, comparisons work to the disadvantage of Deighton, who so far has not been as extensively written about in monographs as the other two subjects. Sauerberg finds the secret-agent formula "more tolerant of variation than, for instance, the formula of the formal detective story" (page 237).

The use of initials to designate book titles in the text can be irritating.

116. Schreuders, Piet. *Paperbacks U.S.A.: A Graphic History, 1939-1959.* Translated from the Dutch by Josh Pachter. San Diego, CA: Blue Dolphin, 1981. 295p. Illus., bibl., index.

As the title suggests, the work of cover artists rather than authors is emphasized here. Many covers are reproduced, most for mysteries and some in color. There is much fascinating information on paperback collecting, histories of individual firms, biographies of artists (few of them covered in other reference sources), and the technical aspects of cover design.

117. **Simon, Reeva S.** *The Middle East in Crime Fiction: Mysteries, Spy Novels, and Thrillers From 1916 to the 1980s.* New York: Lilian Barger, 1989. ix, 226p. Bibl., index.

The author claims not to perform literary criticism but rather to analyze the perception of the Middle East by writers of crime fiction. Though she alludes to pure detection and romantic suspense, it is not surprising that espionage thrillers loom largest. Chapters are topical, covering trends, plots, heroes, villains, and the Arab-Israeli conflict. Among the principal authors discussed are John Buchan, William Haggard, Ian Fleming, Edward S. Aarons, "Nick Carter" (with some quotes from the Carter series writer guidelines), C.A. Haddad, Eric Ambler, Ken Follett, Talbot Mundy, Julian Rathbone, Sax Rohmer, Joan Fleming, and Dennis Wheatley. The author has also turned up numerous lesser-known or one-shot authors, including James H. Hunter, an author of early evangelical Christian thrillers, notably *The Mystery of Mar Saba* (1940). A most valuable feature is the 52-page annotated primary bibliography, followed by a ten-page secondary bibliography.

There are some errors. Dilys Winn, to my knowledge, is not accurately labelled a "mystery writer" (page 2); *Black Mask* and *Dime Detective* are dated too early; and some names are scrambled: Julian "Symonds" and "Mat" Bolan. In an irritating indexing oddity, titles are alphabetized by the initial article A—fortunately, the same is not done with The.

118. **Skenazy, Paul.** *The New Wild West: The Urban Mysteries of Dashiell Hammett and Raymond Chandler.* (Boise State University Western Writers Series, No. 34.) Boise, Idaho: Boise State University, 1982. 52p. Bibl.

As the title implies, Hammett and Chandler's detective stories are compared with the Western fictional tradition, with the urban private eye the equivalent of the cowboy hero. Otherwise, this is a solid if unexceptional survey of the two authors' careers, with a brief discussion of Ross Macdonald and a four-page primary and secondary bibliography.

119. **Skinner, Robert E.** *The New Hard-Boiled Dicks: A Personal Checklist.* (Brownstone Chapbook Series vol. 2.) Madison, IN: Brownstone, 1987. vii, 60p. Bibl.

Intending a continuation of James Sandoe's famous pamphlet (WAM #57), Skinner writes at greater length than his model, following a chapter of history of the hardboiled dicks with individual considerations of Andrew Bergman, James Crumley, Loren D. Estleman, Stephen Greenleaf, Donald Hamilton, Chester Himes, Stuart M. Kaminsky, Elmore Leonard, Robert B. Parker, Richard Stark (Donald E. Westlake), cartoonist Jim Steranko (a surprising choice), and Ernest Tidyman. A bibliography follows each. Sharp critical comments are included and in some cases (fairly rare in secondary sources on the mystery) notes for collectors: Skinner tips Estleman as a particularly good collectible investment. An appendix more briefly cites eleven "other guys": Max Byrd, Max Allan Collins, John Gregory Dunne (misspelled here "Dunn"), Joe Gores, Joseph Hansen, John D. MacDonald, L.A. Morse, Sara Paretsky, Bill Pronzini, Roger L. Simon, and Chris Wiltz.

120. Spencer, William David. *Mysterium and Mystery: The Clerical Crime Novel.* (Studies in Religions, No. 6.) Ann Arbor: UMI Research Press, 1989. xi, 344p. Bibl., index.

This very learned and well-written study of religious detective stories is as much a theological treatise as a critical work on mysteries, but the author clearly has a broad and deep general knowledge of the field. Be warned that the densely theological and scholarly early chapters might scare off some readers who would enjoy the individual treatments of religious sleuths, beginning with the Apocrypha's Daniel, called "the first of the Judeo-Christian clerical detectives" (page 21) and also likened to the 20th-century hardboiled hero. Spencer goes on to cover Harry Kemelman's Rabbi Small, followed by Christian religious detectives both famous (G.K. Chesterton's Father Brown, Charles Merrill Smith's Reverend Randollph, Ellis Peters' Brother Cadfael) and relatively obscure (Stephen Chance's Septimus, Isabelle Holland's Claire Aldington, James L. Johnson's Sebastian). Spencer deals with virtually every series clerical sleuth at novel length (including the current crop of priest and nun detectives created by William X. Kienzle, Andrew Greeley, Ralph McInerny, and Sister Carol Anne O'Marie) along with some one-shots, notably Victor L. Whitechurch's Vicar Westerham. There is an especially good piece on Leonard Holton's (Leonard Wibberley's) relatively undervalued Father Bredder and an extensive consideration of Dorothy Gilman's *A Nun in the Closet.* Aside from Father Brown (and, come to think of it, Daniel),

Spencer generally does not cover short-story characters—thus, some creators of detecting clergy, e.g. Edward D. Hoch and Alice Scanlan Reach, do not appear in the index. The 11-page bibliography includes a checklist of "The Clerical Crime Novel in English" plus an extensive list of other works consulted. The general index is followed by a separate index of fictional characters.

Spencer's is one of the best volumes extant of specialized detective story criticism and is highly recommended.

121. Stafford, David. *The Silent Game*. Toronto, 1988. Revised edition. Athens: U. of Georgia P., 1991. x, 257p. Bibl., index.

The following description is based on the revised edition.

In what may be the first post-Cold War study of spy fiction, the author immediately reassures the reader the form is not dead. In readable style, Stafford parallels the history of spying in Britain with its fictional equivalent. (One early real-life British spy was Boy Scout founder Robert Baden-Powell, who "saw in espionage some of the same virtues he saw in cold baths and rigorous abstention from temptations of the flesh" [page 11].) While most comparable studies have concentrated on the spy fiction of the 1950s on, Stafford gives considerable attention to the oldtimers, not even getting to Eric Ambler until page 128. He devotes much more space to William LeQueux (who has more page references in the index than le Carré!), Valentine Williams, and Francis Beeding than do most other sources. Along with the expected subjects (Buchan, Oppenheim, "Sapper," Greene, Maugham, Compton Mackenzie, Household, Fleming, Deighton) are writers sometimes overlooked (at least as espionage practitioners in the first two cases): A.E.W. Mason, Dennis Wheatley, Ted Allbuery, and the surprisingly obscure (given her credentials) Marthe McKenna. Though the focus is British, Stafford touches briefly on some American spy writers, notably Van Wyck Mason, E. Howard Hunt, Charles McCarry, W.T. Tyler, and William F. Buckley, Jr. For a book from a university press, the approach is surprisingly unscholarly. Stafford has a six-page secondary bibliography but no notes, and at one point he quotes "a recent American author" (page 43) with no documentation whatsoever.

122. Symons, Julian. *The Modern Crime Story*. Edinburgh: Tragara, 1980. 25p.

Published in an edition of 125 copies, this is the slightly revised text of a lecture given at York University, Toronto, in 1975. Most of the information and argument is readily available in *Bloody Murder* (WAM #5 and the present volume #555) and other more widely published writings, though Symons has more to say here about his own novels, specifically *The Players and the Game*, *The Man Who Lost His Wife*, and *The Man Who Killed Himself.*

123. Tani, Stefano. *The Doomed Detective: The Contribution of the Detective Novel to Postmodern America and Italian Fiction.* Carbondale: Southern Illinois UP, 1984. xvi, 183p. Bibl., index.

Tani's subject is the "anti-detective novel," in which mainstream writers use the trappings of the form but subvert it through denying the reader the central feature of a detective novel: a comprehensive, logically-achieved solution. Major works discussed include Leonardo Sciascia's *A ciascuno il suo*, John Gardner's *The Sunlight Dialogues*, Umberto Eco's *Il nome della rosa* (*The Name of the Rose*), Sciascia's *Todo Modo*, Thomas Pynchon's *The Crying of Lot 49*, William Hjortsberg's *Falling Angel*, Italo Calvino's *Se una notte d'inverno un viaggiatore*, and Vladimir Nabokov's *Pale Fire*. While interesting and well-written, the book is not likely to appeal to most fans who value detective fiction for its own sake.

Sensing that Tani's statement that Mike Hammer "hates 'the Reds and the niggers' and his moral commitment is 'to mop them out of America'" (page 26) was probably unfair to Mickey Spillane, I asked Spillane specialist Max Allan Collins (see #331), who writes, "There is no basis in Spillane for the 'nigger' remark, and less for the 'Reds' than one might imagine. Mike Hammer is the friend of the underdog, of lower class losers, and if anything he has sympathy for members of any persecuted ethnic group. . . .

"What slight basis Tani might have is a scene in *I, the Jury* in which Hammer beats up two black guys. However, they attack him—and he is visiting the black bar, where he is regularly a visitor, being on very friendly terms with the black owner/bartender. Some of the dialogue . . . is in a standard-for-the-time stereotypical dialect. Calling this racist shows a lack of understanding of historical context, and extrapolating from any of this that Hammer 'hates the niggers' is ludicrous.

"In the early novels, only one is concerned with 'Reds': *One Lonely Night;* later on, *The Girl Hunters* and *Survival . . . Zero*!; in the latter, the mellowed Hammer seems in favor of detente!"

124. **Van Dover, J. Kenneth.** *Murder in the Millions.* New York: Ungar, 1984. xi, 235p. Illus., bibl., index.

Van Dover discusses three of the mystery field's "Supersellers"— Erle Stanley Gardner, Mickey Spillane, and Ian Fleming—and tries to figure out why they have appealed to such large groups of readers. Though all have their adherents among fans and critics, I doubt anyone would claim they were the three best crime fiction writers of the Twentieth Century, and I doubt many would put more than one of them in the top ten or twenty.

Though Van Dover is an academic (assistant professor of English at Pennsylvania's Lincoln University), he is clearly also a fan, and his prose is smooth and readable. He makes some interesting points about the similarities and differences among his three subjects. For example, Perry Mason and James Bond (dissimilar as they may be in other ways) both have a respect for democratic institutions that Mike Hammer lacks. The works of Spillane and Fleming are full of psychopaths, but no one in a Gardner novel is ever insane. Fleming alone of the three is capable of irony. Fleming can make a real place come to life in his novels, while Gardner's backgrounds are sketchy and Spillane's have the atmospheric exaggeration of opera. Both Spillane and Gardner value a fast pace so much that events (if you bother to chart them) prove to be happening in an absurdly telescoped timeframe. Ultimately, reading Van Dover's book helped me understand why I love Gardner's novels, can't stand Spillane's, and can take or leave Fleming's.

Not unexpectedly, though, I found Van Dover least fair to the writer I most admire. He stereotypes Gardner's novels in a reductive way, very much overdoing the alleged sameness of Perry Mason's adventures and failing to note their changes from the pulp-flavored thirties through the slick-flavored forties and fifties, to the TV-flavored sixties. In dealing with a writer far more prolific than his other two subjects, Van Dover also sometimes trips over his generalizations. It is not true, for example, that no Mason case ever goes to the jury. It happens at least twice: in *The Case of the Terrified Typist* (1956) and again in *The Case of the Fenced-In Woman* (posthumously published in 1972).

The bibliography includes a checklist of the authors' books plus secondary sources on each author and a list of general references. Film and television adaptations are briefly listed and provide most of the volume's illustrations.

125. **Webb, Nancy, and Jean Francis Webb, eds.** *Plots & Pans: Recipes and Antidotes from The Mystery Writers of America.* Illustrated by Gahan Wilson. Introduction by Isaac Asimov. New York: Wynwood, 1989. 287p. Illus., index.

Not examined. According to Edward D. Hoch (*The Year's Best Mystery and Suspense Stories 1990* [see #369]), "[h]undreds of recipes and some brief anecdotes about food from members of MWA" are included.

126. **Whitley, John S.** *Detectives and Friends: Dashiell Hammett's The Glass Key and Raymond Chandler's The Long Goodbye.* (American Arts Pamphlet No. 6.) Exeter: University of Exeter American Arts Documentation Centre, 1981. 31p. Bibl.

Following a combined four-page chronology of the lives of Hammett and Chandler by Richard Maltby, Whitley discusses *The Glass Key* and *The Long Goodbye,* given as examples of the "negative" thriller in Jerry Palmer's 1978 study, *Thrillers* (see WAM #53). The essay is readable and interesting but necessary only to completist collections of the two writers. There are two pages of notes and a four-page secondary bibliography.

127. **Wilt, David.** *Hardboiled in Hollywood.* Bowling Green, OH: Popular, 1991. 189p. Illus., bibl., index.

In an enjoyable book for lovers of pulp mystery fiction and/or B-movies of the '30s through '50s, the print and screenwriting careers of five *Black Mask* writers are considered. Best-known is Horace McCoy, author of *They Shoot Horses, Don't They?,* who has the semblance of a mainstream literary reputation and wrote such major films as *Gentleman Jim* and *The Lusty Men.* The shadowy Peter Ruric, who used the pseudonym Paul Cain on the minor hardboiled classic *Fast One,* did his best screen work on the adaptation of Sue MacVeigh's *Grand Central Murder.* The other three are comparatively obscure: Eric Taylor (who wrote Ellery Queen movies and the Claude Rains version of *The Phantom of the Opera*), Dwight V. Babcock (whose novels about Hannah Van Doren Wilt recommends), and John K. Butler (who was the author of many mystery-flavored western scripts). All but Ruric appear with Hammett, Chandler, and others in the famous group photo, reproduced on page 6, taken at the Los Angeles *Black Mask* dinner in 1936. There are also a good selection of stills and a filmography for each subject.

128. Winks, Robin W. *Modus Operandi: An Excursion into Detective Fiction.* Boston: Godine, 1982. 131p. Index.

A Yale history professor and one of the most respected of American mystery critics, Winks offers some interesting observations on the crime fiction genre, especially its spy and hardboiled subgroupings. Not intended as any kind of definitive statement, the volume provides good critical commentary on such authors as William Haggard, Donald Hamilton, Adam Hall, John D. MacDonald, and William F. Buckley, Jr. Non-contemporaries with numerous page references in the index include John Buchan, Agatha Christie, Raymond Chandler, and Dorothy L. Sayers. Winks is among those who believe the current crime novel is much better than the puzzles of the classical school. Most likely to be offended by his forthright opinions are science-fiction readers and fans of John Dickson Carr. His essay makes for a short book, leading him to pretend worry about landing in library vertical files instead of on the shelf.

129. Wu, William F. *The Yellow Peril: Chinese Americans in American Fiction, 1850-1940.* Hamden, CT: Archon, 1982. ix, 241p. Bibl., index.

As the title of this engaging and well-written book implies, it is not solely devoted to mystery and detective fiction. But much of the negative stereotyping of Chinese immigrants appeared in crime fiction, with all its sinister Oriental villains most typified by Sax Rohmer's Fu Manchu. Among the other writers discussed are Dashiell Hammett, "Grant Stockbridge," Robert J. Hogan, Donald E. Keyhoe, and Hugh Wiley.

For years I've been defending Earl Derr Biggers' Charlie Chan against charges he is an ethnic stereotype, and I've searched in vain for a reasoned explanation of why some Asian-Americans find Chan so offensive, apart from the understandably exasperating fact that he has been played on the screen by a succession of Caucasian actors. To his credit, in attempting to provide such an explanation, Wu bases his points on the Biggers novels alone. And as a Chinese-American himself, he brings a different and presumably more valid perspective to the question.

Still, I'm unconvinced. Wu seems to blame Biggers and Chan more for their uniqueness than for their intrinsic qualities. He overstates the self-effacement of Chan, a character who is ambitious, assertive, and (in his own way) tough. He repeats the pervasive but utterly mistaken charge that Chan speaks in "broken" English—idiosyncratic, yes, but broken or pidgin, never. Wu seems determined to fit Chan into his theme, as "an example of overcompensation in an author's attempt to break away from the Yellow Peril" (page 174) that ultimately is still part of the Yellow Peril, and his efforts are somewhat strained, though they make fascinating reading.

4

COLLECTED ESSAYS AND REVIEWS

130. **Allen, L. David.** *Detective in Fiction.* Lincoln, NB: Cliffs Notes, 1978. 128p. Bibl.

Following an opening chapter that summarizes the detective-story rules of Willard Huntington Wright and Father Ronald Knox and attempts to define detective fiction, Allen offers efficient if somewhat boring critical summaries of Poe's "The Purloined Letter," Collins's *The Moonstone*, Doyle's "The Adventure of the Speckled Band," Sayers's *Whose Body?*, Van Dine's *The Benson Murder Case*, Christie's *The Murder of Roger Ackroyd* and *What Mrs. McGillicuddy Saw*, Allingham's *The Fashion in Shrouds*, Stout's *Black Orchids*, Philip MacDonald's *The List of Adrian Messenger*, and Ellis Peters's *Death and the Joyful Woman*, the latter 1961 novel being the most recent book covered. Given the "pony" function of Cliffs Notes, it shouldn't be surprising that all solutions are revealed. The main text is not badly done but a tad depressing in that its target audience is clearly someone other than the enthusiastic reader of detective fiction. Allen lists the Edgar winners for best novel and best first novel through 1975. A 27-page "Selected Bibliography of Detective Fiction" lacks dates for the titles listed and is misleading when it gives a series detective's name after the author's then fails to tell in which of the listed books the character appears. (Julian Symons's Francis Quarles, for example, is strictly a short-story character and appears in none of the listed novels at all.) Allen also does a disservice to his readers when he lists some of the ersatz Ellery Queen paperbacks about Tim Corrigan along with the real EQ novels. The final page is headed "A Selected Bibliography of Works About Detective Fiction" but actually lists works on true crime and criminology. No real mystery buff needs this book, and the targeted student would be better off reading the assigned texts.

131. Bakerman, Jane S. ed. *And Then There Were Nine . . . More Women of Mystery.* Bowling Green, OH: Popular, 1985. 219p. Bibl., index.

Highlights of this group of essays on female practitioners, a sequel to Bargainnier's *Ten Women of Mystery* (see below), are George N. Dove's fine survey of Dorothy Uhnak's output and the thorough, efficient treatments of Anne Morice and Lillian O'Donnell by the team of Martha Alderson and Neysa Chouteau. Another commendably fresh subject is Craig Rice, though Peggy Moran's essay is too heavy on plot summary and gives away endings for no good reason. Most oppressively academic treatment is accorded E.X. Ferrars. Susan Baker's thesis that Ferrars is not in the classical tradition as usually pegged is unconvincing, mainly because Baker defines the classical mystery far too narrowly—the essay certainly attracts one to Ferrars' books, however. Other subjects and their commentators: Daphne du Maurier (editor Bakerman), Margery Allingham (Rex W. Gaskill), Patricia Highsmith (Kathleen Gregory Klein), and Shirley Jackson (Carol Cleveland). Photographs are included of all the authors save Rice and Jackson. As before, there are chronologies and notes, but this time there is no index. Regrettably in the case of the active writers included, coverage and chronologies end in 1981 or 1982, suggesting the book took an unusually long time to get into print.

132. Bargainnier, Earl F. ed. *Comic Crime.* Bowling Green, OH: Popular, 1987. 195p.

The editor, who died in 1987, was one of the best academic critics of mystery fiction, and this collection is among the most enjoyable of the publisher's essay compilations on the field. Though some of the pieces are better than others, all are eminently worth reading. Following an overview preface by the editor are essays by H.R.F. Keating on five types of humor to be found in British crime novels; Frederick Isaac on humor in the hardboiled school (covering Hammett, Chandler, Macdonald, Stout, Pronzini, Bellem, and Kaminsky, among others); Elaine Bander on the "what-fun" school of British mysteries (Milne, Christie, Knox, Sayers, and most extensively Georgette Heyer); Bargainnier on farce (Michael Innes, Crispin, Dickinson, Brett, Leo Bruce, MacLeod, Gash, Colin Watson, Ross Spencer, Tom Sharpe, but not, surprisingly, John Dickson Carr or William Marshall); Mary Jane DeMarr on the "comic village"

(Christie and Crispin again plus Barnard, Grimes, Anthony Oliver, Aird); Wister Cook on campus humor (many writers, divided between those who celebrate academic life, e.g. Innes, and those who satirize it, e.g. Barnard); Jane S. Bakerman on eccentric detectives (including characters of Christie, Brett, Gash, MacLeod, and Lucille Kallen, among others); and Neysa Chouteau and Martha Alderson on little old ladies (a wide enough designation to take in Gardner/ Fair's Bertha Cool, Dolson's Lucy Ramsdale, Gilman's Mrs. Pollifax, McInerny/ Quill's Sister Mary Theresa, Palmer's Hildegarde Withers, and Carvic's Miss Seeton, as well as the inevitable Miss Marple). The final three essays treat individual writers: Barrie Hayne on humor in the Sherlock Holmes canon, Michael Dunn on Westlake's comic capers, and Lizabeth Paravisini and Carlos Yorio on the parodies of L.A. Morse.

Though most of the contributors are American, British subjects get considerably more space. That may be fair enough, but among American humorists either treated in passing or ignored completely are Craig Rice, Jonathan Latimer, Phoebe Atwood Taylor, Margaret Scherf, and Richard S. Prather.

With so many writers alluded to and many discussed in several of the essays, the lack of an index is unconscionable. The notes at the end of each essay (except for Keating's) serve as a bibliography of the subjects' principal works, but it's unfortunate that Tom Sharpe, the least familiar name discussed in the whole book, does not appear in the notes at the end of Bargainnier's essay, nor does Ross H. Spencer. It's tough to blame Bargainnier, who presumably was not around to put finishing touches on the project, but surely an editor should have made the needed additions.

133. **Bargainnier, Earl F.**, ed. *Ten Women of Mystery*. Bowling Green, OH: Popular, 1981. 304p. Bibl., illus., index.

This is a particularly admirable collection, since at least some of its subjects represent fresh scholarly ground. One highlight is a most welcome essay by Barrie Hayne on under-appreciated pioneer Anna Katharine Green (who finally would be the subject of a book-length work eight years later in Patricia D. Maida's *Mother of Detective Fiction* [see #254]). Jan Kohn's article on Mary Roberts Rinehart does not duplicate material from her 1980 biography, *Improbable Fiction* (see WAM #202), and should satisfy readers who would have liked more discussion of Rinehart's mysteries in that book. Other subjects and their commentators include

Dorothy L. Sayers (Kathleen Gregory Klein), Josephine Tey (Nancy Ellen Talburt), Ngaio Marsh (editor Bargainnier), P.D. James (Nancy C. Joyner), Ruth Rendell (Jane S. Bakerman), Margaret Millar (John Reilly), Emma Lathen (Jeanne F. Bedell), and Amanda Cross (Steven R. Carter). Each essay includes a photograph of the subject, a chronology, and notes. Indexes of characters and titles are provided.

There are a few editing problems. The Sayers article should not have been titled without the obligatory middle initial, and it is puzzling that the name of Margery Allingham (frequently referred to though not one of the ten subjects) should be so consistently misspelled.

134. Bargainnier, Earl F. ed. *Twelve Englishmen of Mystery*. Bowling Green, OH: Popular, 1984. 325p. Bibl., illus.

The format is similar to that of *Ten Women of Mystery* (see above), save for the regrettable absence of an index. The dozen subjects are well-chosen and mostly well-covered in essays by a variety of mystery scholars. Especially good are the treatments of H.C. Bailey (by Nancy Ellen Talburt), Anthony Berkeley Cox (by William Bradley Strickland), Michael Gilbert (by George N. Dove), Nicholas Blake and Simon Brett (both by editor Bargainnier). Only Marty Knepper's article on Dick Francis is seriously flawed. To celebrate her subject (who surely deserves celebrating), Knepper feels she must denigrate the whole school of hardboiled detective fiction, a classification to which thriller/adventure writer Francis doesn't even belong. The critic has a feminist ax to grind, which further skews her view of Francis and leads her to more sweeping denunciations of other writers. (By the way, if Knepper wants to find a writer more solidly in the hardboiled tradition than Francis who certainly does include many useful, independent women among his characters, she need look no further than the much-abused Erle Stanley Gardner.) As for Knepper's statement that "Violence sells books easily" (page 226), there is only one answer: nothing does!

Other subjects and their interpreters: Wilkie Collins (Jeanne F. Bedell), A.E.W. Mason (Barrie Hayne), G.K. Chesterton (Thomas E. Porter), Julian Symons (Larry Grimes), Edmund Crispin (Mary Jane DeMarr), and H.R.F. Keating (Meera T. Clark). The Keating essay is fine on the Inspector Ghote series but ignores his non-Ghote detective novels.

135. **Bennett, Arnold.** *The Evening Standard Years: 'Books and Persons' 1926-1931.* Ed. Andrew Mylett. London: Chatto & Windus; Hamden, CT: Archon, 1974. xxviii, 481p. Index.

This reprint of Bennett's weekly book review columns includes at least nine touching on mystery and detective fiction. In the first of them, dated 8 September 1927, he packs an astonishing amount of provocative opinion into a short article. He is essentially disappointed with most examples of the genre, scorning the emphasis on detection and believing even Poe to have been overrated. He praises Anna Katharine Green's *The Leavenworth Case* but doesn't want to reread it (in a later column he does and suffers the predicted letdown), believes Gaston Leroux's *The Mystery of the Yellow Room* the best mystery of them all (an opinion he repeats in later columns), finds Watson "an authentic human creation" (page 81) but Holmes not, and is unimpressed by Rohmer and Christie. The main subjects of the column are Walter S. Masterman's *The Curse of the Reckavilles* (good puzzle, terrible writing) and A.E.W. Mason's *No Other Tiger* (much better). In other columns, he awards Gaboriau's *The Crime of Orcival* classic status; reads his first Edgar Wallace and much prefers him to Christie or Freeman Wills Crofts (whose admirable construction and logic, he notes in another piece, is counterbalanced by a lack of liveliness); compares J.J. Connington's *The Case with Nine Solutions* unfavorably to Gaboriau; finds John Dickson Carr's *It Walks by Night* unconvincing; and, in the last of the columns on mysteries (15 May 1930), finds much to praise in Philip MacDonald's *The Noose* and Leroux's *The Man of a Hundred Masks* (though he finds the translation mediocre). Bennett had a friendly enemy relationship to the form, receiving entreaties from its advocates to read this or that writer and be converted, much as Edmund Wilson would be a few years later on the other side of the Atlantic (see WAM #85). His main problem with the genre was its unreality, one element of which was its typical murderer, who "usually has the brain of an Einstein joined to the prudence of a political leader and the prophetic vision of an H.G. Wells" (page 279).

136. **Benstock, Bernard, ed.** *Art in Crime Writing.* New York: St. Martin's, 1983. xi, 218p. Bibl., index.

This is a good collection of original essays on eleven crime writers, with Ngaio Marsh, Peter Lovesey, Nicolas Freeling, and the team of Maj

Sjöwall and Per Wahlöö representing the freshest ground at the time the book was published. David I. Grossvogel's Agatha Christie article is in a much more accessible and popular vein than his remarks in *Mystery and Its Fictions* (see WAM #44). Bruce Merry on Dorothy L. Sayers pays more attention than most critics to her short stories. Leon Arden's piece on Raymond Chandler makes high claims for its subject, comparing him not unfavorably to Hemingway, and finds a correlation between the quality of the Marlowe novels and the number of smell references in them! Other subjects include Dashiell Hammett, Ross Macdonald, P.D. James, and Georges Simenon. Nearly all the contributors are academics, few well-known for genre criticism. The essays are usually followed by notes and a chronology of the subject's book titles.

137. Breen, Jon L., and Martin Harry Greenberg, eds. *Murder Off the Rack: Critical Studies of Ten Paperback Masters.* Metuchen, NJ: Scarecrow, 1989. x, 178p. Bibl., index.

Ten mystery writers and critics contribute essays on authors of paperback original crime novels. The subjects (critics in parentheses) are Harry Whittington (Bill Crider), Ed Lacy (Marvin Lachman), Jim Thompson (Max Allan Collins), Vin Packer (editor Breen), Marvin H. Albert (George Kelley), Charles Williams (Ed Gorman), Donald Hamilton (Loren D. Estleman), Peter Rabe (Donald E. Westlake), Don Pendleton (Will Murray), and Warren Murphy (Dick Lochte). Checklists at the end of each essay list only those books referred to the essay.

138. Breen, Jon L., and Martin H. Greenberg, eds. *Synod of Sleuths: Essays on Judeo-Christian Detective Fiction.* Metuchen, NJ: Scarecrow, 1990. viii, 161p. Bibl., index.

Contributors cover various aspects of the treatment of Judeo-Christian religion in mysteries: Edward D. Hoch on Roman Catholic religious sleuths; James Yaffe on Jews in detective fiction; editor Breen on Protestant mysteries, focussing on Charles Merrill Smith and Gaylord Larsen; Marvin Lachman on religious cults in the mystery; and Breen again on Mormonism in mysteries. In a symposium on religious detective fiction, authors Ellis Peters, William X. Kienzle, Harry Kemelman, and Sister Carol Anne O'Marie respond to a series of questions. The bibliography lists novels and stories referred to in the essays, anthologies, and secondary sources about religious mysteries. Though the volume won an Anthony award from Bouchercon .22 for best critical book of its year, some reviewers justifiably lamented that the volume did not have broader coverage and that several of the essays were three years out of date, albeit updated by editor's notes. These faults may be blamed on the first-named editor.

139. Browne, Ray B. *Heroes and Humanities: Detective Fiction and Culture.* Bowling Green, OH: Popular, 1987. 141p.

Of the fifteen essays gathered here, three are from *Clues: A Journal of Detection,* one from *The Armchair Detective,* and the rest apparently original to this volume. All concern writers who "demonstrate their concern with human society" (page 5), and most subjects represent commendably fresh ground. The book starts well with a strong essay on Arthur W. Upfield (whom Browne later would treat at book-length in *The Spirit of Australia* [see #340]) and a good piece on Peter Corris, a more recent Australian writer less well-known in this country. After that, however, things go downhill fast.

If Bill Pronzini ever does a *Gun in Cheek* (see #107 and 108) on critics (and no, I wouldn't be surprised if I were featured prominently in such a compilation), some of Browne's sentences in a well-meant but woolly piece on Judson Philips (a.k.a. Hugh Pentecost) will have to be included. About the Julian Quist books: "Mild tempered, mild styled, they pretty much picture language and life as it is, at least in fiction" (page 33). On Peter Styles: "Like the birth of all classic detectives, Styles was, like Shakespeare's Caesar, torn from his parent's womb, in this case his father's; and like Oedipus he had to slay his father before he could become his own tormented self" (page 34).

Other subjects include Ed Lacy, E.V. Cunningham, Thomas B. Dewey, Michael Z. Lewin, Jonathan Valin, George C. Chesbro, John Ball, Ralph McInerny, Martha G. Webb, Martha Grimes, and Thomas Brace Haughey (author of a series of Evangelical Christian detective stories). A final chapter discusses some current Canadian authors, with primary attention to Ted Wood and none to Howard Engel, supposedly "studied in another paper in this collection" (page 136), but I couldn't find it. All Browne's subjects are worthy ones, and he usually has some valid points to make about them. Thus it's truly regrettable so much of the writing in his book is so bad. It reads like an unedited first draft.

140. **Budd, Elaine.** *13 Mistresses of Mystery.* New York: Ungar, 1986. xiii, 144p. Bibl.

Budd profiles thirteen contemporary female mystery writers in highly readable feature-article style. Most of the articles are based on personal interviews, face to face or by phone. Following the profile is a plot synopsis (without solution) of one major book with some critical analysis. As would be expected, most of the critical comment is favorable, but Budd points out the coincidences and improbabilities of Mary Higgins Clark's *Where are the Children?*, regrets the idiot heroine proclivities of Antonia Fraser's Jemima Shore, and is especially tough on Phyllis A. Whitney's "two-dimensional characters." The sometimes lengthy plot synopses are fine if you like plot synopses, but a critical overview of the authors' whole output would have been preferable.

The greatest value of the articles is as biography, with the piece on Shannon OCork especially interesting, both because she has been less extensively written about elsewhere than most of the others and because of the wealth of frank biographical detail in the subject's own words. There is occasional repetitiousness in some of the articles that tighter editing could have fixed, and the time of writing is often vague. Clark, Amanda Cross, Dorothy Uhnak, and Ruth Rendell are all described as being in their early fifties. Their actual ages in 1986: Clark 56, Cross 60, Uhnak 53, and Rendell 56. Overall accuracy is high, though in her introduction, Budd states Josephine Tey's *A Shilling for Candles* was made into one of Alfred Hitchcock's "first films"—in fact, *Young and Innocent* (1937) came toward the end of Hitch's great British period. In the article on Whitney, she implies *Thunder Heights* (published in hardcover by Appleton in 1960) was a paperback original.

Other authors covered are Dorothy Salisbury Davis, Lucy Freeman, Dorothy B. Hughes, P.D. James, Emma Lathen, and Margaret Millar.

141. **Carr, John C.** *The Craft of Crime: Conversations with Crime Writers.* Boston: Houghton Mifflin, 1983. ix, 349p.

Carr's thirteen subjects are Ed McBain, James McClure, June Thomson, Jane Langton, Gregory Mcdonald, Robert B. Parker, Emma Lathen, Dick Francis, Ruth Rendell, Peter Lovesey, Janwillem van de Wetering, and Mark Smith. Each interview is preceded by a biographical-critical introduction. In many cases, the conversations are less about writing per se than about the subject matter of the authors' books. For example, Carr discusses conditions in South Africa with McClure, the Victorian period with Lovesey, and horse racing with Francis.

Carr as interviewer is provocative without being overly intrusive. Some obvious questions go unasked, however. In a joint interview with the two Lathen collaborators (who seem quite open and friendly), he never inquires about their extreme low profile in the field. Carr is also guilty of numerous solution giveaways, albeit with their authors' full cooperation. He is given to rather sweeping and doubtful statements, both concerning the mystery field (that "the modern police procedural began with McBain" [page 2], and even more mistakenly that McBain's Deaf Man is "the only on-going villain since Conan Doyle's Professor Moriarty" [page 8]) and other things (the statement to Francis that "American racing is rather crooked at the moment" [page 212]). At times, post-interview footnotes would have helped clarify matters. Carr and McBain disagree on how many total books he has written, Carr estimating a hundred and McBain claiming only about sixty. The actual figure (somewhere in between at around eighty at the time the book was published) might have been footnoted.

On the whole, however, the interviews are effective, informative, and very readable. They point out just how seriously these writers, both those who are writing firmly within the detective/crime novel tradition and those who are trying to expand the boundaries of the genre, take their work. The Mcdonald interview, in which the creator of Fletch explains why he regards his novels as postrevolutionary, postcinematic, postexistential, postpsychiatric, and postideologic, is especially interesting. Among the most memorable quotes is Parker's statement about his fellow academics: "the average instructor chooses literature that has to be explained to the kid. Otherwise, what has he got to do?" (page 151).

142. **Cooper-Clark, Diana.** *Designs of Darkness: Interviews with Detective Novelists.* Bowling Green, OH: Popular, 1983. 239p. Illus.

Interview subjects include P.D. James, Jean Stubbs, Peter Lovesey, Margaret Millar, Ross Macdonald, Howard Engel, Ruth Rendell, Janwillem van de Wetering, Patricia Highsmith, Julian Symons, Amanda Cross, Anne Perry, and Dick Francis. For all but Cross (Columbia University professor Carolyn Heilbrun), photographs are included. The lack of a bibliography is unfortunate, particularly in the case of Canadian writer Engel, who at the time of publication was most likely to be unfamiliar to readers, who might have liked to know just how many of his private eye novels about Benny Cooperman had appeared in print, when, and who published them. (Since Cooper-Clark's volume appeared, Engel has been published in the U.S. by St. Martin's.)

The questions Cooper-Clark, a Toronto English professor, asks are those of the academic scholar rather than the fan. (She has also compiled a book of interviews with mainstream novelists.) Many of her subjects seem bemused by her sometimes-comically-pretentious questions, particularly Dick Francis, who is on a different wave-length entirely. (The reader imagines he finds the probings of academic critics utterly pointless drivel but is too polite to say so. Q: "I take it from what you're saying that you are not really interested in reading academic, critical books about the novels that you are writing." A: "No. I'm not a well-read person, I suppose. I don't read nearly enough books.")

The interviews are successful, though, because they are revealing of their subjects. Van de Wetering, surprisingly, is as insistent as Francis that he is just telling stories, and he cautions Cooper-Clark not to read too much Zen symbolism into his Amsterdam police novels. Symons reveals that he turned to historical novels because he felt less able to write about younger contemporary characters, knowing how they talk to him but not to each other. Engel endearingly lists the underrated Frank Gruber as an influence along with Hammett and Chandler.

It may well be that Cross, in a slip of tongue or memory, referred to "John Dickenson and Dickenson Carr" being the same writer, but surely the author or editor should have provided the correct names: John Dickson Carr and Carter Dickson. The lack of dates on the interviews is irritating in the extreme, particularly in the case of Macdonald, who was interviewed after the publication of his last novel, *The Blue Hammer* (1976), but before he was disabled by Alzheimer's Disease. It would be good to know just when the interview took place. The reader wonders how much of the handwriting was already on the wall, especially in Macdonald's last statement in the interview: "I'll write another book, if I can."

143. **Cox, J. Randolph, ed.** *TAD-SHRIFT: Twenty Years of Mystery Fandom in the Armchair Detective.* Madison, IN: Bouchercon XVIII/Brownstone, 1987, vii, 111p.

Several writers who were in at or near the beginning of *The Armchair Detective* in 1967 contribute reminiscences to this anniversary volume. Longest piece is founding editor Allen J. Hubin's "TAD's First Decade," reprinted from the 1986 Garland reprint of the journal's first ten volumes. Other contributors include Bob Adey, Jon L. Breen, Robert E. Briney, Nick Carter (really Michael Avallone, internal evidence suggests), Joe R. Christopher, editor Cox, William K. Everson, John A. Hogan, Cameron Hollyer (introducing a reprinted article by *TAD* pioneer Estelle Fox), Marvin Lachman, Edward S. Lauterbach, Frank D. McSherry, Jr., Francis M. Nevins, Jr., William F. Nolan, John Bennett Shaw, Charles Shibuk, and Donald A. Yates.

144. **Docherty, Brian, ed.** *American Crime Fiction: Studies in the Genre.* Basingstoke: Macmillan; New York: St. Martin's, 1988. x, 146p. Bibl., index.

Not examined. Reading the comments of Walter Albert (*The Armchair Detective,* v. 24, n. 2, p. 208), this "collection of essays by British and Australian academics" which displays "a certain insularity in several of the contributions" (i.e., in the assumption that there has been little serious criticism of detective fiction), sounds like a negligible item for most fans. Subjects include Poe, Hammett, Chandler, James M. Cain, Jerome Charyn, George V. Higgins, and Spillane.

145. **Dove, George N., and Earl F. Bargainnier, eds.** *Cops and Constables: American and British Fictional Policemen.* Bowling Green, OH: Popular, 1986. 204p. Bibl.

Following an eight-page introduction by both editors, this collection is divided into an American section, "Cops," edited by Dove, and a British section, "Constables," edited by Bargainnier. Most of the subjects represent relatively fresh critical ground. The essays are primarily profiles of the various series detectives and, as is often true of this approach, there is less critical differentiation between titles than many readers might desire.

Leading off the "Cops" section, Barrie Hayne provides the best article to date on Anthony Abbot's Thatcher Colt. Also outstanding is Joan Y. Worley's piece on Hillary Waugh's Fred Fellows. Other subjects and their critics include Joseph Harrington's Francis X. Kerrigan (Martha Alderson and Neysa Chouteau), John Ball's Virgil Tibbs and Jack Tallon (editor Dove), Dell Shannon's Luis Mendoza (Mary Jean DeMarr), Collin Wilcox's Frank Hastings (Frederick Isaac), and Tony Hillerman's Joe Leaphorn and Jim Chee (Jane S. Bakerman).

The somewhat briefer "Constables" section is highlighted by Donald C. Wall's concluding roundup chapter on current types and trends in British police fiction, covering briefly the work of Colin Dexter, Patricia Moyes, William McIlvanney, Jack S. Scott, James Barnett, Peter Hill, Reginald Hill, Peter Turnbull, John Wainwright, and G.F. Newman. (The scope of this chapter makes especially regrettable the lack of an index to the whole volume.) Among the individual profiles is the volume's weakest, Liahna Babener's dull treatment of a fascinating writer and character (Christianna Brand and Inspector Cockrill), in which nearly all the author's solutions are given away for no compelling reason. Others given chapter-length treatment are Henry Wade's John Poole (Leah A. Strong), Colin Watson's Walter Purbright (editor Bargainnier), Bill Knox's Thane and Moss (Constance Hammett Poster), and Peter Lovesey's Cribb and Thackery (Jeanne F. Bedell).

On the whole, this is an admirable collection. But the editors make a dubious claim in their introduction: that there were no notable American examples of the "great policeman" in the twenties and thirties aside from Thatcher Colt, Earl Derr Biggers' Charlie Chan, and William MacHarg's short story sleuth O'Malley. What about Helen Reilly's Inspector McKee, Rufus King's Lt. Valcour (according to Howard Haycraft's *Murder for Pleasure* [WAM #1]) nearly as popular as Perry Mason in the thirties), Milton M. Propper's Tommy Rankin, and perhaps most notably George Bagby's Inspector Schmidt, whose career-in-print lasted nearly fifty years?

146. **Fine, David, ed.** *Los Angeles in Fiction: A Collection of Original Essays*. Albuquerque: U. of New Mexico P., 1984. 262p. Index, bibl.

Not too surprisingly, more than half of these dozen lively and readable scholarly essays on fiction set in L.A. are partly or entirely concerned with crime or mystery fiction. Richard Lehan's "The Los Angeles Novel and the Idea of the West" touches on Horace McCoy's *They Shoot Horses, Don't They?*, Chandler's *The Big Sleep*, and John Gregory Dunne's *True Confessions*. Editor Fine's own chapter is devoted to the novels of McCoy and James M. Cain. In a three-essay section on "Los Angeles and the Detective Novel," Paul Skenazy discusses hardboiled fiction generally, touching on Paul Cain's *Fast One* along with the work of Hammett, Chandler, and Ross Macdonald; Liahna K. Babener contributes a chapter on Chandler and Jerry Speir one on Macdonald. Skenazy returns with a chapter on Dunne's *True Confessions* and Thomas Sanchez's *Zoot-Suit Murders,* and Babener's concluding essay discusses the classic Robert Towne/Roman Polanski private-eye film *Chinatown*. A useful bibliographic note is appended to each of the essays save one.

Fine's introduction, after describing what is in the book, identifies some worthy subjects in L.A. fiction not covered except in passing, among them crime writers Roger L. Simon, Andrew Bergman, Stuart Kaminsky, and Joseph Wambaugh.

147. **Fleenor, Juliann, ed.** *The Female Gothic.* Montreal and London: Eden, 1983. 311p. Bibl.

Not examined. According to Albert (see #6), "A collection of essays on 19th and 20th century Gothic novels with an introduction by editor Fleenor and four essays in which there is some treatment of the relationship between Gothic and mystery fiction" (page 58). Among them is Joanna Russ's acute essay from *Journal of Popular Culture,* "Somebody's Trying to Kill Me and I Think It's My Husband: The Modern Gothic." Others writing on the modern gothic are Kay J. Mussell (on the audience), Barbara Bowman (on Victoria Holt), and Kathleen L. Maio (on the "Had-I-But-Known" school of Mary Roberts Rinehart, Mabel Seeley, and others).

148. **Freeman, Lucy, ed.** *The Murder Mystique: Crime Writers and Their Art.* New York: Ungar, 1982. 139p.

Here is a good collection of essays on mystery writing, ostensibly intended for the reader rather the prospective writer of crime fiction. The book is divided into two sections: "On the Genre" and "On Technique."

Bruce Cassiday leads off section one with an interesting account of mystery fiction's recent re-merging with the "mainstream," whence it came in the works of such nineteenth-century novelists as Dickens and Collins. Thomas Chastain, in one of the weaker pieces, writes of private eyes, presenting a scenario for a Spade-Marlowe collaboration I hope nobody ever tries to write. Hillary Waugh is excellent on police procedurals, a form he still seems to like so much one wonders why he quit writing them. Editor Freeman discusses Freudian psychology in the mystery, and Helen Wells offers a very welcome survey of juvenile mystery fiction.

In section two, Ken Follett shows amazing honesty in an article on characterization, candidly describing the tricks he uses and pointing out some of the drawbacks in the plots of his best-sellers. Though *The Eye of the Needle* is as sure a bet for classic status as any thriller of the seventies, Follett insists it would have been a better book if the second half were done differently. D.R. Bensen writes entertainingly of hackery. Franklin Bandy, in a discussion of hardcover-vs.-softcover, relates the story of his Edgar-winning paperback, *Deceit and Deadly Lies*. Edward D. Hoch is interesting on film adaptations of mysteries, and Eleanor Sullivan quotes from some of her interviews (and other people's) with various mystery writers. In the most unusual entry in the book, Shannon OCork presents a little-magazine short story disguised as an article on fictional technique—or is it the other way around?

149. Friedland, Martin L., ed. *Rough Justice: Essays on Crime in Literature.* Toronto: U. of Toronto P., 1991. xxix, 248p.

Despite the title, only the last essay, Josef Skvorecky's "Detective Stories and *Fingerprints*" discusses genre works. The Czech/Canadian writer, a detective story purist, recounts his own entry into the field in the course of reviewing the anthology *Fingerprints,* whose contributors included Howard Engel, Margaret Millar, and a number of less well-known Canadian writers. Subjects of the other essays, from presentations by English professors at a law school seminar, run to the Bible, Chaucer, Fielding, Scott, Dickens (*Our Mutual Friend*), Wilde, Faulkner, Dreiser, and Richard Wright.

150. **Gerber, Samuel M., ed.** *Chemistry and Crime: From Sherlock Holmes to Today's Courtroom.* Washington, D.C.: American Chemical Society, 1983. xiii, 135p. Illus., bibl., index.

Though most of it is not fiction-related, this collection leads off with three essays (35 pages) on chemical applications in mystery fiction. Two concern the Sherlock Holmes saga: Ely Liebow's "Medical School Influences on the Fiction of Arthur Conan Doyle" and editor Gerber's "A Study in Scarlet: Blood Identification in 1875." The third is Natalie Foster's "Strong Poison: Chemistry in the Works of Dorothy L. Sayers." Anne G. Bigler provides some attractive period-flavor illustrations. The essays are of primary interest to specialists.

151. **Hays, Rhys H.** *Selected Writings of Rhys H. Hays.* Ed. Justus F. Paul. Stevens Point, WI: privately printed by the Department of History, University of Wisconsin-Stevens Point and Judge Paul R. Hays, 1977. 213p. Bibl.

Not examined. According to Albert (see #6), "[t]his memorial volume collects the major essays of historian detective story buff . . . Hays (d. 1976). Pages 155-210 contain eleven articles reprinted from *The Armchair Detective.* A bibliography of Hays' writings is included (pp. 211-213)." Among the topics are the novels of Joseph Harrington, Chesterton's Father Brown and Mr. Pond, medieval detection, Lewis Carroll, dying messages, and religious aspects of chess and religion. Having read these articles in their original periodical form, I can highly recommend Hays' avocational fan writings.

152. **Jakubowski, Maxim, ed.** *100 Great Detectives; or The Detective Directory.* London: Xanadu; New York: Carroll & Graf, 1991. 255p. Bibl.

In essays averaging about two pages, the contributors (mostly mystery writers with a sprinkling of knowledgeable critics, scholars, publishers, dealers, and fans) write of their favorite fictional detectives. The editor does not claim the hundred subjects are necessarily the greatest—indeed his introduction steals the thunder of critics by providing a staggering list of well-known characters not included (Perry Mason, Travis McGee, Rabbi Small, and Brother Cadfael, for example). Among those who are

included are some who unquestionably would belong in a list of the top
hundred (Appleby, Archer, Father Brown, Campion, Chan, Dupin, Fell,
Holmes, Maigret, Marlowe, Marple, Poirot, Queen, Wimsey, Wolfe);
those who arguably would—or might some day (Alleyn, Dalziel and
Pascoe, Fen, Ghote, Leaphorn and Chee, McCone, Millhone, Morse,
Nameless, Spenser, Thatcher, Traveler, van der Valk, Warshawski); and
those who unquestionably wouldn't but are still fun to read about (Joseph
Commings' Brooks U. Banner, Peter Cheyney's Lemmy Caution, Doro-
thy L. Sayers's Montague Egg, Sax Rohmer's Moris Klaw, and such
one-shot characters as William Hjortsberg's Harry Angel, Umberto Eco's
William Baskerville, and Marc Behm's The Eye). Among the most
obscure inclusions are Charles Burns' comic-strip sleuth El Borbah and
John Russell Fearn's "Black Maria." Among the oddest are William S.
Burroughs (not, I think, a fictional character); Anthony Trollope's trio of
Mackintosh, Bunfit, and Gager (not generally considered to have occupied detective stories); and Simon Smith's The Clewseys (in an only
occasionally funny hoax entry attributed to Soeur Van Folly).

Among the better-known essayists and their subjects: Joe Gores on
Michael Gilbert's Calder and Behrens, Michael Moorcock on Margery
Allingham's Albert Campion, Susan Dunlap on Joyce Porter's Dover,
Patricia Moyes on Elizabeth Peters' Amelia Peabody Emerson, H.R.F.
Keating on Holmes, Loren D. Estleman on Marlowe, Sharyn McCrumb
on Carter Dickson's Sir Henry Merrivale, Bill Pronzini on Marcia
Muller's Sharon McCone, Simon Brett on Sue Grafton's Kinsey Millhone,
Ed Gorman on Pronzini's Nameless, Edward D. Hoch on Queen, Julian
Symons on Dashiell Hammett's Sam Spade, Catherine Aird on Emma
Lathen's John Putnam Thatcher, Robert Campbell on Robert Irvine's
Moroni Traveler, Carolyn G. Hart on Phoebe Atwood Taylor's Leonidas
Witherall, and Brian Stableford on M.P. Shiel's Prince Zaleski.

The arrangement of entries is alphabetical by character name, followed by sixteen pages of notes on the contributors. Each entry has a
bibliographic checklist appended—most of these require consultation of
other sources for full information, generally giving title and year with no
additional information. Robert Adey's entry on Banner, strictly a short-
story character, has a very thorough checklist—but unfortunately the
asterisks in the two footnotes are unreferenced in the list.

A statement in Aaron Elkins' appreciation of Sir John Appleby needs
correction. He writes, "Only Hercule Poirot matches his extraordinary
achievement in solving crimes in six successive decades." Not so. Ellery

Queen solved cases in six decades (twenties to seventies), and Gladys Mitchell's Beatrice Bradley solved them in seven (twenties to eighties).

153. **Keating, H.R.F.** *The Bedside Companion to Crime.* London: O'Mara; New York: Mysterious, 1989. 192p. Illus., index.

As a joyfully enthusiastic and boundlessly learned mystery commentator, Keating is closest in spirit to the Ellery Queen of the forties. Here he presents short takes on a wide variety of subjects: the appeal of crime fiction, defending it against its detractors; title changes,especially of Agatha Christie's novels; literary writers claimed for crime fiction (Faulkner, Greene) and those who actually wrote it (Snow, Arnold Bennett, Priestley. Walpole, Kipling, Forester, Dickens); authorial mistakes (in his own books and those of Martha Grimes); dullness as a virtue (Woods, Eberhart, Rhode); round-robin mysteries (such as *The Floating Admiral*); prolific writers (the well-known ones plus Leonard Gribble and W. Murdoch Duncan); the great crooks (twenty, including series characters like Fu Manchu, Arsene Lupin, Lovejoy, and Fantomas, and one-shots like Caspar Gutman and Count Fosco); various story types and elements (locked rooms, school backgrounds, parody, trains, religion, history, humor, food); a selection of mystery-related poetry by authors as varied as Auden, Nash, Symons, and Reginald Hill; the first books of Christie, Simenon, Michael Innes, Chandler, and Ross Macdonald; and appreciations of five favorite books (*The Moonstone, The Hound of the Baskervilles, The Maltese Falcon, The Talented Mr. Ripley,* and *A Taste for Death*) and a group of favorite writers male (Freeman, Post, Wallace, Futrelle), female (Rinehart, Mitchell, Allingham), and collaborative (Lathen, Queen). Magazine-style sidebars cover such topics as bungling detectives, unfinished mysteries, red herrings, pseudonyms, Jack the Ripper in fiction, and former criminals as mystery writers.

154. **Macdonald, Ross,** pseudonym of Kenneth Millar. *A Collection of Reviews.* Northridge, CA: Lord John, 1979. xiii, 67p.

This limited edition collects fourteen book reviews by Macdonald, the first three of which bear on crime fiction. The first is a review of A.E. Murch's *The Development of the Detective Novel* (see WAM #2), though (in a fairly incredible editorial lapse) the full title of the book appears nowhere in the article or elsewhere in the volume. He also reviews Barzun and Taylor's famous reference book (see WAM #10) in a piece headed *A Catalog* [sic] *of Crime* and James M. Cain's omnibus *Cain X 3*. Not surprisingly, Macdonald takes issue (courteously and effectively) with the conservative/classical bent of both Murch and the B&T team.

155. **Masters, Anthony.** *Literary Agents: The Novelist as Spy.* Oxford and New York: Blackwell, 1987. viii, 271p. Illus., bibl., index.

In one of the better books on spy fiction, Masters considers a dozen writers, most but not all associated with the thriller genre, who had real-life Intelligence experience. All save E. Howard Hunt are British. Tom Driberg apparently wrote only non-fiction, while Malcolm Muggeridge did not write espionage fiction. Other subjects are Erskine Childers, John Buchan, Somerset Maugham, Compton Mackenzie, Graham Greene, Ian Fleming, John Bingham, Dennis Wheatley, and John le Carré. An epilogue briefly discusses non-spook Len Deighton, who provides a foreword. The essays consider their subject's biographies, espionage activities, and literary achievement. Not surprisingly, the extent of their real-life spying activities is often speculative. (For example, did Fleming really engineer Rudolf Hess's flight to Scotland early in World War II?) Several of the essays, notably those on Muggeridge and Hunt, are enriched by interviews with the author. Masters includes evaluative content: he dislikes the fiction of Fleming and Wheatley, for example, but likes that of the relatively little-known Bingham. In the le Carré chapter, Masters tries to identify the original model for George Smiley. One suspect (not Masters' choice) is Bingham, ironically given Bingham's umbrage at le Carré's jaundiced depiction of the British intelligence community. A good selection of photographs of the subjects is included.

156. **Most, Glenn W., and William W. Stowe, eds.** *The Poetics of Murder: Detective Fiction and Literary Theory.* San Diego: Harcourt Brace Jovanovich, 1983. xv, 394p. Bibl., index.

This highly scholarly collection is notable for its international slant, with several of the essays translated from European languages by the editors or others; its inter-disciplinary approach, with various psychoanalytical, philosophical, and sociological viewpoints; and its concentration on well-known critics and thinkers not usually associated with the genre, e.g. Jacques Lacan, Frank Kermode, Roland Barthes, and Michael Holquist. Many appear in earlier volumes covered in WAM: Geraldine Pederson-Krag's "Detective Stories and the Primal Scene" (see *Dimensions of Detective Fiction* [WAM #72]), Umberto Eco on Ian Fleming (from *The Bond Affair* [WAM #156], David I. Grossvogel on Agatha Christie (from *Mystery and Its Fictions* [WAM #44]), Stephen Knight on early history (from *Form and Ideology in Crime Fiction* [#86]), and Dennis Porter on suspense (from *The Pursuit of Crime* [#106]). There is also D.A. Miller's journal article "The Novel and the Police" (preceding its book-length version in #99), and Roger Caillois's "The Detective Novel as Game," a different translation of the middle section of *The Mystery Novel* (see #64). Stephen Marcus's introduction to the Dashiell Hammett collection *The Continental Op* (1974) is another familiar piece. Other essays of note find East German scholar Ernst Kaemmel writing on detective fiction's capitalist connection and Richard Alewyn persuasively advancing the claim that E.T.A. Hoffmann wrote a modern-style detective story years before Poe. The only original essays are the editors': Most on le Carré (as a writer of detective rather than spy fiction) and Stowe on Chandler.

157. *The Mystery Scene Reader.* Cedar Rapids, IA: Fedora, 1987. 166p.

This was the first and regrettably only issue of a book spinoff from *Mystery Scene* magazine, edited and introduced by Ed Gorman. The volume opens with fifty pages of tributes to the late John D. MacDonald, most a page or two long, by such writers as Lawrence Block, Max Allan Collins, Harlan Ellison, Loren D. Estleman, Mickey Friedman, William Campbell Gault, Joe Gores, Joe L. Hensley, Tony Hillerman, Stephen King, Dean R. Koontz, John Lutz, Donald E. Westlake, Teri White, and Charles Willeford. Following a section of five short stories (including Ellison's Edgar-winning "Soft Monkey") are a group of brief interviews with George Baxt, Koontz, MacDonald, William F. Nolan, comic-book writer-editor Denny O'Neill, Elizabeth Peters, and Jimmy Sangster and an eleven-page autobiographical piece on his pulp-writing career by Todhunter (known to mystery readers as W.T.) Ballard.

158. Nieminski, John. *John Nieminski: Somewhere a Roscoe.* (Brownstone Chapbook Series Volume Three.) Selected and edited by Ely Liebow and Art Scott. Madison, IN: Brownstone, 1987. 61p.

This selection was published for the 1987 Bouchercon, held in Minneapolis, in memory of its posthumous fan guest of honor. As shown in these pages reprinted from his very-small-distribution DAPA-EM fanzine *Somewhere a Roscoe,* Chicago Sherlockian John Nieminski was one of the most talented and entertaining writers ever to hide his light under a fannish bushel. Given the small number of readers he reached, it is virtually impossible to express how good he was and expect to be believed. Those who have never read his work can find out for themselves in this sampler. (One example of Nieminski's creative use of language is his account of first reading "The Speckled Band" in a high school anthology "filled with gunk like the painful self-indulgences of Robert Browning, whose 'My Last Duchess' we were encouraged to commit to memory of all places.")

Among the subjects are Michael Avallone (a hilarious final exam from an "Advanced Seminar" on the works of Ed Noon's creator, all questions drawn from *The Case of the Violent Virgin*); a 1966 meeting with Basil Rathbone (in Chicago to introduce a series of his old Holmes films for a TV station, on his way to Hollywood to appear in *Pajama Party in a Haunted House*); works as varied as Anthony Berkeley's *Dead Mrs. Stratton,* Rufus King's *The Fatal Kiss Mystery,* and Milton K. Ozaki's *The Deadly Pickup;* and the experience of compiling an index to *Ellery Queen's Mystery Magazine* (see WAM #22). Besides an introduction by co-editor Scott, there are concluding tributes by Liebow, Bob Briney, Marv Lachman, Mary Shura Craig, Len and June Moffatt, and Ellen Nehr.

159. Panek, LeRoy L(ad). *The Special Branch: The British Spy Novel, 1890-1980.* Bowling Green, OH: Popular, 1981. 288p.

In his *Watteau's Shepherds* (see WAM #80), Panek wrote one of the best books extant on the classical British detective novel. Here he does nearly as good a job on spy fiction. He offers individual essays on seventeen writers, some pioneers (William LeQueux, E. Phillips Oppenheim, Erskine Childers), some acknowledged masters (John Buchan, Graham Greene, Eric Ambler, Geoffrey Household), some relatively neglected (at least by critics) (Francis Beeding, Manning Coles, Adam

Hall), some figures of controversy (Sydney Horler, Sapper, Peter Cheyney, Ian Fleming), and some contemporary best-sellers (Len Deighton, John le Carré, Frederick Forsyth). Panek puts Fleming in perspective as a minor writer in every way except popular appeal, a commodity the creator of James Bond presumably would have settled for. He points out that le Carré, unlike most of his fellow espionage practitioners, is more a detective story than an adventure writer.

Though this is an excellent book, there are some things to complain about. The lack of both an index and a bibliography is unfortunate. And an appalling number of careless mistakes have been allowed by Panek and his editors to creep into print. Two James Bond heroines are miscalled "Honeychild" Rider and Tiffany "Chase." There are references to authors "Carroll J. Dailey" (Carroll John Daly) and Richard "Osborne" (Usborne). A Nazi figure is misspelled Martin "Borman." And Panek devotes a whole chapter to a writer (Horler), misspelling his first name throughout as "Sidney"!

160. **Prescott, Peter S.** *Never in Doubt: Critical Essays on American Books, 1972-1985*. New York: Arbor, 1986. x, 302p. Index.

The *Newsweek* critic's subjects include a number of crime writers in a section called "The Art of the Thriller": Elmore Leonard (with the much-quoted and somewhat overstated designation, "the best American writer of crime fiction alive, possibly the best we've ever had" [page 88]), Ross Macdonald, John le Carré, Geoffrey Household, Martin Cruz Smith, and George V. Higgins. Subgrouped under the heading "The Art of Trash" are briefer and somewhat less complimentary discussions of Stephen King, W.T. Tyler, Eric Ambler, Len Deighton, and Michael Crichton. The writing is as lively and quotable as you would expect from a newsmagazine critic. Of Higgins: "Attending to his plots as a pot-smoking teenager in a day-care center might attend to her charges, he devotes his energies to the true matter of his fiction: talk" (page 118).

161. **Prescott, Peter S.** *Soundings: Encounters with Contemporary Books*. New York: Coward, McCann, & Geoghegan, 1972. 331p. Index.

In this earlier collection of reviews from various periodicals, Prescott seems to appreciate the crime and mystery genre less than he would in

Never in Doubt (see above). "Taking Crime Seriously" brings together reviews of Roderick Thorp's *The Detective* (found boring, an example of the mistake of trying to do serious fiction in the genre), Ross Macdonald's *The Goodbye Look* and *The Underground Man*, and Helen MacInnes's *The Venetian Affair*, the last an unremitting pan. Also included are reviews of le Carré's *The Looking Glass War* and (in a consideration of science fiction) Michael Crichton's *The Andromeda Strain*. In a most entertaining semi-satirical piece on "How to Write a Spy Novel," among the rules for the High-brow Spy Novel (le Carré, Deighton) is "Be confusing"; among those for the Low-Brow Spy Novel (Fleming, MacInnes), "Pretend to be sophisticated" (page 278). Adam Hall's *The Quiller Memorandum* is seen as a good compromise between the two brow levels. Of associated interest is a hatchet attack on C.P. Snow's murder-trial novel *The Sleep of Reason* titled "Another Snow Job."

162. Rader, Barbara A., and Howard G. Zettler, eds. *The Sleuth and the Scholar: Origins, Evolution, and Current Trends in Detective Fiction.* Westport, CT: Greenwood, 1988. xiii, 138p. Bibl., index.

Consisting of papers presented at a Wesleyan University symposium held October 18, 1986, this may be mystery fiction's first "proceedings" volume. Because of their brevity and their presentation as lectures rather than essays, these pieces are easier to take than some academic criticism and as such offer a good first step into what serious academic analysis of the genre has to offer. Following Robin W. Winks's foreword, Carolyn G. Heilbrun discusses androgyny in the detective story in an interesting keynote address. The other lectures are presented in three sections: "Mystery as Social Criticism," including Dennis Porter on P.D. James, Peter J. Rabinowitz on Chester Himes, and John McAleer on June Thomson (fresher ground here, a writer probably undervalued in this country); "Women and Crime Writing," consisting of B.J. Rahn on Seeley Regester's *The Dead Letter* (a systematic analysis of this 1867 novel's claims to being the first detective novel rather than Anna Katharine Green's *The Leavenworth Case*—Collins's *The Moonstone* being disqualified because the detective fails to solve the crime), Michele Slung on Agatha Christie (a ringing defense of Christie as writer and feminist, unfortunately finishing with a gratuitous sneer at Mary Roberts Rinehart, bracketed with Judith Krantz as, implicitly, a schlock writer), and Marilyn Stasio making "A Sweep Through the Subgenres"; and "Down These

Mean Streets," including William W. Stowe on frontier pamphlet-writer Virgil Stewart, Richard Slotkin on the roots of the hardboiled in James Fenimore Cooper, Allan Pinkerton, and dime novels, and Glenn W. Most on Elmore Leonard. Susan Steinberg's annotated bibliography, primary and secondary, is generally good though it incredibly lists Ordean Hagen's *Who Done It?* (see WAM #16) while omitting the Hubin bibliographies that have completely superseded it. Also, LeRoy Panek's *Watteau's Shepherds* did not win an Edgar award.

As suggested above, the volume has a distinct female bias, clearly the result of the recent efforts of mystery-writing feminists. Stasio celebrates women's contributions to the historical mystery and the formal puzzle without mentioning masculine names like Carr, Queen, and Lovesey. While many little-known women writers are rightly celebrated, virtually no lesser-known men are covered, at least of the present century, and the only contemporary male discussed at length is Leonard. Finally, the female scholars represented tend to be much more readable and informal than the males, if also a bit less obviously rigorous.

163. **Rosenberg, Betty.** *The Letter Killeth: Three Bibliographical Essays for Bibliomaniacs.* Los Angeles: Kenneth Karmiole, 1982. vi, 60p. Index.

In this limited edition, the former UCLA library school professor offers a trio of lively essays on bibliomysteries with library, bookselling and collecting, and publishing backgrounds. Author and title indexes are included.

164. **Salwak, Dale.** *Mystery Voices: Interviews with British Crime Writers.* (Brownstone Mystery Guides Series, Volume 8.) San Bernardino: Borgo, 1991. 112p. Illus., bibl., index.

Subjects include Catherine Aird, P.D. James, H.R.F. Keating, Ruth Rendell, and Julian Symons, with a photo and a chronology preceding each interview and a secondary bibliography following. The interviews (presenting in Q-and-A form without any framing narrative by Salwak) are well-conducted, entertaining, and a valuable source of insights into their subjects. Aird contributes an enjoyable and thoughtful introduction, "On Being a Writer of Detective Fiction."

I suspect the "Dorothy" Yates referred to in the Aird interview (page 17) should be Dornford, especially since she brackets him/her with John Buchan and Sapper. At another point, Margery Allingham's first name becomes "Marjorie."

165. Sampson, Robert. *Deadly Excitements: Shadows and Phantoms.* Bowling Green, OH: Popular, 1989. 223p. Illus., index.

With the same evocative prose and fannish enthusiasm that permeates his *Yesterday's Faces* (see #114), Sampson collects his individual essays on the pulps, many originally published in small-circulation fanzines. Not all the subjects are mystery or detective pulps, with weird and western titles also getting considerable attention. Among the subjects are the Phantom Detective, Doc Savage, the Spider, and Lester Dent's Oscar Sail. Sampson also examines the contents of individual magazine issues, among them *The Shadow* (August 1, 1934); *Black Mask* (November 1921); *Crime Busters* (November 1937); and *Scientific Detective Monthly* (June 1930).

166. Schleh, Eugene, ed. *Mysteries of Africa.* Bowling Green, OH: Popular, 1991. 124p. Bibl.

The editor's opening essay underlines the Eurocentrism of most detective fiction set in Africa but shows how Africans gradually came to be included as real characters rather than just background color. Individual pieces are devoted to Matthew Head (an especially good piece by Earl Bargainnier), Elspeth Huxley (by Sharon A. Russell), John Wyllie (by editor Schleh), Wessel Ebersohn (by Fred Isaac), and James McClure (by Schleh), while the last of the twelve entries is an excellent interview with McClure by Don Wall. (Astonishingly, only one of McClure's Kramer and Zondi novels, considered in Europe and America to be fearless and unrelenting exposes of apartheid, was banned in South Africa, where the books are seen as objective descriptions of "the way things are" [page 117].) Two of the editor's short essays discuss mysteries from the colonial era and the era of independence and cite works by various non-specialist authors. Another introduces a 69-item checklist of detective stories with South African backgrounds, most by non-African authors. Less familiar topics include the Macmillan Pacesetters, a series of novels, most bylined by Black Africans and aimed at African young adults, fascinatingly described in a piece by Mary Lou Quinn and the editor; Africans in West German crime fiction (a body of work rarely written about in English in any aspect), discussed by Dieter Riegel; and Kenyan writer Ngugi wa Thiong'o's *Petals of Blood,* discussed by Steven R. Carter in the volume's longest piece. Most of the essays are followed by a reference list or bibliographic note. Some of them are reprinted from *Clues,* Bowling Green's mystery fiction journal, but most are original to this volume. This is an admirable collection, covering much fresh ground.

167. **Symons, Julian.** *Critical Observations.* London: Faber; New Haven, CT: Ticknor & Fields, 1981. 213p.

The third of this collection's four sections, comprising 47 pages, gathers five essays from the mid- to late seventies on criminous topics. Pieces on Hammett and Chandler are reprinted from *Crime Writers* (WAM #101) and *The World of Raymond Chandler* (WAM #121). New to book form are "The Crime Collector's Cabinet of Curiosities," a fascinating catch-all of oddities turned up during Symons's research for *Bloody Murder* (WAM #5), beginning with an account of Charles Felix's pioneering detective novel *The Notting Hill Mystery* and ending with a celebration of Corey Ford's Philo Vance parody *The John Riddell Murder Case;* a review of Kathleen Tynan's fictionalization of the Christie disappearance, *Agatha* (rightly labelled "contemptible" and "total nonsense" by Symons), along with an appreciation of Christie's own works and their media adaptations; and a collective review of some Simenon novels.

Several essays outside the specialized section also have some genre interest: a not-too-enthusiastic review of Kingsley Amis's *The Riverside Villas Murder,* also touching briefly on the author's spy novel *The Anti-Death League;* an essay on C.P. Snow's *Strangers and Brothers* sequence, which sometimes verged on crime fiction; a piece on the author's friend Ruthven Todd, briefly referring to Todd's rapidly-written mystery novels as R.T. Campbell; and a description of Symons's year as a visiting professor at Amherst, devoting a single paragraph to a course he taught there on crime fiction. As always, Symons the critic is insightful and a pleasure to read.

168. **Symons, Julian.** *Critical Occasions.* London: Hamilton, 1966. 213p.

The section called "Criminal Occasions" (pages 149-182) includes the essay "The Face in the Mirror," reprinted from *Crime in Good Company* (see WAM #68), non-fiction pieces on the Tichborne Claimant and Julia Wallace, and essays on Eric Ambler (from 1956) and Raymond Chandler (from 1962). A 1954 essay on C.P. Snow is of associated interest, though there is no direct discussion of that author's detective fiction.

169. **Walker, Ronald G., and Jane M. Frazer, eds.** *The Cunning Craft: Original Essays on Detective Fiction and Contemporary Literary Theory.* Afterword by David R. Anderson. Macomb, IL: Western Illinois U.P., 1990. vii, 203p. Bibl., index.

Not examined. According to reviewer Dan Crawford (*The Armchair Detective,* v. 24 n. 3, page 343), subjects of the fourteen essays include such writers as Poe, Paretsky, Doyle, Christie (the *Roger Ackroyd* problem), Chesterton, Sayers, and Hammett, "discussed in relation to modernism, feminism, and a host of other '-isms.'" Though generally favorable, Crawford warns, "the language of this book is the language of the professional literary theoretician. It can be read with comfort only by those for whom the use of a word like 'ineluctably' is a natural and unforced thing."

170. **Waugh, Hillary.** *Hillary Waugh's Guide to Mysteries and Mystery Writing.* Cincinnati: Writer's Digest, 1990. x, 196p. Bibl., index.

Combining historical commentary with technical advice, MWA Grand Master Waugh presents a mixed bag of essays, some previously published (two each from *The Mystery Story* [WAM #63] and the revised *Mystery Writer's Handbook* [WAM #95]), one from *The Writer* magazine, and another from the 1978 MWA nonfiction anthology *I, Witness*), most original to this volume.

The book begins well with a good, hard-headed analysis of Poe's contributions, successfully deflating any argument that "The Gold Bug" and "Thou Art the Man" do not qualify as detective fiction. Indeed, he credits Poe with inventing fair-play clueing in the latter story, the very tale Howard Haycraft disqualified from the genre for the lack of it. Waugh makes a clear point that fair play was generally not a factor in early detective fiction.

In discussing Wilkie Collins, Waugh overstates both the length of *The Moonstone* and the minor nature of its detective plot. The discussion of Doyle takes a no-nonsense approach, frankly criticizing the quality of the Holmes stories and treating the Mrs. Watson problem as a writer's dilemma rather than a biographical puzzle.

Subsequent historical chapters concentrate on the best-known names, with special attention to Christie, Hammett, Chandler, and Spillane. Two of the reprinted articles deal with police-procedural form and the work of real police detectives in contrast to fictional. The final historical chapter discusses the currently proliferating female private eyes, including some observations to which feminists are sure to take exception. Twenty-eight pages of how-to-write chapters differentiate the mystery from the general novel and offer sound advice on plotting, characterization, research, and the pros and cons of outlining. There are five pages of recommended reading, mostly familiar highspots in the development of detective fiction.

Knowledgeable as he is about the genre, Waugh makes occasional careless errors, such as spelling the surname of Lew Archer's creator "McDonald." Erle Stanley Gardner fans will surely dispute the statement that the Perry Mason novels are of uniform quality—such an expectation could lead a reader starting with one of the inferior latter-day Masons to discount the whole series. Comprising Waugh's worst offense are his serious misstatements about Charlie Chan, who was not a "stick figure" but a fully-developed, complex character (admittedly, that is a matter of opinion) who spoke beautiful though not perfect English and never confused his l's and his r's (that is a matter of fact).

171. **Williams, John.** *Into the Badlands.* London: Paladin Grafton, 1991. 240p. Bibl.

Not examined. According to Edward D. Hoch (*The Year's Best Mystery and Suspense Stories 1992* [see #369]), the author took a "journey across American in 1989, interviewing some fifteen mystery and crime writers encountered along the way."

172. **Winks, Robin W., ed.** *Colloquium on Crime.* New York: Scribners, 1986. 216p. Index.

Mystery critic Winks asked his fifteen favorite living authors to write essays on their craft, suggesting that they address such matters as how they entered the crime fiction field, how much of themselves goes into the writing, the influence of other authors, their attitudes to critics, the future of the genre, its alleged conservatism, and the effect of its new-found academic attention. Eleven of the fifteen agreed, and their responses make an excellent book.

The authors' approaches to the subject are quite varied, some offering much autobiographical detail, others practically none. Robert Barnard provides tantalizing descriptions of some of his rejected novels and admits to cribbing his unpleasant Australian cop in *Death of an Old Goat* from Joyce Porter's Dover. Rex Burns reveals that the name of his detective, Gabriel Wager, was purposely symbolic. Two writers who seem to pay little attention to Winks's questions are Michael Gilbert, who expands on his controversial thesis that thrillers are harder to write than detective stories, and Donald Hamilton, who offers a motivational lecture for potential writers. Other contributors are K.C. Constantine, Joseph Hansen, Reginald Hill, Dorothy Salisbury Davis, Tony Hillerman, James McClure, and Robert B. Parker.

Winks declines to reveal the four favorites who declined to participate, but what he says about them provides a stimulating puzzle. He tells the reader "that had these four been present, the balance between American and English would have been as exact as an odd number could make it, and that the same would be true between genders . . . " This statement works regarding nationality, where the present score is seven Americans to four British. If all four missing writers were British, the score would be eight to seven. However, by my figuring, even if all four missing writers were women, the score would be only five women to ten men. One must conclude either that Winks, a Yale history professor, is woefully deficient in math skills, or that at least two of the ten writers included I have assumed to be men are actually women!

173. Winks, Robin W., ed. *Detective Fiction: A Collection of Critical Essays.* Englewood Cliffs, NJ: Prentice-Hall, 1980. vi, 246p. Bibl. Revised edition. Woodstock, VT: Foul Play/Countryman, 1988. 301p. Bibl., index.

This description is based on the revised edition.

The only area in which this fine collection of critical essays falls short of Howard Haycraft's *The Art of the Mystery Story* (see WAM #69) and Francis M. Nevins, Jr.'s *The Mystery Writer's Art* (WAM #78) is the relative familiarity of most of the material, nearly all of which is excerpted from books or has been published in earlier collections. The essays are well-selected and arranged, and in many cases the editor's notes add to or clarify points made in the essays. The first section, "The Genre Examined," leads off with W.H. Auden's "The Guilty Vicarage," followed by widely-reprinted pieces by Dorothy L. Sayers, Edmund Wilson, and Joseph Wood Krutch, and the prologue from Gavin Lambert's *The Dangerous Edge* (see WAM #71). "A History of the Type" consists of the introduction to Sayers's *Omnibus of Crime* (see #512), with some interesting notes by Winks, plus separate pieces by George Grella on the classical and hardboiled mystery. "Literary Analysis" reprints Jacques Barzun's introduction to *The Delights of Detection* (see #363) with book excerpts from John Cawelti, Julian Symons, and Eric Routley. "A Closer Look at Specific Authors" consists of Ross Macdonald's "The Writer as Detective Hero" from his *On Crime Writing* (see #191), another excerpt from Cawelti on Christie and Sayers, and Ronald A. Knox's "A Detective Story Decalogue." "Means and Ends" comprises George Dove's "The Criticism of Detective Fiction"; Ernest Mandel's "A Marxian Interpretation of the Crime Story" from his *Delightful Murder: A Social History of the Crime Story* (see #3); editor Winks's perceptive pieces on Donald Hamilton, P.D. James, William Haggard, Robert Duncan/James Hall Roberts, and E. Howard Hunt, all but the latter from *The New Republic;* and his introduction to *The Historian as Detective*. Appendices include Winks's article "Teaching About American Detective Fiction," a selective bibliography of secondary sources, and a nine-page list of his favorite novels in the field. There follow a general index and an author/title index.

The first edition has the same contents minus the Dove and Mandel pieces. In addition, Winks revised and updated the material in the appendices for the second edition, substituting a bibliographic essay for a pair of course syllabi he deems no longer needed and expanding his list of personal favorites.

5
TECHNICAL MANUALS

174. Bendel, Stephanie Kay. *Making Crime Pay: A Practical Guide to Mystery Writing*. Englewood Cliffs, NJ: Prentice-Hall, 1983. vi, 234p. Bibl., index.

Not examined. This fairly recent volume is surprisingly difficult to find, and I was also unable to identify any reviews.

175. Bilker, Harvey L., and Audrey L. Bilker. *Writing Mysteries That Sell*. Chicago: Contemporary, 1982. vii, 134p. Index.

You would have to go back to 1936 and *Murder Manual* (see WAM #93) to find a mystery writer's how-to book as hopelessly inept as this one. Its problem can be summed up simply: no reader unsophisticated enough to profit by the advice given here would be capable of writing publishable mystery fiction or anything else. A few of its offenses: idiotic definitions of story types that either belabor the obvious or betray the authors' confusion, hopelessly hackneyed plotting and suspense technique examples, a paucity of author-title references aside from very obvious ones, and such doubtful statements as calling Robert L. Fish's Schlock Homes series a "pastiche." (Pastiche is serious—when you do it for laughs, it's a parody or a burlesque.)

The selection of market information was of some use at the time of publication but readily available elsewhere. The general writing advice is better than the specifically mystery-oriented advice, but even it is nothing special. The authors are claimed to have published in the mystery field, but the extent and nature of their publications is not specified.

176. **Block, Lawrence.** *Telling Lies for Fun & Profit: A Manual for Fiction Writers.* Introduction by Brian Garfield. New York: Arbor, 1981. 256p. Index.

Like the author's *Writing the Novel: From Plot to Print* (WAM #86), this collection compiled from his *Writer's Digest* columns is addressed to fiction writers generally rather than to mystery writers specifically, but his stature in the genre, even greater today than when this book was published, and the number of examples drawn from the crime/suspense field make its inclusion here appropriate. Some of the chapters are in a question-and-answer format, and Block often addresses by name members of an imaginary writing class. Nearly every aspect of fiction writing is addressed, always entertainingly and instructively.

177. **Block, Lawrence.** *Spider, Spin Me a Web: Lawrence Block on Writing Fiction.* Cincinnati: Writer's Digest, 1988. 243p.

More of Block's *Writer's Digest* columns are collected, with the level of helpfulness and readability high as ever, and the imaginary writing class even more frequently addressed.

178. **Burack, Sylvia K.** *Writing Mystery and Crime Fiction.* Boston: The Writer, 1985. 208p. Bibl.

A well-known group of contemporary practitioners offer tips on writing as well as insights into their own works in this collection of 26 essays, most reprinted from recent issues of *The Writer* magazine. Similar in title to earlier *Writer* collections edited by the late A.S. Burack (the 1945 edition of *Writing Detective and Mystery Fiction* [WAM #87], its 1967 revision [not noted in WAM], and the 1977 revision and retitling, *Writing Suspense and Mystery Fiction* [WAM #88]), this is an all-new collection, eschewing any historical reprints in its emphasis on the current market. The final two chapters, "A Layman's Guide to Law and the Courts" and "Glossary of Legal Terms" are dedicated to helping the writer get the details of jurisprudence right. A two-page bibliography includes both reference sources on mystery fiction and treatises on police history, techniques, and procedures.

Many of the essays reveal a strong strain of iconoclasm. Loren D. Estleman opens a sound and helpful article with a gratuitous slam at Ellery Queen. (If he really believes the thirties novels of Queen and other Golden Age greats are easily solvable by present-day mystery readers, he's a much better armchair sleuth than I am. I suspect he's really thinking of B movie whodunits of the same era.) Max Byrd, also impatient with the traditional mystery plot, takes a somewhat milder swipe at Agatha Christie. Most shocking of all, Stanley Ellin is left cold by Conan Doyle ("A pox, I say, on the posturing Holmes and the goggle-eyed Watson"), believing Doyle lacked the saving grace of irony. Other contributors are Catherine Aird, Jean L. Backus, Cecilia Bartholomew, Rex Burns, Rosemary Gatenby, Sue Grafton, Bill Granger, William Hallahan, Paul Henissart, Clark Howard, P.D. James, Peter Lovesey, Dan J. Marlowe, Patricia Moyes, Marcia Muller, Al Nussbaum, Lillian O'Donnell, Gerald Petievich, Richard Martin Stern, Mary Stewart, Dorothy Uhnak, Michael Underwood, and Phyllis A. Whitney.

179. Corbett, James. *How I Write and Sell Thrillers.* High Wycombe, England: Stebbing, n.d. 11p.

Corbett is a writer best known for his ineptitude (fan reviewer William F. Deeck has made him famous), and this well-intended advisory pamphlet invites wisecracks from its opening sentence: "'There is money—a lot of money—in the well-written shocker', writes Sydney Horler, and how true it is." Corbett begins by differentiating the kind of thriller he writes from the more analytical detective story, but when he starts naming authors and plot elements, the distinction becomes hopelessly blurred.

Obviously no one will go to this antiquarian item for writing advice, but it has some historical interest re the state of the mystery market in Britain at mid-century. (Corbett's *Death Makes a Date,* identified as "my latest thriller," was published in 1950.) Corbett lists 23 British publishers of thrillers and says the following re royalties: "A modern thriller may earn from 50 to 300 and a serial-thriller may bring in a great deal more. I did hear the 'Daily Express' paid four hundred guineas for a serial, and would not be surprised if that is correct. Royalties generally start at 10 per cent an advance-royalty cheque being usually about twenty-five pounds. American publishers often treble our figures." I hope so.

180. **Grafton, Sue, ed.** *Writing Mysteries: A Handbook by the Mystery Writers of America.* Cincinnati: Writer's Digest, 1992. xiii, 208p. Index.

In a successor to the two editions of *The Mystery Writer's Handbook* (see WAM #94-95), Grafton gathers 27 articles, most previously published in writers' magazines. Contributors include some of the top names in the field, e.g. Jeremiah Healy, Faye and Jonathan Kellerman, Julie Smith, Sara Paretsky, Nancy Pickard, Tony Hillerman, Phyllis A. Whitney, Lawrence Block, and John Lutz. Among the most entertaining entries are Dick Lochte's discussion of work schedules and Warren Murphy and Molly Cochran's exchange on collaboration. Most unusual (and potentially among the most useful) is Robert Campbell's description of using the computer as an outlining and organizational tool. Articles on finding an agent and marketing a mystery are followed by a discussion from an editor's viewpoint by Ruth Cavin of St. Martin's. In a section on specialties, Joan Lowery Nixon discusses juvenile mysteries and Edward D. Hoch short stories. A three-page list of mystery writers' reference sources in credited to Bruce Cassiday. This is among the most helpful volumes available for beginning mystery writers.

181. **Jute, André.** *Writing a Thriller.* London: Black, 1986. New York: St. Martin's, 1987. 100p. Index.

Jute takes an anyone-can-do-it approach, exhorting his reader to hard work, perseverance being far more important to this kind of writing than talent. He scorns most fiction manuals but finds John Braine's *Writing a Novel* valuable. Brief but helpful chapters discuss character, plot, research, and cutting and rewriting, offering a page of typescript from his own book as a good example of the latter. Though he includes a taxonomy of the wider crime-detective-suspense field, his main focus is the spy or adventure thriller, and he believes Charles McCarry is the best now writing in the form.

182. **Keating, H.R.F.** *Writing Crime Fiction.* London: A. and C. Black, 1986. New York: St. Martin's, 1987. 88p. Index.

Defining crime fiction as "fiction that is written primarily for its entertainment value which has as its subject some form of crime," Keating begins with a chapter describing the formal detective story as practiced in the Golden Age. Subsequent chapters discuss the "modern variations" (inverted stories, "backgrounders," howdunits, whydunits, the "detective novel" [apparently a finer thing than the mere "detective story"], and the crime novel); the hardboiled novel (pointing out this kind of story can be done by a British writer, he goes so far as to refer favorably to Basil Copper's Mike Faraday books, which Keating believes occur in "an authentic-seeming Los Angeles"), along with procedurals and suspense novels; and other types "on the periphery" (comic and farcical mysteries, romantic suspense, historical mysteries, fiction based on fact, and finally the short story, on the current state of which Keating is overly negative in my opinion). The fifth chapter gives advice on the actual process of putting a crime novel together.

Many will read this for insights into Keating's own product and method. But the book really is full of good advice for potential writers. One litmus test for a book like this is the quality of its allusions, the writers and titles used as examples, and here Keating is outstanding.

The final chapter, "Last Words," presents a problem, at least in the American edition. Any literate reader can tell this is a British book written from a British perspective. After all, we have a reference to Radio 3 and a suggestion to visit the British Library for newspaper research. Why then did the American publisher do an inadequate patch job on the last chapter on markets to make it appear to be American in focus?

183. Koontz, Dean R. *How to Write Best Selling Fiction.* Cincinnati: Writer's Digest Books, 1981. 309p. Index.

This manual is a borderline inclusion in the present work. In contrast to his earlier *Writing Popular Fiction* (see WAM #91), which encourages writers to break in with "category" fiction, Koontz now wants to put genre behind him in the quest for bestsellerdom and suggests others do the same. (Koontz had already largely succeeded in this by 1981, and in more recent years his commercial success has gone right off the charts.) Koontz assumes the blockbuster novel is more difficult than the genre novel and better almost by definition, and he is one of the few writers who think the incursion of the conglomerates into book publishing is a good thing. He has some very harsh words about the mystery genre as it existed circa 1981, finding it "stale, imitative," making one wonder if the boom in mystery publishing since then has produced enough new talent to change his mind. Still, most of his works still have at least one foot in the mystery genre, and a large number of his examples are drawn from the field. His chapter of recommended reading includes such mystery figures as Catherine Aird, Eric Ambler, Mary Higgins Clark, Stanley Ellin, Dick Francis, Adam Hall, Harry Kemelman, Lawrence Sanders, and Donald E. Westlake, among many others. (Statistical note: of the 99 fiction writers Koontz recommends, at least 37 are solidly under the crime/detective/mystery umbrella, and many others have spent some of their time there.) A provocative book, sometimes an irritating one, but get past the controversy and Koontz is still one of the best writing teachers in print.

184. Newton, Michael. *How to Write Action Adventure Novels.* Cincinnati: Writer's Digest, 1989. 159p. Index.

Newton, one of the most prolific of the team of writers creating new adventures for Don Pendleton's Mack Bolan, has written a very helpful guide to prospective writers in a field that overlaps mystery and detective fiction to a large extent. He cites plentiful published examples (even, to his credit, bad ones) to make his points, both from "mainstream" popular writers like Dean R. Koontz, Martin Cruz Smith, and Robert Daley and from his paperback series colleagues. His most important point comes early: any writer of popular fiction, from heralded bestseller to unreviewed series practitioner laboring behind a house name, must believe in what he or she is writing and give it the best effort possible. The slumming author who writes down to an unrespected reader must inevitably fail.

The usual fiction manual topics are covered—subdivisions of the genre, writers to read for an understanding of the category (a fine list), building a plot, opening hooks, characterization (including the naming of the characters), dialogue, marketing—along with those of particular importance to the action/adventure category: authenticity in weaponry, writing physical action, dealing with sex and violence. Newton is especially good on getting plot germs from the newspapers and outlining. He provides an annotated list of the major paperback publishers in the action/adventure category.

Since Newton takes special pains to mention factual sourcebooks in his text, it is regrettable there is no bibliography giving publishers and dates.

Newton is also the author of *Armed and Dangerous: A Writer's Guide to Weapons* (Writer's Digest, 1990), one of the publisher's Howdunit

Series to aid fiction writers in technical details. In the same series, also published in 1990, is *Deadly Doses: A Writer's Guide to Poisons* by Serita Deborah Stevens with Anne Klarner.

185. **Norville, Barbara.** *Writing the Modern Mystery.* Cincinnati: Writer's Digest, 1986. 209p. Bibl., index.

Despite some generalized statements that will irritate the buff—a gratuitous downgrading of the classics, including, like Howard Haycraft's 45 years before, a premature burial of the locked room, saying only Richard Forrest and Orania Papazoglou among recent writers have managed to handle it (what about Bill Pronzini and Francis Selwyn to name two?)—and at least one factual howler (Hitchcock's *Rope* could not have been based on Meyer Levin's *Compulsion,* having been made several years before the novel was published), editor Norville's is one of the most thorough and helpful of technical manuals for writers wanting to enter the field. Offering very much of a nuts-and-bolts approach, she gives specific examples of specialized information useful to the mystery writer and how to obtain it, plus general outlines of books in the various subgenres of the mystery. Her emphasis, though, is on the pure whodunit, and the development of an outline for such a book is covered exhaustively both in the text and an appendix. She alludes to many good and recent examples to support her points.

After an opening chapter on the taxonomy of the mystery genre, subsequent chapters cover getting and developing ideas (a real answer to that most pervasive of questions amateurs ask pros), plotting, characters (the victim, the sleuth, and the murderer in separate chapters plus another on characterization generally), background, style, and finally marketing. The final chapter cites writers' publications and organizations and includes a list of mystery book dealers. The four-page bibliography covers both books on writing and on specialized information for the mystery writer.

186. **OCork, Shannon.** *How to Write Mysteries.* Introduction by Hillary Waugh. Cincinnati: Writer's Digest, 1989. 131p. Index.

Coming from the same Genre Writing Series as Newton's volume (see #184), OCork's brief book offers good nuts-and-bolts advice, including plentiful examples drawn from published work or created for the occasion, along with inspirational encouragement for the potential writer. Following an opening peptalk, OCork deals with subgenres; plotting, constructing an original storyline to illustrate; atmosphere, voice, and point-of-view; heroes, including the question of oneshot-vs.-series; other characters (murderers, suspects, victims); pace, clues, suspense, dialogue, sex, climax and denouement, choice of title, professional discipline, and marketing. The use of very well-known titles for many of the examples (e.g., *The Maltese Falcon, Laura, The Murder of Roger Ackroyd*) is a good idea. OCork finishes with an invitation to write to her personally (in care of the publisher) for more advice.

The author falls down only in her loose grasp of detective story history and her tendency to careless error. There are references to Charlie Chan as a "hard-boiled tough egg," to "Raymond Chandler's San Francisco," to the writing team of "Bill Levenson and Richard Link." In a double error, OCork awards Poirot's companion Hastings a doctorate and implies he appeared later than Philo Vance's chronicler Van Dine. OCork states that Conan Doyle "was not able to gain a readership for his more 'serious' novels" (page 50)—in fact, Doyle had a vast readership for just about everything he wrote, if not as vast as for the Holmes stories. And what of the statement that the puzzle is "not fashionable today—their ilk seems to have gone to television episodes" (page 14)? If this were true, I for one would be watching a lot more television.

187. **Stevenson, John.** *Writing Commercial Fiction.* Foreword by Tony Hillerman. Englewood Cliffs, NJ: Prentice-Hall, 1983. viii, 120p. Index.

Here is a wealth of practical advice for prospective writers of "category" fiction. The genres discussed are romance, suspense, western, occult, action-adventure, mystery, fantasy, and science fiction. After describing the characteristics and conventions of each type with a likeable deadpan humor, the author devotes sections to plot, characterization, and "the actual writing." The treatment seems strongest on romance, western, and action stories, weakest on science fiction, but there are good points made about all categories.

Stevenson, who has been Nick Carter on occasion and is best-known for the espionage novels signed by Mark Denning, states as his purpose to provide the information he would like to have had at the start of his own career. He emphasizes the pleasures a writer can have (and provide to the reader) without venturing outside well-established genre boundaries. Well-chosen examples are drawn from such good and/or representative writers as John D. MacDonald, Brian Garfield, Jerry Pournelle, Gary Brandner, Don Pendleton, Patricia Matthews, and James M. Cain.

6
WORKS ON INDIVIDUAL AUTHORS

ALLINGHAM, Margery

188. **Martin, Richard.** *Ink in Her Blood: The Life and Crime Fiction of Margery Allingham.* Ann Arbor, MI: U.M.I. Research, 1988. Illus., bibl., index.

The author makes large claims for Allingham, finding her work of "considerably greater interest" than that of Christie or Sayers; her novels, in that phrase so grating to the ears of fans, "transcend the narrow limits of the subgenre." (They don't even transcend a full genre!) The opening chapter concerns the debate over the literary merits of detective fiction generally, an odd way to kick off a biography. The stodgy writing style and careless errors (including references to "Nicholas" Freeling and Ngaio Marsh's "Roger" Alleyn) may lose some readers early, but when Martin gets into his rich and previously unexplored biographical material, based on free access to Allingham's papers, matters look up considerably.

Martin alternates biographical chapters with critical examinations covering his subject's twenty novels published between 1929 and 1968, with short stories, novellas, and other works omitted from full study as "incidental." The critical commentary, routinely giving away solutions and sometimes giving Allingham special credit for some very standard detective-story methods, is generally less valuable than that found in Barry Pike's work of a year earlier (see below). While some of Pike's *Armchair Detective* articles on Allingham are cited in the text and bibliography, their gathering in book form is not, and the earlier writer is patronized by Martin when he is credited with "unwittingly" making an important point about one of Allingham's novels.

The bibliography is less useful than it could be. It is a key to references in the text rather than a complete listing, so that the novel *Dance of the Years* appears only in its American edition as *The Galantrys*, and most of the novels are listed in various reprint editions used by Martin, though the year of original publication is given.

189. Pike, B(arry) A. *Campion's Career: A Study of the Novels of Margery Allingham.* Bowling Green, OH: Popular, 1987. 253p. Bibl.

Originally serialized in *The Armchair Detective,* this is an exhaustively thorough survey of all the Albert Campion novels, touching on plot, characterization, style, and theme, by one of the most elegant writers of mystery criticism. Pike avoids giving away solutions, and he has a fine eye for the details and quotable phrases that give the flavor of his subject's work, making this reader at least want to drop everything and go read Allingham. Little biographical information is provided, and the subject's non-Campion novels are discussed only briefly. As in Martin's study (above), the two Campion novels written by Allingham's husband, Youngman Carter, after her death are not covered.

190. Thorogood, Julia. *Margery Allingham: A Biography.* London: Heinemann, 1991. xxii, 423p. Illus., bibl., index.

This will undoubtedly be the standard Allingham biography for years to come, markedly superior to Martin's earlier effort (see #188). Thorogood draws on her subject's diaries, unpublished manuscripts, and papers for a thorough biographical account and also provides more information than other sources on Allingham's lesser-known "hack" writings. One wonders if the crook series *The Darings of the Red Rose* (published in the periodical *Weekly Welcome* in 1930) will ever be published in book form.

The illustrations are especially notable, including besides a fine selection of photographs a number of good cartoon/caricatures, some of them by Allingham friend A.J. "Grog" Gregory. The notes and primary and secondary bibliography and extensive and useful.

In the kind of slip a knowledgable scholar could easily make, Thorogood attributes E.C. Bentley's *Trent's Last Case* to H.C. Bailey.

AMBLER, Eric

191. **Ambler, Eric.** *Here Lies: An Autobiography*. London: Weidenfeld & Nicolson, 1985. New York: Farrar Straus Giroux, 1986. 234p. Illus.

Though it was a deserving Edgar winner for best biographical or critical volume of its year, some of the reviews of Ambler's autobiography were unenthusiastic. It's true Ambler chooses to reveal himself very selectively and unaccountably breaks off the narrative after World War II, with only passing references to his first marriage and a single allusion (buried early on) to his second. Nevertheless, what he does choose to tell—about his parents' show business career, his early work experience in the 1920s, the first part of his novelistic career, and his experiences in World War II as a documentarian working with Carol Reed, Peter Ustinov, and John Huston among others—is beautifully written and informative. Both the book's clever double-meaning title and the first chapter, recounting an automobile accident at age 72 that caused Ambler to fear a loss of creative power, warn us not to expect the whole truth.

Ambler calls John Huston's *The Maltese Falcon* "the sixth remake" of the Dashiell Hammett novel (page 191), while other sources indicate it was only the second. In grousing about the film version of *The Mask of Dimitrios*, so bad it gave him stomach cramps in the projection room, Ambler writes, "An old writer of westerns named Frank Gruber had done the screenplay" (page 224). In fact, Gruber was only forty (about five years older than Ambler) when the film came out.

192. **Lewis, Peter.** *Eric Ambler*. New York: Continuum, 1990. 216p. Bibl., index.

Considering his reputation as one of the greatest and most innovative writers of crime and espionage fiction, it is amazing that this is the first book-length critical study of Ambler. The author, who won an Edgar for an earlier study of John le Carré (see #280), follows an introductory biographical chapter with a book by book consideration of Ambler's career, from the 1936 parody *The Dark Frontier* through 1981's *The Care of Time*. Lewis is as readable as he is rigorous, and the result is an excellent critical guide to Ambler's fiction.

ANDERSON, Frederick Irving

193. **Fisher, Benjamin Franklin IV.** *Frederick Irving Anderson (1877-1947): A Biobibliography.* (Brownstone Chapbook Series, Volume Four.) Madison, IN: Brownstone, 1987. vii, 43p.

Anderson was a writer for *Saturday Evening Post* and other slicks who would be even more deeply vanished into obscurity than he is were it not for the efforts of editor Ellery Queen (Frederic Dannay), who reprinted in anthologies and the early years of *Ellery Queen's Mystery Magazine* tales of detectives Deputy Parr and Oliver Armiston and series rogues Sophie Lang and the Infallible Godahl. Following a ten-page biocritical article, Fisher presents a valuable and meticulous annotated bibliography of all Anderson's publications, a fine starting point for future critical work on an unjustly neglected writer.

BOUCHER, Anthony (William Anthony Parker White)

194. **White, Phyllis, and Lawrence White.** *Boucher: A Family Portrait.* Introduction by Phil McArdle. Berkeley, CA: Berkeley Historical Society, 1985. 21p. Illus.

White/Boucher was an excellent practitioner of the formal detective story as well as the genre's finest critic. A full-scale biography is in order, but, lacking that, look for this charming pamphlet, illustrated with family photos and comprised of remembrances from his widow and one of his two sons. The book begins and ends with mock Berkeley newspaper items, one from *The Case of the Seven of Calvary* (1937) and the other from "The Compleat Werewolf" (1942).

BROWN, Fredric

195. **Baird, Newton.** *A Key to Fredric Brown's Wonderland: A Study and an Annotated Bibliographical Checklist.* Georgetown, CA: Talisman Literary Research, 1981. 63p. Illus., index.

This large-size paperback is to date the only monograph on Fredric Brown. The title essay of seven double-column pages is essentially a critical survey, with most attention to *Night of the Jabberwock;* a four-page chronology provides biographical details. There follow an interview with widow Elizabeth Brown and an article by agent Harry Altshuler, both translated back into English from their original appearances in a French fanzine. There is also a two-page essay by Brown, "It's Only Everything," about his attitude toward religion. The largest section is a full annotated bibliography of Brown's books, stories, poems, articles, radio and TV adaptations, audio readings, plus secondary sources. An appendix covers such supplemental areas as Brown's relationship with Mickey Spillane, a tally of his point-of-view methods, and his pseudonymous and collaborative work. The last ten pages are a thorough index. Illustrations include book covers and small photos.

The series "Frederic Brown in the Detective Pulps," published in various locations by Dennis McMillan, has some interesting secondary information on Brown, usually in the introductions by various well-known mystery and science fiction writers. Most notable of all is volume 16, *Happy Ending* (Missoula, Montana, 1990), which includes a 94-page excerpt from Elizabeth Brown's unpublished *Oh, for the Life of an Author's Wife!*, covering the period of their life in Taos, New Mexico, and providing much insight into Brown's character and his working methods.

CAIN, James M.

196. Hoopes, Roy. *Cain: The Biography of James M. Cain*. New York: Holt, Rinehart, and Winston, 1982. xvi, 684p. Illus., bibl., index.

There may not be a writer of crime fiction more worthy of this kind of full-scale biography than Cain, not only because of his quality and influence as a writer, but because of his uniqueness and complexity as a personality and the range of twentieth-century people and events he was associated with. Prominent in the index are such names as Heywood Broun, Walter Lippmann, James T. Farrell, Alfred Knopf, Arthur Krock, Ring Lardner, Sinclair Lewis, H.L. Mencken, Samson Raphaelson, Harold Ross, and James Thurber. (The very thorough thirty-page index makes an interesting gaffe when it telescopes the entries of novelist Thomas Wolfe and journalist Tom Wolfe.) Hoopes, who had Cain's cooperation

while the novelist was still living, tells his story with unobtrusive effi-
ciency. In accordance with his subject's wishes, he eschews critical
judgements, but his inclusion of quotes from Cain's work and from
contemporary opinions of it gives a very good impression of the kind of
writer Cain was. Eighty-one pages of notes plus a thorough primary
bibliography and filmography are appended. The book won an Edgar
award from Mystery Writers of America for the best biographical or
critical book of its year.

197. **Madden, David.** *Cain's Craft.* Metuchen, NJ: Scarecrow, 1985. xi,
162p. Illus., bibl., index.

Supplementing and updating his 1970 Twayne study (see below),
Madden presents separate essays on various aspects of Cain's career, most
adapted from earlier published material. *The Postman Always Rings Twice*
is compared with Horace McCoy's *They Shoot Horses, Don't They?* and
B. Traven's *The Death Ship.* Cain's career as a novelist is surveyed,
offering more information on the origin of the stories than critical analysis.
(Cain's two posthumously published novels are not discussed.) Following
chapters on Cain and the movies and on Cain's works as "pure novels,"
Postman is compared to Camus' *The Stranger,* much to the French
author's advantage, and *Serenade* is compared to Wright Morris's *Love
Among the Cannibals* in the course of an attempt to formulate an "aesthetics of popular culture." The book ends with an excellent 22-page
primary and secondary bibliography. The camera-ready typescript (complete with elevated a and wobbly underlining) is a distraction, but Madden
again proves his value as a true scholar who can write. Illustrations include
film stills, portraits of Cain, and a page of paperback covers.

198. **Madden, David.** *James M. Cain.* (Twayne's United States Authors
Series, vol. 171.) Boston: Twayne, 1970. 200p. Bibl., index.

The first book-length study of Cain, written while he was still alive
and at work, covers the novels through *The Magician's Wife* (1965).
Ultimately making no exaggerated claims for his subject, Madden covers
a great amount of biographical and critical ground in economical fashion.
Cain's letters to the author are quoted to good advantage. Though some-

what superseded by later writings by Madden himself and others, this remains a most useful introduction.

199. Skenazy, Paul. *James M. Cain.* New York: Continuum, 1989. xix, 203p. Illus., bibl., index.

The author of this thorough, well-written, and probing study warns in the preface he will be "less sympathetic to Cain than Madden or Hoopes [see above]; far less sympathetic, in fact, than I expected to be when I began this study" (page xi). Considering Cain's work chronologically, Skenazy finds his subject written out by 1941 and is very negative on the novels of the '40s through '70s. There is much material on screen versions of Cain's work, especially interesting on the differences between the book and film of *Mildred Pierce*, not always to the film's disadvantage. All the illustrations are movie stills.

CARR, John Dickson

200. Joshi, S.T. *John Dickson Carr: A Critical Study.* Bowling Green, OH: Popular, 1990. ii, 195p. Bibl., index.

Following a biographical introduction, Part I devotes individual chapters to Carr's major series sleuths (Bencolin, Fell, and Merrivale), followed by chapters on his other detectives, his historical mysteries, and his radio and short-story work. Part II offers topical essays on Carr's philosophy (mainly his religious skepticism and political conservatism), detective-writing techniques, use of the supernatural (including a discussion of *The Burning Court*, called "perhaps Carr's greatest novel"), and style and characterization. A four-page conclusion sums up his accomplishment. There is a thorough primary and secondary bibliography.

Joshi advises reading *The Three Coffins (The Hollow Man)* and other Carr novels "twice in succession: the first to be bamboozled, the second to see how it was done" (page 32).

Whether they agree with them or not, readers will find Joshi's outspoken critical judgments refreshing. He calls *The Arabian Nights Murder* "very likely the greatest pure detective story ever written" (page 33), though not necessarily Carr's best novel. He finds the Merrivale books generally inferior to the Fells and Bencolins but applauds their experiments in narrative technique. He values the non-fictional *Murder of Sir Edmund Godfrey* beyond any of Carr's historical novels. He often cites Carr's strained attempts at humor as a major fault, but compares his successful attempts to the work of P.G. Wodehouse. He believes Carr failed at short stories (I disagree!) but excelled at radio plays.

With this volume, we finally have a critical source on the third of the pure detective story's big three to stand with Robert Barnard's *A Talent to Deceive* (on Christie; see WAM #127) and Francis M. Nevins, Jr.'s *Royal Bloodline* (on Queen; see WAM #201).

CHANDLER, Raymond

201. **Brewer, Gay.** *A Detective in Distress: Philip Marlowe's Domestic Dream.* (Brownstone Chapbook Series Volume Five.) Madison, IN: Brownstone, 1989. 68p. Bibl.

Here is yet another reading of the Philip Marlowe novels, albeit an original and well-stated one. Brewer concentrates on the importance of home to the loner detective, including such domestic rituals as making coffee for visitors. The author jousts entertainingly with earlier critics and finds reason to value the final novel *Playback* more than most of them, seeing it not as a diminution of Chandler's powers but as a consistent development of Marlowe's character from the earlier books. A six-page, mostly secondary bibliography is included.

202. **Chandler, Raymond.** *The Notebooks of Raymond Chandler and English Summer: A Gothic Romance.* Illustrated by Edward Gorey. Edited by Frank MacShane. New York: Ecco, 1976. 113p. Illus.

Chandler's notebooks gather story ideas, plans for future work, bits of description, similes, ruminations on writing and language, collections of specialized slang, and excerpts from other writers. Of particular mystery interest in the latter category are descriptions of women by H.C. Bailey, an article by Frank Gruber on mystery novels and their authors, and Mary Roberts Rinehart's notes on the crime novel. Chandler's "Twelve Notes on the Mystery Story" and its addenda constitute one of the best sets of rules for the game ever compiled. One provocative statement: "The perfect detective story cannot be written. The type of mind which can evolve the perfect problem is not the type of mind that can produce the artistic job of writing. It would be nice to have Dashiell Hammett and Austin Freeman in the same book, but it just isn't possible. Hammett couldn't have the plodding patience and Freeman couldn't have the verve for narrative. They don't go together. Even a fair compromise such as Dorothy L. Sayers is less satisfying than the two types taken separately" (pp. 37-38). Among the other inclusions is Chandler's London *Sunday Times* review of Ian Fleming's *Diamonds are Forever*. The final 27 pages are comprised of the short story "English Summer," illustrated by Edward Gorey. Other illustrations include photographs and notebook pages.

203. **Chandler, Raymond.** *Selected Letters of Raymond Chandler.* Ed. Frank MacShane. New York: Columbia U.P., 1981. xx, 501p. Illus.

The early sampler *Raymond Chandler Speaking* (see WAM #118) gave a taste of the author's greatness as a letter-writer. Here is the banquet. The letters are arranged chronologically, from June 15, 1937, to February 21, 1959, followed by an index to subjects and recipients. The volume begins with a two-page chronology of Chandler's life, followed by four pages identifying the recipients, who include agents (Carl Brandt, H.N. Swanson), publishers (Alfred Knopf, Hamish Hamilton), lexicographers (Bergen Evans, Eric Partridge), librarians (Philip Gaskell, Wilbur Smith), motion picture figures (John Houseman, Alfred Hitchcock), and fellow writers (James M. Cain, George Harmon Coxe, Ian Fleming, Erle Stanley Gardner, William Campbell Gault, Michael Gilbert, John Hersey, Howard Hunt, W. Somerset Maugham, S.J. Perelman, J.B. Priestley, and others). MacShane's eight-page introduction gives a short biography of Chandler, discusses the range and mechanics of his correspondence, and identifies sources of letters and editorial procedures. The only illustration is a photo opposite the title page of Chandler and his cat.

204. **Clark, Al.** *Raymond Chandler in Hollywood.* London and New York: Proteus, 1983. 159p. Illus., index.

Not examined. According to Albert (see #6), "Clark went to Los Angeles and interviewed people involved in the production of Chandler's films and people who knew Chandler, and his narrative is a mixture of production information and film analysis. In his preface, Clark describes the sources he will be citing but there are no notes or bibliography. The illustrations include stills, lobbycards and other advertising material for the films" (page 360).

205. Luhr, William. *Raymond Chandler and Film.* New York: Ungar, 1982. xv, 208p. Illus., bibl., index.

Luhr devotes one section to the films for which Chandler wrote screenplays and another to those based on his work. There is an interesting discussion of the "forbidden" subtext in 1940s film noir. Aside from a tendency not to get names quite right—Edgar "Allen" Poe, Warren "Williams," Ross "MacDonald," Robert "P." Parker—Luhr is a reliable commentator. His competent and responsible summary, however, offers little that is new to readers of earlier books about Chandler. A good filmography and primary and secondary bibliography are appended.

206. Marling, William. *Raymond Chandler.* (Twayne's United States Authors Series, vol. 508). Boston: Twayne, 1986. 169p. Illus., bibl., index.

Though he has nothing startlingly fresh to offer, Marling provides an efficient overview of Chandler and his work, drawing effectively on earlier studies while providing his own intelligent readings. The first fifty pages are a good short biography, drawing heavily on Frank MacShane's standard life (see WAM #122) and Chandler's letters. Marling then devotes a chapter to the short stories, considering them in greater detail than have most critical summaries of Chandler's work. The final four chapters deal with the novels chronologically, providing full plot summaries followed by considerations of style, characters, themes, and critical reception.

207. Newlin, Keith. *Hardboiled Burlesque: Raymond Chandler's Comic Style.* (Brownstone Chapbook Series Volume One.) Madison, IN: Brownstone, 1984. 50p. Bibl.

In an adaptation of what clearly was an unusually worthwhile M.A. thesis, Newlin offers a stimulating and well-written examination of Chandler's style, a focus he sees as lacking in earlier studies. The use of "objective realism" is traced from Hemingway to Hammett to Chandler. As is appropriate to a study of style development, the author gives the majority of his space to the early pulp stories, emphasizing Chandler's use of humor and parody and regarding "Pearls are a Nuisance" as Chandler's "best, most sustained" work of this type. "It is this humor, which stems largely from his burlesque of the formula's conventions and style, that enabled Chandler to transform the dullness of the objective method into a richer, more expressive style. Ironically, his burlesque also indicates that his objection to the classic, deductive mystery (that it was not 'honest') applies to the hardboiled species as well" (page 27). Newlin's thesis has Chandler peaking with *Farewell, My Lovely, The High Window,* and *The Lady in the Lake,* declining markedly thereafter. The final novel *Playback* is not even deemed worthy of discussion, putting Newlin at odds with another Brownstone Chapbook author, Gay Brewer (see #201). A good five-page primary and secondary bibliography follows five pages of notes.

208. **Speir, Jerry.** *Raymond Chandler.* New York: Ungar, 1981. x, 166p. Bibl., index.

The author of an early Ross Macdonald study (see WAM #192) begins with a good biographical chapter before considering the novels in order of publication. Speir defends Chandler as a plotter, suggesting much of *The Big Sleep*'s reputation for impenetrable confusion is based on the movie version. In an interesting reading of that novel, Speir contends that much of what is usually seen as sloppy plotting is really a statement of Chandler's theme. Speir appreciates *The Long Goodbye,* perhaps the most controversial of the Philip Marlowe novels in the way it divides readers and critics, and is not merely dismissive of *Playback,* though not making lofty claims for it. Plot summary is excessively detailed when discussing such readily available texts, but that criticism apart, Speir has done a good, readable summary.

Following consideration of the novels are a thorough discussion of the earlier short stories, focussing on the "cannibalization" process, and chapters on the character of Marlowe and Chandler's style and themes.

Speir goes too far in claiming Chandler "despised" the English detective story (page 106), especially in view of his subject's praise of R. Austin Freeman.

209. Thorpe, Edward. *Chandlertown: The Los Angeles of Philip Marlowe.* London: Vermilion, 1983. New York: St. Martin's, 1984. 112p. Illus.

Englishman Thorpe visits present-day L.A., takes lots of nice pictures, and writes about the city and Chandler's view of it in the thirties through fifties. Approach is topical, with chapters devoted to architecture, sex, men, women, cars, food, and culture. Since he writes rather well himself and has Chandler's books to draw on for quotations, Thorpe manages to produce an entertaining and readable book, albeit one that gives a hostile visitor's narrow and distorted view of Southern California. The author is much better on Chandler's work than on the reality of the area today, which he explains like an anthropologist who hasn't been at his post long. What he describes are aspects of Los Angeles, but he presents them as the whole story.

It took Chapter 11, on the culinary and cultural scene, to make this tolerant Californian fighting mad. Thorpe seems abysmally ignorant of L.A. as theatre town, and his statement that the city has only one outstanding restaurant makes the reader wonder how many he could have visited. (And if there is only one, he certainly ought to have named it.)

Thorpe has a tendency to swallow Chandler whole, not only in his acceptance as literal truth of Marlowe's narrative hyperboles. He quotes passages to suggest Marlowe may have been homosexual or bisexual, but then rejects the idea simply because the private eye expresses hatred of gays in other passages. Doesn't he think such behavior is consistent with a repressed closet homosexual of that time? (I'm not saying Marlowe was gay, merely pointing out Thorpe is naive to reject the idea so easily.) Thorpe's favorite noun for homosexual is "queer," which may still be acceptable in polite circles in Britain but grated on the American ear by the eighties.

A matter not directly related to Chandler and Marlowe epitomizes Thorpe's sloppy pigeon-holing. Dividing actors into those who have stuck to a "tough-guy" image (Eastwood, Bronson, Reynolds, Stallone) and those who have "sought a wider range" (Beatty, Redford, Nicholson), he places both Marlon Brando and Paul Newman in the former category. In

Newman's case it may at least be arguable, but surely no actor, for better or worse, has tackled a more varied range of screen roles than Brando.

210. Ward, Elizabeth, and Alain Silver. *Raymond Chandler's Los Angeles.* Woodstock, NY: Overlook, 1987. 234p. Illus., bibl.

Superficially similar to Thorpe's volume (see above) but more friendly to Los Angeles, this one has less secondary text to accompany the many photographs of Southern California landmarks and settings used in Chandler's writings, sometimes the structures themselves but more often "a visual equivalent." Quotes directly from Chandler's novels and stories usually caption the photos, intermingled with the authors' well-written commentary on the city and on Chandler's (and Marlowe's) life there. The closest equivalent to this book is probably Don Herron's Dashiell Hammett tour of San Francisco (see #257), though a specific route is not suggested here, and Chandler's far-flung sites certainly don't lend themselves to a walking tour. The authors provide nine pages of bibliography (primary and secondary) and filmography.

211. Wolfe, Peter. *Something More Than Night: The Case of Raymond Chandler.* Bowling Green, OH: Popular, 1985. 242p.

The author of earlier studies of Hammett (see WAM #180) and Ross Macdonald (WAM #193) completes his consideration of the private-eye novel's big three with one of the best critical volumes to date on Chandler. From the rat-a-tat biographical opening to the concluding appreciation of *Playback* (Chandler's "most misread and underrated work"), Wolfe's work is dense and sometimes difficult but ultimately rewarding. Among other delights, Wolfe presents a dissenting view of *Farewell, My Lovely,* which he believes too highly ranked both by Chandler and his critics; a fascinating catalog of the contradictions of Chandler and Marlowe, e.g., their racial attitudes; a good chapter on Chandler's use of the tools and conventions of classical detective fiction; and an excellent consideration of Marlowe's first-person style.

Some readers will find Wolfe's attempt to psychoanalyze Chandler through his writing distasteful, and he occasionally makes some rather extreme assumptions—see, for example, page 17, on the Freudian significance of Chandler's use of firearms, and page 51, on his alleged homosexual tendencies.

CHRISTIE, Agatha

212. **Adams, Tom.** *Agatha Christie Cover Story.* Commentary by Julian Symons. Introduction by John Fowles. London: Dragon's World, 1981. As *Agatha Christie: The Art of Her Crimes: The Paintings of Tom Adams.* New York: Everest, 1981. 144p. Illus., index.

Adams is the best-known designer of covers and dust jackets for Agatha Christie's novels. This handsome volume reproduces more than ninety of his paintings in full cover with a running commentary by the artist and Julian Symons. Their remarks are quite honest and often at odds, adding to the reader's enjoyment. Impressive as they are in isolation, Adams's paintings are particularly admirable when one realizes how carefully he tried to reflect the mood and content of the novels. One of the most interesting products in the boom of Christie secondary sources, this handsome book will be of interest to art as well as mystery collections.

213. *Agatha Christie.* New York: Harper, 1990. 98p. Illus., bibl.

This large-format trade paperback is offered in celebration of the Christie centenary. Presented magazine-style and generously illustrated with photographs, book covers, and play and movie ads, many in color, it covers the usual ground and offers little unfamiliar information. One surprising item is a reprint of the obscure 1923 story "Trap for the Unwary."

Lynn Underwood is credited as editor and wrote many of the chapters. Other contributors include Christie biographers Charles Osborne (see #222) and Janet Morgan (see #220), Peter Haining, Sir William Collins, and the subject's daughter Rosalind Hicks and grandson Matthew Prichard.

214. **Gill, Gillian.** *Agatha Christie: The Woman and Her Mysteries.* New York: Free Press, 1990. xii, 243p. Illus., bibl., index.

This is the most recent biographical/critical study of Christie and one of the best. Though there is no new information, the book is expertly written and succeeds in offering a deeper and fuller analysis of Christie's character than most of its predecessors. For example, the discussion of Christie's early anti-Semitism is more probing than that found in Charles Osborne's book (see #222), and Gill offers one of the most thorough considerations of the 1926 disappearance, drawing on but sometimes differing from the theory of Janet Morgan (see #220).

Gill presents a close analysis of Christie's clueing and puzzle-building technique in (as well as nearly every other aspect of) her first novel, *The Mysterious Affair at Styles*, drawing from this book advice for the reader on what to look for in solving a Christie mystery. The author states in her introduction that only five solutions will be revealed; interestingly, *The Murder of Roger Ackroyd* is not among them. Novels chosen for in-depth treatment are *The Secret of Chimneys, Cards on the Table, The Body in the Library,* and *Nemesis.* Some of the novels written as Mary Westmacott also receive a close reading—notably *Unfinished Portrait* for its autobiographical elements and *The Rose and the Yew Tree,* seen as an expression of Christie's political and religious views.

Gill believes Christie has been underrated and patronized, castigating some of her mystery writing critics, both friendly (H.R.F. Keating) and unfriendly (Jessica Mann), for overstating Christie's banality. (She does this, by the way, as part of her 19 pages of notes, this being one of those books in which the notes are often as entertaining and informative as the text itself.) But I think her contention of a lack of appreciation of Christie's quality as a writer is a straw man—what, then, were all those earlier studies about? And her opinion that "[m]any other Golden Age novelists offered equally good puzzles" (page 7) is arguable—in fact, only Queen and Carr consistently did so.

In an amusing but non-crucial (because obvious) error, *Absent in the Spring* is described as a "fifty-thousand-page novel . . . written in three days flat" (page 151).

The bibliography lists secondary sources only. The sole illustration is a frontispiece portrait of Christie.

215. Gregg, Hubert. *Agatha Christie and All That Mousetrap.* London: Kimber, 1980. 170p. Illus., index.

This is the first book to focus attention on Christie's plays rather than the rest of her output, and as such it is valuable despite some irritating features. Gregg directed *The Hollow* (and starred in it during its pre-London run), was one of several to direct *The Mousetrap* (though not the first), and also staged *The Unexpected Guest*. His style is cutesy-chatty, sometimes amusing, almost Wodehousian at its best, but frequently annoying. He provides a sketchy early biography of his subject and pays considerable attention to the disappearance mystery—here is one commentator on the case who seems to sympathize more with Archie Christie than with Agatha. There is also much autobiographical information on Gregg, some of it interesting, and much theatrical material unrelated to Christie, e.g. a treatise on stage lighting and a jeremiad on the inability of today's actors to tie a bow tie or to wear evening clothes correctly. Gregg also discusses his mounting of Audrey and William Roos's *Speaking of Murder,* a play he thinks highly of, as a rival for *The Mousetrap* (in the theatre next door!)

Gregg is fairly patronizing toward his subject's work. Of her books, he claims to have read only *The Murder of Roger Ackroyd.* He awards himself a large part of the credit for her stage success, including naming *The Mousetrap* when the title *Three Blind Mice* was rendered unavailable, and creating the ending for the play *The Witness for the Prosecution,* though he turned down the chance to direct it.

Gregg is scrupulous about warning the reader when he is about to give away a secret, but he often doesn't tell you which secret he is going to give away—for example, he reveals the solution to *The Mousetrap* while discussing *Go Back for Murder.*

216. **Haining, Peter.** *Agatha Christie: A Murder in 4 Acts.* London: Virgin/Allen, 1990. 159p. Illus.

Not examined. According to Edward D. Hoch (in *The Year's Best Mystery and Suspense Stories 1991* [see #369]), it is an "[i]llustrated survey of Christie's work on stage, film, radio, and television."

217. **Hart, Anne.** *The Life and Times of Hercule Poirot.* New York: Putnam, 1990. 286p. Bibl., index.

The author of an earlier biographical account of Miss Marple (see below) now turns to Poirot. The first six chapters give a chronological treatment of the Belgian sleuth's career through *Elephants Can Remember* (1972). There follow chapters on Poirot's appearance, sartorial elegance, and attitudes; his relations with the English; his Watson-Boswell, Captain Arthur Hastings; his domestic arrangements, travels, male and female friends, clients and associates, and methods. The final chapter discusses his swan song in *Curtain*.

Many of the quoted passages recall to mind the charm and social observation of Christie's writing. The litmus test of all Christie commentators is how they deal with the *Roger Ackroyd* problem. Hart guards the secret beautifully. The volume ends with a 31-page Poirot bibliography, a very brief list of film and TV adaptations, and a two-page list of references quoted in the text.

218. **Hart, Anne.** *The Life and Times of Miss Jane Marple.* New York: Dodd, Mead, 1985. x, 161p. Illus., bibl.

The author, a librarian at Memorial University of Newfoundland, presents an appropriately brief and charmingly-written biography of the most celebrated of little-old-lady sleuths. The approach is only semi-Sherlockian, a "creator" being mentioned in the first sentence though never referred to again. Content is biographical rather than critical, so don't look here to find out which Marple adventures are the best or least. Special features are a map of the village of St. Mary Mead, a bibliography of Marple books listing both hardcover and paperback editions, a short-story checklist identifying appearances in collections, a listing of motion picture and television adaptations, and a one-page list of secondary references. This is one of the less essential additions to the groaning shelf of Christie studies, but fans will want to have it.

219. **Maida, Patricia D., and Nicholas B. Spornick.** *Murder She Wrote: A Study of Agatha Christie's Detective Fiction.* Bowling Green, OH: Popular, 1982. 199p. Illus.

Here is a solid, commendable effort that could easily be lost in the shuffle of Christie studies. There is more information on Christie's literary progenitors than in most other studies and also more attention to the short stories not about Poirot and Marple but lesser-known characters like Parker Pyne, Harley Quin, and Tuppence and Tommy Beresford. The

parodies in *Partners in Crime* starring the latter team are given considerable coverage, though sometimes the target characters are named without
identification of their authors. The only illustration is a portrait of Christie
opposite the title page. Though there is no bibliography, there are five
pages of notes. The notes to Chapter IX are unaccountably omitted. (And
I really wanted a source for the doubtful statement quoted on page 192
that Christie produced "more short stories than O'Henry [sic], Ernest
Hemingway, and Damon Runyon combined.") Other problems are the
identification of Elizabeth Bowen and Muriel Spark as "detective writers"
(page 60) and the implication that neither Christie nor other writers reused
the *Roger Ackroyd* trick (page 81). While on that subject, by the way,
solutions are freely revealed without warning.

220. **Morgan, Janet.** *Agatha Christie: A Biography.* London: Collins,
1984. New York: Knopf, 1985. xvii, 393p. Illus., index.

This is the only authorized biography, produced with the cooperation
of Christie's family and full access to her papers. Thus, it includes
information and insights unavailable to earlier biographers and almost
automatically supersedes Gwen Robyns' *The Mystery of Agatha Christie*
(see WAM #126) as the standard life. Morgan's account is far from being
the piece of well-laundered hagiography that such works sometimes
threaten to be. She offers, for example, the fullest and most intelligent
account to date of Christie's disappearance in 1926, and certainly she does
not overrate her subject's literary importance. Christie comes across as a
thoroughly admirable and likeable persons whose quirks are more endear-
ing than annoying.

Among the fresh elements included here are financial details, including her enormously complicated tax problems; a continuing account of
how carefully and tactfully her British and American agents handled their
star client and protected her from unwanted attentions of fans and media;
examples of how her notebook jottings were developed into mystery plots;
and specifics on how Eden Phillpotts encouraged Christie early in her
career. Her correspondence with family, agents, and publishers (which
might be worth a book of its own) is quoted extensively. Especially
entertaining is her reaction to a proposed jacket illustration for the Collins
edition of *The Labours of Hercules.* She wrote, "It suggests Poirot going
naked to the bath!!! All sorts of obscene suggestions are being made by

my family . . . Put statuary on the cover but make it clear it is statuary—not Poirot gone peculiar in Hyde Park!!!" (page 224).

Though Morgan has no track record as a mystery commentator, she is (or has made herself) decently knowledgeable about the field generally. Her critical comments on Christie's books are sound, and she admirably avoids solution giveaways—except in the case of *Roger Ackroyd,* which the subject tipped herself in her autobiography. Obvious factual errors are at a minimum, though there are some lapses in information. In some book references, Morgan is vague about whether the volume in question is a novel or a collection, and she never explains that the actor referred to repeatedly as Larry Sullivan was professionally known as Francis L. Sullivan, or that another Larry (Bachmann), Christie's liaison with M.G.M. during the production of the Miss Marple films with Margaret Rutherford, was also an accomplished mystery writer as Lawrence P. Bachmann.

The only major disappointment of the book is the illustrations, which include few recognizable likenesses of the subject. To make matters worse, throughout the text there are tantalizing references to photographs and illustrations (e.g., Poirot going to the bath) that have not been reproduced in the book. Both the Robyns biography and Dame Agatha's own reticent autobiography (WAM #129) are superior in this department—but in no other.

221. Morselt, Ben. *An A to Z of the Novels and Short Stories of Agatha Christie.* Bushey, Hertfordshire, UK: Phoenix, 1985. 255p. Bibl., index.

The author summarizes Christie's plots, with 66 novels and 143 short stories arranged chronologically in separate sections. A feature not available in other Christie sources is the solution listing, separated from the synopses to avoid undesired giveaways. It is arranged by entry number and reveals who did it in stories where that question is a factor. Morselt doesn't tell all, however: he finds himself unable to summarize the solution of *Murder on the Orient Express,* for example. There is also an alphabetical index by title, including variants, a listing of short story collections with contents identified by entry numbers, and an index to series detectives. There is no critical content. Though the summaries of individual short stories have some reference value, this volume is vital only to completist collections.

222. Osborne, Charles. *The Life and Crimes of Agatha Christie.* London: Collins, 1982. New York: Holt, Rinehart, Winston, 1983. 256p. Illus., bibl., index.

This literary biography is definitely one of the better Christie secondary sources, not because it provides much information not available elsewhere but because of its infectious enthusiasm and intelligent execution. It is pleasingly written, critically acute, and possibly unique in offering individual critical consideration to all her books, even including the poetry and collaborative works like the Detection Club's *The Floating Admiral.* Stage and film adaptations as well as Christie's own plays are discussed, including the final play, *Fiddlers Three,* often overlooked by other commentators. Osborne is generally more interested in and charitable toward Christie's non-detective works than some other writers, celebrating the Mary Westmacott novels and the play *Akhnaton.* Biographical details are intermingled with the professional history—Osborne agrees with Edgar Wallace's theory that Christie vanished deliberately in 1926 to get back at husband Archie.

Osborne, a music historian and broadcaster, probably has more to say about musical references in Christie than any other writer. Far from an unfailingly favorable commentator, he also records many of the anti-Semitic comments of Christie's characters and points out careless errors in her plots. His discussion of her later books illustrates a sad truth: that very successful veteran novelists often get no editorial help when they need it most. Other features include an excellent selection of illustrations and a chart identifying all of Christie's parody targets in the Tuppence and Tommy collection *Partners in Crime* (1929).

Osborne assures the reader in his preface that no solutions will be revealed, and he seems very upset that Christie herself tipped the solution to *Murder on the Orient Express* in *Cards on the Table* and the names of killers in four other novels in *Poirot Loses a Client.*

223. Ryan, Richard T. *Agatha Christie Trivia.* Boston: Quinlan, 1988.

Not examined. According to Dan Crawford's review in *The Armchair Detective* (v.22, n.2, page 201), this is a challenging book of Christie quizzes that differs from Andy East's *Agatha Christie Quizbook* (WAM #130) in its eschewing of true/false and multiple choice questions.

224. **Sanders, Dennis, and Len Lovallo.** *The Agatha Christie Companion.* New York: Delacorte, 1984. xxvii, 523p. Bibl., index. Revised edition, New York: Berkley, 1989. xxviii, 498p. Bibl., index.

More a consolidation of material from other sources than an original work, this volume is careful, competent, and complete enough to be the best Christie reference handbook. The authors cover her detective fiction book by book, offering contemporary biographical details, an account of the critical reaction, a plot summary (avoiding solution giveaways), a list of characters, identification of British and American first editions including pagination and price, and reference to media adaptations if any. One unique feature is the identification of the dedicatees of most of Christie's books. Non-mystery works are covered in a separate section, as are stage, film, and television adaptations, including critical reception and main cast credits in most cases. A section of Christie Lists identifies which books various series characters appear in (including both main characters like Poirot and Marple and a few secondary characters like Ariadne Oliver and Inspector Japp); plus a bibliography of secondary sources and a chronology.

Errors are relatively few, though page 327 has reference to books called *The Chronicles of Mark Hewitt* (should be *Martin*)—here it must be admitted they are accurately quoting Christie's own autobiography, but a parenthetical sic would be appropriate—and to Michael Gilbert's *Small Bones Deceased* (should be *Smallbone*). In their discussion of *The Murder of Roger Ackroyd* (1926), the authors imply that novel was preceded by the founding of the Detection Club in 1928. Language purists will shiver at a sentence than commits two teeth-grinding errors in syntax, announcing "One reason why . . . was because . . . " (page 253).

In a few cases, the authors are unfair to their subject. While it is true that Christie's novels, like many of the time, were full of racist attitudes, it is hardly fair to say a reference in dialogue to that "damned dago" was "made by Christie" (page 142). And surely the following statement is a serious disservice to her: "If Agatha had been killed during one of the raids on London in the 1940s . . . , she would now probably be remembered as just a good solid mystery writer of the prewar years" (page 374). On the contrary, she would be remembered, as she was already regarded, as one of the consummate masters of the form. Possibly her work would not have enjoyed the same kind of runaway commercial success had she not lived on into the sixties and seventies, but given the revival in the seventies of interest in Dorothy L. Sayers, who did all her work in the mystery field before World War II, even blitzed Christie as commercial phenomenon cannot be entirely ruled out.

In the revised edition, some biographical facts and later media adaptations have been added, but none of the errors noted above have been corrected.

225. Wagoner, Mary S. *Agatha Christie*. (Twayne's English Authors Series, vol. 432.) Boston: Twayne, 1986. 162p. Illus., bibl., index.

Though I'd have sworn there was no need for yet another Christie study, Wagoner has done an excellent and very thorough job here, covering material not usually considered in earlier studies and providing some fresh insights. A short biographical chapter leans heavily on Christie's autobiography, turning to Robyns (see WAM #136) and Morgan (see #220) only regarding the disappearance. The second chapter, oddly, concerns the short stories, giving more critical attention to them and to adaptation of their elements into novels than other sources. The next five chapters deal chronologically with the detective novels. There follow separate chapters on the thrillers and spy novels (generally disparaged), the Mary Westmacott novels, the plays, autobiographical writings, and finally "Bits and Pieces" (including the verse, a children's book, and Christie's participation in the Detection Club collaborative projects, *The Floating Admiral, Behind the Screen*, and *The Scoop*). Wagoner avoids revealing solutions almost entirely, managing an interesting analysis of *The Murder of Roger Ackroyd* without actually giving it away. As is appropriate in a study of Christie, criticism is focussed on the novels as detective stories with much attention to their plot structure and provision of clues. Strictly as a critical account, Wagoner's book ranks behind only Robert Barnard's *A Talent to Deceive* (WAM #127) and perhaps the books of Gillian Gill (see #214) and Charles Osborne (see #222).

COLLINS, Wilkie

226. Clarke, William. *The Secret Life of Wilkie Collins*. London: Allison & Busby, 1988. xii, 239p. Illus., bibl., index.

The husband of Collins's great-granddaughter essays a look into the mysterious corners of his subject's life, specifically his relationship with mistresses Caroline Graves and Martha Rudd, the latter of whom bore him children. Family trees of both are included. There is much on Collins's early family life, based partly on his mother's diary, considerable detail on his American visit in 1873-74, and much more than other sources on the family life of his later years. The section on the years after Collins's death traces the lives of his legatees and explains how his careful plans to provide for them went awry. Clarke has done some fine scholarly detective work and produced one of the better biographies.

Clarke's genre references are sometimes shaky. He claims Collins was called "the father of the detective story" (page ix), a title almost invariably applied to Poe, and even more inaccurately that *The Moonstone* "is still regarded as the first detective story" (page 116). In fairness, the note to the latter statement contradicts it, appropriately noting Charles Felix's *The Notting Hill Mystery* as a novel that preceded *The Moonstone*.

Challenge for puzzle-fanciers: Try to figure out in what order the bibliography is arranged. (By author? No. By title? No. By date? No.)

227. **Heller, Tamara.** *Dead Secrets: Wilkie Collins and the Female Gothic*. New Haven, CT: Yale U.P., 1972. ix, 201p. Index.

In a volume of criticism best appreciated by specialists in feminism and nineteenth-century fiction, Heller sees the female gothic (e.g. Anne Radcliffe's *The Mysteries of Udolpho*, Mary Wollstonecraft's *Marie*, Mary W. Shelley's *Frankenstein*) as "important source material from which Collins derives inspiration for his representation of gender and . . . class" (page 9). She finds a struggle in her subject's career between the sensationalism that connects him with women writers of the time and the literary professionalism that associates him with his male contemporaries. Heller devotes more attention than most sources to Collins's memoir of his father, the early novels *Antonina* and *Basil*, and the short-story collection *After Dark*, while also devoting full chapters to *The Woman in White* and *The Moonstone*. Though there is no bibliography, there are 27 pages of notes.

228. **Lonoff, Sue.** *Wilkie Collins and His Victorian Readers: A Study in the Rhetoric of Authorship.* (AMS Studies in the Nineteenth Century, No. 2.) New York: AMS, 1982. xii, 298p. Illus., bibl., index.

As the title of this lively and useful study suggests, Lonoff devotes her attention to the author-reader relationship as demonstrated in Collins's novels, their prefaces, and his other writings on fictional techniques and purposes. She also discusses Dickens's role as a critical reader, noting the drop-off in quality of Collins's work after his mentor's death, and Collins's prickly relationship with reviewers, while revealing that he sometimes was one himself (usually anonymously, as was the general rule in Victorian times). The early chapters are perfect for the reader more intrigued by accounts of writing careers than by close critical readings of individual texts or non-literary biographical details. The chapter on Collins's use of the novel as a game between author and reader is of special interest to students of detective fiction. A chapter on Collins's writing for himself, with no reader in mind, considers his treatment of women and of the mentally and physically aberrant. *The Moonstone* is used as a case study of the author-reader relationship, with an appendix listing its divisions as originally serialized.

229. **O'Neill, Philip.** *Wilkie Collins: Women, Property and Propriety.* Basingstoke, UK: Macmillan, 1988. vii, 238p. Bibl., index.

Believing Collins's categorization as a detective or sensation novelist did much to deny him his due in English literature, and that T.S. Eliot was "a poor ally" whose "faint praise may have done more to condemn Collins to the critical twilight than would a sustained and polemical dismissal of his novels" (page 2), O'Neill devotes more space to the generally scorned novel *The Fallen Leaves* than to either *The Moonstone* or *The Woman in White*. Other novels accorded extended discussion are *Armadale, Basil, Man and Wife*, and *No Name*. The author devotes a chapter to his subject's subtly and ambivalently feminist treatment of women and concludes that the contemporary women's movement should herald a revival and reevaluation of Collins. Purely critical rather than biographical, this is a readable and stimulating piece of scholarship.

230. **Peters, Catherine.** *The King of Invention: A Life of Wilkie Collins.* London: Secker & Warburg, 1991. xiii, 498p. Illus., bibl., index.

Collins is a prime subject for biography, not only for his significance as a writer but because he led an eventful life with its share of mystery and controversy, had important associates (notably Dickens), and was apparently a complex, unconventional, and extremely likeable person. Combining original research in previously untapped primary sources, notably an autobiographical account by Collins's mother, with the fruits of earlier scholars' probings, Peters has produced a thorough and highly readable account, superseding Kenneth Robinson's book (see WAM #144 and the present volume #553) as the standard life. Like Clarke (see #226), Peters describes Collins with the phrase "the father of the detective story" (page 434), a tag recently and inaccurately applied.

231. **Taylor, Jenny Bourne.** *In the Secret Theatre of Home: Wilkie Collins, Sensation Narrative, and Nineteenth-Century Psychology.* London and New York: Routledge, 1988. 220p.

Not examined. It is cited by Tamara Heller (see #227) as using "a feminist perspective to assess Collins' work" (page 4).

CRICHTON, Michael

232. **Crichton, Michael.** *Travels.* New York: Knopf, 1988. xi, 377p.

Crichton's is either an autobiography disguised as a collection of travel essays, a travel book disguised as an autobiography, or a book on paranormal phenomena disguised as both. "Freud once defined life as work and love, but I have chosen to discuss neither, except as my travel experiences impinge on them" (page xi). He admits to having changed "names and identifying characteristics" of all physicians and medical patients appearing in the early chapters and of some of the individuals in the larger post-medical section. He is consistently uninformative about dates, and the large amount of quoted dialogue suggests either a tape-recorder memory or a fiction writer's embellishment. There is relatively little about his writing, but he does refer briefly to writing paperback originals for money in his sparse spare time as a medical student and about the best-novel Edgar award threatening to blow his cover as Jeffrey Hudson, pseudonymous author of *A Case of Need.* He also devotes a chapter to his experience in Ireland directing Sean Connery in the film of his novel, *The Great Train Robbery.* Other books and films are mentioned only in passing or (more frequently) not at all.

DEIGHTON, Len

233. **Milward-Oliver, Edward.** *Len Deighton: An Annotated Bibliography.* Foreword by Julian Symons. Maidstone, UK: Sammler, 1985. 64p. As *Len Deighton: An Annotated Bibliography 1954-1985.* Santa Barbara, CA: Santa Teresa, 1988. 100p.

Not examined. The original was a limited edition distributed with a boxed set of Deighton's *Game, Set, Match* trilogy.

234. **Milward-Oliver, Edward.** *The Len Deighton Companion.* London: Grafton, 1987. 332p. Bibl.

Entries in the alphabetical main section include titles of works (including books, articles, short stories, and film versions with main credits), characters, locales, devices (e.g. Watson role, jokes), subjects (e.g. abduction, actors, children, music), intelligence agencies and organizations, espionage terms, other allusions (e.g. Checkpoint Charlie), influences (e.g. *Beat the Devil,* which inspired *The IPCRESS File;* Raymond Chandler), and persons with some Deighton connection (e.g. Michael Caine). Among the entries are selections of opening and closing lines, which the readers are challenged to identify, and a 50-question quiz. Other features include a good 15-page interview (part of which appeared in the author's Len Deighton bibliography [see above]), a chronology of first editions 1962-1987, a descriptive bibliography of Deighton's fiction and non-fiction books through 1987, and a list of characters by nationality.

Among the odd bits of information: the recently-published *Mamista!* is discussed as an abandoned novel, and *Bomber* (written in 1968-69) is claimed to be the first novel to be written on a word processor.

Though San Antonio is miscalled "a Texas border town" (page 245), the author is generally painstakingly accurate. The entries have no critical content. A critical reading and/or biography of Deighton would be of greater value, but this work serves its intended function well.

DENT, Lester

235. Cannaday, Marilyn. *Bigger Than Life: The Creator of Doc Savage.* Bowling Green, OH: Popular, 1990. 201p. Illus., bibl., index.

This is a welcome full-scale biography of the prolific writer-adventurer-treasure hunter who wrote most of the Doc Savage novels. Both main events of his life and a summary of his writings are included. There is a fine selection of photos, plus Frank Hamilton drawings of Dent and of his detective character Oscar Sail. Appended are "Doc Savage, Supreme Adventurer," a 1932 "character and plot outline, said to have been written by Street and Smith executives Henry Ralston and John Nanovic, which was the genesis of future Doc Savage stories" (pages 146-167); two Dent articles from *Writer's Digest Yearbook,* "The Pulp Paper Master Fiction Plot" and "Tag 'Em" (on character tags); and a chronological list of Dent's published fiction.

236. Farmer, Philip José. *Doc Savage: His Apocalyptic Life.* Garden City, NY: Doubleday, 1973. 226p. Illus., bibl. Corrected and expanded edition. New York: Bantam, 1975. 269p. Illus., bibl.

In a follow-up to the author's *Tarzan Alive,* which fits many of the great heroes and villains of popular fiction into the same family tree, Doc Savage is given the Sherlockian treatment. Following a chapter comparing Dent's nightmare visions to those found in the works of E.E. (Doc) Smith, Henry Miller, and William S. Burroughs, there is a chapter of Dent biography, including some critical comments on the Savage novels but only passing mention of his other mystery fiction. The rest is a biography of Doc, with a description of his milieu and profiles of his associates, mainly from evidence found in the novels. There is more Sherlockian silliness than some readers will want to tolerate, but the descriptions of the individual adventures certainly whet the appetite. Appended are a discussion of the family tree shown on the endpapers, a chronology of Doc's adventures, and a listing in the order they appeared in print. Illustrations include a map and floorplan of Doc's headquarters. The same features appear in the paperback edition with some corrections and updatings.

237. **Weinberg, Robert, ed.** *The Man Behind Doc Savage.* Oak Lawn, IL: Weinberg, 1974. 127p. Illus., bibl., index.

This handsome paperback, with a cover and interior illustrations by Frank Hamilton along with many black-and-white reproductions of book and magazine covers (mostly from the *Doc Savage* pulp), includes a biographical chapter by the editor, three essays each by knowledgeable pulp historians Will Murray (on the Doc Savage saga) and Robert Sampson (mostly on Dent's non-Doc writings), an account by Philip José Farmer of the writing of Doc's biography (see above), and a reprint of Dent's "Pulp Paper Master Fiction Plot." Two of Sampson's essays have short bibliographic checklists, but there is no full list here of the Savage novels. There are a pair of Dent's pulp short stories along with the secondary material.

DU MAURIER, Daphne

238. **Kelly, Richard.** *Daphne du Maurier.* (Twayne's English Authors Series, vol. 437.) Boston: Twayne, 1987. 156p. Illus., bibl., index.

For a writer of such enormous popularity, Du Maurier has been little written about outside of book reviews. This fine first monograph does her justice. Following the usual Twayne pattern, the only illustration is a portrait of the subject opposite the title page, and a chronology precedes a biographical chapter. Kelly then considers Du Maurier's novels chronologically, with *Rebecca* accorded a separate (and excellent) chapter. The penultimate chapter discusses the short stories. Kelly addresses screen adaptations along with their sources, offering a particularly interesting account of the differences between the book and film versions of *Rebecca*, along with some ill-advised and rejected ideas of director Alfred Hitchcock that would have made the movie still more different. In the short-story chapter, Kelly excoriates Hitch's version of "The Birds" while celebrating Nicholas Roeg's adaptation of "Don't Look Now."

Kelly mistakenly (if understandably) assumes that Beverley Nichols, who wrote about Du Maurier in a 1956 *Ladies Home Journal* article, was female.

FLEMING, Ian

239. Bennett, Tony, and Janet Woollacott. *Bond and Beyond: The Political Career of a Popular Hero.* London: Macmillan; New York: Methuen, 1987. xi, 315p. Illus., bibl., index.

Some of the topics in this often stimulating study include the economics of Bond (with much information on copies sold, film budgets, etc.); the use of Bond in advertising, toys, and other products; the "Bond" girls and changing sexual mores; political changes in the series in deference to the world market; and the earlier critical readings of Bond by Ann Boyd (see WAM #154) and Umberto Eco (see WAM #156). In the extensive discussions of the screen Bond, including a full chapter comparing the book and movie versions of *Goldfinger* and another on the making of *The Spy Who Loved Me,* they sometimes leave Bond for pages at a time to discuss other films. Since the authors are dealing here with "the Bond phenomenon" rather than just the books and films per se, the authorized pastiches of Kingsley Amis and John Gardner are treated as full-fledged Bond texts along with Fleming's.

Suggesting that American critics took hardboiled detective fiction as the point of comparison for the Bond novels, the authors over-estimate American ignorance of the spy-thriller tradition, and they show the obvious influence of such works on Fleming at unnecessary length.

The book's wealth of interesting material unfortunately is rendered in a turgid, heavily academic style. When the authors start explaining the difference between "inter-textuality" and "intertextuality," they sound almost as parodic as some of the Bond films.

The illustrations, in a book that certainly lends itself to such, amount only to three book covers. Errors include some carelessness about names (film reviewers Rex "Read" and Joel "Siegal," producer Kevin "McLory" [sometimes correctly rendered as McClory], and the publisher "Arbour" House) and an implication that the film of *Casino Royale* was a Woody

Allen product. Allen appears in the film but can hardly be called its "auteur"—and I suspect he would not want to be.

240. **Bennett, Tony, et al.** *The Making of The Spy Who Loved Me*. Milton Keynes, UK: Open U.P., 1977.

Not examined. In *Bond and Beyond* (see above), it is described as "a case-study" that "consisted of interviews with the Bond production team combined with filmed and written accounts of a number of the planning meetings where policy decisions were made . . . " (page 175).

241. **Benson, Raymond.** *The James Bond Bedside Companion*. New York: Dodd, Mead, 1984. xiii, 256p. Illus., bibl., index.

This thorough oversize volume occupies approximately the same place among the mountain of Ian Fleming sources as Sanders and Lovallo's *The Agatha Christie Companion* (see #224) among the abundance of works on their subject: a consolidation of mostly familiar information available in other sources but hitherto not in one place. Sections include a chronological overview of "The James Bond Phenomenon," a biographical remembrance of Fleming, a portrait of the character of Bond, a critical survey of the novels and short story collections about Bond (including the pastiches of Kingsley Amis and John Gardner), and a critical survey of the Bond films (through the 1983 productions of *Octopussy* and *Never Say Never Again*). Novel entries include a plot summary plus glosses of style and themes, characters, and "Highlights and Other Ingredients." Film entries include detailed summaries of production, screenplay, direction, actors and characters, and other aspects. In viewing both the novels and the films, Benson proves a refreshingly hard to please critic. His facts and opinions are equally interesting and worthy of the fan's attention, and the whole book has a meticulous and authoritative feel. Benson includes a one-page glossary of Bondian terms, acronyms, and initialisms. Appendices list other secondary sources on Bond and Fleming and book-by-book lists of Bond's weapons and injuries. An updated edition (published in 1988) was not examined.

242. **Brosnan, John.** *James Bond in the Cinema*. London: Tantivy; South Brunswick, NJ: Barnes, 1972. 176p. Illus. Second edition. San Diego: Barnes; London: Tantivy, 1981. ix, 309p. Illus.

The first edition was not examined. The following description is based on the second.

This is an entertaining summary of Bond's film career through *Moonraker* (1979), with plentiful illustrations and full credits. Many readers may find the synopses over-detailed, but it's easy to skim the plot summaries. Unlike Rubin's *The James Bond Films* (see #246), Brosnan's work devotes most of an appendix to the all-star big-money travesty *Casino Royale*, to that point the only Bond film not produced by the Albert Broccoli/Harry Saltzman team. He also refers to the forthcoming *Warhead*, to be produced by Kevin McClory with Sean Connery returning to his Bond role. (This was eventually filmed as *Never Say Never Again* and released in direct competition to a United Artists Bond starring Roger Moore.)

243. **Campbell, Iain.** *Ian Fleming: A Catalog of a Collection: A Preliminary to a Bibliography*. Liverpool, 1978. viii, 71p. Index.

As far as I know, this self-published catalog of Campbell's own collection, with some listings of significant items not in his collection, is still the closest approach to a descriptive bibliography of Fleming's works. For each of the James Bond volumes, plus Fleming's non-fiction books and the children's book *Chitty Chitty Bang Bang*, Campbell describes the first edition and (where applicable) proof and inscribed copies, source materials, anthologies and serials, book reviews, U.K. book club editions, U.K. paperbacks, foreign editions, films, film reviews, and miscellaneous. He also lists Fleming's articles and interviews, in book or periodical form; miscellaneous items with some Fleming association; parodies, pastiches, and cartoons; books with publicity quotes comparing them to Fleming (a very small selection of what must be hundreds in this category); Fleming biographies in books and periodicals; other secondary sources with some reference to Fleming or James Bond; and sources on the films. The general cut-off date is 1965 (the year of Fleming's death), but later items of importance are listed. There are separate indexes to periodical references and non-fictional names. Campbell's cutesy and complicated cataloging system includes 007 in each item number. Coverage of American editions is sparse, but this is undoubtedly a necessary item for the serious Fleming collector.

244. **Haining, Peter.** *James Bond: A Celebration.* London: Allen, 1987.

Not examined. According to Edward D. Hoch (in *The Year's Best Mystery and Suspense Stories, 1988* [see #369]), Haining discusses both the books and films about James Bond.

245. **Rubin, Steven Jay.** *The Complete James Bond Movie Encyclopedia.* Chicago: Contemporary, 1990. viii, 467p. Illus.

Entries include names of characters, performers and behind-the-scenes artists, titles, and allusions. Full credits are given for all of the films, including *Casino Royale,* not included in the author's earlier *The James Bond Films* (see below). Much of the material is adapted from the earlier source.

246. **Rubin, Steven Jay.** *The James Bond Films.* Westport, CT: Arlington, 1981. vii, 183p. Illus., index. Revised edition. Westport, CT: Arlington, 1983. vii, 183p. Illus., index.

Rubin covers the United Artists Bond movies from *Dr. No* through *For Your Eyes Only* (1981). Rubin emphasizes behind-the-scenes information rather than plot summary or critical analysis, and many of the tidbits about the production are fascinating. (For example, the dramatic account of the rush to finish Pedro Armendariz's role as Kerim Bey in *From Russia with Love* before his terminal cancer made him too sick to work.) The selection of photographs is excellent. Rubin's style lacks panache, however, and the punctuation is distractingly wrongheaded at times. Generally, he bests John Brosnan (above) in illustrations and production details while falling short in quality of writing. (I have not examined the revised edition, which, though identical in catalog description, reportedly carries the coverage through *Octopussy* and *Never Say Never Again.*)

FRANCIS, Dick

247. **Barnes, Melvyn.** *Dick Francis.* New York: Ungar, 1986. xvi, 184p. Bibl., index.

Following a brief, efficient biographical chapter, Barnes discusses all Francis' novels through *The Danger* (1983), chronologically except for the two Sid Halley novels, *Odds Against* and *Whip Hand*, which are covered together. Barnes assesses the books both as general novels and as mysteries, avoids solution giveaways (usually a question of how or why rather than who with Francis), and makes an effective (i.e., restrained) use of plot summary. Barnes generally values the more recent novels over the earlier ones and seems to like *Trial Run* best of all. Aside from some repetitiousness—we are assured more times than necessary that Francis is not just a writer of racing thrillers—Barnes has done his work thoroughly and well, making the reader want to seek out Francis' work, whether again or for the first time. The bibliography lists Francis' novels through *Break In* (1985); his short stories, anthologies, and nonfiction; and three pages of secondary sources. (Barnes is mistaken in his belief that Francis has won three Edgars. *Forfeit* and *Whip Hand* were winners, but *Reflex* wasn't even a nominee.)

248. **Davis, J. Madison.** *Dick Francis.* (Twayne's English Authors Series, vol. 464.) Boston: Twayne, 1989. 156p. Illus., bibl., index.

As the entry above shows, the author's claim in the preface that this is the "first book-length study" of his subject's writings is mistaken. But this second Francis study, covering the novels through *Bolt* (1987), is a good one that nicely complements Barnes. Following the customary chronology and biographical chapter (more detailed than in Barnes), Davis takes a topical rather than chronological approach to the novels, addressing in separate chapters Francis's central characters, his use of father-son and male-female relationships, and his villains. He also devotes a six-page postscript to the short stories, not discussed by Barnes.

Davis's division of mystery fiction into "British" and "hard-boiled" seems dubious, as does his categorization of Francis with the latter school. By his own description, Francis's formula seems to conform more to a British pattern: the Buchan or Ambler reluctant-amateur thriller. The bibliography incorporates two questionable decisions: the edition listed is usually a paperback reprint, with no indication of original date given, and the novels are listed alphabetically rather than in order of publication.

FREEMAN, R. Austin

249. Mayo, Oliver. *R. Austin Freeman: The Anthropologist at Large.* Hawthorndene, South Australia: Investigator, 1980.

Not examined. According to Robert E. Briney, writing in Albert (see #6), this biography "presents the results of Mayo's extensive research in the records of the British Colonial Service . . . [and] reflects the cooperation of Freeman's niece, and includes many previously unpublished and revealing letters. The implied thesis . . . is that . . . Dr. Thorndyke was a thinly disguised version of Freeman himself."

GABORIAU, Emile

250. Curry, Nancy E. *The Life and Works of Emile Gaboriau.* New York: Garland, 1979. 273p.

Not examined. According to E.F. Bleiler, writing in Albert (see #6), Curry's PhD thesis, "based on extensive research in France, is the only thorough study of Gaboriau in any language, with much unique information about [his] life, his books, and hitherto-unknown periodical contributions. Dr. Curry also covers the social milieu both around and within Gaboriau's novels."

GARDNER, Erle Stanley

251. Kelleher, Brian, and Diana Merrill. *The Perry Mason TV Show Book: The Complete Story of America's Favorite Television Lawyer by Two of His Greatest Fans.* New York: St. Martin's, 1987. xi, 201p. Illus., bibl.

The Mason show was probably the best (and certainly the longest running) TV series based on an established fictional sleuth, and the authors have done a good, thorough reference on the show's original 1957-1966 run. Though some of the writing is clumsy, especially early on, there is a tremendous amount of interesting information. Slightly under half the book consists of chapters on Gardner, the program's history (including reference to the earlier movie and radio incarnations, mostly unsatisfactory to Gardner), the program's regular actors (separate chapters on Raymond Burr as Mason, Barbara Hale as Della Street, William Hopper as Paul Drake, William Talman as Hamilton Burger, and the cops beginning with Ray Collins as Lt. Tragg), and the early entries in the recent series of TV movies about Mason. Then the 271 episodes are listed in chronological order of airing, with directing and writing credits, a brief plot summary with other comments (usually concerning notable performers in the guest cast), and main acting credits.

Most readers of the present book would probably have liked more on the writers of the series, whose ranks included such notable authors of print mystery fiction as Jackson Gillis, Philip MacDonald, Robert C. Dennis, Jonathan Latimer, Robert Bloomfield, William O'Farrell, Helen Nielsen, Robert Leslie Bellem, and Henry Farrell. We're told that Gardner's favorite Mason scripter was the otherwise unfamiliar Seeleg Lester. Unfortunately, there is no index, so anyone wanting to trace all the Mason credits of a particular director, writer, or actor can only browse for them. (I was positive a very famous mystery novelist had done at least one Mason script, but I missed his name first time through and didn't have the time to try again.)

GIBSON, Walter B.

252. Cox, J. Randolph. *Man of Magic and Mystery: A Guide to the Works of Walter B. Gibson*. Metuchen, NJ: Scarecrow, 1988. xxiv, 382p. Illus., bibl., index.

If Gibson had written only the Shadow novels, he would be counted as an extraordinarily prolific writer. Add to them his extensive works on magic, true crime, gambling, and occult subjects (often under pseudonyms or as a ghost writer), and you can see what a daunting task faced bibliographer Cox in attempting to account for it all. He has done a thorough job and—in the introduction's personal glimpses of Gibson in his later years, in the biographical information sprinkled throughout the "Books and Pamphlets" section, and in the extensive annotations, including brief plot summaries of all the Shadow tales in whatever format—an entertaining one.

The main body of the work is divided into six sections: "Books and Pamphlets," further subdivided by decade; "Contributions to Periodicals," the largest section, including all the Shadow novels in their original pulp appearances; "Contributions to Books and Pamphlets by Other Writers," "Syndicated Features," "Comic Books and Newspaper Strips," and "Radio Scripts and Miscellaneous Works." Appendices list all of Gibson's pseudonymous and ghostly bylines, periodicals he edited or contributed to, Shadow novels and other works published as by Maxwell Grant and written by persons other than Gibson, Shadow adaptations in other media (including credits and summaries of several feature films and serials), and secondary sources about Gibson. Cox provides a checklist of the books and pamphlets covered in the first section (187 items) and title and name indexes. Illustrations include a Frank Hamilton drawing of Gibson and the Shadow, opposite the title page, and a few reproductions of books and magazine covers.

GOULD, Chester

253. **Maeder, Jay.** *Dick Tracy: The Official Biography.* New York: Plume, 1990. v, 218p. Illus., index.

Warren Beatty's Dick Tracy film brought forth numerous tie-in books, among the most enjoyable this combined biography of the character Tracy and his creator Chester Gould. The account is extensively illustrated with examples from the strip, some in color. For this reader at least, the material on Gould and his successors as artists and writers of the Tracy strip held more interest than the plot summaries, however entertainingly presented.

GREEN, Anna Katharine

254. **Maida, Patricia D.** *Mother of Detective Fiction: The Life and Works of Anna Katharine Green.* Bowling Green, OH: Popular, 1989. 120p. Illus., bibl., index.

Among the greats of detective fiction, the author of *The Leavenworth Case* (1878) has been underappreciated—this is the first book-length study of her work. Maida does an excellent job of setting Green in the context of her times and conveying the value of her writings as social history, without downplaying her gifts for storytelling, puzzle-spinning, and characterization. The biographical chapter presents many details of Green's life not previously encountered. Separate chapters deal with the subject's non-mystery writings, religious convictions, and views of women's rights and roles. Maida includes eight pages of notes plus a three-page primary and secondary bibliography.

HAMMETT, Dashiell

255. **Dooley, Dennis.** *Dashiell Hammett.* New York: Ungar, 1985. xv, 174p. Bibl., index.

This capably written critical volume may seem rather superfluous given all the other Hammett studies on the market. Its main distinguishing feature is its emphasis on the short stories, consideration of which fills about half the book. Though generally reliable, Dooley commits a few careless errors, including a reference to "Edward" Lockridge's Mr. and Mrs. North; an astonishing misstatement that Willard Huntington Wright was killed in a 1933 car crash; and a claim that in the film of *The Maltese Falcon,* Sam Spade tells secretary Effie the falcon is "the stuff that dreams are made of." He actually makes the statement to Detective Tom Polhaus.

256. **Gregory, Sinda.** *Private Investigations: The Novels of Dashiell Hammett.* Carbondale: Southern Illinois U.P., 1985. xiv, 205p. Bibl., index.

An opening chapter discussing Hammett's life and contrasting the traditions of classical and hardboiled detective fiction is followed by a long chapter on each of the five full-length Hammett novels. A short concluding summary precedes fifteen pages of notes, a three-page primary and secondary bibliography, and an index. Gregory's is one of the best critical studies of Hammett's fiction. She offers the kind of real insights that make a reader want to rush back to the less highly regarded *Red Harvest* and *The Dain Curse* for a rereading. (She even made me want to reconsider *The Thin Man,* a book I thought his weakest.) And she explicates Hammett's themes without ignoring his novels as detective stories, with attention to their use of clues and devices drawn from the classical and pulp schools. She also avoids the frequent analyst's error of ignoring Hammett's peers, citing Paul Cain, Jonathan Latimer, Raoul Whitfield, Carroll John Daly, and even as obscure a figure as J.J. Des Ormeaux. Francis M. Nevins, Jr. contributes an illuminating foreword.

257. **Herron, Don.** *Dashiell Hammett Tour.* (Herron's Literary Walks in San Francisco, #1.) San Francisco: Dawn Heron, 1982. 95p. Illus., bibl.

Following a good 11-page biographical chapter, Herron takes the reader on a splendidly worked-out tour, with numerous street maps showing the locations and a mix of historical and contemporary photos of the various sites. As an example of the interesting insights afforded by the guide, Herron points out that all the hotels in *The Maltese Falcon* appear under false names but all the restaurants Sam Spade eats in (some of which still survived in 1982) appear under their real names, with the implication former adman Hammett got some free meals out of the deal. There is a good annotated bibliography, not of critical sources on Hammett but of items providing information for the tour. (In a rare miscue, Herron misspells Nathanael West's first name "Nathaniel," an easy mistake to make—I'm grateful to an anonymous copy editor who once saved me from it.)

258. **Johnson, Diane.** *Dashiell Hammett: A Life.* New York: Random, 1983. xxi, 344p. Illus., bibl. index.

This was the last of a trio of major Hammett biographies published in the early 1980s and, because of the author's reputation as a novelist and the blessing of Hammett's executor Lillian Hellman in giving her free access to the subject's papers, perhaps the most eagerly anticipated. Though Johnson mines her source material for some interesting quotes and insights, the "official" biography is ultimately disappointing. There is a certain sketchiness and vagueness, an occasional lack of clarity. Johnson sometimes seems to be going from one clipping to another in desultory fashion. Editing is sloppy: on page 54, Johnson introduces a quote as "a high-minded essay on style for *Western Advertising*," then says on the next page following the long quotation, "This appeared in a magazine called *Western Advertising* in 1926." There are careless errors: Ben Ray Redman was not a *Black Mask* writer; *Ellery Queen's Mystery Magazine* did not absorb *Black Mask* in 1941; and the *Wind Over Wisconsin* Hammett read in jail was presumably by August Derleth, not someone named "Cerletti." For a full account of Hammett, readers need this book along with the others, but Layman and Nolan (see the next two entries) essentially did better jobs, presumably because they had more rapport with Hammett's hardboiled milieu and thus more knowledge of the context of his work.

259. Layman, Richard. *Shadow Man: The Life of Dashiell Hammett.* New York: Harcourt Brace Jovanovich/Bruccoli Clark, 1981. xviii, 285p. Illus., bibl., index.

Since Layman was denied any access to the Hammett papers controlled by Lillian Hellman, this first of the full-scale Hammett biographies is undeniably sparse on information in some areas. But it is a highly responsible, well-documented, and painstaking job, most notable for its critical summaries of the subject's work. It offers an especially interesting account of Hammett's early work for *Smart Set*. In contrast to Johnson (see above), Layman devotes more than half the book to the period of Hammett's major productivity as a writer, covering his life from 1934 to his death in less than a hundred pages.

260. Nolan, William F. *Hammett: A Life at the Edge.* New York: Congdon & Weed, 1983. xiv, 276p. Illus., bibl, index.

The author of the first book-length Hammett study, *Dashiell Hammett: A Casebook* (see WAM #179), weighs in with his contribution to the biography stakes, intended as a "more personal" approach than Richard Layman's (see above). Nolan offers more information than other sources on the comic strip "Secret Agent X-9," more on Hammett's post-*Thin Man* writing and his influence on Hellman's plays, and more credit to Ellery Queen as reprinter of Hammett's pulp work. Stronger on anecdote than literary criticism, the book is very readable but still left room for the definitive biography, which Diane Johnson's authorized volume (see #258) unfortunately would not provide.

261. Symons, Julian. *Dashiell Hammett.* (HBJ Album Biographies.) San Diego: Harcourt, Brace, Jovanovich, 1985. xiii, 178p. Illus., bibl., index.

The first book-length Hammett study by a British critic is both extensively illustrated and, as would be expected from its author, beautifully written. Since Hammett's biography has been treated at greater length by Richard Layman (see #259), William F. Nolan (see above), and Diane Johnson (see #258), it's just as well that Symons's emphasis is more critical than biographical. Symons manages to discuss the novels without the tedious plot summaries that shackle some critical studies.

In comparing the novel and film versions of *The Maltese Falcon,* Symons gives John Huston's adaptation too little credit for staying true to Hammett in the censorious Hollywood of the early forties. He states, "Wilmer is no longer Gutman's boy. Cairo is a primping popinjay but not an obvious homosexual . . . " (page 131). On the contrary, the nature of the trio can be read between the lines as surely as the heterosexual innuendo of Bogart and Bacall's racetrack dialogue in *The Big Sleep.*

HILLERMAN, Tony

262. Erisman, Fred. *Tony Hillerman.* (Boise State University Western Writers Series, No. 87.) Boise, Idaho: Boise State University, 1989. 51p. Bibl.

Following an identification of Hillerman as a "local color" novelist and a biographical summary with some interesting details (he once wrote radio commercials for Purina Pig Chow), Erisman devotes several pages to his subject's generally undervalued non-fiction writings before discussing his fiction, including the non-series *The Fly on the Wall* (1971), the juvenile *The Boy Who Made Dragonfly* (1972), and all the Joe Leaphorn and/or Jim Chee novels through *A Thief of Time* (1988). One might carp that solutions are revealed too freely, but otherwise this first Hillerman monograph is a well-written and valuable critical summary. A primary and secondary bibliography is included.

263. **Hieb, Louis A.** *Tony Hillerman—A Bibliography*. Tucson: Press of the Giant Hound, 1990. 88p. Illus.

This handsomely produced limited edition is a descriptive bibliography of advance proofs, American and British first editions of Hillerman's books, fiction and non-fiction, through *Talking God* (1989). Reprint editions, Hillerman's short works, and secondary sources are also listed. The only illustrations are covers of proof copies.

264. **Hillerman, Tony.** ***Words, Weather, and Wolfmen: Conversations with Tony Hillerman***. Ed. Ernie Bulow. Art by Ernest Franklin. Gallup, NM: Southwesterner, 1989. xii, 124p. Illus. **Revised as Tony Hillerman and Ernie Bulow,** *Talking Mysteries: A Conversation with Tony Hillerman*. Albuquerque: U. of New Mexico P., 1991. 135p. Illus., bibl.

The original edition was limited to 400 copies, but its revised version, on which the following description is based, has been distributed much more widely. Though it is a thin book, even briefer in text than the pagination would suggest, it tells a great deal about Hillerman and his writing technique.

The opening essay by Bulow surprises the reader with a bluntly negative critique of Hillerman's first novel, *The Blessing Way*, for its distortion of Navajo culture among other problems, and goes on to charge later (and better) Hillerman novels with continuing to make cultural errors. (In a footnote, Hillerman mildly refutes some of the errors charged but agrees with Bulow's low opinion of *The Blessing Way*.) There follow a piece by Hillerman on his life and work, citing the influence of Arthur W. Upfield as well as such writers as Ambler, Chandler, and Greene. In the longest section, Bulow interviews Hillerman, repeating some of the information in the essay but offering a detailed discussion of his writing technique, including some depth on *A Thief of Time* and plotting problems on *Talking God,* the novel in progress when the interview took place. Also included are the Jim Chee short story "The Witch, Yazzie, and the Nine of Clubs"; biographies of the authors and illustrator Franklin; and a 12-page section of uncaptioned Franklin drawings illustrating Hillerman's work. Scattered through the text are several photos of Hillerman and one each of Bulow and Franklin.

HIMES, Chester

265. Lundquist, James. *Chester Himes.* New York: Ungar, 1976. ix, 166p. Bibl., index.

Not examined. Per Muller (see below), it is a "[s]urvey of Himes's life and career, providing detailed summaries of early novels and perceptive treatment of the detective fiction" (page 132).

266. Muller, Gilbert H. *Chester Himes.* (Twayne's United States Authors Series 553.) Boston: Twayne, 1989. xv, 138p. Illus., bibl., index.

Muller begins with a telling observation credited to Ralph Ellison: "that American readers reject serious fiction until its time has passed and it has lost its cutting edge" (page ix). The author over-estimates (I hope) Himes's unknownness as an American literary figure, but he has produced one of several excellent studies of a writer who seems to bring out the best in critics. Following a biographical chapter, Muller considers all of his subject's output, with one chapter devoted to the Harlem detective stories and another to the unfinished final entry in the Grave Digger-Coffin Ed series, "Plan B," published only in French and not considered in Skinner's volume of the same year (see below). Muller disagrees with Skinner about Himes's knowledge of detective fiction before he started writing it, saying Himes "had read crime and detective fiction since his days as a young convict" and was a subscriber to *Black Mask* (page 80). As with Skinner, the only illustration is a smiling frontispiece portrait of the subject, a different one but displaying a cheerfulness equally incongruous considering the anger and bitterness of Himes.

267. Skinner, Robert E. *Two Guns from Harlem: The Detective Fiction of Chester Himes*. Bowling Green, OH: Popular, 1989. 190p. Illus., bibl., index.

This is unique among Himes studies in its concentration on the eight Harlem detective stories about Coffin Ed and Grave Digger, with only passing reference to Himes's other novels. The biographical first chapter is very well done, pointing up the painful irony of a writer having to take jobs like porter, janitor, and bellhop to make ends meet while producing periodical and book-length fiction for prestigious markets. After a series of topical chapters (profiling the two sleuths, describing the Harlem background, and discussing the use of color as a determinant of character), Skinner presents an exhaustive book-by-book account with much plot summary, identification of themes and techniques, and perceptive critical evaluation. There are three pages of notes but a bibliography that lists only the eight novels under discussion, those not in first edition but in the reprint editions used by the author.

It's surprising that Skinner, a widely-published detective fiction critic (see #55 and 119), should find it necessary to sneer at the genre in the course of praising his subject. He is too negative about '50s hardboiled fiction, not choosing to mention that the first black private eye, created by white writer Ed Lacy, debuted in that decade. He takes a cheap shot at Richard S. Prather as a writer of "hack work" (page 2). And while mystery critic Marvin Lachman might be amused to be called a member of the "white literary establishment," it is surely unnecessary to accuse him of "unrealized prejudice" (page 2) because he happens to disagree with Skinner about Himes's work.

There are scattered errors, including a reference to Edgar "Allen" Poe. And Skinner is mistaken about the order of American publication of some of his subject's works. *Cotton Comes to Harlem*, though published in France after *The Heat's On*, was in fact the first Himes detective novel to appear in American hardcover.

HOCH, Edward D.

268. **Moffatt, June M., and Francis M. Nevins, Jr., compilers.** *Edward D. Hoch Bibliography 1955-1991*. Introduction by Marvin Lachman. Pasadena, CA: BoucherCon .22, 1991. xii, 112p.

Here is a meticulously prepared and most valuable bibliographic guide to the work of the mystery genre's most prolific writer of short stories. Following a four-page overview by Lachman, an abbreviation guide describes all 24 of Hoch's series in chronological order of first appearance, usually giving the total number of stories in the series to date. (Captain Leopold is the leader with 87 appearances, followed by Nick Velvet with 64, Simon Ark with 48, and Dr. Sam Hawthorne with 43.) The bibliography proper includes sections on Hoch's novels, short story collections (including lists of contents with original magazine sources), and anthologies edited (noting stories by Hoch included); short stories as by Hoch, arranged by source periodical and date (including series designation and appearances in reprint where appropriate), followed by a chronological list of stories not from magazines; short stories published under pseudonyms (Anthony Circus, Stephen Dentinger, R.L. Stevens, Mr. X, Pat McMahon, Irwin Booth) with the same arrangement under each; ghost-written material as Ellery Queen (one novel and one short story); contest novels under pseudonyms; non-fiction (by byline); stories on audio tape; film adaptations; and finally chronological lists by series character (with, conveniently, reprint information repeated from the earlier sections).

HORLER, Sydney

269. **Horler, Sydney.** *Excitement: An Impudent Autobiography.* London: Hutchinson, 1934.

Not examined. I had no idea this autobiography existed until I read the reviews quoted in the work following.

270. **Horler, Sydney.** *Strictly Personal: An Informal Diary.* London: Hutchinson, n.d. [1934]. 287p. Illus., index.

According to the foreword, this publication of the author's diary of September 1933 to February 1934 (years unspecified but divined from internal evidence) sprang from his frustration at having his letters to the editor so frequently rejected. This is as unpleasant a work as you might expect from its homophobic, racist, anti-Semitic, anti-feminist, and hideously reactionary author, but there's no denying the fascination of its comments on the films, sports, politics, literature, and issues of the day. Horler vents his outrage at the BBC's hiring of a female announcer, fills in his readers on his servant problems, grouses about the lack of thank-you letters from recipients of his Christmas presents, quotes the laudatory notices of his autobiography *Excitement* (see above), touches on collecting detective fiction, and expresses his opinions of many of his fellow crime and thriller writers: he is unimpressed with Sherlock Holmes; finds A.E.W. Mason "the greatest living writer of mystery-adventure fiction" (page 168); is bewildered by John Dickson Carr and bored by E. Phillips Oppenheim, but writes favorably of Edgar Wallace and Valentine Williams. He also shows us his letter to Dorothy L. Sayers deploring her bad review of a novel by Francis Beeding. Generally disparaging of critics, he believes for one author to review another's book is simply not cricket. The sole illustration is a frontispiece caricature of the author.

271. Horler, Sydney. *More Strictly Personal: Six Months in My Life.* London: Rich & Cowan, 1935. 273p.

This is more of the same, beginning with quotes of reader comments and reviews of *Strictly Personal*. The dates this time are explicit, the diary covering June 21, 1934, through February 4, 1935. There are fewer comments on other mystery or thriller writers, but some revelations surface: Horler much preferred S.S. Van Dine to Dashiell Hammett and found the gathering-of-the-suspects finale of the film *The Thin Man* a Van Dine rip-off; though he acquired Edgar Wallace's desk, chair, Dictaphone, and secretary, he denies claiming to be Wallace's successor ("The distinction has been thrust upon me" [page 5]); and he includes Dornford Yates (along with Aldous Huxley, Jeffrey Farnol, and others) on "a list of novelists whose work I cordially dislike" (page 201).

INNES, Michael (John Innes MacKintosh Stewart)

272. Scheper, George L. *Michael Innes.* New York: Ungar, 1986. xv, 224p. Bibl., index.

The first book-length study of Innes is an excellent appreciation of one of detective fiction's longest and most productive careers. Scheper values Innes's books both for their general literary virtues and for the ingenious use of detective story/thriller conventions. Following a good biographical chapter, Scheper covers the first three John Appleby novels together before treating the subsequent books in four categories: thrillers, academic novels, art mysteries, and country-house stories. Scheper seems to like all of Innes but has some of his highest praise (perhaps surprisingly) for *Stop Press* (1939; U.S. title *The Spider Strikes*), which he calls "his most ambitious novel and arguably the best country-house mystery ever written" (page 155). The author makes a frequent and serious misuse of the term "sealed-room," using it when he really means "closed-circle." Solution giveaways are constant, as the author warns at the outset, claiming that with Innes it doesn't matter much. Scheper may lose fans of Raymond Chandler (among others) almost immediately with his first-page claim that his subject is universally regarded as "far and away the finest writer among the practitioners of detective fiction." The claim may well be true, but surely it would at least produce a lively argument.

273. **Stewart, J(ohn) I(nnes) M(ackintosh).** *Myself and Michael Innes: A Memoir.* New York: Norton, 1988. 206p. Illus., index.

This is accurately called a memoir rather than a full-scale autobiography. In some ways a patchwork job, it interpolates a radio play and a short story to fill out the pages. As would be expected from the author, however, it includes some beautiful English prose. Some of the most interesting material concerns the life of an Oxford student and a visiting university professor in Australia between the world wars. There are anecdotes about major literary figures—F.R. Leavis, T.S. Eliot, Joyce Cary—but none about mystery fiction figures save (glancingly) Simenon. However, Stewart devotes more pages to discussing his Michael Innes detective fiction than the mainstream novels published under his own name, and the discussions include some interesting self-criticism, notably of The Secret Vanguard and *Hare Sitting Up*. He identifies *The Journeying Boy* as "to my mind the best of the Michael Innes stories" (page 27) and discusses it at considerable length. A separate essay on detective fiction (pages 175-183) discusses Doyle, Christie, and the ethics of clue-planting. (His comments on *The Murder of Roger Ackroyd* stop short of giving away the solution, but he talks and quotes around it rather cleverly.)

JAMES, P.D.

274. **Gidez, Richard B.** *P.D. James.* (Twayne's English Authors Series, vol. 430.) Boston: Twayne, 1986. 153p. Illus., bibl., index.

While sharing with Norma Siebenheller's earlier study (see below) an over-emphasis on plot summary and a determination to reveal every solution with or without a good reason, Gidez's work has several advantages over its predecessor. It gives full coverage to James's short stories and considers the author's output through *The Skull Beneath the Skin* (1982). Its bibliography is more thorough, both on primary and secondary sources. Gidez presents slightly more biographical information, including the standard Twayne chronology. He also does a better job of putting his subject in the context of detective fiction history, even if he overstates his case in claiming that the classical detective novel has been "long dominated by women" (page 7)—what of Queen, Carr, Crispin, Blake, Innes, Berkeley, Freeman, Crofts, Van Dine, Stout, Philip MacDonald, Kemelman, and quite a few others?

On the whole, Gidez does a good, efficient, if not especially exciting job. Aside from the introduction and conclusion and a separate chapter on the short stories, the novels are treated chronologically with a chapter devoted to each. Gidez values *Death of an Expert Witness* most highly and gives very unfavorable notices to the mainstream bestseller *Innocent Blood* and to *Unnatural Causes,* discussed as a parody of classical detective fiction, as is *The Skull Beneath the Skin.*

275. **Siebenheller, Norma.** *P.D. James.* New York: Ungar, 1981. x, 154p. Bibl., index.

The first full-length critical study of James begins with a brief and somewhat unpromising overview chapter: in championing her subject's importance, the author denigrates earlier women puzzle-makers more than necessary and proves overly prone to generalizations, especially about the American detective story. Approximately the first half of the book offers a chronological survey (including somewhat excessive plot summary) of the novels through *Innocent Blood* (1980), of which the author makes the truly fatuous statement, "One cannot savor the unsavory" (page 72). The reader is warned at the outset that no attempt will be

made to avoid solution giveaways. Things begin to look up in the second
half of the book, with good chapters profiling series sleuths Adam
Dalgliesh and Cordelia Gray followed by a topical treatment of James's
themes, secondary characters, and style. Siebenheller decries James's
distasteful treatment of women: aside from Cordelia and Dalgliesh's Aunt
Jane, almost all the other women are "fussy, neurotic, sadistic, simple,
scheming, or evil. They are, on the whole, a depressing lot" (page 128).
The author makes some interesting points in support of her implication
that James dislikes women, but she may be unfair in assuming Dalgliesh's
views necessarily are shared by his creator.

In summary, this is a good, thorough job, better overall than the early
chapters might lead one to expect. A valuable feature of the bibliography
is a listing of selected reviews of James's novels, all from general review
media rather than specialized mystery publications.

KEENE, Carolyn (Harriet Stratemeyer Adams, et al.)

276. **Farah, David.** *Farah's Guide to the Nancy Drew Mystery Series*.
Grand Blanc, MI, 1985. 224p. Second printing. Grand Blanc, MI, 1987.

Not examined. Of the second printing (actually "an extensively
revised second edition"), Walter Albert writes (*The Armchair Detective*,
v. 24, n. 3, p. 328), "Farah's bibliography of the Nancy Drew series is a
mammoth undertaking, accomplished with bibliographic economy and
clarity. One of the few essential juvenile series reference books."

LE CARRÉ, John (David John Moore Cornwell)

277. **Barley, Tony.** *Taking Sides: The Fiction of John le Carré*. Milton
Keynes, UK, and Philadelphia: Open U.P., 1986. vii, 175p. Bibl., index.

Concentrating his attention on his subject's "political and psychological materials" (page 2), Barley discusses le Carré's relationship to the
spy/thriller genre, then devotes a separate chapter to each novel from *The
Spy Who Came in from the Cold* to *The Little Drummer Girl*, with the
exception of the non-espionage experiment *The Naive and Sentimental
Lover*, which is mentioned only in passing. The first two novels, *Call for*

the Dead and *A Murder of Quality* are seen as "more akin to the classic English detective story than to the spy-thriller" (page 3). Though some have called le Carré an ideologue, Barley finds his novels draw much of their interest from the lack of a clear or consistent political position. Barley analyzes the neurotic George Smiley in Freudian terms and confronts the critical barbs hurled at *The Honourable Schoolboy* by Clive James and others, drawing a comparison of that novel with Graham Greene's Vietnam novel *The Quiet America,* to which le Carré's book responds. This is a substantial if somewhat stodgily written study.

278. **Bloom, Harold, ed.** *John le Carré.* (Modern Critical Views series.) New York: Chelsea, 1987. viii, 180p. Bibl., index.

Eleven essays are gathered in this stimulating collection, all but one previously published in books or periodicals, constituting what editor Bloom calls "the best criticism available" on le Carré's work. Bloom's own introduction considers *The Perfect Spy* and *The Little Drummer Girl* and does not seem overly impressed, finding le Carré too reminiscent of Greene and Conrad and taking offense at his pro-Palestinian stance. Contributors include Stefan Kanfer (a *Time* review of *The Honourable Schoolboy*), Andrew Rutherford (an overview article from his 1978 book *The Literature of War*), LeRoy Panek (the le Carré chapter from *The Special Branch* [see #159]), Abraham Rothberg (on the character of George Smiley in *Call for the Dead, Tinker, Tailor, Soldier, Spy,* and *Smiley's People*), Holly Beth King (on *Tinker, Tailor . . .*), Helen S. Garson (on *Call for the Dead*), Glenn W. Most (on le Carré as detective novelist, from *The Poetics of Murder* [see #156]), Lars Ole Sauerberg (on Britain's relations with America and Germany, from his *Secret Agents in Fiction* [see #115]), William F. Buckley, Jr. (a *New York Times Book Review* notice of *The Little Drummer Girl*), David Monaghan (on le Carré's metaphors, from his *The Novels of John le Carré* [see #281]), and Susan Laity (an original article on *A Perfect Spy*). A chronology of the subject's life and a secondary bibliography are appended.

279. **Homburger, Eric.** *John le Carré.* (Contemporary Writers.) London and New York: Methuen, 1986. 112p. Bibl.

In the course of discussing the packaging of bestsellers, which one hopes is not quite as cynical and non-author-driven as he thinks, at least on the fiction side, Homburger calls his subject "one of the few writers in England today who is 'popular' and 'serious'" (page 13). Following a short biography and some spy-fiction history (giving more attention to his subject's forbearers than one might expect in such a short book), the author discusses the novels through *A Perfect Spy*, giving more attention to *The Naive and Sentimental Lover* than most of le Carré's critics. This is an adequate short introduction, if slight and superficial in comparison with works of writers like Barley (see #277) and Lewis (see below). Homburger makes one notably silly statement: that the title of *The Quest for Karla* "denies the trilogy full seriousness" (page 88). Three long novels can lose their seriousness because they are given a bad overall title?

280. Lewis, Peter. *John le Carré.* New York: Ungar, 1985. 228p. Bibl., index.

The first book on George Smiley's creator is an excellent work of genuine literary criticism, offering a clear and careful cataloging of le Carré's themes and attitudes, his techniques of plotting and character-building, his symbols and allusions. Not every reader will want or enjoy this deep a probing, but few who persevere will feel their time has been wasted. Lewis frequently quotes other critics' views tellingly. The book devotes a chapter to each of the novels through *The Little Drummer Girl* (1983) with the exception of *The Naive and Sentimental Lover*, a non-mystery or spy novel that is accorded three pages of analysis. Lewis's book won the Mystery Writers of America Edgar award for best biographical or critical volume of 1985.

281. Monaghan, David. *The Novels of John Le Carré.* Oxford and New York: Blackwell, 1985. xv, 207p. Bibl., index.

Taking a topical approach, Monaghan gives full-chapter consideration only to *The Little Drummer Girl,* the most recent le Carré novel at the time of the book's publication. Following an introduction that serves as a bibliographic essay on previous secondary sources as well as a summary of what is to come, the author devotes chapters to le Carré's "dualistic vision of experience," his use of locale descriptions as metaphor, and his place in the spy novel tradition, including such extended discussions of Joseph Conrad's *The Secret Agent* and several novels by Graham Greene that the book seems to be as much about them as le Carré. Pointing to some dark aspects in the works of Buchan, Oppenheim, and LeQueux, Monaghan gives these traditional spy writers more credit than most for influencing le Carré.

Department of mistaken prophecy: "There can be little doubt that *Smiley's People* brings to an end the cycle of George Smiley novels" (page 123).

282. **Monaghan, David.** *Smiley's Circus.* London: Orbis; New York: St. Martin's, 1986. 207p. Illus., bibl., index.

In a Sherlockian-type guide to le Carré's fictional intelligence organization, Monaghan begins with a chapter on its history from 1918 to 1978, with plot summary and/or reference to the seven "Circus" novels through *Smiley's People;* chronologies of five major Circus operations (with discussion of the dating process); a hierarchy of the Circus; a description of its headquarters; and the largest section, called a "Who's Who" but including intelligence organizations, jargon terms, places, and other allusions along with characters from the novels. Illustrations include maps and photos of various locales.

This is one of those books that overwhelm the reader with the amount of labor that must have gone into them—and given the large casts and sometimes staggeringly complicated nature of le Carré's works, it might actually be a useful reference to have at hand while reading some of the novels. (I'll certainly have it at my elbow if I ever give *The Honourable Schoolboy* another try.)

283. **Wolfe, Peter.** *Corridors of Deceit: The World of John le Carré.* Bowling Green, OH: Popular, 1987. 275p.

His previous studies of Hammett (see WAM #180), Chandler (see #211), and Ross Macdonald (see WAM #193) have established Wolfe as one of the premier academic critics of mystery and detective fiction, a writer who seems equally at home in genre fiction and the wider world of literature. His le Carré study confirms that status. Beginning with several topical chapters—covering such subjects as le Carré's "tendency to disrupt and thus disallow narrative flow" (page 34), a practice as French as his pseudonym; his religious imagery and school-days allusions; and a portrait of George Smiley—Wolfe devotes a full and very detailed chapter to each novel through *The Little Drummer Girl,* including the non-espionage work *The Naive and Sentimental Lover.* He pronounces the very difficult *The Honourable Schoolboy* "le Carré's most ambitious and perhaps best book" (page 227).

There are notes but no bibliography. Given the range of topics Wolfe explores, the book badly needs an index.

LE FANU, Sheridan

284. **Begnal, Michael H.** *Joseph Sheridan Le Fanu.* (Irish Writers Series.) Lewisberg: Bucknell U.P., 1971. 87p. Bibl.

This good compact bio-critical introduction prizes Le Fanu's psychological insight and understanding of women but makes only mild claims for him: "Though it would be a bit exuberant to call for a revival of Le Fanu, several of his novels certainly merit a reprinting . . . " (page 82). They have since received it.

285. **McCormack, W. J.** *Sheridan Le Fanu and Victorian Ireland.* Oxford: Clarendon, 1980. xi, 310p. Illus., bibl., index.

The standard Le Fanu biography is concerned, as the title suggests, with putting its subject, the son of a Protestant clergyman and an anti-Catholic activist, in the context of Irish society, religion, and politics. McCormick's work shows how much literary biographers can glean from preserved correspondence—and suggests how little such intimate details will be available to future biographers with subjects living in our own telephonic, non-letter-writing age. Of Le Fanu's works, greatest attention is paid to *Uncle Silas,* subject of a 47-page chapter. In an appendix, McCormack does some interesting detective work, attributing to Le Fanu the anonymous magazine serial *Loved and Lost* and speculating on the authorship of a pseudonymous novel, *My Own Story.* A good selection of illustrations appears, untypically, at the very end of the book.

286. **Melada, Ivan.** *Sheridan Le Fanu.* (Twayne's English Authors Series, vol. 438.) Boston: Twayne, 1987. 142p. Illus., bibl., index.

Adhering to the reliable Twayne pattern, Melada follows a chapter of biography with a chronological consideration of his subject's novels, and finishes with several pages of notes, a primary bibliography, and an annotated secondary bibliography. The famous *Uncle Silas* is accorded a separate chapter. In a chapter on suspense novels, four are grouped as "Novels of Mystery": *Wylder's Hand, Guy Deverell, All in the Dark,* and *The Evil Guest.* Le Fanu is shown as an early cannibalizer, turning short stories and novelettes into three-decker novels, not always advisedly.

LEONARD, Elmore

287. **Geherin, David.** *Elmore Leonard.* New York: Continuum, 1989. xiii, 158p. Illus., bibl., index.

The first book-length study of the author Geherin considers "America's greatest living crime writer" (an arguable statement) is thorough, well-written, efficiently organized, and most valuable. Following a three-page chronology and a biographical chapter, Geherin discusses his subject's early western fiction in the 1950s, his transition from westerns to crime novels in the '60s, and (in greater depth) his "fifteen major crime novels" from *Fifty-Two Pickup* (1974) to *Freaky Deaky* (1988). The final chapter is an excellent analysis of Leonard's technique and the reasons for his success.

Identified as major influences are the works of Hemingway and George V. Higgins's 1972 novel *The Friends of Eddie Coyle.* One quote from *Time* writer R.Z. Sheppard expresses what is for some the downside of Leonard's work: his "eerie ability to get inside empty heads" (page 107).

LEVINSON, Richard, and William Link

288. **Dawudziak, Mark.** *The Columbo Phile: A Casebook.* New York: Mysterious, 1989. xiv, 353p. Illus., bibl., index.

If you share my conviction that Columbo, whose original run spanned 45 cases between 1968 and 1978 and who has recently been revived, is the greatest of television detectives, you will be enthralled by this detailed record of the raincoat-wearing Los Angeles police lieutenant's career. For each of the first 45 programs, Dawudziak provides original air date, complete credits, a plot synopsis (including in these usually inverted mysteries the key clues to the solution), and a critical assessment, usually with some behind-the-scenes details of the production. Interviews with creators Richard Levinson and William Link, star Peter Falk, and many of the other writers, producers, directors, and actors involved in the program help provide an insider's view.

289. Levinson, Richard, and William Link. *Stay Tuned: An Inside Look at the Making of Prime Time Television.* New York: St. Martin's, 1981. xvi, 253p. Index.

Though Levinson and Link, a team first formed in junior high school, made their professional debut with an *Ellery Queen's Mystery Magazine* first story and later contributed to *Alfred Hitchcock's Mystery Magazine,* they made their greatest mark as TV writer-producers, not always but perhaps most prominently in the crime-mystery genre. Their book is an autobiography only in a professional sense—one never has a chance to tell Levinson from Link. Essentially it's a fascinating and sometimes depressing account of how network TV operates. The description of the pressures on writer-producers causes amazement that *Columbo* ever made it at all in the form it did: no action (in the car chase or menace-in-the-parking-garage sense), a main character who arrives late and experiences no romance, no "family" of continuing characters aside from a raincoat, car, basset hound, and never-seen wife. Principal genre-related content is the 26-page *Columbo* chapter, but there are also comments on the *Mannix* and *Ellery Queen* series and many other mystery references throughout, most of them not indexed. The one irritant of this informative and insightful account is the authors' aversion to specifying dates.

MCBAIN, Ed (Evan Hunter)

290. **Dove, George N.** *The Boys from Grover Avenue: Ed McBain's 87th Precinct Novels.* Bowling Green, OH: Popular, 1985. 166p. Bibl., index.

The author of the first book length study of the police procedural novel (see #74) here offers a readable and welcome treatment of the longest-running and possibly best procedural series of them all. Taking a topical approach, Dove first describes the "Imaginary City" of the novels (obviously based on New York), then discusses the time frame of the books, including the way in which the characters age at different rates. (Meyer Meyer, for example, ages not at all, staying 37 throughout the series.) These early chapters may lose some readers with limited tolerance of Sherlockian-style nitpicking. More diverting, though, are chapters on the series' use of procedure, the relationships of the cops with the public and the criminals they seek, thumbnail sketches of the major and minor recurring characters, and a discussion of McBain's distinctive style. In appendices, Dove presents a checklist of the novels, 1956-1983; some questions and answers about the "Imaginary City"; a description of the Precinct Station House; a chronology of the cases, not always the same as the order published; crime statistics of the 87th; and lists of police injuries and deaths. There are five pages of notes and a one-page index.

MACDONALD, John D.

291. **Brogan, John.** *The Official Travis McGee Quiz Book.* Introduction by John D. MacDonald. New York: Fawcett Gold Medal, 1984. 114p.

There are thirty quizzes, all multiple choice, divided into three categories: "Apprentice Detective," "Super Sleuth," and "Salvage Expert." The degree of difficulty increases appropriately. There is fun to be had here for the devoted McGee fan, but neither the quizzes nor the subject's good-natured introduction have any real reference or scholarly value.

292. **Geherin, David.** *John D. MacDonald.* New York: Ungar, 1982. ix, 202p. Bibl., index.

This is the first book-length critical study of MacDonald. Following a brief biographical chapter, Geherin devotes a mere 31 pages to his subject's pulp apprenticeship and non-series novels. Chapters three through seven, the major portion of the book, are devoted to a title-by-title discussion of the Travis McGee series and a delineation of McGee's character. Whether the emphasis on McGee is justified is arguable, but the volume does an excellent job of presenting MacDonald's strengths and weaknesses as a novelist and pinpointing his place in contemporary American literature. Geherin chooses exemplary quotes with particular effectiveness. As is so often the case with critical volumes in the genre, the use of plot summary sometimes seems a bit excessive.

293. **Hirshberg, Edgar W.** *John D. MacDonald.* (Twayne's United States Authors Series, vol. 486.) Boston: Twayne, 1985. 132p. Illus., bibl., index.

Though it has many of the attributes expected from the generally reliable Twayne series—the biographical chapter, based on interviews with JDM, is probably the most extensive yet published—the critical content of this second book-length study is somewhat disappointing, with many of the comments superficial and/or obvious and far too much repetitiousness and tangent-chasing for such a short book. In his preface, Hirshberg says of the MacDonald canon, "less than half his work properly belongs in the field of mystery and suspense," a view that embodies an excessively narrow definition of the field. Trying to defend this highly doubtful proposition, even claiming the Travis McGee series "defies classification in this or any other specific category" (page 27) takes up too much of the author's energy. In celebrating JDM, Hirshberg can't resist denigrating the genres to which he contributed—the generalizations about science fiction are equally insulting. (The human concerns of MacDonald's s.f. are those that have always preoccupied the really good writers in the genre.)

After a chapter on the early novels, Hirshberg takes a topical approach, generally giving less attention to the McGees than to the non-series novels and stories. Topics include point-of-view, morality, and social criticism. The sum-up chapter gives some attention to MacDonald's non-fictional writings. Though MacDonald was still alive and writing at the time the book was published, only his last book, *Barrier Island,* is missing from the bibliography.

According to Hirshberg, in 1947, JDM "probably had read" Chandler's *The Long Goodby* (sic)(page 32), a novel not published until 1953.

294. MacLean, David G. *John D. MacDonald: A Checklist of Collectible Editions & Translations.* Indiana (city unknown): Americana, 1987. 32p.

Not examined. The only evidence I have of its existence is a listing in a Gravesend Books catalog.

295. Rowan, Dan, and John D. MacDonald. *A Friendship: The Letters of Dan Rowan and John D. MacDonald 1967-1974.* New York: Knopf, 1986. x, 239p.

We have long been told by those who knew him that MacDonald was always more interested in talking about the other person's specialty than his own. Thus, it isn't surprising that this entertaining collection of correspondence tells us quite a bit more about Rowan and Martin's *Laugh-In* than about the writing of the Travis McGee novels. We also learn more about Rowan the man than we do about JDM. Both men are first-rate letter-writers, and the history of their friendship makes fascinating reading, down to the painful last few letters (apparently with right and wrong on both sides) that resulted in a seven-year silence between them. MacDonald, a prolific correspondent, is a natural candidate for a full-scale letter collection a few years down the line.

296. Shine, Walter and Jean. *A Bibliography of the Published Works of John D. MacDonald with Selected Biographical Materials and Critical Essays.* Gainesville: Patrons of the Libraries, University of Florida, 1980. xii, 209p. Illus., index.

Building on Len and June Moffatt's *The JDM Master Checklist* (see WAM #189), the Shines present a staggering amount of information. The section on MacDonald's published works begins with a chronology, listing books and shorter works in one month-by-month sequence, including word count, followed by chronological and alphabetical checklists of MacDonald's books, their American and British publishing histories and appearances in translation; magazine and newspaper fiction, arranged by publication title, and fiction in anthologies and collections, alphabetical by story title; non-fiction and media adaptations. The shorter biographical and critical section includes a six-page biographical sketch reprinted from *MD;* a chronological listing of biographical articles; listings of honors and awards, professional and civic activities, and education, military service, and employment; and a listing of secondary sources, including a chronological list of critical essays and a listing of book reviews, arranged alphabetically by title. Illustrations include book and magazine covers, the subject's letterheads, and some photos. Separate indices are included of English titles and translated titles. Though inevitably incomplete, since MacDonald was still alive and working at the time of its publication, this is an impressive compilation.

297. **Shine, Walter and Jean.** *An Index to the JDM Bibliophile: An Amateur Publication Devoted to the Life & Work of John D. MacDonald, Issues No. 1 through 30.* Privately printed, 1982. 33p.

Not examined. According to Albert (see #6), it is "[a]n index by title, subject and author. Letters to the editor are indexed separately by name."

298. **Shine, Walter and Jean.** *John D. MacDonald: A True Bibliophile.* Privately printed, 1985. 54p. Bibl.

Not examined. According to Walter Albert (*The Armchair Detective,* v. 21, n. 1, p. 78), it includes "[a] collection of comments by MacDonald on his wide reading, with introductory and connecting commentary by the Shines. There are excerpts from MacDonald's published reviews of fiction, . . . a section on his views on detective writers and fiction, and . . . a checklist of published—and unpublished—material by JDM on writers and writing. The Shines also describe the contents of books from the working library donated by MacDonald to the University of Florida at Gainesville."

299. **Shine, Walter and Jean.** *A MacDonald Potpourri—Being a Miscellany of Post-perusal Pleasures of the John D. MacDonald Books for Bibliophiles, Bibliographer, and Bibliomaniacs.* Gainsville: U. of Florida Libraries, 1988. xii, 219p. Illus.

As the subtitle suggests, this volume serves mainly as a collector's guide to the JDM corpus, including much more extensive information on the identification of American editions than was included in the 1980 bibliography (see #296). Among the features are a section on book numbering systems and other categories of book identification; listings of MacDonald's books by publisher; contents of his omnibus volumes and short story collections; books that made New York *Times, Publisher's Weekly,* or *Time* best-seller lists, including number of weeks on the list, highest position reached, and position each week (his only #1, by the way, was *Cinnamon Skin*); totals of copies printed and sold; foreign editions listed by country; typographical errors, epigraphs, working titles, dedications, photographers of JDM (with a four-page section of cover and jacket photos), jacket and cover artists and designers (with a 34-page section of variant covers), and a book-by-book table of identification features. Reproduction of the illustrations is sometimes murky. A three-page selected bibliography consists mostly of works on book collecting. Though the work may be somewhat complicated to use, it is indispensable to the serious JDM collector.

300. **Shine, Walter and Jean.** *Special Confidential Report: Subject: Travis McGee.* Florida Center for the Book, The Literary Landmarks Association, and Bahia Mar Resort, 1987. 32p.

Not examined. According to Walter Albert (*The Armchair Detective,* v. 24, n. 4, p. 459), this booklet is a "detailed record based on a comprehensive review of the world of Travis McGee . . . published on the occasion (Feb. 21, 1987) of the renaming of one of the boat slips at Bahia Mar Resort and Yachting Center in honor of MacDonald, with a brass plaque designating it as a 'literary landmark.'"

MACDONALD, Ross (Kenneth Millar)

301. **Bruccoli, Matthew J.** *Ross Macdonald.* (HBJ Album Biographies.) San Diego: Harcourt, Brace, Jovanovich, 1984. xxi, 147p. Illus., bibl., index.

Eventually, Millar/Macdonald will be the subject of a long, full-scale biography, but until that day comes, Bruccoli's extensively-illustrated, skeletal preliminary will fill the gap. The author's scholarly prose is smooth, readable, and unpretentious. This is decidedly a literary biography, with some tragic personal events in the subject's life alluded to but treated very discreetly. Like many writers on the handful of critically fashionable authors of mystery fiction, Bruccoli tends to treat the rest of the field rather slightingly. Typical is a snide swipe at *Ellery Queen's Mystery Magazine* (page 17).

Among the interesting tidbits: One of the early title possibilities for Macdonald's *The Galton Case* was *Skull Beneath the Skin,* a title later used by P.D. James. Macdonald once reviewed for the *New York Times* a book by a friend that he had read in draft form and even provided the title for.

302. **Bruccoli, Matthew J.** *Ross Macdonald/Kenneth Millar: A Descriptive Bibliography* (Pittsburgh Series in Bibliography). Pittsburgh: U. of Pittsburgh P., 1983. xv, 259p. Illus., index.

In the same format as earlier series volumes on Chandler (see WAM #117) and Hammett (WAM #177), Bruccoli catalogs first American and British editions of all the author's works, first as Millar, then as John Macdonald, as John Ross Macdonald, and finally as Ross Macdonald, the John having been phased out to avoid confusion with John D. MacDonald. Dust jackets, title pages, and copyright pages are reproduced. Following the section on separate publications are listings of contributions to books, first periodical appearances, and blurbs. Two brief appendices include the compiler's notes and a four-item list of books and articles about Macdonald. This supersedes Bruccoli's earlier *Kenneth Millar/Ross Macdonald: A Checklist* (WAM #190).

303. **Macdonald, Ross.** *Self-Portrait: Ceaselessly Into the Past.* Foreword by Eudora Welty. Edited and with an afterword by Ralph B. Sipper. Santa Barbara: Capra, 1981. iv, 129p. Bibl.

This collection of Macdonald's non-fiction writings, most previously published in journals or as forewords to his own and other people's books, includes quite a bit of scattered autobiographical detail. Most of the topics are literary, but there are two *Sports Illustrated* articles on ecological subjects, the near-extinction of the California condor and the Santa Barbara oil spill—the latter is also discussed in the foreword to Robert Easton's *Black Tide.* The two essays in Macdonald's *On Crime Writing* (WAM #191) reappear here. The only previously unpublished pieces are a speech given at the World Crime Writer's Conference in 1978; a short notebook entry on F. Scott Fitzgerald and Millar's 1948 novel *The Three Roads;* and an introduction of Eudora Welty at a writers' conference.

304. **Mahan, Jeffrey Howard.** *A Long Way From Solving That One: Psycho/Social and Ethical Implications of Ross Macdonald's Lew Archer Tales.* Lanham, MD, and London: University Press of America, 1990. xxiv, 141p. Bibl., index.

Mahan's subject has great potential interest, with major chapters offering a Freudian interpretation of *The Moving Target* and a discussion relating *The Underground Man* to Christian theology, specifically the "ethics of responsibility" of H. Richard Niebuhr. An appendix discusses the differences between novels and films. Unfortunately, this is a dissertation reproduced from typescript, and its plodding style and schematic nature combine to make it numbingly dull. It is an academic exercise rather than a real book, and I don't think it serves scholarship, the subject, or the author to publish it in this form.

305. **Schopen, Bernard A.** *Ross Macdonald.* (Twayne's United States Authors Series, volume 557.) Boston: Twayne, 1990. xiv, 149p. Illus., bibl., index.

In the preface to this well-written and provocative survey, the author indicates Macdonald has been overrated by some commentators and promises a tough critical analysis. Following a chronology and biograph-

ical chapter, Schopen discusses the detective genre, placing himself firmly
in the giants-and-hacks school of literary criticism: Hammett, Chandler,
and Macdonald are geniuses, all others chopped liver. He then devotes
chapters to Macdonald's works in groups, beginning with the novels
published as Kenneth Millar (not highly regarded by Schopen) through
the first Lew Archer book, *The Moving Target,* and ending with a brief
discussion of the final two, *Sleeping Beauty* and *The Blue Hammer,* which
represented a decline in the author's powers. Two books are considered
important enough for full-chapter consideration: *The Doomsters* (called
both "the last superior effort in the Chandler tradition" and "the finest
novel in the strictly hardboiled manner" [page 69]) and *The Underground
Man.* The six-page bibliography includes useful annotations to secondary
sources. Julian Symons' surname is consistently misspelled "Symonds."

306. **Sipper, Ralph B., ed.** *Inward Journey: Ross Macdonald.* Santa
Barbara: Cordelia, 1984. 161p. Illus.

Two previously unpublished Macdonald pieces—one the transcript
of a talk on mystery fiction given at the University of Michigan in 1954,
the other a 1952 letter to Alfred A. Knopf regarding his desire to go beyond
Raymond Chandler—are followed by tributes and short takes on various
aspects of Millar/Macdonald by fellow mystery writers Margaret Millar,
Julian Symons, Robert B. Parker, and John D. MacDonald; poets Donald
Davie, Reynolds Price, and Diane Wakoski; and mainstream novelists
Thomas Berger, William Goldman, and Eudora Welty, among others. In
a moving afterword, editor Sipper recounts Macdonald's final struggle
with Alzheimer's disease. A good selection of photographs is included.

MARSH, Ngaio

307. **Gibbs, Rowen, and Richard Williams.** *Ngaio Marsh: A Bibliography.* Scunthorpe: Dragonby, 1990. 51p.

Not examined. According to Edward D. Hoch (*The Year's Best
Mystery and Suspense Stories 1991* [see #369]), it is a "booklet that
includes valuations of first editions."

308. **Lewis, Margaret.** *Ngaio Marsh: A Life.* London: Chatto & Windus, 1991. x, 276p. Illus., bibl., index.

Among the four "Queens of Crime" of the 1930s, Lewis finds Marsh "reigns supreme for excellence of style and characterization" (page x). Though proponents of Allingham and Sayers would no doubt argue the point, it may well be true—certainly she surpasses my own favorite of the group, Christie, in those two areas. Along with the most thorough personal biography yet published, Lewis provides a knowledgeable discussion of Marsh's detective fiction, touching on both her strengths and weaknesses, as well as much detail on her theatrical career. There is a moving account of the health problems and self-doubts attending the writing of Marsh's last few novels, written in her eighties (her real year of birth being 1895 instead of the long-reported 1899). Even without allowing for these difficulties, those last books found her at or very near top form.

This is an excellent biography with an especially fine selection of photographs. There are some errors, however. The 1978 Edgar Awards presentation, at which Marsh was made a Grand Master, was in New York rather than Los Angeles; the definition of "English cosy" as "a novel set entirely in an English country village" (page 59) is much too narrow; and H.R.F. Keating was hardly "a very young arrival on the literary scene" (page 225) in 1974—he was by then extremely well-known and loomed nearly as large in the mystery genre as he does today.

309. **McDorman, Kathryne Slate.** *Ngaio Marsh.* (Twayne's English Authors Series, vol. 481.) Boston: Twayne, 1991. xiv, 162p. Illus., bibl., index.

In a useful addition to the reliable Twayne series, McDorman takes a thematic approach. Following the standard chronology and biographical chapter, she discusses Marsh's New Zealand novels, her use of setting generally, her continuing and supporting characters, her use of theatrical backgrounds, and finally her "legacy." Comparing Marsh to the other three of the Big Four of female Golden Age British writers (Christie, Sayers, and Allingham), she is always favorable to Marsh (regarded, she says, as second only to Sayers in quality and to Christie in popularity) and not always fair to the others. She also identifies and discusses some contemporaries influenced by the Big Four: P.D. James, Patricia Moyes, Martha Grimes, Amanda Cross, and (more briefly) June Thomson and

Sheila Radley. This is a well-written critical volume, displaying a firm grasp of general detective fiction (at least in the English tradition by female writers) and including a good primary and secondary bibliography, the latter helpfully annotated.

MASON, A.E.W.

310. Overton, Grant. *A.E.W. Mason: Appreciations—with Biographical Particulars and Notes on His Books.* New York: Doran, n.d. 222p.

Not examined. Listed in Albert (see #6) by Robert E. Briney, who also has not examined it.

MURPHY, Warren, and Richard Sapir

311. Murphy, Warren, and Richard Sapir. *The Assassins' Handbook.* New York: Pinnacle, 1982. 285p. **Revised as** *Inside Sinanju.* Compiled and edited by Will Murray. New York: Pinnacle, 1985. 268p.

The following is based on the revised edition.

Somewhat along the lines of the Don Pendleton Executioner secondary sources (see #312-313) but (as would be expected) much more tongue-in-cheek, this volume has more fiction than anything else: the 55-page novella "The Day Remo Died" and a number of short comic pieces, plus the text that gives the book its title, by Remo Williams' guru Chiun. The non-fictional pieces of biographical or critical interest are Murray's selection of "The Ten Best Destroyer Novels," a section profiling the major continuing characters, an interview with Murphy and Sapir on "Creating the Destroyer," and a selection of fan letters.

PENDLETON, Don

312. Pendleton, Don. *The Executioner's War Book.* New York: Pinnacle, 1977. 201p. Illus.

At the time this handbook appeared, the pioneering "splatterman" Mack Bolan had appeared in 28 novels. Since then, many more have appeared, some of them ghost-written by the two Executioner fans who have contributed essays to this handbook, Mike Newton and Stephen Mertz. Following an exchange of letters between Pendleton and a fan who compares Mack Bolan to Sherlock Holmes (!) and a two-page foreword by the great Mafia-fighter's creator, Mertz offers "Behind the Executioner," an admiring chapter of biography of Pendleton. Newton's "The Bolan Saga" summarizes the series to date. "The Gallery" is an index of characters appearing in the novels. "The Arsenal" describes and pictures and various the various weapons used by the Executioner. "Interiors" and "Exteriors" offer some choice quotes from the novels. Finally, "Feedback" prints letters from fans and Pendleton's responses. Of very limited biographical or critical interest, this volume is only for the most devoted followers of the series.

313. **Pendleton, Don.** *The New War Book.* Toronto: Gold Eagle, 1984. 187p. Illus.

This is more of the same as above. The character index is updated; more weapons are illustrated; more correspondence between fans and Pendleton is published. This time, there are also two short stories, considerable series hype, and a list of Marines killed and wounded in Beirut.

PETERS, Ellis (Edith Pargeter)

314. **Whiteman, Robin.** *The Cadfael Companion: The World of Brother Cadfael.* Introduction by Ellis Peters. London: Macdonald, 1991. 392p. Illus.

Not examined. According to Robert E. Briney, writing in his small-circulation fanzine *Contact is Not a Verb* (#67, March 1992, page 4), "This is an 'A to Z of People, Places, and properties' (both real and fictional) mentioned in the Cadfael books. There are five carefully drawn maps and several appendices, listing plants and herbs mentioned in the books, the Brothers and Officers of Shrewsbury Abbey, and the Kings, Emperors, Popes, and Archbishops of the tenth through twelfth centuries."

QUEEN, Ellery (Frederic Dannay and Manfred B. Lee)

315. **Christopher, Joe R.** *Queen's Books Investigated; or Queen is in the Accounting House.* Stephenville, TX: Carolingian Press, 1983. 35p.

Christopher, an English professor, reviewer, and frequent fanzine contributor, gathers his Queenian essays in a small pamphlet limited to thirty numbered and signed copies. It is surely destined to be one of the rarest collector's items in the field of mystery scholarship, as well as a highly entertaining gathering. Most of the short pieces have been previously published, three in *The Armchair Detective*, five in the *Queen Canon Bibliophile* (including a revision of one of the *TAD* articles), and one in *Jabberwocky: The Journal of the Lewis Carroll Society*. Several of the pieces are newly revised. Not previously published is a short parody, "The Persian Fez Mystery," which represents one of the best attempts to imitate the Queen prose style for comic effect.

316. **Nevins, Francis M., Jr., and Ray Stanich.** *The Sound of Detection: Ellery Queen's Adventures in Radio.* Madison, IN: Brownstone, 1983. vii, 109p. Illus.

Nevins presents a narrative history of the *Ellery Queen* radio show, followed by an episode-by-episode chronological listing of the series prepared in collaboration with Stanich. Though ostensibly of greatest interest to radio buffs, this entertaining book should be read by all Queen fans, since it includes considerable biographical information about Frederic Dannay and Manfred B. Lee that was not available to Nevins at the time he wrote his definitive Queenian study, *Royal Bloodline* (see WAM #201).

Among the book's most interesting revelations is the involvement of Anthony Boucher in writing many of the later Queen radio scripts in collaboration with Lee when Dannay was too busy with other projects. It is appropriate that Boucher, as directly influenced by Queen as any detective novelist of his time, at least for a time was Ellery Queen.

317. **Sullivan, Eleanor.** *Whodunit: A Biblio-Bio-Anecdotal Memoir of Frederic Dannay "Ellery Queen."* New York: Targ, 1984. 45p. Illus., bibl.

Dannay's successor as editor of *Ellery Queen's Mystery Magazine* recounts the EQ story and her own experiences working with him in a warm and informative tribute quoting such authorities as Dorothy Parker, Stanley Ellin, and Anthony Boucher. This handsome book was limited to 150 copies, signed by Sullivan with a signed frontispiece drawing of Dannay by John Groth. The full text was reprinted in *EQMM*, March 1991.

ROHMER, Sax (Arthur Henry Sarsfield Ward)

318. **Day, Bradford M.** *Sax Rohmer: A Bibliography*. Denver: Science-Fiction & Fantasy Publications, 1963. 34p.

Rohmer's books are listed alphabetically, including U.S., British, and reprint editions with a cover description of the first. Contents of collections are listed, with dates of original periodical publication. There is also a chronological list of magazine stories, a page and a half of biography, and a slightly shorter account of films based on Rohmer's work. Duplicated from a typescript on 8 1/2 x 11 pages, this scarce item may still be the most complete extant. The bibliography compiled by Robert E. Briney for Cay Van Ash's Rohmer biography *Master of Villainy* (WAM #204) does not extend to periodical appearances.

SAYERS, Dorothy L.

319. **Brabazon, James.** *Dorothy L. Sayers: A Biography*. Preface by Anthony Fleming. Foreword by P.D. James. New York: Scribners, 1981. xviii, 398p. Illus., bibl., index.

Having the advantage of the official sanction of the subject's heir and consequent access to papers unavailable to earlier writers, this volume far surpasses all previous Sayers biographies, including even Ralph E. Hone's Edgar winner (WAM #212). Brabazon captures Sayers on paper as no other writer could. The section on Dante translating made me want to run off and read Dante (almost). One fascinating revelation: Lord Peter Wimsey may have originally been intended as a secondary character in a Sexton Blake novel!

320. Clarke, Stephan P. *The Lord Peter Wimsey Companion.* New York: Mysterious, 1985. 563p. Illus., bibl., index.

Clarke's massive compilation provides for the Wimsey series what Jack Tracy's *Encyclopedia Sherlockiana* did for the Holmes canon: a dictionary of characters, places, and allusions keyed by abbreviations to the story or stories in which they appeared. There are 7509 numbered entries presented alphabetically in the main section. The eight-page bibliography includes primary sources (Sayers's books) and secondary sources of information, mostly non-fictional. Wimsey and the other characters are treated as historical personages; thus, there is no entry in the main body for Dorothy L. Sayers, nor any listing in the bibliography of works strictly about mystery fiction. The index goes from story or novel title to numbers of references. Among the plentiful illustrations: photographs of buildings, streets, and other landmarks occurring in the Wimsey stories; maps; and three pages of diagrams to illustrate the extensive explanation of cricket.

In many ways, Clarke's book is an extraordinary achievement, a labor of love that must have taken years of painstaking research, and this reader at least could not fault its accuracy or clarity. But only the most deeply committed Sayers buffs will find it essential.

321. Gaillard, Dawson. *Dorothy L. Sayers.* New York: Ungar, 1981. xi, 123p. Bibl., index.

Gaillard's brief critical study is entirely devoted to Sayers's detective fiction, beginning with a chapter on the short stories that fails to mention her most famous story, "Suspicion." (Admittedly, it's more a pure crime story than a detective story, but still . . .) The study is smoothly written and unexceptionable but not too exciting.

322. Kenney, Catherine. *The Remarkable Case of Dorothy L. Sayers.* Kent, OH: Kent State UP, 1990. xvii, 309p. Bibl., index.

The latest Sayers study is critically acute, entertainingly written, and carefully documented. Following 119 pages on the detective fiction for which the subject is best-known, with especially detailed attention to *The Nine Tailors* and *Gaudy Night,* Kenney devotes substantial sections to

Sayers's views of women (also to a great extent based on her novels) and her religious writings.

In most ways an admirable piece of work, the book has much to antagonize the mystery fan. Kenney has done her homework on the wider mystery field and is little given to factual error. But like many academic critics who choose a subject in genre fiction, Kenney has an annoyingly condescending attitude to the rest of the subject's genre. She implies that Sayers was the one great Twentieth-Century novelist in the detective-fiction field rather than one of a score or more who have executed the form with literary distinction. Consider for example this fatuous statement: "It has been said that there are two kinds of people who read mysteries: people who read only mystery fiction, and those who read only Dorothy L. Sayers" (page xii). Illogical as it is, I can't determine exactly what that means, but I can tell it's an insult to mystery readers as a group.

In a discussion of Sayers's reviewing, Kenney sometimes finds it unnecessary to identify the title and author of the book under review (e.g., the interesting historical novel described on pages 35-36). The volume even has a snobbish index. A number of Sayers's detective novelist contemporaries are substantively discussed in the book (e.g., Ellery Queen, E.R. Punshon), but their names usually do not appear in the index. On page 78, Kenney quotes both Flannery O'Connor and Robert Barnard. O'Connor is indexed. Barnard is not.

On page 33, Kenney lists some authors praised in Sayers's review columns, a largely distinguished group (Doyle, Chesterton, Rhode, Gardner, Freeman, Iles, Bailey, Queen, Christie, Rinehart, Carr, Wodehouse, Le Fanu, John Meade Falkner), and follows the list with this statement: "It is certainly a generous mind and an expansive definition of mystery fiction that will admit such a motley crew" (my italics). I realize that expression can have a neutral meaning of a varied group, but I think to most readers a pejorative connotation is suggested. Then she adds, to make it worse, "It is also ironic that Sayers herself could enjoy many more crime writers than do most of her admirers." How presumptuous of Kenney to speak for such a large group of readers.

323. **Reynolds, Barbara.** *The Passionate Intellect: Dorothy L. Sayers' Encounter with Dante.* Foreword by Ralph E. Hone. Kent, OH: Kent State U.P., 1989. xvii, 267p. Illus., bibl., index.

The author knew Sayers personally and was the scholar selected to complete her translation of Dante's *Paradiso,* of which twenty out of thirty-three cantos had been completed at the time of her death in 1957. Though there are references to the Lord Peter Wimsey saga, the book deals almost entirely with work outside mystery fiction and is included here in the interest of completeness.

324. Ryan, Elizabeth Bond, and William J. Eakins. *The Lord Peter Wimsey Cookbook.* Drawings by Francesca Green. New Haven: Ticknor & Fields, 1981. xii, 138p. Illus., index.

Wimsey joins Nero Wolfe (WAM #222) and Mme. Maigret (WAM #215) as fictional characters accorded the honor of fronting a cookbook. After an opening chapter commenting on Sayers's gastronomic interests and speculating about her role in her husband Atherton Fleming's *The Gourmet's Book of Food and Drink,* the authors arrange their presentation chronologically through the day: breakfast, lunch, tea, dinner, and supper. The description of a meal mentioned in the Wimsey canon is followed by the recipes needed to reproduce it. My cookbook consultant approvingly notes that a list of ingredients for each dish precedes the method, and that U.S. equivalents are sometimes given to substitute for hard-to-find items. A separate chapter is devoted to Lord Peter's wine expertise and some of his "more exotic tipples." An appendix lists California equivalents to the French vintages referred to in the stories. The index provides access by names of dishes, ingredients, and book and story titles.

325. Tischler, Nancy M(arie Patterson). *Dorothy L. Sayers: A Pilgrim Soul.* Atlanta: John Knox, 1980. 160p. Index.

This stimulating and enjoyably written study is a sort of spiritual biography, concentrating on Sayers's religious faith as seen in her life and works. Over half the book discusses the detective novels, followed by considerations of Sayers the playwright, the essayist, and the translator. A chronology of works follows each section.

326. Youngberg, Ruth Tanis. *Dorothy L. Sayers: A Reference Guide.* Boston: Hall, 1982. xxi, 178p.

To the primary Sayers bibliographies of Colleen Gilbert (WAM #207) and Harmon and Burger (WAM #210) add this annotated secondary bibliography of books and periodical articles about the subject's work. Arrangement is chronological, from 1917 (a *Times Literary Supplement* review of a Sayers poetry collection) to 1981 (the Brabazon biography [see #319] and Gaillard critical survey [see #321]). This is an admirable piece of work, thorough and wide-ranging with lucid, informative annotations that are usually descriptive rather than critical. (A supplement or updated edition covering all the material published since 1981 would be most welcome.)

SIMENON, Georges

327. **Bresler, Fenton.** *The Mystery of Georges Simenon.* London: Heinemann; New York: Beaufort, 1983. x, 260p. Illus., index.

Though several sources offer more extensive critical commentary, this work is certainly the fullest and best Simenon biography in English. Bresler was able to draw on the *Mémoires intime* (see #329), published in French in 1981, as well as extensive interviews with Simenon himself, both his wives, other family members and friends, including his Connecticut neighbors in the early '50s. Bresler gives much attention to the legend of Simenon's 10,000 sex partners and offers more detail than other sources on his subject's wartime activities in occupied France. This is a journalistic rather than a scholarly biography, with no bibliography and sparse footnotes, and Bresler has the journalist's habit of hyping the revelations to come. The authorized nature of the work—Simenon offered full cooperation and urged others to do the same—doesn't prevent Bresler from coming down quite hard on his subject's humanity in the final chapter. A very good selection of photographs is included.

One of Bresler's undocumented statements is the claim that Simenon was the favorite mystery writer of both Hammett and Chandler. Maybe so, but Simenon doesn't even appear in the index of Chandler's *Selected Letters* (see #203).

328. **Eskin, Stanley G.** *Simenon: A Critical Biography.* Jefferson, NC: McFarland, 1987. xiii, 304p. Illus., bibl., index.

This is one of the better books on Simenon, especially from the mystery scholar's point of view: there is much more material on the subject's pre-Maigret apprentice writing than in any other biographical/critical source, and there is a good account of the birth of Maigret, with much detail on the initial critical response and the early movie adaptations. In all, three chapters are devoted to the famous detective character, the last a profile and biography. Eskin sees the widely-travelled Maigret as having more in common with hardboiled private eyes than real cops. He offers this summation of the incredibly prolific Simenon: "The novels are an extraordinary series of first drafts. . . . Simenon was like a photographer quite uninterested in darkroom work but endowed with a very good eye, who took enough shots that some came out entirely right, while most of them, in any case, had something worth looking at" (page 242). The bibliography is arranged by publisher, with English titles given following the French and included in the index to facilitate access. There is also an abbreviated filmography and a good selection of photographs.

329. Simenon, Georges. *Intimate Memoirs, Including Marie-Jo's Book.* Translated from the French by Harold J. Samuelson. San Diego: Harcourt, Brace, Jovanovich, 1984. 815p. (French title: *Mémoires intimes.*)

As a novelist, Simenon was noted for brevity, but as an autobiographer, he takes another route entirely. As the title suggests, the emphasis is personal rather than professional. The author is vague on literary details— early on, he doesn't even refer to his publishers by name. He has almost nothing to say about his works save where he was when he was writing them. (The book badly needs an index of names and titles, so that scholars can more easily pinpoint what the Belgian novelist was writing when.) It's a self-serving account, of course, much given to name dropping, as in a reference to "my friend Picasso" (page 412). Simenon seems to have had more friends among film people than literati: other pals included Orson Welles, Jean Cocteau, Jean Renoir, and Henry Miller.

A listing of limitations is somewhat beside the point in considering a substantial and sometimes masterful work of literature. The book is written with considerable suspense and some mystery, with a great novelist's hand clearly at work in a piece of purported non-fiction. There are hints of a terrible secret, tantalizingly withheld until the end.

Simenon states that his previous autobiographical work *Quand j'etais vieux* (*When I Was Old*; see WAM #218), often mined by scholars for biographical insights, was distorted and misleading because "the better part . . . was written to keep a woman, my wife, from slipping into the abyss" (page 479).

The book takes the form of an extended letter to Simenon's dead daughter, Marie-Jo, who died a suicide in 1978. The last 151 pages are comprised of Marie-Jo's writings, mostly poetry and letters.

SJÖWALL, Maj, and Per Wahlöö

330. **Van Dover, J. Kenneth.** *Polemical Pulps: The Martin Beck Novels of Maj Sjöwall and Per Wahlöö.* (Brownstone Mystery Guides Series, Volume 11.) San Bernardino, CA: Borgo, forthcoming.

Not examined for good reason. After initially indicating this book had been published (hence its listing and assignment of a number here), the publisher informs me it is still forthcoming. Along with several other titles from Borgo (including Frank D. McSherry's long-awaited essay collection *Studies in Scarlet*), *Polemical Pulps* has been listed in *Books in Print* as far back as 1987—it has most recently been listed there with a 1991 publication date—without ever actually appearing. When this one does turn up, it will be the first monograph (at least in English) on its subjects, and, judging from Van Dover's track record (see #124 and 337), should be well worth reading.

SPILLANE, Mickey

331. **Collins, Max Allan, and James L. Traylor.** *One Lonely Knight: Mickey Spillane's Mike Hammer.* Bowling Green, OH: Popular, 1984. 186p. Illus., bibl.

Two true believers present the case for Mickey Spillane as an important writer of mystery fiction. Though the book is over-heavy on plot summary and is not likely to convince skeptics, it is important and welcome as the first book-length study of one of the great publishing phenomena of the century. The authors' honesty serves (for this reader anyway) to neutralize the effect of their argument: they admit many of Spillane's failings as a writer and don't leave enough standing to explain their high regard for his work. They offer quotes to illustrate their points, but the quotes don't always support the claims made for them. A fairly effective atmospheric description on page 84, we are told, is "outside the range" (!!) of such writers as Hammett, Chandler, Cain, and the "various MacDonalds."

Other points: Be warned that nearly all of Spillane's vaunted surprise endings are revealed by the authors, necessarily or not. There is a good bibliography of Spillane's book and magazine writing since 1947, as well as books and articles about Spillane. It would be interesting to know exactly what Spillane wrote for the slicks, where he reputedly started out.

Both Spillane's fans and his detractors will find this an invigorating book.

STOUT, Rex

332. **Anderson, David R.** *Rex Stout.* New York: Ungar, 1984. x, 134p. Bibl., index.

The Nero Wolfe books deserve and will eventually inspire a critical monograph as good as Francis M. Nevins, Jr.'s *Royal Bloodline* on Ellery Queen (see WAM #201) or Robert Barnard's *A Talent to Deceive* on Christie (WAM #127). But this study, albeit of some usefulness, is not the book. Following a chronology, a brief biographical chapter on Stout, and an overview of the Wolfe saga, Anderson devotes three chapters to a discussion of 19 of the 33 novels. Since most of his comments on the individual novels are comprised of plot summary, his failure to cover all the Wolfe novels is especially unfortunate. Anderson eschews solution giveaways, even of *A Family Affair* (whose windup is unconscionably revealed in Robert Goldsborough's otherwise admirable pastiche, *Murder in E Minor*), though he comes so close, one wonders why he bothers. Subsequent chapters discuss Wolfe, Archie, the other continuing characters, and Stout's place in the genre.

On the whole, Anderson is far too totally admiring of Stout. He makes little distinction in quality between the novels, seeming to find them uniformly excellent. In answering Stout's critics, Anderson erects straw men and never addresses the author's main shortcoming as a writer of detective fiction: his failure to create a solid fair-play puzzle plot most of the time. While Stout was virtually unmatched in style and characterization, his plots, while just as artificial, are far less satisfying than those of Queen, Christie, or Carr—or for that matter, Gardner, Coxe, or Halliday.

333. Darby, Ken. *The Brownstone House of Nero Wolfe.* Boston: Little, Brown, 1983. 178p. Bibl.

Ostensibly the work of Archie Goodwin, this compilation locates the famous brownstone (not on West 35th Street), describes it room-by-room (with detailed floorplans), and profiles the various continuing characters in the Wolfe series. Archie expresses outright anger at the inaccurate floorplan that appeared in William S. Baring-Gould's *Nero Wolfe of West 35th Street* (see WAM #220). The novels are extensively quoted throughout. Near the end of a fairly pleasurable book (the amount of pleasure in proportion to the reader's tolerance for the Sherlockian approach), Darby introduces the ersatz Wolfe letters that have made this a controversial work. Here, Darby saddles Wolfe with his own reactionary opinions on social issues not addressed in Stout's books. Overall, Darby has done a good job of what he set out to do, but the homophobic jeremiad attributed to Wolfe represents a serious lapse in taste and judgment.

334. McAleer, John. *Queen's Counsel: Conversations with Ruth Stout on Her Brother Rex Stout.* Ashton, MD: Pontes, 1987. ii, 89p.

Not examined. According to Robert E. Briney (*The Armchair Detective,* v. 24, n. 4, p. 465), these interviews "cover various family memories, Ruth Stout's opinions of her brother's work, information about friends, and some of her own concerns: gardening, writing, and a run-in with the FBI. Nothing of major importance, but an engaging portrait of an interesting and individualistic woman."

335. McAleer, John. *Royal Decree: Conversations with Rex Stout.* Ashton, MD: Pontes, 1983. 74p.

Even in the 621 pages of his massive biography of Stout (see WAM #221), McAleer was not able to use all the material provided him by his subject in several years' worth of interviews. Thus, this diverting compilation of Q-and-A, divided into four sections: "Stout on his Craft," "Stout on his Peers," "Nero and Archie," and "The Wolfe Corpus." The collection of explanations, opinions, and one-liners cannot fail to amuse and fascinate loyal fans of the series.

336. **Townsend, Guy M.; John J. McAleer, Judson C. Sapp, and Arriean Schemer, eds.** *Rex Stout: An Annotated Primary and Secondary Bibliography.* (Garland Reference Library of the Humanities, Vol. 239.) New York: Garland, 1980. xxvi, 199p. Illus., index.

Following a succinct twelve-page biographical introduction, the compilers list Stout's novels, including references to all editions and selected book reviews (using +/- symbols to differentiate favorable from unfavorable). Listings of Stout's short stories and other works follow in a classified arrangement. (There are even a couple of pages of jacket blurbs, though the compilers don't begin to provide full coverage of Stout's output in that category.) Secondary items include movies based on Stout's works, *Nero Wolfe* radio broadcasts, pastiches, interviews, and critical sources. Most items are annotated, usually descriptively but occasionally critically. The single illustration is a frontispiece portrait of Stout in 1929. This is a most valuable volume for students of one of the finest American mystery writers and (possibly) the greatest of all fictional sleuths after Holmes.

337. **Van Dover, J. Kenneth.** *At Wolfe's Door.* (The Milford Series Popular Writers of Today, Volume Fifty-Two.) San Bernardino, CA: Borgo, 1991. 120p. Bibl., index.

All Stout's works of mystery fiction from 1934 to 1975, both about Nero Wolfe and other sleuths, are described and evaluated, including under each title victims, clients, other principals (including the murderers, not unmasked as such), synopsis, and comment. The comments are often sharply critical and constitute the book's most important contribution, no other source to date having provided a similar service. The final chapter compares Wolfe and Perry Mason, very much to latter's disadvantage, though rightly noting Erle Stanley Gardner's superiority as a plotter.

THOMPSON, Jim

338. **Collins, Max Allan, and Ed Gorman.** *Jim Thompson: The Killers Inside Him.* Cedar Rapids, IA: Fedora, 1983. 104p. Illus., bibl.

This limited-edition paperback is a marginal inclusion, since well over half the contents are fiction: Thompson's previously unpublished novella, "This World, Then the Fireworks." Still, it is packaged as a secondary source, and it includes some useful material: portraits of Thompson and wife Alberta, Gorman's four-page introduction, a three-page remembrance by Thompson's Lion Books editor Arnold Hano, eleven pages of interviews with Thompson's widow and with Hano, the 15-page Collins essay that gives the book its title, and a single-page bibliography of Thompson's fiction. The Collins essay appeared in revised and expanded form in *Murder Off the Rack* (see #137).

339. **McCauley, Michael J.** *Jim Thompson: Sleep with the Devil.* New York: Mysterious, 1991. 340p. Illus., bibl., index.

The first book-length Thompson study clearly doesn't tell the whole story of a writer whose stature continues to increase, but later writers will owe a debt to McCauley's preliminary effort. The book is about equally divided between biography and critical analysis, with information on Thompson's life drawn from interviews with friends and professional colleagues and (admittedly well-filtered) from family members. Much is extrapolated from Thompson's novels and from his fictionalized autobiographies *Bad Boy* (1953) and *Roughneck* (1954)—this can be a risky course, but the subject was among the most transparently autobiographical of novelists, at least at times, and McCauley is careful to separate fact from speculation. Some readers will get bogged down in the extensive, albeit efficiently done, plot summaries, but they add to the book's value as a resource for later commentators. Appendices include as full as possible a listing of Thompson's published work, though much of his work for true crime magazines is not readily findable and the listing of English-language reprint and French editions for some reason breaks off in 1977. Of special interest is a 21-page annotated list of Thompson's unpublished and/or unfinished novels. Like the main text, they include extensive quotations from his writing. The quotes more than the connecting matter demonstrate what an original and formidable writer Thompson was and whet the reader's appetite both for reading Thompson's own writings and learning more about his tortured life.

A couple of mild quibbles: McCauley states Thompson's novels were the "first paperback originals of any kind to be reviewed in the (N.Y.) *Times*" (page 190). According to my index of paperback original reviews in Anthony Boucher's "Criminals at Large" column, *The Girl in the Pictorial Wrapper* (WAM #11), the first Boucher column to review paperback originals was March 29, 1953, and the first Thompson book to be reviewed there, *Savage Night,* was not covered until September 6 of that year. The *New York Times Index* shows no earlier review of a Thompson paperback original. Thompson's two short stories about Mitch Allison in *Alfred Hitchcock's Mystery Magazine,* "The Cellini Chalice" (December 1956) and "The Frightening Frammis" (February 1957) are characterized as "novellas"—the former may marginally qualify for the term, but the latter is surely a short story.

UPFIELD, Arthur W.

340. **Browne, Ray B.** *The Spirit of Australia: The Crime Fiction of Arthur W. Upfield.* Bowling Green, OH: Popular, 1988. 266p. Illus., bibl.

First the good news. As a work of research and scholarship, this first book-length critical study of Inspector Napoleon Bonaparte's creator is admirable. It's thorough, meticulous in providing maps for the sites of the stories, full of insights and acute observations (such as Bony's tendency to become lighter-skinned as the series goes on), sensitive to the racial politics of Australia and Upfield's ambivalence, and obviously deeply felt in its desire to celebrate an important and possibly undervalued writer of detective fiction. Now the bad news. As a piece of writing, it's exasperating, full of tortured sentences that are often nonsensical or self-contradictory if taken literally, and badly in need of a good editing job to weed out the repetitiousness along with the stylistic infelicities. This is a book worth perusing as it stands, but it could have been so much better.

Following a biographical chapter, Browne provides a valuable plot and critical summary of all Upfield's novels. The remainder of the book takes a topical approach, exploring the subject's locales, themes, and recurring elements. Browne identifies *The Will of the Tribe* (1962) as

Upfield's masterpiece. The claims for Upfield's importance may be a trifle overdone. Bony is "one of the three or four outstanding operatives of all crime fiction" (page 32), and Upfield is "the first to write crime fiction as a genre larger than detective fiction," producing "works in cultural and anthropological philosophy" that "develop on a plane far above the level of mere detective fiction" (page 14). Many of the authors used for comparison are from outside the mystery genre, including Frank Norris, Jack London, Robert W. Service, James Fenimore Cooper, and Herman Melville.

According to Browne, Australian writer Joe Kovess was at work on a biography of Upfield, possibly to "be published within the next two or three years" (page 1). Browne reveals that the first published Upfield biography, *Follow My Dust* (WAM #224), was actually written by Upfield himself and edited by ostensible author Jessica Hawke.

VAN DINE, S.S. (Willard Huntington Wright)

341. **Loughery, John.** *Alias S.S. Van Dine.* New York: Scribners, 1992. xxii, 296p. Illus., bibl., index.

Few writers of detective fiction are as natural biographical subjects as Van Dine, a complex, formidable, and tortured character, no more likable than some exasperated readers have found his mannered sleuth Philo Vance but undeniably fascinating. Even aside from the Vance novels, which had an impact in the twenties hard to appreciate from a distance of over sixty years, Willard Huntington Wright was an early editor of some significance, an associate of H.L. Mencken and George Jean Nathan who bought for *Smart Set* the works of avant garde literary figures like Ezra Pound and D.H. Lawrence, and a critic who pioneered American appreciation of modern art, often in the course of publicizing the work of his brother, talented painter Stanton Macdonald-Wright. Himself an art critic, Loughery may bring a somewhat surer hand to the discussion of that aspect of Wright's work than to his detective fiction, but he has written an excellent biography of a difficult subject. Wright made the biographer's task harder by telling lies about himself all his life, and his heirs continued to discourage biographers in the years after his death, often destroying letters and other primary materials.

Some of Loughery's odd critical views invite argument. He is surprisingly negative on the quality of his subject's detective fiction, referring to "eight or nine bad novels" (page 230) out of twelve. (Even tough critics of Van Dine usually credit him with a decent job on his first six.) His criticism of the old-hat qualities of the locked room in *The Kennel Murder Case* seems unduly harsh—after all, when the book was published, locked-room master John Dickson Carr was barely starting out—and he also underrates the film version, which many (this writer included) regard as a classic screen whodunit despite one oversized plot hole. On the other hand, he tends to overrate the abysmal *Kidnap Murder Case,* which is by far the nadir of the Vance series, worse even than the embarrassing *Gracie Allen Murder Case.*

The creator of rural detective Philo Gubb, Ellis Parker Butler, mistakenly becomes "Joseph Ellis" Butler—and I doubt that humorous correspondence-school sleuth could have been a conscious inspiration for Vance's first name. Loughery has Van Dine not minding a Philo Vance takeoff in an Abbott and Costello film—since that team didn't make their first film until 1940, the year after Van Dine's death, I suspect the author is thinking of Laurel and Hardy. A more serious and puzzling error is Loughery's repeated tendency to understate the word-count of the Philo Vance novels: *The Benson Murder Case* 50,000 words (the book runs 348 pages in its first edition—surely 80,000 or 90,000 is a closer estimate); *The Gracie Allen Murder Case* 20,000 words (it's short but at 227 pages surely no less than 50,000 words); and *The Winter Murder Case* 20,000 words (Jon Tuska [see WAM #225] gives a more plausible 30,000-word figure for the final Vance novel, which did not go through the customary expansion to book length).

An oddity of the generally good photo section (and one that is quite likely not the author's fault) is the lack of a single picture of several Wright family members who feature prominently in the story: his brother (some of whose art is reproduced), his mother, his first wife, and his daughter.

VAN GULIK, Robert

342. **Evers, A.M., ed.** *Bibliography of Dr. R.H. Van Gulik.* Boston: Boston University Libraries, n.d. [ca. 1968]. 82p.

Not examined. Douglas G. Greene writes in Albert (see #6), that the pamphlet "begins with material on van Gulik's life and continues with descriptions of all his articles, scholarly books, poems, reviews, dictionaries, and novels, including a listing of the Judge Dee books in all languages through 1967. The pamphlet also includes van Gulik's notes about the composition of the Judge Dee stories. An excellent reference work which deserves to be better known and widely used" (page 701).

343. **Van de Wetering, Janwillem.** *Robert Van Gulik: His Life and Work.* Miami Beach: Dennis McMillan, 1987. 147p. Illus., bibl.

The author and subject are the two greatest names in Dutch detective fiction, and there is much to admire in this beautifully made and illustrated volume, limited in its first edition to 350 numbered and signed copies. However, mystery fans may grow impatient in such a short book with the tangential material on Taoist religion and Chinese law. Employing a topical rather than a chronological approach, van de Wetering presents van Gulik in all his varied roles: the diplomat, the scholar of Eastern culture and religion, the novelist, the eroticist, the linguist, and the gibbon-keeper. Illustrations include photographs, some of the subject's own drawings, a sample page of the Chinese text of one of van Gulik's books, and a drawing of van Gulik dreaming of naked Chinese maidens by Joe Servello, who also designed the attractive dust jacket and remarkable endpapers (a specialty of the publisher). The bibliography at the end of the book is confined to the subject's scholarly books and articles, but earlier a table of the Judge Dee series is reprinted from the Scribner edition of *Judge Dee at Work.* Van de Wetering also provides a chronology of the subject's life for the more linear-minded among us.

WALLACE, Edgar

344. **Kiddle, Charles.** *A Guide to the First Editions of Edgar Wallace.* Dorset (town unknown): Ivory Head, 1981. 88p.

Not examined. Listed in a Gravesend Books catalog.

WILLEFORD, Charles

345. **Willeford, Charles.** *I Was Looking for a Street.* Woodstock, VT: Countryman, 1988. 143p. Illus.

This gem of a memoir describes the author's Los Angeles boyhood in the '20s and his teenage years on the road as a "bum" (his term). For all their horrors and deprivations, the Depression years seem a gentler time than today in Willeford's vivid account. In an unusual author's note, he says he changed most names "for euphonious reasons." Though there are flash-forwards in references to the film of his novel *Cockfighter* and to college literature teaching, plus a passing reference to novelistic technique, there is nothing about Willeford's writing career per se.

346. **Willeford, Charles.** *Something About a Soldier.* New York: Random, 1986. 255p. Illus.

I have not examined this memoir of Willeford's pre-World War II U.S. Army experiences, but based on the quality of the book above, it has to be better than the rather discouraging reviews in *Library Journal* (April 16, 1986, p. 76) and *Publishers Weekly* (March 7, 1986, p. 90) suggest. The latter notice quotes an ironic remark, following "brutally frank" descriptions of drinking and whoring: "If a man wasn't careful the Army could coarsen him, and I had to protect my sensitivity if I was ever going to write anything first-rate."

WILLIAMS, Valentine

347. **Williams, Valentine.** *The World of Action: The Autobiography of Valentine Williams.* London: Hamilton, 1938. 479p. Illus., index.

Williams's readable account is mostly about his experiences as a journalist and soldier, though he devotes a chapter to the creation of *The Man with the Clubfoot* while recuperating from injuries sustained in the Battle of the Somme in 1916. He identifies Sherlock Holmes (with no mention of anyone named Conan Doyle) as the influence that set his course toward crime fiction and devotes about three pages to detective fiction technique, emphasizing that detective stories are much harder to write than romantic fiction.

WOOLRICH, Cornell

348. **Nevins, Francis M., Jr.** *Cornell Woolrich: First You Dream, Then You Die.* New York: Mysterious, 1988. ix, 613p. Illus., bibl., index.

The first book-length work on Woolrich is so thorough in its coverage, it will be the definitive reference on this haunted and remarkable writer for years to come. Nevins makes the most of the sparse biographical information available while synopsizing all of Woolrich's published works, including the unreprinted early novels and obscure (not always deservedly so) magazine pieces, as well as the suspense novels and stories that made his reputation. Coverage of radio, television, and film adaptations is also extensive. Appendices include a 25-page checklist of books and magazine appearances, a 19-page filmography, listings of radio and TV adaptations, and a secondary bibliography. The book was awarded an Edgar for best biographical or critical work of its year.

349. **Nielsen, Bjarne.** *Bibliography in Black: The Works of Cornell Woolrich.* Copenhagen: Antikvariat Pinkerton, 1988. 40p.

Not examined. Description is from the British fanzine *Crime & Detective Stories (CADS)* as noted by Albert (*The Armchair Detective*, v. 24, n. 4, p. 468). Despite the place of publication, the work is reportedly in English.

350. **Woolrich, Cornell.** *Blues of a Lifetime: The Autobiography of Cornell Woolrich.* Edited by Mark T. Bassett. Bowling Green, OH: Popular, 1991. xv, 152p. Bibl.

The reader of this volume will come away with some understanding of Woolrich's life and personality, to the extent he chose to reveal it, but more strikingly with a renewed appreciation of the magic of his prose.

The five autobiographical pieces collected here are uninformative of specific facts and dates and are structured more like short stories than parts of an extended narrative. The editor's introduction provides a context to the pieces, stressing the shadowy nature of Woolrich and the unanswered questions about his life. Extensive notes define and clarify Woolrich's references and allusions, puzzle over the many internal contradictions, and identify the frequent popular-song references. An appendix gathers fragments from Woolrich's fictional writings that may illuminate an event not addressed in the autobiographical pieces (his failed marriage) and presents the haunting paragraph with which Woolrich intended to end his autobiography, beginning with the words, "I was only trying to cheat death."

YATES, Dornford (Cecil William Mercer)

351. **Smithers, A.J.** *Dornford Yates: A Biography.* London: Hodder and Stoughton, 1982. x, 241p. Illus., bibl., index.

Yates/Mercer, a cousin of H.H. Munro ("Saki"), was consistently published in the United States in his lifetime, but he clearly did not have the same impact here as in Britain, where he is apparently still read and revered. With "Sapper" and John Buchan, he formed a triumvirate of British thriller writers celebrated in Richard Usborne's *Clubland Heroes* (WAM #60). Smithers's book is a thorough, readable biocritical account that falls short of hagiography but is clearly simpatico with its subject. The author does not deny Yates's antisemitism, for example, but takes pains to make it seem understandable.

352. **Yates, Dornford.** *As Berry and I Were Saying.* London: Ward, Lock, 1952. 285p.

353. **Yates, Dornford.** *B-Berry and I Look Back.* London: Ward, Lock, 1958.

Not examined. According to Smithers (see above), Yates "had the ability to withdraw into his study, shut the door and live in a dream-world that was as real to him as the one outside. It became so impossible to disentangle the two that his quasi-autobiographies . . . need to be read with care" (page 3).

7
ANTHOLOGIES

354. Adrian, Jack, ed. *Detective Stories from the Strand Magazine.* Foreword by Julian Symons. Oxford and New York: Oxford U.P., 1991. xxiii, 374p.

Since Adrian is one of the top present-day anthologists and ranks among the best of all time in the quality and scholarship of his editorial notes, there could hardly be a better volume to lead off this section. Secondary matter—Symons's foreword, the overall introduction and those to six individual sections—totals 28 pages, recounting the history of the *Strand* (1891-1950) and offering biographical and critical notes on the contributors, who range from famous mystery writers (Doyle, of course, along with Christie, Chesterton, Wallace and others) to less widely-remembered old-timers (H. Warner Allen, Will Scott, Sapper, Seamark) to renowned writers more often associated with other areas (Aldous Huxley, Somerset Maugham, Quentin Reynolds). Some names are almost totally unfamiliar—Augustus Muir, D.L. Murray, Hylton Cleaver, Loel Yeo—but in each case there is either biographical detail or at least (in the case of the last-named) learned speculation.

355. Adrian, Jack, ed. *Sexton Blake Wins.* London: Dent, 1986. 460p. Bibl.

Not examined. Contento (see #14) indicates this collection of Sexton Blake novelettes by various hands includes an introduction by Adrian (starting on page vii) and a two-page "Select Bibliography." It is the only such collection I know of, and Adrian likely has some interesting information to convey.

356. Adrian, Jack, and Robert Adey, eds. *Murder Impossible: An Extravaganza of Miraculous Murders, Fantastic Felonies & Incredible Criminals.* London: Xanadu; New York: Carroll & Graf, 1990. ix, 306p.

Besides gathering some relatively unfamiliar tales, this collection of 21 locked-room and impossible-crime mysteries has some of the best and most informative story introductions extant, many of them a full page or longer. Particularly useful are the notes on the contributions of such little-written-about mystery practitioners as Hake Talbot, Vincent Cornier, Arthur Porges, John F. Suter, Joseph Commings, and Jeffrey Wallman. The editorial enthusiasm recalls the best days of Ellery Queen.

357. Allen, Dick, and David Chacko, eds. *Detective Fiction: Crime and Compromise.* New York: Harcourt, Brace, Jovanovich, 1974. xiv, 480p. Bibl.

Intended as a text for a college-level course on the genre, this volume is about a third secondary material, including the overall introduction, notes on each section, study questions at the end of each selection, six pages of possible research topics, ten pages of primary and secondary sources, and (most notably) the essays collected in the fourth section, "Theories." To four very familiar pieces (Sayers's ubiquitous *Omnibus of Crime* introduction [see #512], Chesterton's "Defence of Detective Stories," Chandler's "Simple Art of Murder," and Auden's "Guilty Vicarage"), the editors add George Grella's "Murder and the Mean Streets: The Hard-Boiled Detective Novel," Robert Daley's "Police Report on the TV Cop Shows" (he doesn't like them one bit), and Fred Graham's strictly non-fictional "Contemporary History of American Crime." The three sections of fiction take every opportunity to downplay the distinction between genre writing and literature: "Manifestations" includes selections from Frost, Hemingway, Shirley Jackson, Stevenson, Browning, and Greene along with Christie; "The Detective" includes Poe, Doyle, Futrelle, Chesterton, Hammett, Chandler, Ross Macdonald, Simenon, Thomas Flanagan, and Twain; "The Genre Extended" offers Henry James, Borges, William Burroughs, Barthelme, and novel excerpts from Macdonald and Hammett.

358. **Ambler, Eric, ed.** *To Catch a Spy.* London: Bodley Head, 1964. New York: Atheneum, 1965. 224p.

Ambler's sixteen-page introduction is a good short history of spying in fact and fiction. The notes on stories by John Buchan, Somerset Maugham, Compton Mackenzie, Graham Greene, the editor, Ian Fleming, and Michael Gilbert tend to be critical rather than biographical, and the eminence of the commentator gives them special value. Like Allen Dulles (see #399), Ambler found good spy short stories scarce, but most of his selections are short stories or novelettes rather than excerpts from novels.

359. **Apostolou, John L., and Martin H. Greenberg, eds.** *Murder in Japan.* Foreword by James Melville. New York: Dembner, 1987. xiv, 224p.

Fourteen stories by ten authors are collected here with only Seicho Matsumoto and Shizuko Natsuki recurring from Ellery Queen's earlier *Japanese Golden Dozen* (see #488). The stories are arranged chronologically. All had appeared in English translation prior to their reprinting here. Melville's brief foreword discusses the large Japanese market for mysteries. Apostolou contributes a six-page historical introduction, and the individual stories have biographical notes on the authors.

360. **Asimov, Isaac; Charles G. Waugh, and Martin H. Greenberg, eds.** *The Best Crime Stories of the 19th Century.* New York: Dembner, 1988. x, 325p.

Asimov's four-page introduction discusses some of the biblical and classical pre-history of the mystery form, but the greatest reference value lies in ten pages of very substantial biographical notes on the fifteen contributors, who range from major literary figures (Collins, Doyle, Hardy, Hawthorne, Poe, Twain) to mystery writers well-known or faintly familiar (Grant Allen, Robert Barr, Richard Harding Davis, Arthur Morrison, Rodriguez Ottolengui, Melville Davisson Post, William Russell ["Waters"], Israel Zangwill) to one name totally unknown to me (Harry Stillwell Edwards, whose first novel *Sons and Fathers,* we are told, "has been called the best mystery novel ever written by an American" [page 320]—by whom, we aren't told).

361. **Asimov, Isaac; Martin Harry Greenberg, and Charles G. Waugh, eds.** *The Thirteen Crimes of Science Fiction*. Garden City, NY: Doubleday, 1979. 455p.

Thirteen mystery sub-genres (e.g., hardboiled, spy, inverted, locked room, police procedurals) are seen in science-fictional manifestations. Asimov's four-page introduction discusses such crossovers generally, and the individual story introductions often refer the reader to other occurrences, usually with regrettably little specificity as to titles.

362. **Barnard, Allan, ed.** *The Harlot Killer*. New York: Dodd, Mead, 1953. 248p.

Though fictional entries (including the expected by Anthony Boucher, Thomas Burke, Marie Belloc Lowndes, and Robert Bloch) outnumber factual in this anthology, its value is undoubtedly greater as a Jack the Ripper reference than as a mystery fiction reference. The longest section is comprised of reprints of contemporary newspaper accounts of the crimes, compiled by Richard Barker for his factual anthology, *The Fatal Caress*. Still, Barnard's introduction (a dozen pages in the Dell reprint) includes a survey of films and fictional works inspired by the Whitechapel killer.

363. **Barzun, Jacques, ed.** *The Delights of Detection*. New York: Criterion, 1961. 381p.

Barzun's introductory essay, "Detection and the Literary Art," runs fifteen pages and sets out his distinction between the novel and the tale. One of the key texts in defense of the classical detective story, it is reprinted in both Nevins's *The Mystery Writer's Art* (see WAM #78) and Winks's *Detective Fiction* (see #173). The seventeen selections (divided into classic, modern, and historic tales) have no individual introductions.

364. **Barzun, Jacques, and Wendell Hertig Taylor, eds.** *Classic Short Stories of Crime and Detection*. (50 Classics of Crime Fiction, 1950-1975.) New York: Garland, 1983. 304p.

Though it has a five-page introduction on recent trends in the mystery field, this volume has less secondary interest overall than its predecessor (see below). There is no information on the authors of the individual selections.

365. Barzun, Jacques, and Wendell Hertig Taylor, eds. *Classic Stories of Crime and Detection*. (Fifty Classics of Crime Fiction, 1900-1950, volume 1.) New York: Garland, 1976. 361p.

The introduction, of nine unnumbered pages, discusses the fourteen selections and provides brief biographical identifications of the contributors, some very famous (Berkeley, Carr, Queen, Starrett), others less so (Belton Cobb, Leonard Gribble, Owen Johnson).

366. Beach, Stewart, ed. *This Week's Stories of Mystery and Suspense*. Introduction by Alfred Hitchcock. New York: Random, 1957. xii, 330p.

Neither Hitchcock's introduction nor the very brief story notes offer much that is special, but appended is a 19-page article by editor Beach on "How to Write the Mystery and Suspense Story" and a single-page "Glossary of Writers' Terms."

367. Berbrich, Joan D., ed. *Stories of Crime and Detection*. New York: McGraw-Hill, 1974. 296p.

Not examined. Per Contento (see #14), there is a general introduction plus an introduction to each of six sections to which the 23 stories are assigned: "All in the Family," "The Mind of a Criminal," "Footprints and Fingerprints," "Celebrating Sleuths," "Things Are Seldom as They Seem," and "Murder Up-To-Date."

368. Bernkopf, Jeanne F., ed. *Boucher's Choicest: A Collection of Anthony Boucher's Favorites from Best Detective Stories of the Year*. Introduction by Allen J. Hubin. New York: Dutton, 1969. 320p.

Following a two-page tribute to Boucher by Hubin, his successor as editor of *Best Detective Stories of the Year* (see below) and as *New York Times* mystery critic, Dutton editor Bernkopf presents 24 stories, four from each of Boucher's volumes in the series, that she knew to be his special favorites. Boucher's original story notes are included.

369. *Best Detective Stories of the Year.* New York: Dutton, annual, 1946-1968, 1970-1981. **Edited by David C. Cooke (1946-1960), Brett Halliday (1961-1962), Anthony Boucher (1963-1968), Allen J. Hubin (1970-1975), and Edward D. Hoch (1976-1981).** Continued as *The Year's Best Mystery and Suspense Stories.* New York: Walker, 1982-. **Edited by Edward D. Hoch.**

The annual anthology has always been worthwhile purely as a gathering of good stories, and from the early days under Cooke the story notes were frequently valuable and informative. But the series first gained significant reference value under Boucher's editorship, beginning in 1963 with the eighteenth annual volume, which introduced a 10-page appendix called "The Yearbook of the Detective Story," a feature continued by Hubin and Hoch. The first yearbook included a bibliography of anthologies, single-author collections, and critical volumes published in the preceding year; a list of the year's awards; a necrology; and an honor role of the best stories published during the year. The 1991 volume's yearbook runs 19 pages, including all the features mentioned above plus a selection of the year's best novels in the genre, the rest of the increase accounted for by the greater length of the bibliography and awards listings. A complete set of this annual from Boucher's first year on provides a ready-reference guide to developments in the mystery field that is not available anywhere else in as convenient form.

Boucher's last volume, published in 1968 and covering the short-story crop of 1967, was compiled while the editor was ill and unable to produce a yearbook aside from a shortened honor role, and Hubin's first, published in 1970, covered the stories of 1969, leaving the year 1968 in limbo, joining in that state 1959: the fifteenth annual volume and Cooke's last, *Best of the Best Detective Stories,* published in 1960, included one story from each of the first fourteen annuals and only a single tale to represent 1959. For other anthologies derived from the *Best Detective Stories* series, see Bernkopf (above) and Hubin (#431).

370. Blaustein, Albert P. *Fiction Goes to Court: Favorite Stories of Lawyers and the Law Selected by Famous Lawyers.* New York: Holt, 1954. xii, 303p.

This collection of legal fiction may not be a mystery anthology per se, but many of the eighteen authors represented are solidly (Melville Davisson Post, Arthur Train, Octavus Roy Cohen, Erle Stanley Gardner) or tangentially (Irvin S. Cobb, A.A. Milne, William Faulkner) in the crime fiction field. Lawyers as varied as then-Vice President Richard M. Nixon, Adlai E. Stevenson, Fred M. Vinson, Oscar Hammerstein 2d, Elmer Rice, and Jerry Giesler are invited to select their favorite examples of lawyer fiction. (Only Gardner appears both as selector and selectee.) Blaustein's six-page introduction discusses the selectors rather than the stories they have chosen. The selectors' introductions to their choices are briefer than one might wish, usually no more than a sentence or two, but include occasional interesting tidbits: one-time presidential candidate John W. Davis calls Post "an old friend of West Virginia days—a friend who sometimes borrowed my law books to do research for his magnificent lawyer stories" (page 2).

371. Bleiler, E.F., ed. *Eight Dime Novels.* New York: Dover, 1974. xv, 190p.

Bleiler's nine-page introduction to this large-format paperback is a brief, scholarly history of dime novels. Personalities represented in the selections (not confined to detectives) include Old King Brady, Frank James, Nick Carter, Deadwood Dick, Buffalo Bill, The Steam Man, Frank Merriwell, and Horatio Alger. Though it has less reference material than Hoppenstand's similar collection (see #428), more of the reprinted stories have type of readable size (the Deadwood Dick and Steam Man entries being notable exceptions).

372. Bleiler, E.F., ed. *Three Victorian Detective Novels.* New York: Dover, 1978. xvi, 302p.

The chosen trio are Andrew Forrester's *The Unknown Weapon,* Wilkie Collins's *My Lady's Money,* and Israel Zangwill's *The Big Bow Mystery.* The editor's ten-page introduction discusses the careers of the three authors and their contributions to the development of the form. Since Forrester is by far the most obscure of the three, the material on him no doubt has the most reference interest. *The Big Bow Mystery* is prefaced by Zangwill's own introduction, written for an 1895 edition.

373. **Bleiler, E.F., ed.** *A Treasury of Victorian Detective Stories.* New York: Scribners, 1979. vi, 496p. Bibl.

The five-page introduction makes the claim that virtually all the sub-types we associate with the detective story in the 20th century have their Victorian equivalents. The 23 contributors include some famous names (Dickens, Gaboriau, Collins, Doyle, Post, Green, Harte), but a majority are virtually forgotten today (Andrew Forrester, Jr., "Waters," Tom Fox, E. and H. Heron, Cutcliffe Hyne, C.L. Pirkis), and on these especially, Bleiler's brief story notes are most informative. The two-page bibliography lists the original sources of the stories.

374. **Bond, Raymond T., ed.** *Famous Stories of Code and Cipher.* New York: Rinehart, 1947. xxvi, 342p. Illus.

Bond's introduction is a meaty non-fictional survey of codes, and more code lore (along with the usual biographical information) appears in the story notes. The notes on Poe's "The Gold Bug" and Doyle's "The Adventure of the Dancing Men" are especially lengthy and interesting, catching both authors in code-making errors. With this volume and his collection of poisoning stories (see below), Bond compiled two of the best theme anthologies in the mystery genre.

375. **Bond, Raymond T., ed.** *Handbook for Poisoners: A Collection of Famous Poison Stories Selected, with an Introduction on Poisons.* New York: Rinehart, 1951. vi, 311p.

This is one of the most reference-worthy anthologies of them all, including a scholarly introduction of 76 pages which recounts the history of poisoning, with reference to many celebrated cases, concluding with an annotated list of twenty poisons "which are most commonly met in real life and in fiction" (page 68) and bibliographic notes. The individual introductions to the dozen stories are also longer than most anthologies offer—in addition to (and sometimes instead of) the usual biographical notes are comments on the poisons used in the individual stories. In some cases (Dorothy L. Sayers's "Suspicion," Miriam Allen DeFord's "The Oleander," Phyllis Bottome's "The Liqueur Glass," and Irvin S. Cobb's "An Occurrence up a Side Street"), additional poisoning notes follow the stories. Other tales included are Anthony Wynne's "The Cyprian Bees," E.C. Bentley's "The Clever Cockatoo," Anthony Berkeley's "The Avenging Chance," Rudyard Kipling's "Reingelder and the German Flag," Agatha Christie's "Accident," R. Austin Freeman's "Rex v. Burnaby," Nathaniel Hawthorne's "Rappaccini's Daughter," and G.K. Chesterton's "The Quick One."

376. **Boucher, Anthony (William A.P. White), ed.** *Four-&-Twenty Bloodhounds.* (Mystery Writers of America anthology). New York: Simon and Schuster, 1950. vii, 406p.

Boucher borrows the gimmick used in Kenneth MacGowan's *Sleuths* (see #451) and invites each of the authors of these 25 stories to present a *Who's Who*-type biography of the series detective concerned. Only characters whose creators declined to provide biographical details are Ellery Queen and (for obvious reasons) Robert Arthur's radio mystery man the Mysterious Traveler. Brett Halliday discusses his best-known character in the essay "Michael Shayne as I Know Him" rather than a *Who's Who* bio. Along with widely-known creations of authors like Carr, Masur, Boucher, Rawson, and Coxe, are such relatively little-known characters as Verne Chute's Shadrach Arnold, W.T. Brannon's Jim Burgess, Joseph Commings's Senator Brooks U. Banner, and Ken Crossen's Mortimer Death. Interesting bits of trivia abound: August Derleth's Solar Pons published a monograph called *An Examination of the Cthulhu Cult and Others;* Q. Patrick's Timothy Trant collects neckties; Kelley Roos's Jeff Troy is a member of the Betty Grable Fan Club; and Stuart Palmer's Hildegarde Withers wrote for an education journal an article titled "Hoodlumism in Children Six to Twelve."

377. **Boucher, Anthony (William A.P. White), ed.** *Quintessence of Queen: Best Prize Stories from 12 Years of Ellery Queen's Mystery Magazine.* New York: Random, 1962. xiii, 560p.

Though there are no story notes and nothing specific about the *EQMM* prize contests (for which see *The Queen's Awards* and *Ellery Queen's The Golden 13* [see #490]), Boucher's five-page introduction, first published in the February 26, 1961, *New York Times Book Review* as "There Was No Mystery in What the Crime Editor Was After," recounts the early history of the magazine.

378. Breen, Jon L., and Rita A. Breen, eds. *American Murders: 11 Rediscovered Short Novels from the American Magazine 1934-1954.* (Garland Reference Library of the Humanities, Vol. 610.) New York: Garland, 1986. xiv, 452p. Illus., bibl.

An introduction discusses the *American's* short mystery novel series, and a twelve-page appendix lists all the novels in the series chronologically, noting series characters, specialized backgrounds, and subsequent book publications.

379. Brodkin, Sylvia Z., and Elizabeth J. Pearson, eds. *Seven Plays of Mystery & Suspense.* Globe, 1982. 212p.

Not examined. Per Contento (see #14), this is a textbook, with an overall introduction and such familiar school-days features as Questions for Final Review, Vocabulary Review, Glossary, and Writing Manual. The seven selected plays are Robert F. Carroll's "Heat Lightning," Arthur Hailey's "Flight Into Danger," Rod Serling's "I Shot an Arrow," Marjorie R. Watson's "The Dogs of War," Susan Glaspell's "Trifles," Louis N. Parker's "The Monkey's Paw" (from W.W. Jacobs' story), and Hamilton Deane and John L. Balderston's **Dracula** (from the Bram Stoker novel), the latter apparently the only full-length play included.

380. Bruccoli, Matthew J., and Richard Layman, eds. *A Matter of Crime,* vol. 1 through 4. San Diego: Harcourt, Brace, Jovanovich, 1987-1988.

The successor to the editors' *New Black Mask* (see #443), it follows the same pattern, though with a reduced rack-sized format and slightly less emphasis on the hardboiled school—though admittedly the choice of interview subjects tends not to bear the latter statement out. Volume 1 includes an interview with James Ellroy, volume 2 with Joe Gores and Linda Barnes, volume 3 with George V. Higgins, and volume 4 with Andrew Vachss.

381. **Burns, Rex, and Mary Rose Sullivan, eds.** *Crime Classics: The Mystery Story from Poe to the Present.* New York: Viking, 1990. xxv, 295p. Bibl.

The seventeen stories, from Poe's "Murders in the Rue Morgue" to McBain's "Sadie When She Died," are so familiar, the volume must rise or fall on the basis of its secondary material. The seventeen-page introduction and the story notes offer little that is new to the mystery buff but are reliable enough to make this an adequate choice for a course textbook. (I don't know where the editors got the idea Agatha Christie specialized in "witty literary allusion," however.)

Co-editor Burns, a solid but hardly ground-breaking author, is discussed in the introduction, and his *Strip Search* is among eighteen fiction titles listed under "Suggestions for Further Reading." Such self-serving behavior by historians and anthologists is not unheard-of, but when the rest of the list is made up of names like Dickens, Collins, Christie, Hammett, Sayers, and Chandler, with P.D. James the only active contemporary aside from Burns, it is unusually blatant. There is also an eighteen-item list of critical and bibliographic sources.

382. **Cartmell, Van H., and Bennett Cerf, eds.** *Famous Plays of Crime and Detection.* Introduction by John Chapman. Philadelphia: Blakiston, 1946. xv, 910p.

This pioneering collection of stage mysteries includes less detailed information than Stanley Richards's two volumes (see #503 and 504), but Chapman's introduction discusses each play in an interesting few paragraphs and cast credits for first Broadway production are included for most. The thirteen selections, little overlapping those of Richards, are William Gilette's *Sherlock Holmes,* Bayard Veiller's *Within the Law,* George M. Cohan's *Seven Keys to Baldpate* (with no cast credits), Elmer Rice's *On Trial* (credited with introducing the flashback), Roi Cooper Megrue's *Under Cover,* Veiller's *The Thirteenth Chair,* John Willard's *The*

Cat and the Canary, Mary Roberts Rinehart and Avery Hopwood's *The Bat*, Philip Dunning and George Abbott's *Broadway*, Jeffrey Dell's *Payment Deferred*, Edward Chodorov's *Kind Lady*, Emlyn Williams's *Night Must Fall*, and Patrick Hamilton's *Angel Street*.

383. **Cassiday, Bruce, ed.** *Roots of Detection: The Art of Deduction Before Sherlock Holmes.* New York: Ungar, 1983. vi, 195p.

In one of the few anthologies devoted entirely to detection pre-Doyle (and sometimes even pre-Poe), Cassiday provides a five-page introduction and informative story notes to selections (usually excerpts from longer works rather than short stories) from Herodotus, the Book of Daniel, the *Arabian Nights,* Voltaire, Hoffmann, Bulwer-Lytton, Vidocq, Poe, Dumas, Dickens, Collins, Mrs. Henry Wood, Charles Felix, and Gaboriau.

384. **Charteris, Leslie, ed.** *The Saint's Choice.* n.p.: Bond-Charteris, 1945. 119p.
  The Saint's Choice, volume 2. n.p.: Jacobs, 1945. 125p.
  The Saint's Choice of True Crime Stories. n.p.: Jacobs, 1945. 128p.
  The Saint's Choice of Humorous Crime. Hollywood: Shaw, 1945.
      142p.
  The Saint's Choice of Impossible Crime. Hollywood: Bond-Charteris,
      1945. 125p.
  The Saint's Choice of Hollywood Crime. Hollywood: Saint Enterprises,
      1946. 128p.
  The Saint's Choice of Radio Thrillers. Hollywood: Saint Enterprises,
      1946. 125p.

Charteris, always quick with a provocative opinion, explains his choices in individual introductions, sometimes running more than a page, to the stories in this enjoyable series. The first two volumes are devoted to stories by English and American writers respectively, with the editor managing to include himself in both categories. The misleadingly-titled fourth volume actually has a theme of science fiction, probably making it the pioneering collection of s.f./mystery hybrids. These paperbound volumes, besides being a nightmare for bibliographers with all those changes in publisher imprint, are undoubtedly hard to find now, but they're worth seeking out for the editor's commentary. A later series from 1959 and 1960, Saint Mystery Library, lacks secondary interest.

385. Clark, Mary Higgins, ed. *Murder on the Aisle.* (Mystery Writers of American Anthology.) New York: Simon and Schuster, 1987. x, 213p.

Clark's brief introduction lays out the theme and glosses the stories (fifteen tales with show business and sports backgrounds). But the concluding section of contributor biographies runs five pages and gives more information than average for such notes, of interest for famous names like Ellin, Hoch, Nolan, Slesar, and Treat, and even more so for short-story specialists like Betty Buchanan, J.F. Pierce, Joan Richter, Isak Romun, John F. Suter, and Gerald Tomlinson.

386. Clarke, Stephan P., ed. *Crimes and Clues.* (Prentice-Hall Passport Series.) Englewood Cliffs, NJ: Prentice-Hall, 1978. 273p.

Not examined, information per Contento (see #14). A "Logical Thinking and Writing" text, it includes an introduction, a portion of Sayers's "Aristotle on Detective Fiction," and presumably the usual textbook accoutrements.

387. Clute, Cedric E., Jr., and Nicholas Lewin, eds. *Sleight of Crime: Fifteen Classic Tales of Murder, Mayhem, and Magic.* Chicago: Regnery, 1977. viii, 301p. Illus., bibl.

Though beaten to the post by another anthology of magic-oriented mystery stories, Otto Penzler's *Whodunit? Houdini?* (see #474), this volume has equally fine contents and even greater reference value. The story notes give considerable information on the lives and works of writers like Clayton Rawson, Grant Allen, Chelsea Quinn Yarbro, Philip Mac-Donald, Walter B. Gibson, and Manly Wade Wellman, and most of the fifteen stories (including two vignettes by Stephen Leacock) have postscripts discussing their real-life inspirations and parallels. A nine-page photo section is headed "Intermission: A Pictorial Glimpse into the Magicians' World of Magic and Illusion," enjoyable albeit better suited to a nonfiction book on magic than to a mystery anthology. Finally, there is a two-page bibliography citing book-length "magical mysteries" (some pretty obscure) by eight authors.

388. Cooke, David C., ed. *My Best Murder Story.* New York: Merlin Press, 1955. 384p.

The original editor of *Best Detective Stories of the Year* (see #369) here asked fourteen American mystery writers to pick their best stories and tell why. Lengths of the authors' introductions (all interesting for one reason or another) run from a paragraph by Mignon G. Eberhart on "Spider" to three pages by Stuart Palmer on "Snafu Murder"; most run a page or more. Other contributors include Lawrence G. Blochman, Leslie Charteris, Octavus Roy Cohen, Frank Gruber, Vincent Starrett, John and Ward Hawkins, Q. Patrick, Hugh Pentecost, Ellery Queen, Craig Rice, Sax Rohmer, and editor Cooke.

(Only authors to appear both in Cooke's book and 28 years later in Josh Pachter's similar *Top Crime* [see #469] are Charteris and Queen, both of whom chose different stories for the latter volume. Charteris chose "The Arrow of God" for Cooke and "The Pearls of Peace" for Pachter, Queen "The Mad Tea Party" for Cooke and "The Adventure of Abraham Lincoln's Clue" for Pachter. Queen, who for the early volume *My Best Mystery Story* [a 1939 British anthology unfortunately bereft of any editorial apparatus at all] picked still another story, "The Adventure of the One-Penny Black," did his or their best choosing for Cooke, in my opinion.)

389. Coxe, George Harmon, ed. *Butcher, Baker, Murder-Maker.* (Mystery Writers of America anthology.) New York: Knopf, 1954. viii, 341p.

As in some of the other early MWA annual collections, the authors were asked to introduce their own stories. This time, Raymond Chandler made a rare appearance, introducing "I'll Be Waiting" as "the only thing I ever wrote deliberately to please a slick magazine." Rex Stout's "Cop's Gift" is described as "the only detective story of less than eighteen thousand words I have ever written. . . . As you will see when you read it, the characters are taken from stock . . . " Others include Robert Arthur, Ben Benson, Anthony Boucher, Stanley Ellin, Bruno Fischer, Michael Gilbert, Brett Halliday, Morris Hershman, William Byron Mowery, Stuart

Palmer, Q. Patrick, Maurice Procter, Ellery Queen, Clayton Rawson, Sidney Rowland, Walter Snow, and Thomas Walsh. Not providing comments on their contributions are Lillian de la Torre and Georges Simenon. (The introduction to Simenon's "Stan the Killer" "was written from material submitted by Mme. Simenon.")

390. Craig, Patricia, ed. *The Oxford Book of English Detective Stories.* Oxford and New York: Oxford U.P., 1990. xxi, 554p.

Craig's thirteen-page introduction discusses the selected stories in the course of a scholarly and readable historical commentary. There are also five pages of brief but informative biographical notes on the contributors. Most of the selections are by the expected well-known writers, with only Clarence Rook, about whom virtually nothing is known, a truly obscure name.

391. Creasey, John, ed. *Crime Across the Sea.* (Mystery Writers of America Anthology.) Preface by Herbert Brean. New York: Harper and Row, 1964. xiv, 235p.

In one of the more original MWA theme anthologies, Americans write British backgrounds and British write American. Neither Creasey's very short introduction nor Brean's preface offer much of special interest, but the five pages of author biographies are a bit more informative than usual. British entrants include Josephine Bell, Michael Gilbert, Bill Knox, and Julian Symons, while less well-known American names include Gladys Cluff, James Holding, Fred Levon, James McKimmey, and John F. Suter.

392. *Crime Wave: World's Winning Crime Stories 1981.* Introduction by Desmond Bagley. London: Collins, 1981. 287p.

As part of the Third Crime Writers' International Congress, held in Stockholm in 1981, a short-story competition was held with a Saab Turbo as the first prize. Frank Sisk's "A Visit with Montezuma," one of over 400 entries, won the car, and that story is published here along with second and third prize winners by Dwight Steward and Tony Hillerman and a dozen other entrants. Bagley's two-page introduction is amusing, and the volume concludes with three pages of notes on the authors. Despite the international nature of the event, only the Dutch Janwillem van de Wetering (who lives in the U.S. and writes in English) and Czechoslovakian Jaroslav Veis are neither English nor American.

393. Davenport, Basil, ed. *13 Ways to Dispose of a Body.* New York: Dodd, Mead, 1966. ix, 277p.

In this follow-up to *13 Ways to Kill a Man* (see below) the editor comments briefly on each disposal method in a postscript, sometimes discussing the efficacy of the method chosen, sometimes referring to other fictional or factual instances of the method.

394. Davenport, Basil, ed. *13 Ways to Kill a Man.* New York: Dodd, Mead, 1965. xx, 232p.

In a chatty ten-page introduction and story notes ranging from a paragraph to several pages, Davenport discourses on the various means of murder available and cites their employment in fact and fiction. Especially meaty are the essay on strangling preceding C.S. Forester's "The Turn of the Tide," the notes on stabbing at both ends of Edgar Jepson and Robert Eustace's "The Tea Leaf," and the survey of "The Animal Kingdom" introducing Maurice Level's "The Kennel." Other methods and the stories presented to illustrate them: "The Simplest of All" (Henry Slesar's "The Candidate"), beating (Roald Dahl's "Lamb to the Slaughter"—and Davenport does explain why he doesn't call it clubbing or bludgeoning instead), shooting (Melville Davisson Post's "The Adopted Daughter"), poison (Phyllis Bottome's "The Liqueur Glass"), burning (Edgar Allan Poe's "Hop-Frog"), starvation (Ronald A. Knox's "Solved by Inspection"), explosion (Anthony Berkeley's "The Policeman Only Knocks Once"), vehicular homicide (Robert Arthur's "Weapon, Motive, Method—"), electrocution (Stanley Ellin's "The Question My Son Asked"), and finally "One to Kill a Woman" (John Collier's "Back for Christmas").

395. Davis, Dorothy Salisbury, ed. *A Choice of Murders.* (Mystery Writers of America Anthology.) New York: Scribner, 1958. vii, 312p.

In some earlier MWA anthologies, the authors introduced their stories. This time they offer postscripts which, though usually only a few sentences and far less informative, sometimes include interesting tidbits. Ross Macdonald provides a postscript for wife Margaret Millar's story as well as his own. Others commenting include Stanley Ellin, Robert Turner, Stephen Marlowe, Mignon G. Eberhart, John Basye Price, Wenzell Brown, Anthony Gilbert, Anthony Boucher, Helen Kasson, Margaret Manners, Stuart Palmer, Andrew Garve, Marc Seymour, Lawrence Treat, James A. Kirch, and Michael Gilbert. Not taking the opportunity to comment are Ellery Queen, Ruthven Todd, Robert Arthur, Lawrence G. Blochman, and Ryerson Johnson.

396. Dickensheet, Dean, ed. *Men and Malice: An Anthology of Mystery and Suspense by West Coast Authors.* Garden City, NY: Doubleday/ Crime Club, 1973. xi, 248p.

Dickensheet's three-page introduction is mostly concerned with championing John Rollin Ridge, author of the purely fictitious *Life and Adventures of Jaoquin Murietta, The Celebrated California Bandit,* as "the earliest major crime writer on the West Coast . . . " The seventeen stories (mostly originals) have informative introductory notes and, in two cases, postscripts discussing the stories: Dickensheet on Jessamyn West's "Up a Tree" and Frank McAuliffe on his own Hammett/Chandler homage "The Maltese Falcon Commission." Among the other authors represented are Joe Gores, William F. Nolan, Richard Deming, Chelsea Quinn Yarbro, Ray Russell, and Randall Garrett.

397. Dozois, Gardner, and Susan Casper, eds. *Ripper.* New York: TOR, 1988. xx, 428p. Bibl.

Except for two obligatory classics, Robert Bloch's "Yours Truly, Jack the Ripper" and Harlan Ellison's "The Prowler in the City at the Edge of the World," the 19 stories (mostly supernatural) inspired by the Ripper's crimes are all originals. Bloch's eight-page foreword is a factual summary of the case, while the often substantial individual story introductions give considerable biographical information on the authors. Most contributors are better known as science fiction or horror writers than mystery writers, among them Karl Edward Wagner, Gene Wolfe, and Charles L. Grant. A very brief and non-comprehensive Further Reading list cites two earlier anthologies, four non-fiction references on the case (two unaccountably listed without their authors), and a list of eight other short story treatments of the crimes.

Another anthology commemorating the Ripper centennial, *Red Jack* (DAW, 1988), edited by Martin H. Greenberg, Charles G. Waugh, and Frank D. McSherry, Jr., consisting of reprints, including the Bloch and Ellison tales listed above, has less material of secondary interest.

398. Drew, Bernard, ed. *Hard-Boiled Dames: Stories Featuring Women Detectives, Reporters, Adventurers, and Criminals From the Pulp Fiction Magazines of the 1930's.* Preface by Marcia Muller. New York: St. Martin's, 1986. xix, 331p. Illus.

Muller's preface alludes to some of the current crop of female detectives, most of them created by women writers. But the stories Drew selects are all the work of men, and the female spotlighted is not always the main character. Drew's nine-page introduction offers a general discussion of women in the pulps, and the notes on individual stories provide biographical material on the authors when possible. The stories are reprinted directly from the original magazines with illustrations and some ads intact. Authors included range from the fairly well-known, such as Cleve F. Adams, Jean Francis Webb (as Roswell Brown), Frederick Nebel, Frederick C. Davis, Richard Sale, Judson P. Philips (better-known as Hugh Pentecost), and Hulbert Footner, through the faintly well-known (Theodore Tinsley, T.T. Flynn, Whitman Chambers) to the utterly forgotten (D.B. McCandless, Lars Anderson, Perry Paul, C.B. Yorke, Eugene Thomas).

399. Dulles, Allen, ed. *Great Spy Stories From Fiction.* New York: Harper, 1969. xiv, 433p.

In an anthology completed shortly before his death, the famous American spymaster offers plenty of information and provocative opinion in a four-page foreword and substantial introductions to each of twelve sections and the 32 individual entries, most of them excerpts from novels rather than short stories.

400. Furman, A.L., ed. *The Mystery Companion.* New York: Gold Label, 1943. 438p.
Second Mystery Companion. New York: Gold Label, 1944. viii, 410p.
Third Mystery Companion. New York: Gold Label, 1945. x, 395p.
Fourth Mystery Companion. New York: Lantern, 1946. viii, 396p.

I have examined only the fourth. The eight-page "Biographies" section at the end of the book includes a paragraph or two on each of the nineteen authors, sometimes in their own words. Among those offering autobiographical notes are George Harmon Coxe, Mignon G. Eberhart, William MacHarg, Hugh Pentecost, and Vincent Starrett. The very short mirror bios of Cornell Woolrich and William Irish are intentionally misleading: both are said to be 36 years old (43 being more accurate at the time), "brown hair, blue eyes, height 5 foot 9. Born in New York." But Irish has "a rotten disposition," Woolrich a "fair" one, and while Irish is "married on Tuesdays, Thursdays, and Saturdays," Woolrich is married on "Mondays, Wednesdays, and Fridays." (Ellery Queen once speculated that Woolrich/Irish must have been a bachelor on Sundays.) Along with the well-known writers are less familiar names like Walter C. Brown, Louis Paul, and Frederick Skerry. According to Contento and Greenberg (see #14), the first volume in the series lacks this separate feature, but the second and third have it. The third is also a source of considerable information on Woolrich according to *Blues of a Lifetime* (see #350).

401. Gardiner, Dorothy, ed. *For Love or Money.* (Mystery Writers of America Anthology.) Garden City, NY: Doubleday/ Crime Club, 1957. 233p.

Though this MWA anthology doesn't have the meaty secondary information of some of its predecessors, there are brief biographical notes before each story, often in the author's own words. Along with the usual suspects (Allingham, Blochman, Coxe, Fischer, Queen, Simenon, Treat, etc.) are some less familiar names, including Gladys Cluff, Margaret Manners, Sidney Rowland, and C.L. Sweeney, Jr.

402. Garfield, Brian, ed. *The Crime of My Life: Favorite Stories by Presidents of the Mystery Writers of America.* New York: Walker, 1984. x, 269p.

President of MWA at the time this book was compiled, Garfield asked all living past presidents to select their favorite stories and tell why. Thirteen such tales appear, introduced by their authors, and Garfield's preface includes a list of all MWA presidents to date. Contributors include Helen McCloy, Richard Martin Stern, John D. MacDonald, Edward D. Hoch, Lawrence Treat, Harold Q. Masur, Robert Bloch, Stanley Ellin, Hillary Waugh, Lillian de la Torre, editor Garfield, Georges Simenon, and Dorothy Salisbury Davis.

It's irresistible to compare the choices of those writers who also responded to the same request for Josh Pachter's *Top Crime* (see #469), published in the U.S.A. in the same year. Hoch picked "The Leopold Locked Room" for both volumes. Treat picked "Give the Devil His Due" for Garfield, "L as in Loot" for Pachter. Simenon chose "Blessed are the Meek" for Garfield, "Seven Little Crosses in a Notebook" for Pachter.

403. Gilbert, Elliot L., ed. *The World of Mystery Fiction*. Del Mar, CA: University Extension, U. of California, San Diego, in cooperation with Publisher's Inc., 1978. xxxi, 441p.

Intended as a text for a college course on mystery fiction, this large anthology was accompanied by a separate instructor's guide (see WAM #42). With a very high familiarity quotient in the selections, the book's greatest value is in its editorial apparatus: a scholarly 25-page introduction, including an annotated bibliography of ten secondary sources, and unusually extensive story notes. The sections include "In the Beginning" (Vidocq, William Russell, Dickens), "Poe and the First Great Detective" (reprinting "Murders in the Rue Morgue," "The Purloined Letter," and surprisingly "The Tell-Tale Heart," advanced as an example of the crime story as opposed to the detective story), "The Game's Afoot" (three Sherlock Holmes stories), "More Great Detectives" (Futrelle, Chesterton, Post, Bramah), "The Golden Age" (Sayers, Queen, Simenon), "The Black Mask School" (Hammett, Chandler, Woolrich, Macdonald), and "The Limits of Detection" (Barr, Christie, Borges).

404. Godfrey, Thomas, ed. *Murder for Christmas*. Illustrated by Gahan Wilson. New York: Mysterious, 1982. xi, 465p. Illus., bibl.

This large collection of stories, cartoons, and verse includes a twelve-title checklist, briefly annotated, of Christmas mystery novels and excellent biographical and critical notes on the contributors, most well-known in the mystery field (Doyle, Christie, Queen, Ellin, Simenon, Stout) and outside it (Woody Allen, Runyon, O. Henry, Dickens, Stevenson, Hardy). Some of the individual story introductions include leads on criminous Christmas stories not included here.

405. Godfrey, Thomas, ed. *English Country House Murders.* New York: Mysterious, 1988. xvii, 348p.

This work, along with *Murder for Christmas* (see above), marks Godfrey as one of the best, if not most prolific, present-day anthologists. A good tongue-in-cheek introduction lays out the rules of this specialized branch of the formal detective story, and the individual story notes are very good as well. Among the 22 contributors are the inevitable (Doyle, Chesterton, Christie, Sayers, Marsh, Carr, etc.), usually represented by less frequently-reprinted stories, along with some surprises (P.G. Wodehouse, Ethel Lina White, James Miles).

406. Godfrey, Thomas, ed. *Murder at the Opera.* London: O'Mara, 1988. New York: Mysterious, 1989. vi, 250p.

This Godfrey anthology is an equally wide-ranging and tasteful compilation but contains less editorial apparatus than the other two. Most interesting part of the three-page introduction is the account of Helen Traubel's "The Ptomaine Canary," apparently actually written by the famed soprano, though her novel *The Metropolitan Opera Murders* (1951) is known to have been ghosted by Harold Q. Masur. Each story is headed with the place, year, and opera being performed.

407. Goodstone, Tony, ed. *The Pulps: Fifty Years of American Pop Culture.* New York: Chelsea, 1970. xvi, 239p. Illus., bibl.

Following eight pages of general pulp history and a selection of color plates reproducing an even hundred covers, Goodstone divides the pulps into ten categories, introducing each in a couple of pages and reprinting complete stories from all but the Hero Pulps, represented by some excerpts from Shadow and Doc Savage novels. The Detective and Mystery section totals 43 pages and presents stories by Rodrigues Ottolengui, Dashiell Hammett, T.T. Flynn, Robert Leslie Bellem, MacKinlay Kantor, and Ray Bradbury. There is overlapping mystery interest in some of the other categories, particularly adventure (including tales by Edgar Wallace and William P. McGivern) and "Straight Out Sex" (with another Bellem contribution).

408. Gorman, Edward, ed. *The Black Lizard Anthology of Crime Fiction*. Berkeley, CA: Black Lizard, 1987. x, 335p.

Gorman's four-page introduction to this gathering of noir fiction celebrates the 1950s paperback originals of Gold Medal that influenced and inspired many present-day writers of harder edged crime fiction. His brief notes on the individual stories are more appreciations than biographies, and they often capture the special qualities of their various subjects very well. Most of the contributors are very familiar names (e.g. Bill Pronzini, William Campbell Gault, Harlan Ellison, Jim Thompson, Clark Howard), with a few relatively lesser-known pros (Robert Edmond Alter, James Reasoner, Michael Seidman), and one newcomer (Barbara Beman).

409. Gorman, Ed, ed. *Dark Crimes: Great Noir Fiction from the '40s to the '90s*. New York: Carroll & Graf, 1991. 464p.

Along with nineteen short stories, most preceded by very brief bio-critical notes, this generous anthology includes two novels by '50s paperback original specialists, both of which (ironically) originally appeared in hardcover. Gil Brewer's *The Red Scarf* has a moving 14-page introduction by Bill Pronzini, describing Brewer's troubled life and career, while Peter Rabe's *Anatomy of a Killer* is preceded by obituaries by editor Gorman and Bill Crider. All this secondary material originally appeared in *Mystery Scene* magazine and deserves the relative permanency of book form. The volume is indicated to be the first in an annual series, and a second volume has been announced for January 1993 publication.

410. **Gorman, Ed, ed.** *The Second Black Lizard Anthology of Crime Fiction.* Berkeley, CA: Black Lizard, 1988. xiii, 664p.

This time, Gorman's three-page introduction celebrates *Manhunt,* one of the greatest of the mystery digests, and again the story introductions are thoughtful and brief. Main reference value, though, lies in Donald E. Westlake's introduction to Peter Rabe's novel *Murder Me for Nickels,* essentially an abridged version of his essay on Rabe in *Murder Off the Rack* (see #137). A story by the late literary agent Ray Puechner is preceded by two-page tribute from one of his clients, Joe Lansdale.

411. **Gorman, Edward; Robert J. Randisi, and Martin H. Greenberg, eds.** *Under the Gun: Mystery Scene Presents the Best Mystery and Suspense Fiction.* New York: New American Library, 1990. xiii, 401p.

Originally projected as the first in an annual series of best-of-the-year volumes, this generous compilation includes a five-page introduction by Randisi reviewing mystery-related events of 1988; story introductions credited to Jim Frenkel; an eight-page article on paperback writer J.M. Flynn from Bill Pronzini's "Forgotten Writers" series in *Mystery Scene* magazine; a three-page recommended reading list of the best novels and short stories of 1988; and finally a short half-page history of *Mystery Scene.* (Though no second volume of *Under the Gun* appeared, the Gorman-Greenberg team have continued their efforts to establish a year's-best alternative to the long-running series edited by Edward D. Hoch [see #369], and a volume on 1990 was scheduled for publication by Carroll & Graf in late 1992 under the title *The Year's 25 Finest Crime and Mystery Stories.)*

412. **Goulart, Ron, ed.** *The Great British Detective.* New York: New American Library, 1982. xiv, 369p. Bibl.

Goulart contributes a six-page introduction, substantial individual story notes averaging about a page, and an eight-page lightly-annotated checklist of books about the series detectives appearing in his fifteen selections, plus a list of a half dozen anthologies containing British detective fiction. The emphasis is historical, with only Ruth Rendell's Inspector Wexford having debuted after World War II. Apart from the expected sleuths of Doyle, Morrison, Freeman, Chesterton, Bailey, Christie, Sayers, Allingham, Carr, and Vickers, Goulart includes Sexton Blake (in a 1906 case, "The Rajah's Bodyguard," by William Murray Graham), C.L. Pirkis's Loveday Brooke, Grant Allen's Colonel Clay, and Robert Barr's Eugene Valmont (for once represented by a story other than "The Absent-Minded Coterie"). That the same editor could produce this volume and the one that follows bespeaks a catholic taste indeed.

413. Goulart, Ron, ed. *The Hardboiled Dicks.* Los Angeles: Sherbourne, 1965. xviii, 296p. Bibl.

A good eight-page introduction on mysteries in the pulps leads off this strong collection. The individual story notes give sparse biographical information about the eight contributors (Norbert Davis, John K. Butler, Frederick Nebel, Raoul Whitfield, Frank Gruber, Richard Sale, Lester Dent, and Erle Stanley Gardner). The four-page "Informal Reading List" enumerates (unfortunately without publisher or date) some of the books of prominent pulp writers, including several not represented in the anthology.

414. Green, Jen, ed. *Reader, I Murdered Him: Original Crime Stories by Women.* Introduction by Alison Hennegan. New York: St. Martin's, 1989. 234p.

The reference value of this gathering of sixteen mostly original tales lies in the twelve-page introduction, recounting some detective story history from a feminist perspective and defending the form against Q.D. Leavis's attack on it in the thirties, and in the three pages of biographical notes on the contributors, some celebrated (Amanda Cross, Susan Dunlap, Sara Paretsky, Sheila Radley, Margaret Yorke) but most relatively little-known.

415. Greenberg, Martin H., ed. *Masterpieces of Mystery and Suspense.* New York: St. Martin's, 1988. xvi, 651p.

With forty entries, this is one of the largest and most all-encompassing of one-volume mystery anthologies. The six-page historical introduction is an efficient short summary, and the notes to the stories are often substantial, though with the familiarity of most of the contributors, there is little information not available elsewhere.

416. Greenberg, Martin, ed. *The New Edgar Winners*. (Mystery Writers of American Anthology.) Introduction by Donald E. Westlake. New York: Wynwood, 1990. 255p.

The ten Edgar-winning short stories for 1979 through 1988 are gathered with a four-page introduction by Westlake and a couple of pages of abbreviated author bios. Main reference value is a 17-page list of all Edgar winners and nominees in adult fiction categories from 1945 through 1988.

417. Greenberg, Martin H., and Ed Gorman, eds. *Cat Crimes*. New York: Fine, 1991. x, 260p.

Co-editor Gorman combines biographical snippets with interesting evaluative comments in his four pages of notes on the seventeen contributors to this original anthology, but of even greater interest is the remarkably candid autobiographical account of his own relationship with cats in the three-page introduction. Contributors combine the very well-known (Lovesey, Pronzini, Hughes, Lutz) with some less prominent and hence less written about (e.g. Christopher Fahy, Douglas Borton, and Barbara Collins.) The follow-up volume, *Cat Crimes II* (Fine, 1992) has an equally impressive list of contributors but less secondary interest.

418. Greene, Douglas G., and Robert C.S. Adey, eds. *Death Locked In: An Anthology of Locked Room Stories*. New York: International Polygonics, 1987. 553p.

Though this generous anthology is more notable for the quality of its contents than for its reference value, Greene's three-page introduction traces the early history of locked room and impossible crime situations, and the notes to the 24 stories are often informative.

419. Greene, Hugh, ed. *The Rivals of Sherlock Holmes: Early Detective Stories.* London: The Bodley Head; New York: Pantheon, 1970. 352p. Illus.

Greene's four anthologies of the works of Doyle's contemporaries all include valuable historical information along with fine and usually unfamiliar stories. The twelve-page introduction to this first volume provides biographical notes on the authors and keys the various detectives and rogues to their haunts on a double-page map of London circa 1898. There are thirteen tales, two by Arthur Morrison (about Martin Hewitt and Dorrington & Hicks), two by Baroness Orczy (concerning Lady Molly of Scotland Yard and the Old Man in the Corner), three by R. Austin Freeman (one as himself about Dr. Thorndyke and two in collaboration as Clifford Ashdown, about Romney Pringle), and single tales about Max Pemberton's Bernard Sutton, Guy Boothby's Klimo, L.T. Meade and Robert Eustace's Eric Vandeleur, William LeQueux's Duckworth Drew, William Hope Hodgson's Carnacki, and Ernest Bramah's Max Carrados. (Note that for convenience the listing of further Greene anthologies below follows a chronological rather than the usual alphabetical arrangement.)

420. Greene, Hugh, ed. *More Rivals of Sherlock Holmes: Cosmopolitan Crimes.* London: The Bodley Head, 1971. As *Cosmopolitan Crimes: Foreign Rivals of Sherlock Holmes.* New York: Pantheon, 1971. 348p.

Greene's second set of stories from the period between 1891 (Holmes's *Strand* debut) and 1914 (the beginning of World War I) moves away from London, with the exception of one investigation there by a French detective, and to locales on the Continent, in North America, and in South Africa. As in the previous volume, the introduction (shorter this time at ten pages) includes notes on the authors and the final page gives the sources for the stories. Authors and characters represented include Grant Allen's Colonel Clay (two stories), George Griffith's very obscure Inspector Lipinski, Arnold Bennett's Cecil Thorold, Robert Barr's Eugene Valmont, Jacques Futrelle's Thinking Machine (two stories), Maurice Leblanc's Arsene Lupin (two stories), Baron Palle Rosenkrantz's Lieutenant Holst, Balduin Groller's Dagobert Trostler, E. Phillips Oppenheim's Mr. Laxworthy, and H. Hesketh Prichard's November Joe.

421. Greene, Hugh, ed. *The Crooked Counties.* London: The Bodley Head, 1973. As *The Further Rivals of Sherlock Holmes.* New York: Pantheon, 1973. 319p. Bibl.

The theme this time is British detection outside London, and the format is as before. Greene opens his ten-page introduction with the prediction that this will be his last anthology of pre-World War I detective stories. ("I doubt whether there are many more discoveries to be made.") Recurring from earlier volumes are Arthur Morrison (one story each about Hewitt and Dorrington), Jacques Futrelle (about a house detective in a seaside hotel), and Ernest Bramah (about Max Carrados). Newcomers include Catherine Louisa Pirkis's Loveday Brooke, Dick Donovan, M. McDonnell Bodkin's Paul Beck and Dora Myrl (in one story each), Fergus Hume's Hagar Stanley, L.T. Meade and Clifford Halifax's Gilchrist, J.S. Fletcher's Archer Dawe, Richard Marsh's Judith Lee, and Victor L. Whitechurch's Thorpe Hazell.

422. Greene, Hugh, ed. *The American Rivals of Sherlock Holmes.* London: The Bodley Head; New York: Pantheon, 1976. 350p. Bibl.

Crediting brother Graham with the idea, the editor returns for one last stand, the format as before. Futrelle's Thinking Machine makes a return appearance. Other characters included are Hugh C. Weir's Madelyn Mack, Rodriguez Ottolengui's Barnes and Mitchell (two stories), Josiah Flynt and Francis Walton's New York cops and robbers, William MacHarg and Edwin Balmer's Luther Trant (two stories), Samuel Hopkins Adams's Average Jones, Francis Lynde's Scientific Sprague, Charles Felton Pidgin and J.M. Taylor's Quincy Adams Sawyer, Arthur B. Reeve's Craig Kennedy, Frederick Irving Anderson's Infallible Godahl, and Richard Harding Davis's District Attorney Wharton (in a story the editor admits is "very much a borderline case"). The eight-page introduction is packed with interesting information about the authors. Greene's four-volume series ranks high among historical anthologies of the form.

423. Hale, T.J., ed. *Great French Detective Stories.* New York: Vanguard, 1984. 284p.

This is one of the most reference-worthy anthologies because of the concise history of French detective fiction recounted in the thirty-page introduction. Some of the subjects (and contributors) are well-known to English readers: Vidocq, Gaboriau (whose influence on Conan Doyle is discussed at length), Leblanc, Leroux, and Simenon. Others are little-known because seldom or never translated: Jacques Decrest, Pierre Very (whom Hale believes "a more stylish and amusing writer than Agatha Christie" [page 33]), Jype Carraud, and Leo Malet (the French equivalent of Hammett and Chandler). Putting the French writers in their historical context, Hale also touches on William Godwin's *Adventures of Caleb Williams* and Poe's Dupin stories.

Hale calls Simenon "the only Continental writer of detective stories to have had any widespread recognition outside his own country in the last fifty years" (page 27). Don't the Scandinavians, most notably Maj Sjöwall and Per Wahlöö, count as "Continental"?

424. Haycraft, Howard, ed. *The Boys' Book of Great Detective Stories*. New York: Harper, 1938. viii, 315p.

Haycraft's preface is very brief, but the individual story notes, often running to a page or more, present much early history of the detective-story form and serve as a precursor to the author's *Murder for Pleasure* (WAM #1). Biographical information on the authors is considerable. Included are Poe, Doyle, Barr, Futrelle, Freeman, Leblanc, Orczy, Balmer & MacHarg, Samuel Hopkins Adams, Chesterton, Post, and Reeve.

425. Haycraft, Howard, ed. *The Boys' Second Book of Great Detective Stories*. New York: Harper, 1940. viii, 352p.

In the same format as the volume above, Haycraft introduces stories by Bentley, Bramah, O'Higgins, Fletcher, Christie, Bailey, "Sapper," Anderson, Sayers, the Coles, Cohen, Rhode, Berkeley, and Wallace. Only three American writers appear, giving the volume an even more striking British bias than its predecessor, which had six. Though both these books were directed at adolescents (and of only one gender at that!), they are uncondescending and perform fine as adult anthologies.

426. Hoch, Edward D., ed. *All But Impossible: An Anthology of Locked Room and Impossible Crime Stories by Members of the Mystery Writers of America.* (Mystery Writers of America Anthology.) New York: Ticknor and Fields, 1981. xi, 359p.

In his three-page introduction, Hoch gives the results of a poll he conducted of seventeen mystery scholars to select the best locked room/impossible crime novels. Top vote-getter was John Dickson Carr's *The Three Coffins (The Hollow Man)*, and three other Carr products appear in the top ten, along with books by Hake Talbot (whose *Rim of the Pit* was a surprising second), Gaston Leroux, Israel Zangwill, Clayton Rawson, Ellery Queen, and H.H. Holmes (Anthony Boucher).

427. Hoch, Edward D., and Martin H. Greenberg, eds. *Murder Most Sacred: Great Catholic Tales of Mystery and Suspense.* New York: Dembner, 1989. ix, 213p. Bibl.

Hoch's three-page introduction provides a brief history of the Catholic connection in mystery fiction, including an account of the first identifiable use (in a play by Paul Anthelme) of the classic situation where a priest hears a murderer's confession and must keep silent despite compelling reasons to want the truth to come to light. The biographical introductions to the eleven stories (by writers as varied as Boucher, Chesterton, Muller, and Simenon) are brief but informative. Best reference feature of the book is a six-page, lightly annotated bibliography of Catholic mystery fiction. An earlier Catholic mystery anthology, *Bodies and Souls* (Doubleday/Crime Club, 1961), edited by Dan Herr and Joel Wells, lacks secondary interest.

428. Hoppenstand, Gary, ed. *The Dime Novel Detective.* Bowling Green, OH: Popular, 1982. 254p. Bibl.

Following a page-and-a-half preface by Edward T. LeBlanc and a two-page introduction by the editor, this large format paperback reprints (usually in dauntingly small type) stories from five dime novel detective series: New York Detective Library (featuring Old King Brady), Old Cap Collier, Old Sleuth Library, Bob Brooks Library, and Secret Service (featuring Old and Young King Brady), each with an individual introduction by the editor and followed by an undated numerical checklist of the series. Nick Carter, though featured on the cover, does not appear in the book.

429. **Hoppenstand, Gary, and Ray B. Browne, eds.** *The Defective Detective in the Pulps.* Bowling Green, OH: Popular, 1983. 119p. Illus.

In a seven-page introduction provocatively titled "I'd Kiss You Sweetheart, But My Lips are Missing," the editors recount an unusual pulp-magazine phenomenon: detectives with physical and mental defects, most of whom inhabited the pages of *Dime Mystery Magazine,* though the earliest example, Paul Ernst's "Madam Murder—and the Corpse Brigade" (about Seekay, a private detective with no face), appeared in *Strange Detective Mysteries.* Other characters represented (in stories reprinted directly from the pulps complete with illustrations and ads) are John Kobler's Peter Quest (glaucoma), Warren Lucas's Lin Melchan (super-sensitive hearing), Grendon Alzee's Tom (blind), Dick (deaf), and Harry (twisted legs); Nat Schachner's Nicholas Street (amnesia), and Edith and Ejler Jacobson's Nat Perry (hemophilia).

430. **Hoppenstand, Gary; Garyn G. Roberts, and Ray B. Browne, eds.** *More Tales of the Defective Detective in the Pulps.* Bowling Green, OH: Popular, 1985. 172p. Illus.

Another seven-page introduction puts the "defective" detectives in their 1930s historical context, likening them to the handicapped President Roosevelt, and comments on the stories. Recurring from the earlier collection in two stories each are the Jacobsons' Nat Perry and Kobler's Peter Quest. Featured in three stories is Russell Gray's (Bruno Fischer's) Ben Bryn, a polio victim with withered legs but a well-developed upper body. Leon Byrne's deaf sleuth Dan Holden appears in a single tale. Again, the stories are reproduced directly from their original pulp-magazine appearances, with illustrations and ads included.

431. **Hubin, Allen J. ed.** *Best of the Best Detective Stories: 25th Annual Collection.* New York: Dutton, 1971. 380p.

The same year Hubin took over editorship of Dutton's long-running _Best Detective Stories of the Year_ (see #369), he edited this anthology of stories from the series' first twenty-four volumes, one from each year and with no duplication with the 1960 _Best of the Best Detective Stories_ volume edited by David C. Cooke or _Boucher's Choicest_ (1969), selected by Jeanne Bernkopf (see #368) from Anthony Boucher's volumes in the series. The two-page introduction, recounting the series' history, and the story notes are fairly negligible, but a ten-page checklist indexes the 24 volumes from 1946-1971. Most frequent contributors to that point included Ellery Queen (11 entries), Jack Ritchie (10), Craig Rice, Richard Deming, and Edward D. Hoch (6 each).

432. Huffman, Grant, ed. *12 Detective Stories: Their History and Development.* Toronto: McClelland & Stewart, 1965.

Not examined. Per Contento (see #14), it is a secondary school anthology with an introduction, "A Defence of Detective Fiction," by the editor. The extent of additional editorial apparatus is not known.

433. Hutchison, Don, ed. *The Super Feds: A Facsimile Selection of Dynamic G-Man Stories from the 1930s.* (Starmont Popular Culture Study No. 8.) Mercer Island, WA: Starmont, 1988. v, 158p. Illus., bibl.

Not examined. According to Walter Albert (writing in _The Armchair Detective,_ v. 24 n. 3, p. 326), the 13-page introduction discusses "the popular image of J. Edgar Hoover and the FBI in the 1930s and, in particular, the G-Man as he was portrayed in the pulps," and the bibliography "lists the contents of _Ace G-Man Stories_ by issue; there is also a checklist of 'Main Series Characters' . . . " Better-known names among the contributors (per Contento [see #14]) are Emile C. Tepperman, William R. Cox, Wyatt Blassingame, and Day Keene.

434. Jakubowski, Maxim. *New Crimes.* London Robinson, 1989. New York: Carroll & Graf, 1990. xiv, 253p.
   New Crimes 2. London: Robinson, 1990. New York: Carroll & Graf, 1991. 244p. Bibl.

New Crimes 3. London: Robinson, 1991. New York: Carroll & Graf,
1992. 272p.

The four-page introduction to the first volume of this stimulating
original anthology series briefly profiles the contributors, but the main
secondary interest comes from two features: a six-page Patricia Highsmith
interview (in journalistic rather than transcript style) by John Williams
and ten pages by John Conquest from the introduction to his private eye
reference book *Trouble is My Business* (see #13), covering such topics as
ethnic, homosexual, and female private eyes, mystery reviewers, and
Conquest's choice for the "10 best non-American PI writers." British
novelist Nancy Spain heads the list.

The second and third volumes do not have as much reference interest
as the first, though in each case there is an introduction with notes on the
contributors. *New Crimes 2* also has the editor's enjoyable six-page piece
on Jim Thompson (followed by a Thompson checklist) and a four-page
reprint of a 1947 article on the Black Dahlia case written by David Goodis
for the Los Angeles *Herald-Examiner.* (More interesting than either might
have been the piece that did not materialize, according to the introduction,
"a well-deserved demolition piece on that princess of the cozies, American
author Martha Grimes, demonstrating how bad her knowledge of Britain
and British customs was.") Only other item of secondary interest in *New
Crimes 3* is John Dickson Carr's seven-page Sherlockian piece, "Another
Glass, Watson!"

435. Kahn, Joan, ed. *Chilling and Killing.* Boston: Houghton, Mifflin,
1978. 332p.

Not examined. Per Contento (see #14), it includes a preface by
Jacques Barzun as well as Kahn's introduction and the customary section
of biographical notes, as in the volumes below.

436. **Kahn, Joan, ed.** *The Edge of the Chair.* New York: Harper and Row,
1967. x, 560p.

Like most of Kahn's subsequent anthologies, this one alternates
fiction with true-crime articles. The introduction and story notes are
negligible, but the eight pages of biographical notes, credited to Onica

Friend, are well-organized and informative. (With at least one error, however—Ray Bradbury, precocious but not that precocious, was born in 1920 rather than 1930.) The variety of authors represented by the 34 stories is a tribute to Kahn's editorial net—along with Buchan, Chesterton, Christie, Ellin, Sayers, and Doyle, we have Faulkner, Flanner, Kipling, Pinter, Pushkin, Saint-Exupery, and science fictionist Lewis Padgett (Henry Kuttner and C.L. Moore).

437. Kahn, Joan, ed. *Hanging by a Thread.* Boston: Houghton, Mifflin, 1969. xix, 604p.

Kahn's second anthology, with 36 stories of fact and fiction, boasts a foreword (in verse, of course) by Ogden Nash and a five-page introduction by Eudora Welty. The nine pages of biographical notes, credited to Mary McGinn, cover some writers best-known for mystery fiction (Armstrong, Hammett, John D. MacDonald) or true crime (Pearson, Roughead) but even more from other branches of literature (Borges, Budrys, Bulwer-Lytton, Camus, Gorky, Heyerdahl, Paton, Tacitus, Dylan Thomas, Thurber, H.G. Wells).

438. Kahn, Joan, ed. *Open at Your Own Risk.* Boston: Houghton, Mifflin, 1975. xiii, 506p.

Another 25 entries are followed by seven pages of biographical notes by Sherry Knox. Again the mainstream names (Maugham, Sir Walter Scott, Osbert Sitwell, Wilde, Wodehouse) at least equal the genre names (Michael Gilbert, Lustgarten, Offord, Symons).

439. Kahn, Joan, ed. *Trial and Terror.* Boston: Houghton, Mifflin, 1973. xv, 569p.

The mixture as before (albeit with fewer entries, 25) finishes with nine pages of biographies compiled by Ann O'Hara. Kahn's three page introduction is a ringing defense of the mystery (short and long), quoting from several earlier commentators. The collection has a loose courtroom theme, but most of the trials described are in the nonfictional pieces. The contributors again are a stimulating mix of genre (Hammett, Sayers,

Wallace, Halliday) and mainstream (Roger Angell, Sartre, Balzac, Kafka, Flannery O'Connor).

440. Kittredge, William, and Steven M. Krauzer, eds. *The Great American Detective*. New York: New American Library, 1978. xxxiv, 414p. Bibl.

The editors recount the history of American detective fiction in a meaty 25-page introduction, and their extensive story notes average a page and a half. The fifteen detectives selected range from the inevitable (Queen, Spade, Marlowe, Wolfe, Mason, Archer) through the historically important (Nick Carter, Carroll John Daly's Race Williams), three selected female representatives (Eberhart's Susan Dare, Woolrich's one-shot Jerry Wheeler, and Palmer's Hildegarde Withers) to some welcome if unexpected choices: the Shadow in a radio play by Tom McKnight and Jerry Divine, Robert Leslie Bellem's Dan Turner, Brett Halliday's Michael Shayne, and Don Pendleton's Mack Bolan. The 19-page appendix, "Some Suggestions for Further Reading," includes a short list of out-of-print dealers, checklists of the included authors, and a secondary bibliography. An admirably thorough job, the book ought to have been published in a more permanent form than paperback original.

441. Knight, Stephen, ed. *Dead Witness: Best Australian Mystery Stories*. Ringwood, Victoria: Penguin, 1989. xxv, 259p.

The 17-page introduction provides an informative history of the mystery short story in Australia, undoubtedly fresh ground for most British and American readers. Three stories are set in Australia by British writers (Doyle, Meade and Eustace, and Hornung). Of the thirteen other contributors, a few are familiar (A.E. Martin, Arthur W. Upfield, Peter Corris) but most new to the Up Over reader.

442. Knox, Father Ronald, and H. Harrington, eds. *The Best Detective Stories of the Year 1928*. London: Faber, 1929. As *The Best English Detective Stories: First Series*. New York: Liveright, 1929. 420p.

Knox's fifteen-page introduction defines the detective story and reprises his famous ten rules for writing one. Then he performs a service to the reader that may be unique in anthological annals: he tells (when possible) exactly at what point in each of the stories "to stop, put the book down, light a fresh pipe, take a turn round the garden, and try to solve the mystery . . . "

443. Layman, Richard, and Matthew J. Bruccoli, eds. *The New Black Mask*, numbers 1 through 8. San Diego: Harcourt, Brace, Jovanovich, 1985-1987.

This title is somewhere on the borderline between an anthology series and a magazine—in fact, the first two volumes carried the title *The New Black Mask Quarterly*—but its distribution as a trade paperback makes it appropriate for this listing. The series featured original and reprinted short stories, most but certainly not all in the hardboiled tradition, with informative introductory notes, often quoting from the authors about their backgrounds or the inspiration of the story at hand. Also, each issue includes an interview (usually between six and twenty pages) with a major writer of crime fiction, followed by either a short story or a novel excerpt and sometimes including the author's commentary on the featured work. Subjects of the interviews include Robert B. Parker (in #1, with an excerpt from his Edgar-winning novel *Promised Land* and a commentary on his introduction of Hawk, Spenser's black sidekick, in that book); Elmore Leonard (#2, with a commentary of *La Brava*, also an Edgar winner); Donald E. Westlake (#3, with a commentary on series crook Dortmunder preceding an excerpt from *Good Behavior*); Loren D. Estleman (#4); William Haggard (#5, a definite departure from the *Black Mask* school, including a commentary on his short story, "Timeo Danaos"); Georges Simenon (#6, a very short interview of only three pages); Ed McBain (#7); and John D. MacDonald (#8). Issues 5 and 6 also include a two-part serialization of Dashiell Hammett's screen treatment for *After the Thin Man*, with a three-page introduction, about the series and Hammett's troubled relationship with MGM, and a postscript describing how Hammett's treatment differs from the finished film. (The series was succeeded by *A Matter of Crime* [see #380].)

444. Liebman, Arthur, ed. *Thirteen Classic Detective Stories: A Critical History of Detective Fiction.* New York: Rosen, 1974. xii, 237p. Bibl.

A two-page introduction recounts some of the rules of detective fiction. Each of the thirteen sections is preceded by two to four pages of history, with a single paragraph introducing each of the individual stories, which are almost all anthology staples. With over fifty pages of history and bibliography, this textbook anthology has much more extensive scholarly content than most, but its extremely conventional approach seems to belong to a period twenty to thirty years before its publication date. Already outmoded as a text when it was published, it is even more so today; there's scarcely a point made that Howard Haycraft's *Murder for Pleasure* (see WAM #1) hadn't made better over thirty years before. And there are too many errors in so derivative a collection, including garbled names ("Frances" Steegmuller, Anna "Katherine" Green, "Caroline" Wells, "A.E." Freeman) and dubious statements (e.g. that "the output of female authors began to decline" in the 20s with the coming of the hardboiled school [page 115] or that the Perry Mason novels succeeded in TV because they were "rarely complex in plot, structure, or solution" [page 207].) Worst of all, the introduction to the Poe story seems to confuse first and third person, an especially serious lapse in a textbook for the literary neophyte. A six-page annotated listing of significant detective novels and collections suggests some admirable titles, but places and dates of publication are frequently inaccurate or misleading. The two-page list of important anthologies and collections is a good one.

The volume's back cover advertises several other volumes in the "Masterpieces of Mystery" series, presumably in a comparable format: *Tales of Horror and the Supernatural: The Occult in Literature, Classic Crime Stories: The Criminal in Literature,* and *Tales of Espionage and Intrigue: The Secret Agent in Literature.* These have not been examined for the present work.

445. Lockridge, Frances and Richard, eds. *Crime for Two.* (Mystery Writers of America Anthology.) Philadelphia: Lippincott, 1955. 256p.

In the preface, the Lockridges state the one requirement for submissions: "that two persons be involved in the action, and, preferably, in the solution of the crime." The authors introduce the stories by telling how they came to be written, and if their answers usually aren't quite as detailed or memorable as the story introductions in *Maiden Murders* (see #453), they do add something to the reader's pleasure. Among the more interesting story notes is Brett Halliday's on "Dead Man's Code," a Michael Shayne story that was a actually a collaboration of Halliday and wife Helen McCloy (and, it sounds like, mostly hers). The Anthony Boucher, David Alexander, and Stuart Palmer introductions are also of unusual interest. Others include Robert Arthur, Charles B. Child, Lawrence G. Blochman, Will Oursler, Jerome Barry, Ellery Queen, Thomas Walsh, Q. Patrick, Michael Gilbert, John D. MacDonald, Bruno Fischer, Margery Allingham, and Lawrence Treat. Only Simenon declines to tell how he came to write his story, saying he has written too many of them to be able to say.

446. McCloy, Helen, and Brett Halliday, eds. *20 Great Tales of Murder.* (Mystery Writers of America Anthology.) Preface by Baynard Kendrick. New York: Random, 1951. xv, 336p.

Kendrick's four-page preface gives his own account of the origins of MWA. But Brett Halliday's introduction sets out the uniqueness of the organization's fourth anthology: it is a theme anthology in which the theme is a secret and the reader is invited to guess it. Not until Helen McCloy's postscript is it revealed. Notes to the stories are longer than average but usually not biographically informative.

447. McComas, J. Francis, ed. *Crimes and Misfortunes: The Anthony Boucher Memorial Anthology of Mysteries.* New York: Random, 1970. xv, 459p.

This book and a companion volume of science fiction, *Special Wonder,* were prepared as memorials to Anthony Boucher, and their reference value lies in the brief but often telling story introductions in which the authors recount their memories of the field's premiere critic, not to mention one of the formal detective novel's better American practitioners. McComas's three-page introduction provides a biographical overview. Among the 29 other bylines represented are such luminaries as Fredric Brown, John Dickson Carr, John D. MacDonald, Ross Macdonald, Margaret Millar, Ellery Queen, Georges Simenon, Rex Stout, and Donald E. Westlake.

448. McCullough, David Willis, ed. *City Sleuths and Tough Guys.*
Boston: Houghton, Mifflin, 1989. xvi, 586p. Bibl.

The use of an urban background brings together writers as diverse as
Vidocq, Poe, Wallace, Hammett, Vickers, Simenon, Thompson, Spillane,
Ellin, McBain, Himes, Westlake, van de Wetering, and Paretsky. The
editor's eight-page introduction and sometimes extensive story notes are
informative and learned. The book leads off with Chandler's much-re-
printed essay, "The Simple Art of Murder," and finishes with his screenplay, written with Billy Wilder, of James M. Cain's *Double Indemnity.*

449. McCullough, David Willis, ed. *Great Detectives: A Century of the*
Best Mysteries from England and America. New York: Pantheon, 1984.
xv, 728p.

McCullough introduces one of the most ambitious of historical
anthologies with a good seven-page foreword, and the thorough story
notes each run most of a page and occasionally more. Leading off with
Israel Zangwill's pioneering locked-room novella *The Big Bow Mystery,*
McCullough selects two full-length novels (Ross Macdonald's *The Chill*
and Ruth Rendell's *Death Notes*) and sixteen short stories and novelettes,
including all three of Dashiell Hammett's Sam Spade shorts and selections
of varying degrees of familiarity by Sayers, Chesterton, Christie, van
Gulik (who the editor admits belies the subtitle, being neither English nor
American), Faulkner, Crispin, Chandler, Queen, Stout, Bradbury, P.D.
James, Westlake, and McBain. In the introduction to the Christie entry,
McCullough misspells Margery Allingham's first name as "Marjorie,"
and he refers in both the Ray Bradbury and Ross Macdonald introductions
to James M. "Caine." And important as *Ellery Queen's Mystery Magazine*
has been, at no time was it the "only . . . outlet for the detective story" as
McCullough asserts (page 266).

450. Macdonald, Ross, ed. *Great Stories of Suspense.* New York: Knopf,
1974. xvii, 823p.

In a nine-page introduction, the editor briefly sketches the history of
mystery fiction and discusses the reasons for his selections, which include
four novels (Francis's *Enquiry,* Christie's *What Mrs. McGillicuddy Saw,*

Fearing's *The Big Clock,* and his own *The Far Side of the Dollar),* Stevenson's novella *The Strange Case of Dr. Jekyll and Mr. Hyde,* and short stories by Greene, Dahl, Hammett, Michael Gilbert, Margaret Millar, Cheever, Flannery O'Connor, Ellin, Highsmith, Collier, and James M. Cain. It's primarily the eminence of the introducer that gives this very generous anthology its reference value.

451. MacGowan, Kenneth, ed. *Sleuths: Twenty-Three Great Detectives of Fiction and Their Best Stories.* New York: Harcourt, Brace, 1931. xv, 595p. Bibl.

MacGowan precedes each story with a *Who's Who* biography of the detective concerned, sometimes prepared by the editor and sometimes by the author when living and willing. Generally the editor's biographies are based on details in the stories without the elaborations provided by the contributors to Anthony Boucher's *Four-&-Twenty Bloodhounds* (see #376), but many of the authors get into the spirit of things and provide full data on their creations. Authors providing information about their characters include Arthur Morrison on Martin Hewitt, Arthur B. Reeve on Craig Kennedy, R. Austin Freeman on Dr. Thorndyke, Gelett Burgess on Astro, E.C. Bentley on Philip Trent, Ernest Bramah on Max Carrados, H.C. Bailey on Reggie Fortune, Octavus Roy Cohen on Jim Hanvey, G.D.H. and M.I. Cole on Superintendent Wilson, Dorothy L. Sayers on Lord Peter Wimsey, and T.S. Stribling on Prof. Poggioli. Escaping the biographical treatment for various reasons are Orczy's Old Man in the Corner, Post's Uncle Abner, and Chesterton's Father Brown. MacGowan appends a ten-page bibliography/checklist of important detective stories, arranged chronologically by author, and a listing of a dozen notable detective anthologies.

452. **McSherry, Frank D., Jr.; Charles G. Waugh, and Martin H. Greenberg, eds.** *Sunshine Crime.* Nashville: Rutledge Hill, 1987. x, 224p.

Each of the thirteen stories gathered here is set in a different Southern state. McSherry's two-page introduction is more an evocation of the region than a discussion of the stories, but the author notes at the end of each tale are concise and informative. Some contributors are very well-known (John D. MacDonald, Clark Howard, Melville Davisson Post), but others are less widely familiar: Gloria Norris, Doug Hornig, Thomas Adcock, Wyc Toole, Merle Constiner, Bryce Walton. Mainstream writers included are Guy Owen, Jesse Stuart, O. Henry, and Wilbur Daniel Steele. A companion collection, *Dixie Ghosts* (Rutledge Hill, 1988), gathers ghost stories set in Southern states and includes such mystery writers as Richard Hardwick, Talmage Powell, Howard Rigsby, and Donald Hamilton. The same editors' *A Treasury of American Mystery Stories* (Bonanza, 1989) manages to find a story set in each of the fifty states plus the District of Columbia but lacks secondary interest.

453. *Maiden Murders*. (Mystery Writers of America Anthology.) Introduction by John Dickson Carr. New York: Harper, 1952. xiv, 302p.

In one of the most interesting and reference-worthy of the MWA anthologies, twenty writers (or in a couple of cases, collaborative bylines) present their first stories and describe the circumstances of writing and selling them, often even revealing the purchase price. In not all cases were these first fiction publications: some of the writers, including Ellery Queen and Kenneth Millar, were already established as novelists before making their first short-story sales, and others, including William Campbell Gault, had previously published fiction in other genres. In addition to Carr's six-page introduction, Lawrence G. Blochman describes the book's genesis in a two-page preface, crediting Queen with the idea. Blochman also introduces his own first story, which Carr does not—and how interesting it would have been if he had. Other contributors: Hugh Pentecost, Veronica Parker Johns, Georges Simenon, Stuart Palmer, Lawrence Treat, Harry Stephen Keeler, Jerome and Harold Prince, August Derleth, David Alexander, Ruth Wilson, Jerome Barry, Lillian de la Torre, Joseph Fulling Fishman, Day Keene, Anthony Boucher, and Stanley Ellin.

454. **Maling, Arthur, ed.** *When Last Seen*. (Mystery Writers of America Anthology.) New York: Harper and Row, 1977. xi, 337p.

After several years of little or no editorial matter in MWA anthologies, editor Maling returned in this gathering of missing-person stories to the abandoned practice of asking the contributors to comment on how their stories came to be written. Most of them do, and even for those who don't, the story notes are unusually thoughtful and informative. Authors quoted are Ross Macdonald, Stanley Ellin, Pauline C. Smith, Joe Gores, Michael Gilbert, Edward D. Hoch, Gerald Tomlinson, Dorothy Salisbury Davis, Bill Pronzini, James Holding, Lillian de la Torre, Stanley Cohen, Patrick O'Keeffe, and Dan J. Marlowe. Others contributing are Henry Slesar and Vincent Starrett.

455. Malzberg, Barry N., and Bill Pronzini, eds. *Dark Sins, Dark Dreams: Crime in Science Fiction.* New York: Doubleday, 1978. xii, 224p.

The fifteen mystery/s.f. hybrids collected here come both from writers best known for mystery (Westlake, Lutz, Hoch, Pronzini) and those best known for science fiction (Anderson, Silverberg, Budrys, Malzberg), and the editors divide up the informative story notes mostly along those lines. They also take two pages each to consider the interface of the genres, Pronzini in the introduction, Malzberg in an afterword.

456. Mason, Tom, ed. *Spicy Detective Stories.* Newbury Park, CA: Eternity, 1989. 96p. Illus.

A single-page foreword by the editor and another page introduction by John Wooley provide some information about the naughty pulp that flourished from 1934 to 1942, continuing as *Speed Detective* until 1946. There's also a one-page "Tough Guy Dictionary," defining with questionable necessity such familiar terms as bimbo, gat, roscoe, and shamus. The seven tales are newly typeset, but some original illustrations and ads are reproduced. Only familiar name on the contents page is Robert Leslie Bellem, with a Dan Turner story, but Wooley suggests at least some of the other stories may be Bellem using pseudonyms or house names. A two-page case for comic strip character Sally the Sleuth is also included.

457. *Match Me Sidney!* London: No Exit Press, 1989. 557p.

Not examined. According to Contento (see #14), this is an expanded version of the Private Eye Writers of America anthology *An Eye for Justice* (1988), edited by Robert J. Randisi. Among the added features are

"Murder One's Top Books of the Year," a "Crime Crossword," and a lengthy feature by Graham Lovatt called "1990 Crime Diary."

458. **Muller, Marcia, and Bill Pronzini, eds.** *Chapter and Hearse: Suspense Stories About the World of Books.* New York: Morrow, 1985. 372p.

Two specialists in theme anthologies select sixteen stories about book people—dealers, collectors, librarians, writers, publishers. Though just over four pages, the introduction cites a number of specific titles of bibliographic mysteries, and the individual story notes offer biographical information on the authors.

459. **Muller, Marcia, and Bill Pronzini, eds.** *Child's Ploy: An Anthology of Mystery and Suspense Stories.* New York: Macmillan, 1984. viii, 307p.

The introduction provides the most extensive discussion imaginable in a mere four pages of the role of children in suspense fiction, citing such works as Maurice Leblanc's *The Secret Tomb* (1923), George Ade's *Bang! Bang!* (1928), Harvey J. O'Higgins's *Adventures of Detective Barney* (1915), and Craig Rice's *Home Sweet Homicide* (1944). The story notes are also substantial. The nineteen contributors range from major literary figures (D.H. Lawrence, Katherine Mansfield, William Saroyan, Willa Cather) to lesser-known mystery writers (Betty Ren Wright, Jean L. Backus).

460. **Muller, Marcia, and Bill Pronzini, eds.** *Dark Lessons: Crime and Detection on Campus.* New York: Macmillan, 1984. 264p.

This time, the theme is school settings, from kindergarten to university. Once again, the editors manage to mention many titles, some fairly obscure, in their four-page introduction, and the story notes are frequently informative. Most interesting nugget: Evan Hunter's "To Break the Wall," the story that was expanded into *The Blackboard Jungle*.

461. Muller, Marcia, and Bill Pronzini, eds. *Kill or Cure: Suspense Stories About the World of Medicine.* New York: Macmillan, 1985. 306p.

The theme is crime among the doctors and nurses, and the five-page introduction manages to mention a large number of examples. (Though the editors fail to mention my favorite, admittedly obscure, medical mystery specialist, James G. Edwards, M.D., a Doubleday/Crime Club fixture of the thirties and forties.) The story notes provide brief biographical information on the sixteen stories' authors, most of them well-known in the field.

462. Muller, Marcia, and Bill Pronzini, eds. *The Web She Weaves: An Anthology of Mystery and Suspense Stories by Women.* New York: Morrow, 1983. 514p.

Typically for these two editors, the six-page introduction and brief but meaty story notes offer a great deal of information about women as writers of crime fiction. The 23 authors represented include the expected specialists (Christie, Sayers, Highsmith), mainstream literary figures (Mansfield, Wharton, Millay) and a few more recent writers (Susan Dunlap, Joyce Harrington, and editor Muller).

463. Muller, Marcia, and Bill Pronzini, eds. *The Wickedest Show on Earth: A Carnival of Circus Suspense.* New York: Morrow, 1985. 335p.

In one of their more specialized theme anthologies, the editors note a number of mystery novels and films with circus backgrounds in the five-page introduction and provide the usual biographical information in the seventeen story notes.

464. *Murder Cavalcade.* (Mystery Writers of America Anthology.) Preface by Richard Lockridge. New York: Duell, Sloan, and Pearce, 1946. ix, 432p. Bibl.

This was the first of the still-vital MWA anthologies, which more frequently had reference value in their early years than they do today. The twenty contributions are divided into sections: Fiction (sub-divided "Professionals in Detection," "Professionals in Crime," "Murder for Fun," and "Crimes Passionels"), Fact-Fiction, Fact, and Verdict of Two, with an introduction to each. But the book's real reference value lies in the last section, comprised of Ellery Queen's "The Golden Twenty," selecting the ten most important books of short stories and the ten most important novels in the form to date, and Howard Haycraft's "The Whodunit in World War II," a supplement to the author's *Murder for Pleasure* (see WAM #1) which also appeared in his *Art of the Mystery Story* (WAM #69).

465. Nava, Michael, ed. *Finale.* Boston: Alyson, 1989. 287p.

Though writers like George Baxt, Richard Stevenson, Sandra Scoppettone, and Joseph Hansen have seen mainstream publication, most writers of mystery fiction on gay and lesbian themes are relatively unknown to readers outside the homosexual community. Thus, although Nava's introduction covers only four pages and the author notes only two, this collection of eight stories has considerable informational value, introducing such writers as Phil Andros, a pioneer of gay fiction who also writes (as Samuel Steward) detective novels featuring Gertrude Stein and Alice B. Toklas; Katherine V. Forrest, creator of lesbian L.A. cop Kate Delafield; Richard Hall, credited (depending on whether you are reading the introduction or the author notes) with either the first or one of the first gay mysteries, *The Butterscotch Prince;* and editor Nava, who writes novels about gay lawyer/detective Henry Rios.

466. Nevins, Francis M., Jr., and Martin Harry Greenberg, eds. *Hitchcock in Prime Time.* Introduction by Henry Slesar. New York: Avon, 1985. 356p.

In an anthology equally notable for quality and reference value, the editors have gathered twenty stories that were adapted for Alfred Hitchcock's TV program between 1955 and 1965. Slesar's seven-page introduction describes his experiences working on the show. Each story is followed by the main credits for the TV version and a commentary on the adaptation, usually by the author and ranging from a couple of sentences (by Stanley Ellin) to more than a page (by Charles Runyon). The authors' comments are often fascinating, particularly from those who were not completely thrilled with what had been done to their work, notably John D. MacDonald and Dorothy Salisbury Davis. Other authors providing comments are Clark Howard, Lawrence Treat, Slesar, Harold Q. Masur, Harry Muheim, Robert Bloch, James Yaffe, Helen Nielsen, and Edward D. Hoch. In the case of deceased authors or those declining comment, co-editor Nevins provides the postscript.

467. **Nolan, William F., ed.** *The Black Mask Boys: Masters in the Hard-Boiled School of Detective Fiction.* New York: Morrow, 1985. 273p. Bibl.

Few anthologies in the mystery field have as great reference value as this one. Besides reprinting eight little-known stories from *Black Mask,* Nolan offers one of the best historical treatments of that great pulp. The sixteen-page introducion, with an excellent overview, concludes with an alphabetical list, with year of first appearance, of important contributors not included in the anthology. Each story is preceded by a biographical/critical introduction of several pages and is followed by a listing of the author's *Black Mask* stories. Authors included are Carroll John Daly, Dashiell Hammett, Erle Stanley Gardner, Raoul Whitfield, Frederick Nebel, Horace McCoy, Paul Cain, and Raymond Chandler. An appendix lists alphabetically other pulp magazines in the crime and mystery field, and the acknowledgements section guides the reader to other anthologies of hardboiled stories and general references on detective and mystery fiction.

468. **Noone, Edwina (Michael Avallone), ed.** *Edwina Noone's Gothic Sampler.* New York: Award, 1966. 159p.

Examples of gothic fiction from the Anne Radcliffe/Monk Lewis period are the subject of much academic criticism and generally fall outside the limits of this volume, but the romantic suspense novels of the sixties and seventies that revived the term "gothic," usually written by mystery writers (often men under female pseudonyms) and with roots in the had-I-but-known school of Mary Roberts Rinehart and Mignon G. Eberhart as much as Daphne DuMaurier's *Rebecca,* do not. Since the modern gothics rarely had short-story equivalents, this paperback original anthology is one of the few (perhaps the only) to come out of the sixties gothic craze. The four page "Dark and Brooding Preface" describes and defines the form, while the individual notes hype the stories rather than offering much biographical information. Contributors range from Mary W. Shelley to more contemporary names like Eberhart and Phyllis A. Whitney. The editor, who contributes as "herself" and as Priscilla Dalton, is a thinly disguised nom de plume of the creator of private eye Ed Noon.

469. **Pachter, Josh, ed.** *Top Crime.* London: Dent, 1983. New York: St. Martin's, 1984. xi, 365p.

Pachter asked 24 contemporary writers of short detective stories to select their best single story and tell why. The contributors, ranging from some of the biggest names in the genre (Queen, Simenon, McBain, Symons) to excellent writers somewhat less well-known (Gary Brandner, Florence V. Mayberry), introduce the stories at varying length, usually several paragraphs and often providing some biographical details in addition to the reasons for choosing the story. Queen (one sentence) and Simenon (two) are the briefest, their remarks filled out by the editor's comments. Only Patricia Highsmith provided no quotable comment at all. Other contributors include Asimov, Avallone, Charteris, Ellin, Michael Gilbert, Gores, Hoch, James Holding, Keating, Lovesey, McGerr, Nevins, Pronzini, Slesar, Treat, van de Wetering, and Pachter himself.

470. **Paretsky, Sara, ed.** *Beastly Tales.* (Mystery Writers of America Anthology.) New York: Wynwood, 1989. 288p.

Paretsky's five-page introduction discusses the anthology's animal theme and glosses the stories, finishing with an environmentalist's appeal to people's responsibility for other creatures. The four-page biographical section is more informative than average with some lesser-written-about authors (Hope Raymond, Joan Richter, Dick Stodghill, Edward Wellen) among the well-known names.

471. **Paretsky, Sara, ed.** *A Woman's Eye.* New York: Delacorte, 1991. xiv, 448p.

Paretsky's learned eight-page introduction recounts the plight of the woman author through history, both generally (from Sappho to Kate

Chopin) and in the mystery/detective field. The brief introductory notes to the 25 stories, mostly by relatively well-known female writers (Grafton, Muller, Pickard, Fraser, Hughes) but some by less familiar names (Mary Wings, Gillian Slovo, Maria Antonia Oliver) provide little information not available elsewhere.

472. Parry, Michel, ed. _Jack the Knife._ St. Albans, England: Mayflower, 1975. 160p. Bibl.

The one-page bibliography lists nonfictional accounts of the Jack the Ripper mystery, and the nine-page introduction surveys the notorious case in fact as well as fiction. But the body of the book consists of ten fictional treatments of Jack, with an emphasis more on fantasy and horror than detection—contributors include such writers as R. Chetwynd Hayes, Philip Jose Farmer, Ramsey Campbell, and Harlan Ellison along with the inevitable Marie Belloc Lowndes and Robert Bloch.

473. Parry, Michel, ed. _The Supernatural Solution: Stories of Spooks and Sleuths._ St. Albans, England: Panther, 1976. 222p.

This is the only anthology I know of devoted strictly to psychic detectives, and the eight-page introduction provides a brief survey of the type, though there are no individual story notes. Sleuths included are J.S. Le Fanu's Martin Hesselius, E. and H. Heron's Flaxman Low, William Hope Hodgson's Carnacki the Ghost-Finder, L.T. Meade and Robert Eustace's Bell the Master of Mysteries, Dion Fortune's Dr. Taverner, Arthur Machen's Dyson, Seabury Quinn's Jules de Grandin, Manly Wade Wellman's John Thunstone, and Dennis Wheatley's Neils Orsen. Most notable omission is Algernon Blackwood's John Silence.

474. Penzler, Otto, ed. _Whodunit? Houdini?: Thirteen Tales of Magic, Murder, Mystery._ New York: Harper & Row, 1976. xi, 283p.

The founder of Mysterious Press and the Mysterious Bookshop, Penzler is among the most learned of mystery fiction experts, as shown in the brief introduction and longer-than-average story notes to this volume. The subject is usually the story, sometimes the author, sometimes the wider world of magic and conjuring. Authors included combine the expected (Rawson, Dickson, Gibson, Gardner) with the less so (Kipling, Rafael Sabatini, Manuel Peyrou, Ben Hecht).

475. Peyton, Richard, ed. *Deadly Odds: Crime and Mystery Stories of the Turf.* London: Souvenir Press, 1986. 366p.

Peyton gathers 23 criminous horse racing stories, beginning with Dick Francis's "The Day of the Losers" and concluding with my own Francis parody, "Breakneck." While the overall introduction is a brief two pages, the story notes are longer than average and quite informative, especially on such lesser-known writers (in the U.S.A. at least) as Angus Reach, Guy Boothby, Banjo Paterson, Frank Johnston, Ralph Straus, Geoff O'Hara, and the celebrated Nat Gould, credited with creating "the first Turf sleuth in literature," Valentine Martyn. Also represented is Barclay Northcote, a writer Peyton calls "America's Nat Gould." Though I consider myself a connoisseur of racing mysteries, I confess I'd never heard of him.

476. Preiss, Byron, ed. *Raymond Chandler's Philip Marlowe: A Centennial Celebration.* New York: Knopf, 1988. xiv, 370p. Illus.

Philip Marlowe is probably the only fictional detective outside of Sherlock Holmes to have a whole volume devoted to pastiches by various hands, including writers as various as Max Allan Collins, Joyce Harrington, Sara Paretsky, Julie Smith, Paco Ignacio Taibo, Simon Brett, Edward D. Hoch, and Robert Campbell. Editor Preiss tells how the project came about in a two-page preface, while Chandler biographer Frank MacShane contributes a six-page introduction. Each of the 23 pastiches has an illustration and an afterword by the author, and there are two pages of biographical notes on both the authors and artists. Also included is Chandler's only Philip Marlowe short story, "The Pencil."

477. Pronzini, Bill, ed. *The Arbor House Treasury of Detective and Mystery Stories from the Great Pulps.* New York: Arbor, 1983. 342p.

Besides collecting fifteen little-known stories from the pulps, Pronzini provides a large amount of historical and biographical information in the five-page overall introduction and the individual story notes of one or two pages. Particularly valuable is the information on lesser-known names like Paul Cain and Norbert Davis and two nearly forgotten ones, Dane Gregory and D.L. Champion. Others represented include Hammett, Daly, McCoy, Nebel, Woolrich, Fredric Brown, John D. MacDonald (two stories), Bellem, Gault, and Jakes.

478. Pronzini, Bill, ed. *The Edgar Winners.* (Mystery Writers of American Anthology.) New York: Random, 1980. xii, 420p.

In a volume that seemed long overdue, short-story Edgar winners between 1947 (when Ellery Queen, represented here by the much earlier story, "The Adventure of the Mad Tea-Party," won for general contributions to the form) and 1978 were collected, with a few gaps. Pronzini's four-page introduction includes some history of MWA and the Edgars, and a ten-page appendix lists all Edgar and Special Award winners from 1945 to 1978.

479. Pronzini, Bill, ed. *Midnight Specials: An Anthology for Train Buffs and Suspense Aficionados.* Indianapolis: Bobbs-Merrill, 1977. xii, 272p. Bibl.

One of our best contemporary anthologists presents a railroad lover's delight, collecting stories by literary figures as diverse as Dickens, Twain, Wharton, Noyes, and James M. Cain along with mystery specialists like Lutz, Hoch, Woolrich, Queen, and Simenon. The editor's introductions to these nineteen stories include interesting biographical and critical notes, but the book's greatest reference value lies in the twelve-page bibliography of railroad suspense, divided into short stories in anthologies and collections, short stories in magazines, novels, non-fiction books, plays, and films. Pronzini has starred his favorites.

A series of Pronzini anthologies for Arbor House, though more horror than mystery collections as such, are also notable for their introductions and bibliographies and contain much of interest to mystery readers: *Werewolf!* (1979), *Voodoo!* (1980), *Mummy!* (1980), *Creature!* (1981),

The Arbor House Necropolis (1981; including *Voodoo!*, *Mummy!*, and the original *Ghoul!*), and *Spectre!* (1982).

480. Pronzini, Bill, and Martin H. Greenberg, eds. *The Ethnic Detectives: Masterpieces of Mystery Fiction.* New York: Dodd, Mead, 1985. xiii, 360p.

Toughest task for the editors of this collection of seventeen stories about "ethnic" detectives is to define how a character qualifies as ethnic. Is Poe's Dupin, a Frenchman working among Frenchmen, an ethnic detective? Yes, because "it was the English and Americans who were the primary audience for his cases . . . " (Dupin does not appear in the collection, but Simenon's Maigret does, as by similar logic do Keating's Inspector Ghote and van de Wetering's Inspector Saito.) Among the real ethnic detectives represented (in the sense of a member of a minority group) are Manly Wade Wellman's David Return (American Indian), James Yaffe's Mom (Jewish), John Ball's Virgil Tibbs (black), Tony Hillerman's Jim Chee (American Indian), and Marcia Muller's Elena Olivarez (Chicana). The five-page introduction and some of the story notes mention other detective characters in the various ethnic groups who are not represented in the anthology.

481. Pronzini, Bill, and Martin H. Greenberg, eds. *Great Modern Police Stories.* New York: Walker, 1986. xii, 223p.

The four-page introduction discusses the history of police forces and the police procedural form, explaining why European police gained both real and fictional respect earlier than their American counterparts. In the note to the first story, Cornell Woolrich is cited as one of the few pulp writers to show any respect for the police. Among the other contributors are Treat, McBain, Simenon, the Lockridges, Michael Gilbert, Hoch, and Susan Dunlap.

482. Pronzini, Bill, and Martin H. Greenberg, eds. *Uncollected Crimes.* New York: Walker, 1987. xi, 203p.

There have been several anthologies devoted to tales from the detective pulps, but this one casts its net among the mystery digests for previously unreprinted stories. Though only three pages long, the introduction gives a brief survey of these publications, highlighting seven of the most important and influential. The individual story notes are also brief but packed with interesting tidbits of information about the fourteen authors and their magazine contributions.

483. **Pronzini, Bill; Martin H. Greenberg, and Charles G. Waugh, eds.** *Murder in the First Reel.* Introduction by Isaac Asimov. New York: Avon, 1985. 344p. Bibl.

Not examined. According to Contento (see #14), co-editor Waugh contributes "A Selected List of Short Fiction Behind Mystery Movies."

484. **Pronzini, Bill; Martin H. Greenberg, and Charles Waugh, eds.** *The Mystery Hall of Fame: An Anthology of Classic Mystery and Suspense Stories Selected by the Mystery Writers of America.* New York: Morrow, 1984. 467p.

Though lacking individual story notes and including only four pages of introductory matter, this book takes its reference value from the way its contents were selected: by a poll of MWA members to select "the best mystery and suspense stories of all time." Top five stories on points were Stanley Ellin's "The Specialty of the House" (13 first-place votes, 31 total), Roald Dahl's "Lamb to the Slaughter" (8 and 25), Edgar Allan Poe's "The Purloined Letter" (8 and 16), Thomas Burke's "The Hands of Mr. Ottermole" (4 and 14), and Arthur Conan Doyle's "The Adventure of the Speckled Band" (3 and 15). These are included along with sixteen others, most highly familiar. Unfortunately, the full scorecard of stories receiving votes is not included, but the editors indicate Agatha Christie's "The Witness for the Prosecution" and Shirley Jackson's "The Lottery" would have been included had reprint rights been available.

485. **Pronzini, Bill; Barry N. Malzberg, and Martin H. Greenberg, eds.** *Mystery in the Mainstream: An Anthology of Literary Crimes.* New York: Morrow, 1986. 391p.

Along the lines of Ellery Queen's *The Literature of Crime* (see #492), this volume is devoted to the ventures into crime and mystery fiction of writers like Dickens, Kipling, Tolstoy, Huxley, Oates, Malamud, and Mailer, among others. The introduction (four pages plus) cites some other examples of mainstream writers who wrote in the genre, and the story notes provide biographical information.

486. Pronzini, Bill, and Marcia Muller, eds. *The Deadly Arts.* New York: Arbor, 1985. xiv, 313p.

The arts for purposes of this 23-tale theme anthology are divided into fine (e.g. ballet, opera, poetry, sculpture, classical music, painting, theater), popular (e.g. filmmaking, jazz, cartooning, television, cabaret singing), and the unconventional (e.g. vaudeville, burlesque, wax museum, magic). An introduction of five pages plus surveys the interface of the arts and crime fiction, mentioning a commendable number of specific titles in a short space, while the brief story notes confine themselves to biographical information on the authors.

487. Queen, Ellery (Frederic Dannay and Manfred B. Lee), ed. *Challenge to the Reader.* New York: Stokes, 1938. vii, 502p.

The first of the long and distinguished line of Queen anthologies is based on a tantalizing gimmick that doesn't really work. In the nine-page opening chapter, J.J. McC., the shadowy introduction-writer of the early Queen novels, comes to visit sleuth and book-collector Ellery in his New York apartment. Ellery is trying to think of an original idea for an anthology of mystery stories, and in the course of their discussion he comes up with one: he will publish adventures of famous detectives with their names (and those of continuing secondary characters) changed and challenge the reader to identify the famous detective. He tries out his selections on McC., and that Watsonian character's guesses—his batting average isn't bad, by the way—followed by Ellery's revelations provide a postscript to each story. The problem, of course, is that you either know them or you don't: if you're familiar with the detective character, the problem is too easy, and if you aren't, it's impossible. Still the Queen-McC. conversations are enjoyable, and some good tidbits of mystery-story lore are dropped along the way. Among the 25 characters represented are the still famous (Holmes, Father Brown, Poirot, Spade, Queen) and the comparatively obscure (Anthony Wynne's Dr. Hailey, Octavus Roy Cohen's Jim Hanvey, G.D.H. and M.I. Cole's Superintendent Wilson, and Gelett Burgess's Astro).

488. Queen, Ellery, ed. *Ellery Queen's Japanese Golden Dozen.* Rutland, VT: Tuttle, 1978. 288p.

Queen's six-page introduction offers a bit of history of the Japanese detective story and a description of the market. Introductions to the twelve stories, all new to English translation, offer some biographical details on the authors, most hitherto unknown to western readers, though the notes are regrettably less extensive those in Apostolou and Greenberg's *Murder in Japan* (see #359). Authors included are contemporary—the historically important Edogawa Rampo is not represented.

489. Queen, Ellery, ed. *Ellery Queen's Poetic Justice.* New York: New American Library, 1967. xvi, 300p.

Gathering 23 examples of crime/mystery fiction by world-famous poets, Queen contributes a six-page introduction and story notes that average more than a page. Chronologically arranged, the selections start with Chaucer and end with twentieth-century poets Ogden Nash, Muriel Rukeyser, and Dylan Thomas.

490. Queen, Ellery, ed. *Ellery Queen's The Golden 13.* New York: World, 1970. xvi, 347p.

The winners of *Ellery Queen's Mystery Magazine's* annual short-story contests, which ran from 1945 to 1956 with a one-year revival in 1961, are gathered together for the first time. Queen's eight-page introduction provides some interesting statistics on the contests and gives a description of how the judging process went in three early contests (unfortunately without specifying which), and the substantial story notes are more concerned with the stories than their authors. For further information, see #495.

491. Queen, Ellery, ed. *The Female of the Species: The Great Women Detectives and Criminals.* Boston: Little, Brown, 1943. xii, 422p.

The five-page introduction is a compact history of women as leading characters in mystery fiction and includes a list of characters that could not be included because they do not appear in short stories. The 21 tales are divided into Detectives: American (ten), Detectives: English (seven), Criminals: American, and Criminals: English (two each). In a similar collection today, the proportion of female authors would undoubtedly be greater. Though all the leading characters are female, fifteen of their creators are men. Queen's story notes are less standardized than those of most editors—sometimes a sentence, sometimes a page or more; sometimes a comment on the story, sometimes on the author, sometimes on the subject—and also more interesting.

492. Queen, Ellery, ed. *The Literature of Crime: Stories by World-Famous Authors.* Boston: Little, Brown, 1950. xi, 405p.

Two things gave Queen the editor (who was usually the Dannay half of the collaboration) special delight: publishing the first stories of new writers and uncovering criminous works by mainstream literary figures. This volume is the first anthology devoted to the latter. The introduction runs three pages, and the story notes are substantial and interesting, though never as long and unfettered as in some of the Queen anthologies of the forties. The 26 contributors range from Dickens, Kipling, and de Maupassant to Buck, Lardner, Thurber, and Runyon.

493. Queen, Ellery, ed. *Murder by Experts.* (Mystery Writers of America Anthology.) Chicago: Ziff-Davis, 1947. 387p.

This was the second MWA anthology, ostensibly the result of Ellery Queen's fault-finding with the first, *Murder Cavalcade* (see #464). The initial suggestion of a collection of first stories (later realized in *Maiden Murders* [see #453]) was rejected as too low in quality potential, and the second idea, having each author pick his or her best story, had been done before. Robert Arthur is credited with suggesting the format finally selected: having each author select a favorite story by someone else. Queen's introduction gives a more detailed account of the birth of an anthology idea and the actual process of compiling it than I have found anywhere else. And the critical introductions by the selectors, ranging from a paragraph to two pages, are often delightful. The selectors and their choices: Clayton Rawson on John Dickson Carr's "The Locked Room" (discussing the origin of the "I do not love thee, Doctor Fell" rhyme), Helen McCloy on Brett Halliday's "Human Interest Stuff," Leslie Charteris on G.K. Chesterton's "The Blast of the Book," Dorothy B. Hughes on Percival Wilde's "P. Moran, Diamond-Hunter," Howard Haycraft on Melville Davisson Post's "The Age of Miracles," Mabel Seeley on Agatha Christie's "The Witness for the Prosecution," Margaret and Kenneth Millar on William Faulkner's "The Hound," Q. Patrick on Cornell Woolrich's "The Dancing Detective," Anthony Boucher on Thomas Burke's "The Hands of Mr. Ottermole" (with a one-paragraph introduction but a much lengthier afterword), George Harmon Coxe on Cora Jarett's "The Little Dry Sticks," Baynard Kendrick on Ernest Bramah's "The Last Exploit of Harry the Actor," Helen Reilly on Patrick Quentin's "Puzzle for Poppy," Edward D. Radin on Edward Hale Bierstadt's "Death Draws a Triangle" (the one true-crime inclusion), Lillian de la Torre on Carter Dickson's "Persons or Things Unknown," Hugh Pentecost on William MacHarg's "Almost Perfect," August Derleth on R. Austin Freeman's "Mr. Ponting's Alibi," Percival Wilde on Harry Klingsberg's "Remember Galileo," Lawrence Treat on Robert Louis Stevenson's "Story of the Young Man with the Cream Tarts," Vincent Starrett on Frederick Irving Anderson's "The Infallible Godahl," and Craig Rice on Ellery Queen's "The Adventure of the President's Half Disme." Only author to be selected twice is Carr (as himself and Carter Dickson). Only authors to both select and be selected are Wilde and Q. Patrick/Patrick Quentin.

Appended is a list of the membership of MWA at the time the book was compiled. The British edition, published by Sampson, Low in 1950, omits this feature as well as the stories by Post and Woolrich.

494. Queen, Ellery, ed. *101 Years' Entertainment: The Great Detective Stories, 1841-1941*. Boston: Little, Brown, 1941. xviii, 995p.

Compiled to commemorate the hundredth anniversary of Poe's invention of the modern detective story, this is one of the best and most influential anthologies of detective and crime stories ever published. The 14-page introduction is a compact history of the detective short story, with

the customary Queenian thoroughness, accuracy, and enthusiasm. The
story notes are short and, as is usual with Queen, more often devoted to
appreciation of the stories than to the biographies of the authors. The fifty
tales are divided into six categories: The Great Detectives (28 tales), The
Great Women Detectives (three), The Great Humorous Detectives (three),
The Great Thieves (five), The Great Crime Stories (ten), and The Detective
Story to End Detective Stories (Ben Ray Redman's "The Perfect Crime").
Only authors to appear more than once are Agatha Christie (three entries!),
Maurice Leblanc and Dorothy L. Sayers (two each).

495. Queen, Ellery, ed. *The Queen's Awards.* Annual. Boston: Little,
Brown, 1946-1953. As *Ellery Queen's Awards,* Boston: Little Brown,
1954-1955, New York: Simon and Schuster, 1956-1957. Title of the first
four volumes followed by a year (1946-1949), the rest with a Series
number (Fifth through Twelfth).

This annual series presented winners of the twelve annual short story
contests sponsored by *Ellery Queen's Mystery Magazine.* (A thirteenth
contest was held in 1961 after a gap of several years, but there was no
anthology specifically labelled an awards volume.) The first volume has
a three-page introduction on the contest, revealing there were 838 manuscripts received, including contributions from every state save North
Dakota, which is roundly chastised, plus the District of Columbia and
several foreign countries. In the style of '40s Queen anthologies, there are
long story notes, often running two to three pages. The second volume,
reporting fewer (623) but better manuscripts received, also has much
editorial matter, including a foreword on each author and an afterword on
each story. The nine-page introduction to the third volume (862 entries
received) describes the judging process in the first three contests, and
again there are lengthy notes on the individual stories. The fourth and fifth
volumes include substantial introductions with the customary statistical
bent (793 and 915 entries respectively), but the individual story notes
shrink to the vanishing point. From the sixth volume on, there is only a
list of the winners with no overall introduction or story notes. All thirteen
first-prize winners were later gathered as *Ellery Queen's The Golden
Thirteen* (see #490).

496. Queen, Ellery, ed. *Rogue's Gallery: The Great Criminals of Modern Fiction.* Boston: Little, Brown, 1945. viii, 562p.

By the time this meaty anthology was published, Queen the editor was at his peak as a commentator and story introducer, filling the pages of *Ellery Queen's Mystery Magazine* with all kinds of mystery lore. Here we have a four-page foreword, a two-page betweenword, and a three-page afterword, plus remarkable story notes that often run more than a page. There are 32 stories, their leading miscreants divided into murderers, thieves, confidence men, "criminal" lawyers, and assorted crooks. (Ellery Queen, for his obligatory appearance, is featured in the radio play, "Ellery Queen, Swindler.") No mystery reference collection should be without this or any of the other Queen anthologies of the forties—if they can be found.

497. Queen, Ellery, ed. *Sporting Blood: The Great Sports Detective Stories.* Introduction by Grantland Rice. Boston: Little, Brown, 1942. 362p.

For many years, this was the only anthology devoted to sports mysteries, and there still are very few, though a present-day editor would have more possibilities to choose from than Queen did. Not all the sports covered are truly athletic. Poker and chess are allowed in under Indoor Sports, and collecting (of butterflies, stamps, coins, and books) is admitted under the rubric Hobby Sports. Rice's introduction is a page long and negligible, but Queen's story notes frequently identify novels and tales about the various sports other than the ones being reprinted. (See especially the sports of golf, fishing, hunting, chess, and book collecting.) Among the twenty tales are three by editor Queen, who advances "Man Bites Dog" and "Trojan Horse" rather sheepishly as the only short stories in the genre about baseball and football, but presents the stamp-collecting tale, "The One-Penny Black," not the only one available, without apology. Introducing Doyle's racing mystery "Silver Blaze," Queen quotes from the author's own admission of the turf errors in the story and gives the results of an *Observer* poll to pick the five best Sherlock Holmes stories.

498. Queen, Ellery, ed. *To the Queens' Taste: The First Supplement to 101 Years' Entertainment Consisting of the Best Stories Published in the*

First Four Years of Ellery Queen's Mystery Magazine. Boston: Little, Brown, 1946. xviii, 606p.

The subtitle says not quite all. Queen's eight-page foreword recounts the failure of the anthology *Challenge to the Reader* (see #487), the stepping up of the Queen book collecting activities, the compilation of *101 Years' Entertainment* (see #494), the founding of *EQMM*, and a summary of some recent great book finds. The 36 tales are organized similarly to the parent volume, separating American and English detective and crime stories, while adding sections of French detective stories and riddle stories. The story notes are often lengthy, frequently surprising, and nearly always stimulating. For example, in introducing Craig Rice's "His Heart Could Break," Queen discusses the author's appearance on a *Time* cover but hotly disputes the magazine's claim that "[w]omen have always excelled as detective-story writers." The introduction to S.J. Perelman's Chandler parody "Farewell, My Lovely Appetizer" brings forth a description of the Queens' radio game show *Author! Author!*, on which Perelman also appeared. Some of the same material recurs in *In the Queens' Parlor* (see WAM #82), and of course most of it first appeared in *EQMM*.

499. Queen, Ellery, ed. *Twentieth Century Detective Stories*. Cleveland: World, 1948. 288p. Bibl.

This time, Queen writes no introduction, and the fourteen story notes are mere taglines. But a 62-page appendix constitutes the first book publication of "Queen's Quorum" (see WAM #27), an annotated selection of the most important books of detective-crime short stories. This version carries the listing through #101, Roy Vickers's *The Department of Dead Ends*.

Note: Throughout the sixties and seventies (and posthumously right up to the present), Ellery Queen fronted many more anthologies, usually consisting of stories selected from past issues of *EQMM* and published both in hardcover and paper, sometimes under different titles. Generally, these later compilations have shorter story notes or none at all and less informative introductions than the great Queen anthologies of the forties and fifties, but there are scattered editorial gems (too scattered to discuss them all here) discussing the stories collected.

500. Randisi, Robert, ed. *The Eyes Have It.* (Private Eye Writers of America anthology.) New York: Mysterious, 1984. 327p.

All the PWA anthologies provide good reading, but only this one (the first) has real reference value. Each of the seventeen original stories is introduced by its author, sometimes perfunctorily but frequently offering something of real biographical, technical, or historical interest. Characters represented include Lawrence Block's Matt Scudder, Max Allan Collins's Nate Heller, Michael Collins's Dan Fortune, Loren D. Estleman's Amos Walker, Stephen Greenleaf's John Marshall Tanner, Edward D. Hoch's Al Darlan, Richard Hoyt's John Denson, Stuart M. Kaminsky's Toby Peters, Rob Kantner's Ben Perkins, Michael Z. Lewin's Freddie Herring, John Lutz's Nudger, Marcia Muller's Sharon McCone, William F. Nolan's Bart Challis, Sara Paretsky's V.I. Warshawski, Bill Pronzini's Nameless, editor Randisi's Miles Jacoby, and L.J. Washburn's Hallam.

One of the later PWA anthologies, *An Eye for Justice* (1988), was expanded into a British volume with some secondary interest, *Match Me Sidney!* (see #457).

501. Randisi, Robert J., and Marilyn Wallace, eds. *Deadly Allies: Private Eye Writers of America/Sisters in Crime Collaborative Anthology.* New York: Doubleday, 1992. ix, 370p.

In their three-page foreword, the editors provide some history for their respective organizations and deny that they are in competition. The twenty stories are presented in thematic pairs with a paragraph explaining the pairing and a biographical introduction to each story. Contributors include some of the biggest names in contemporary mystery fiction (e.g. Grafton, Dunlap, Lutz, Estleman, Paretsky), with a couple of newcomers, Sarah Andrews and Jan Grape. Max Allan Collins's "Louise" is miscalled "the first prose story to feature . . . comic-book lady PI, Ms. Tree." There are at least two others: "The Little Woman," reprinted in Ed Gorman's *Second Black Lizard Anthology* (see 410) and "Red Light," reprinted in Gorman's *Dark Crimes* (see #409).

502. Rhode, John, ed. *Detection Medley.* London: Hutchinson, 1939. 528p. Revised as *Line-Up.* New York: Dodd, Mead, 1940. 378p.

Not examined, but the table of contents listed by Contento (see #14) reveals much of secondary interest. In addition to a large selection of stories, the volume includes a foreword by editor Rhode, an introduction by A.A. Milne, and several non-fiction articles: G.K. Chesterton's "The Best Detective Story," J.J. Connington's "A Criminologist's Book-Shelf," R. Austin Freeman's "The Art of the Detective Story," and two by Milward Kennedy: "Are Murders Meant?" and "Murderers in Fiction." The two Kennedy articles are dropped from the American edition.

503. Richards, Stanley, ed. *Best Mystery and Suspense Plays of the Modern Theatre.* New York: Dodd, Mead, 1971. xi, 800p.

In a general introduction of three pages and notes on the individual plays that average about the same length, Richards presents considerable information about these ten stage classics, their authors, and theatrical mysteries generally. Cast and technical credits for the New York and London productions are included. The plays are Agatha Christie's *The Witness for the Prosecution*, Frederick Knott's *Dial "M" for Murder*, Anthony Shaffer's *Sleuth*, W. Somerset Maugham's *The Letter*, Robert Marasco's *Child's Play*, Joseph Kesselring's *Arsenic and Old Lace*, Patrick Hamilton's *Angel Street*, Maxwell Anderson's *Bad Seed*, J.B. Priestley's *Dangerous Corner*, and Hamilton Deane and John L. Balderston's *Dracula*.

504. Richards, Stanley, ed. *10 Classic Mystery and Suspense Plays of the Modern Theatre.* New York: Dodd, Mead, 1973. xi, 887p. Illus.

In the same format as his earlier volume, Richards introduces Agatha Christie's *Ten Little Indians*, Joseph Hayes's *The Desperate Hours*, Jack Roffey's *Hostile Witness*, Edward Chodorov's *Kind Lady*, William Archibald's *The Innocents*, Emlyn Williams's *Night Must Fall*, J.B. Priestley's *An Inspector Calls*, Thomas Job's *Uncle Harry*, Edward Percy and Reginald Denham's *Ladies in Retirement*, and George M. Cohan's *Seven Keys to Baldpate* (the latter from the Earl Derr Biggers novel). Included are eight pages of photographs from the original New York productions.

505. Richardson, Michael, ed. _Maddened by Mystery: A Casebook of Canadian Detective Fiction._ Toronto: Dennys, 1982. 304p.

Not examined. According to Contento (see #14), Richardson contributes a preface and a feature called "Who's Who in Canadian Mystery Fiction" begins on page 287.

506. Roberts, Garyn G., ed. _A Cent a Story: The Best from Ten Detective Aces._ Bowling Green, OH: Popular, 1986. 179p. Illus.

The six-page introduction recounts the history of the pulps generally and specifically of _Ten Detective Aces,_ which mixed the hardboiled and "Avenger" formulae developed in other magazines. Roberts also discusses the stories selected, which are reprinted straight from the original magazines with illustrations. Authors represented are Harry Widmer, Paul Chadwick, Norvell Page, Carl McK. Saunders, Lester Dent, Frederick C. Davis, Richard B. Sale, Alexis Rossoff, G.T. Fleming-Roberts, and Emile C. Tepperman.

507. Roberts, Garyn G.; Gary Hoppenstand, and Ray B. Browne, eds. _Old Sleuth's Freaky Female Detectives (From the Dime Novels)._ Bowling Green, Ohio: Popular, 1990. 112p.

In nine fact-crammed 8 1/2 x 11, double-column pages, the editors discuss the history of dime novels generally, the Old Sleuth series, and finally the three early examples of female detectives reproduced in small-print facsimile: _Lady Kate, The Dashing Female Detective_ (1886), _The Great Bond Robbery, or Tracked by a Female Detective_ (1885, reproduced from a 1908 reprint), and _Madge The Society Detective, Or A Strange Quest Among The Four Hundred_ (1911). They point out that women private eyes disappeared with the demise of the dime novel, to return only relatively recently.

508. Ruhm, Herbert, ed. _The Hard-Boiled Detective: Stories from Black Mask Magazine, 1920-1951._ New York: Vintage, 1977. xviii, 396p.

The fourteen chronologically-arranged stories (from Carroll John Daly's "The False Burton Combs" in 1922 to Bruno Fischer's "Five O'Clock Menace" in 1949) lack individual notes, but Ruhm's scholarly eleven-page introduction is a good short history of the greatest of the pulps.

509. **Russell, Alan K., ed.** *Rivals of Sherlock Holmes.* Secaucus, NJ: Castle, 1978. xii, 484p. Illus.

Not to be confused with Hugh Greene's anthology of the same title (see #419), which Russell acknowledges in his introduction, this volume reprints forty stories in facsimile, complete with illustrations, as they appeared in the *Strand* and other British magazines of the late Victorian and Edwardian period. Six pages of forematter identify the sources and give biographical information on the authors when known, though unfortunately Russell has little to offer on the lesser-known authors included: Clarence Rook, Newton MacTavish, and Fred M. White. The volume is more valuable for the scarcity of some of its contents—by writers like Grant Allen, C.L. Pirkis, L.T. Meade (with Clifford Halifax or Robert Eustace), and Robert Barr—and the original appearance of more widely available material—by Morrison, Doyle, Orczy, Richard Harding Davis, Arnold Bennett, and H.G. Wells—than for its editorial apparatus.

510. **Russell, Alan K., ed.** *The Rivals of Sherlock Holmes Two.* Secaucus, NJ: Castle, 1979. xv, 502p. Illus.

Russell's second volume of reprints is even more impressive than the first, with more stories (46), more obscure authors (including utterly forgotten names like Angus Evan Abbott, George A. Best, Julius Chambers, and Guy Clifford with vaguely remembered ones like George Griffith and Cutcliffe Hyne), and seven pages of informative introduction, including additional illustrations: a shot of William LeQueux in his forty-horsepower Napier and an autographed drawing of L.T. Meade. Famous names like Doyle, Futrelle, Hornung, and Orczy also appear.

511. **Sandoe, James, ed.** *Murder: Plain and Fanciful with Some Milder Malefactions.* New York: Sheridan, 1948. viii, 628p. Bibl., index.

This generous anthology gathers a dozen true crime accounts, three examples of fiction based on fact, and thirteen purely fictional short stories. The principal reference value lies in a 32-page annotated bibliography, "Criminal Clef: Tales and Plays Based on Real Crimes." Arrangement is alphabetical by author, giving title, date, and an identification of the real crime that provided the inspiration for the fiction. Mainstream works like Richard Wright's *Native Son* and Robert Penn Warren's *All the King's Men* are included along with detective and mystery novels, stories, and plays. A case and personal name index permits the reader to access the list by subject. There are six index references each to Lizzie Borden and Madeleine Smith, compared to only three for Jack the Ripper, who surely would be the champ if such a bibliography were prepared today.

512. Sayers, Dorothy L., ed. *Great Short Stories of Detection, Mystery, and Horror*. 3 volumes. Volume 1, London: Gollancz, 1928. 1229p. As *The Omnibus of Crime*. New York: Payson and Clarke, 1929. 1177p. Volume 2, London: Gollancz, 1931. 1147p. As *The Second Omnibus of Crime*. New York: Coward-McCann, 1932. vi, 855p. Volume 3, London: Gollancz, 1934. 1069p. As *The Third Omnibus of Crime*. New York: Coward-McCann, 1935. viii. 808p.

Among the most famous of crime/mystery anthology series, and justifiably so, the three volumes are more likely to be collected for their stories and as basic Sayers items than purely for their reference value. The introduction to the first volume (39 pages in the American edition) is an important early history of the form, published three years before the first book-length history, H. Douglas Thomson's *Masters of Mystery* (see WAM #7), but it has been reprinted again and again, beginning with Howard Haycraft's *The Art of the Mystery Story* (WAM #69). The second volume also offers a substantial introduction (16 pages), discussing developments in the form since the first volume. Interestingly, she is a little alarmed by the number of serious literary studies of the genre, making the form too solemn and self-conscious, and concerned by the shrinking importance of the mystery short story (mainly because of shortened magazine length requirements). This at a time when fanzines were unknown and full-length studies of the genre less than a handful, when countless pulp and slick magazines were publishing mystery shorts by the bushel. What would she think of the situation sixty years later? Though the volume of stories is still large, the introduction to the third volume has shrunk to a mere seven pages, and as before, there are no individual story notes. Also as before, the selections are divided into 1) Detection and Mystery, and 2) Mystery and Horror. The story contents of the British and American editions sometimes differ.

513. Schwartz, Saul, ed. *The Detective Story: An Introduction to the Whodunit.* Skokie, IL: National Textbook, 1975. iv, 441p. Illus., bibl.

This high school text includes a great deal of detective fiction history, including some photographs of authors, in its story introductions and connecting material, and there are more suggested research activities and study questions than found in most such sources. One hopes the editor's obvious enthusiasm proves infectious. Schwartz accords separate sections to Poe, Doyle, and Queen. Most of the authors and detectives represented are very big names, William Brittain and science teacher Mr. Strang being welcome exceptions. Schwartz provides many lists of additional titles by the authors included, but dates and publication information are lacking.

514. Seabourne, Edward A. ed. *Detective in Fiction: A Posse of Eight.* London: Bell, 1931. 239p.

Not examined. Per the listing in Contento (see #14), judging by the length of the editor's introduction—the first story, Poe's "The Murders in the Rue Morgue," doesn't begin until page 37—and the presence of a feature called "Questions and Exercises," this may be the first example of mystery anthology as school textbook, beating its American equivalent, Blanche Colton, Williams's *The Mystery and the Detective: A Collection of Stories* (see #536) by seven years. Seabourne's selections are more familiar than Williams's, including well-known tales of Doyle, Chesterton, Post, Christie, Bramah, Orczy, and Leacock.

515. Sellers, Peter, ed. *Cold Blood: Murder in Canada.* Introduction by Edward D. Hoch. Oakville, Ontario: Mosaic, 1987. 164p.
   Cold Blood II. Oakville, Ontario: Mosaic, 1989. 186p.
   Cold Blood III. Oakville, Ontario: Mosaic, 1991. xviii, 208p.

The editor's first collection of Canadian detective stories (all by Canadian writers except for Hoch's "The Impossible 'Impossible' Crime," which has a Canadian setting) is less informative about its contributors than it should be. Though Hoch offers a two-page introduction with a bit of Canadian genre history, there are no notes on the authors or stories. The second collection, with thirteen tales all original and all by Canadian writers (including Eric Wright, Ted Wood, Charlotte MacLeod, and William Bankier with others less familiar) does better: the editor's two page introduction and the individual story notes are brief but informative. The third volume is best of all for reference purposes, having a three-page introduction recounting the history of the series, plus six pages of notes on the sixteen individual stories and their authors. The amount of biographical information varies, but on writers like golfing computer analyst John North, former pro boxer and "roughneck" Jack Paris, and wine writer Tony Aspler, it is unlikely to be duplicated elsewhere.

516. Shaw, Joseph T., ed. *The Hard-Boiled Omnibus: Early Stories from Black Mask*. New York: Simon and Schuster, 1946. ix, 468p.

Possibly the first anthology to concentrate on the tough pulp, it has less reference value than one might hope: only a five-page introduction by editor Shaw and no notes on the authors. Still, it's worthwhile for the view of *Black Mask*'s most famous editor on how it all happened.

517. *Six Against the Yard*. London: Selwyn and Blount, 1936. 302p. As *Six Against Scotland Yard*. Garden City, NY: Doubleday, Doran, 1936. vi, 302p.

Besides being an early example of an anthology of original mystery stories, this volume has a unique gimmick. Six writers—Margery Allingham, Anthony Berkeley, Freeman Wills Crofts, Ronald A. Knox, Dorothy L. Sayers, and Russell Thorndyke—each present a short story outlining the perfect murder. In afterwords ranging from six to twelve pages, ex-Superintendent Cornish of the C.I.D. tells where they went wrong and how the murderer actually would have been caught.

518. Slung, Michele B., ed. *Crime on Her Mind: Fifteen Stories of Female Sleuths from the Victorian Era to the Forties.* New York: Pantheon, 1975. xxx, 380p. Bibl.

This is an important historical anthology and one of the highest in reference value. Following a scholarly introduction that traces the history of the female detective in sixteen pages, each of the stories has a page of biographical introduction to the author and the detective character, though even Slung is defeated by the shadowy Clarence Rook, creator of Miss Van Snoop. Other characters represented are C.L. Pirkis's Loveday Brooke, George R. Sims's Dorcas Dene, L.T. Meade and Robert Eustace's Florence Cusack, Baroness Orczy's Lady Molly of Scotland Yard, Hugh C. Weir's Madelyn Mack, Anna Katharine Green's Violet Strange, Arthur B. Reeve's Constance Dunlap, Hulbert Footner's Madame Storey, E. Phillips Oppenheim's Baroness Clara Linz, Mignon G. Eberhart's Susan Dare, William Irish's Jerry Wheeler, G.D.H. and M.I. Cole's Mrs. Warrender, Gladys Mitchell's Beatrice Bradley, and Stuart Palmer's Hildegarde Withers. The appendix, "The Women Detectives: A Chronological Survey," is a useful 21-page annotated list, followed by a two-page secondary bibliography.

519. Starrett, Vincent, ed. *Fourteen Great Detective Stories.* New York: Modern Library, 1928. xv, 400p.

Only reference value of this good early anthology lies in Starrett's seven-page introduction, which, among other things, decries the lack of variety of setting in detective stories, always (at that time) set in New York or London, never in Belfast, Ohio. Howard Haycraft later re-edited this anthology, replacing some of the stories with examples from more recent writers.

520. Starrett, Vincent, ed. *World's Great Spy Stories.* Cleveland: World, 1944. 445p.

The four-page introduction of this pioneering anthology provides a short history of spy stories, finding examples in the Bible as well as Thackeray and Zola. The 25 story notes, presenting entries from detective-story writers (Doyle, Carr, Gruber, Boucher), espionage specialists

(Ambler, Wheatley, Oppenheim), and general literary figures (Maugham, Conrad, Leacock) are varied and informative. World published several other anthologies in the forties (one edited by Anthony Boucher and two by Will Cuppy), but they do not have the reference value of this one.

521. **Stout, Rex, ed.** *Eat, Drink, and Be Buried.* (Mystery Writers of America anthology.) New York: Viking, 1956. 246p.

Not examined. According to Contento (see #14), it includes "end-notes by each story's author." Among the contributors are the usual '50s MWA stalwarts plus names less frequently seen: Ben Benson, Joseph Commings, Veronica Parker Johns, James A. Kirch, Henry Kuttner, Fred Levon, and Dana Lyon.

522. **Symons, Julian, ed.** *The Penguin Classic Crime Omnibus.* London: Penguin, 1984. 378p.

Symons is such an all-around expert on crime fiction, it's surprising this excellent compilation is his only general anthology of the genre. The four-page introduction discusses the detective story's roots in the short form and his attempts to represent famous writers with less frequently reprinted stories. The notes to the 25 selected are among the most enjoyable and substantial extant, at least partly because they are more frankly critical than is usual—catch, for example, the raking of Lord Peter Wimsey in the introduction to Dorothy L. Sayers's non-Wimsey tale "The Man Who Knew How." Most of the authors represented are the expected specialists (Carr, Chesterton, Christie, Doyle, Ellin, James, Poe, Queen, Rendell, Simenon), with a couple from mainstream literature (Faulkner and Greene), but the first and last (by alphabetical accident) are the most surprising: American journalist and mystery man Ambrose Bierce and South African writer Arthur Williams, whose only published work is reprinted here several decades after its first appearance in *Ellery Queen's Mystery Magazine.*

523. **Talburt, Nancy Ellen, and Lyna Lee Montgomery, eds.** *A Mystery Reader: Stories of Detection, Adventure, and Horror.* New York: Scribners, 1974. 458p. Bibl.

Not examined. Per Contento (see #14), the editors contribute essays on the Golden Age and on "The Hardboiled School and After," reprint essays by Rex Stout ("Watson Was a Woman"), Ross Macdonald ("The Writer as Detective Hero") and Frank D. McSherry, Jr. ("The Shape of Crimes to Come"), and offer a bibliography "For Further Reading." Albert (see #6) describes it as a "school text, with an introduction, notes and study aids. The critical notes are sketchy and would require considerable additional material to give students any substantive understanding of the field" (page 111).

524. Tenn, William (Philip Klass), and Donald E. Westlake, eds. *Once Against the Law.* New York: Macmillan, 1968. xvii, 330p.

Like Queen's *The Literature of Crime* (see #492) and Pronzini, Malzberg, and Greenberg's *Mystery in the Mainstream* (see #485), this anthology collects crime stories by literary figures normally seen as outside the genre. Among the 22 contributors are Steinbeck, Chaucer, Dickens, Browning, Balzac, Tolstoy, and Pirandello. There are no story notes, but Westlake's 11-page introduction entertainingly discusses why crime is such a popular fictional subject and mentions numerous other examples not included in the book.

525. *The Times of London Anthology of Detective Stories*. London: Cape, 1972; New York: Day, 1973. 252p.

This volume gathers the winners and selected other tales from a competition sponsored by the London *Times* and judged by Agatha Christie, Tom Stoppard, and others. Only first prize-winner John Sladek will be a familiar name to many. Of the other nine, only *Avengers* novelizer John Garforth and Alex Josey (with a self-published volume) have an entry through 1985 in Hubin's crime fiction bibliographies (see WAM #18 and present volume #548). Thus, the biographical notes at the ends of the stories offer information unlikely to be found elsewhere.

526. *Verdict of 13: A Detection Club Anthology*. Introduction by Julian Symons. London: Faber, 1978. New York: Harper and Row, 1979. x, 239p.

In four economical pages, Symons's introduction recounts the history of the Detection Club from an organization of Golden-Age purists to its present relaxed membership requirements that let in outstanding spy and thriller writers along with those of pure detection. The thirteen stories, all concerning juries (literally or metaphorically), do not have individual notes. (Symons adds to and partially corrects his Detection Club history in the introduction to the U.S. edition of *The Scoop & Behind the Screen* [Harper and Row, 1983].)

527. Wagenknecht, Edward, ed. *Murder by Gaslight: Victorian Tales.* New York: Prentice-Hall, 1949. 437p.

Not examined. The length of the introduction (beginning on page 3 with the first story beginning on page 17 per Contento [see #14]) and the editor's scholarly reputation suggest substantial secondary interest. Authors included are Mary Elizabeth Braddon, Charles Dickens, Wilkie Collins, Charles Reade, and Amelia B. Edwards.

528. Wallace, Marilyn, ed. *Sisters in Crime.* New York: Berkley, 1989. xiii, 306p.
Sisters in Crime 2. New York: Berkley, 1990. xii, 292p.
Sisters in Crime 3. New York: Berkley, 1990. xii, 324p.
Sisters in Crime 4. New York: Berkley, 1991. xii, 352p.

Each volume of this admirable original anthology series has a two or three page introduction by editor Wallace, mostly of negligible reference interest, plus individual story notes on the contributors. The reference feature that may be unique, however, is the inclusion of photographs of all contributors on the inside front and back covers.

529. Waugh, Carol-Lynn Rössel; Martin H. Greenberg, and Frank D. McSherry, Jr., eds. *Murder and Mystery in Boston.* New York: Dembner, 1987. 298p.

Though lacking the overall introduction of its Chicago equivalent (see below), this volume offers good biographical notes on its contributors, especially valuable on the comparatively little-known Hayden Howard and S.S. Rafferty. Others include David Alexander, Linda J. Barnes, George Harmon Coxe, David Ely, Robert L. Fish, Jacques Futrelle, George V. Higgins, Edward D. Hoch, Charlotte MacLeod, Phoebe Atwood Taylor, and Donald E. Westlake.

530. Waugh, Carol-Lynn Rössel; Martin H. Greenberg, and Frank D. McSherry, Jr., eds. *Murder and Mystery in Chicago.* New York: Dembner, 1987. x, 258p.

Robert Bloch's four-page introduction recounts his memories of Chicago and that city's contribution to popular literature. The seven pages of author biographies are more extensive and informative than most such in anthologies. Contributors besides Bloch include Sara Paretsky, Fredric Brown, Howard Browne, Edward D. Hoch, Craig Rice, James M. Ullman, Jon L. Breen, Ray Russell, Richard Connell, and Dorothy B. Hughes, whose previously unreprinted 1945 novelette "The Spotted Dog" comprises nearly a third of the book.

531. Waugh, Charles G.; Frank D. McSherry, Jr., and Martin H. Greenberg, eds. *Murder and Mystery in Maine.* New York: Dembner, 1989. 208p.

A state volume in the format of the two city volumes above, this one also has good author biographies in its six-page concluding section. It also has a higher proportion of lesser-known writers—Alfred Kuan (Harvey A. Dodd), Edmund Ware Smith, Robert G. Denig, Holman F. Day, Mary Amlaw, Kit Reed, and Henry T. Parry—to go with famous names like Kemelman, Highsmith, and Hoch.

532. Waugh, Charles; Martin Greenberg, and Joseph Olander, eds. *Mysterious Visions: Great Science Fiction by Masters of Mystery.* Foreword by Isaac Asimov. New York: St. Martin's, 1979. xxvi, 516p.

Waugh contributes a scholarly eight-page introduction, "The Fantastic Mystery: A Neglected Genre," discussing earlier treatments of the topic and classifying genre crossovers in ten different categories. A number of writers besides the 26 represented in the anthology are referred to.

533. Wells, Carolyn, ed. *American Detective Stories.* n.p.: Oxford U. P., American Branch, 1927. xiii, 250p.

In her ten-page foreword to this pioneering anthology, Wells defends the literary value of detective fiction, quoting among others Houdini, Woodrow Wilson, Julian Hawthorne, and one of her contributors, Brander Matthews.

534. Wells, Carolyn, ed. *Best American Mystery Stories of the Year.* 2 volumes. New York: Tudor, 1931 and 1932.

This first attempt at an annual "best" collection lasted only two years but provided an interesting survey (and a wide-ranging one, drawing on pulps and slicks alike) of the short mystery story of its day. There are no individual story notes, but Wells provides interesting introductions, twelve pages in the 1931 volume, including an early discussion of the pre-history of the detective story (partly from the revised edition of her *Technique of the Mystery Story* [WAM #99]), and a less rewarding seven pages in the 1932 collection, adapted from the introduction to her *American Detective Stories* (see above).

535. Weinberg, Robert; Stefan R. Dziemianowicz, and Martin H. Greenberg, eds. *Hard-Boiled Detectives: 23 Great Stories from Dime Detective Magazine.* New York: Gramercy, 1992. xiii, 434p.

Though this sizable anthology lacks individual author or story notes, Dziemianowicz's excellent five-page introduction provides a concise history of hardboiled detective fiction and, more uniquely, of the source periodical, described as a "looser and more varied magazine than *Black Mask.*" *Dime Detective* "allowed both humor and horror into its fiction and wound up accommodating some of the unlikeliest crime stoppers to make the printed page." Contributors range from famous names like Gardner, Brand, Chandler, and John D. MacDonald to writers better-known for science fiction (C.M. Kornbluth, Murray Leinster, William Tenn) to relatively forgotten pulsters like John Lawrence, D.L. Champion, Merle Constiner, Julius Long, and Robert Turner.

536. Williams, Blanche Colton, ed. *The Mystery and the Detective: A Collection of Stories.* New York: Appleton-Century, 1938. xii, 364p.

Though it was beaten to the post by a British volume (Seabourne's *Detective in Fiction* [see 514]), it seems fairly certain that this was the first American mystery anthology designed to be used as a textbook, in this case high school level. The four-page introduction discusses the rules of the detective story, and each selection is followed by a paragraph to a page of author biography and about a page of study questions. Though some of the authors are somewhat to very familiar (Pain, Blackwood, Post, Oppenheim, Brander Matthews, Stockton, Poe, W.W. Jacobs, O. Henry) or ring at least a faint bell (John Russell, F. Marion Crawford, Henry Syndor Harrison), a surprising number are utterly forgotten: Richard Washburn Child, Carolyn Darling, Charles Caldwell Dobie, Frederick Stewart Greene, Theodore White, E.M. Winch, Corinne Harris Markey, and H.D. Umbstaetter. For Winch and White, no biography is provided, but many of the others have impressive resumes for all their present obscurity.

537. *World's Greatest Detective Stories.* London: Syndicate, 1934. 1024p.

Not examined. Per Contento (see #14), the volume has a fairly lengthy foreword (beginning on page 7, with the first story not beginning until page 23) by Howard Spring, who later would reveal the ending of an Agatha Christie novel in the course of an unfavorable review and come to be regarded as an enemy of the genre.

538. Wright, Lee, ed. *The Pocket Mystery Reader.* New York: Pocket Books, 1942. x, 363p.

One of the mystery field's most celebrated book editors, Wright compiled several anthologies in paperback original, usually (as here) without substantial introductions or story notes. But this varied volume includes, besides a Hammett novelette, a selection of short stories, true-crime articles, an Ellery Queen radio play, and sections of poems and puzzles, half a dozen articles about the genre, three satirical (Stephen Leacock's "Twenty Cents' Worth of Murder," Rex Stout's celebrated and castigated "Watson was a Woman," and P.G. Wodehouse's "About These

Mystery Stories") and three more serious (Elliot Paul's "Whodunit," Edmund Pearson's "The Perfect Murder," and Howard Haycraft's "Dictators, Democrats, and Detectives," the latter reprinted from *Murder for Pleasure* [WAM #1]).

539. Wright, Willard Huntington, ed. *The Great Detective Stories: A Chronological Anthology.* New York: Scribners, 1927. viii, 483p.

The 35-page introduction, like Dorothy Sayers's to *Omnibus of Crime* (see #512), is an important early history of the detective genre published before the first book-length studies. Also like the Sayers piece, it has been reprinted, notably in Haycraft's *The Art of the Mystery Story* (see WAM #69). Unlike Sayers, Wright also provides substantial biographical introductions to the seventeen stories. If they offer little that is unfamiliar about the famous (Poe, Collins, Doyle, Chesterton, etc.), they are useful on the relatively unfamiliar or forgotten, such as Bennett Copplestone (Frederick Harcourt Kitchen), Dietrich Thieden, and Balduin Groller. Wright, of course, was better-known by his pseudonym S.S. Van Dine, under which name the anthology was later reissued.

540. Wrong, E(dward) M(urray), ed. *Crime and Detection.* London: Oxford U.P., 1926. xxx, 394p.

Wrong's 22-page introduction, like those of Sayers and Wright (see above), is a substantial study of the genre published before the first book-length histories and has been reprinted in Haycraft's *Art of the Mystery Story* (WAM #69). There are no individual story notes or any other editorial apparatus.

541. Yates, Donald A., ed. *Latin Blood: The Best Crime and Detective Stories of South America.* New York: Herder and Herder, 1972. xv, 224p.

Yates is undoubtedly the ranking English-writing expert on his subject, and he has created an anthology that is both admirable and unique. Its title is a misnomer, however, since Mexico (a part, I believe, of North America) is one of the dominant countries, along with Argentina and Chile, from which these seventeen stories are drawn. In his five-page introduction, Yates uses the now-disparaged descriptor Spanish America. Each story is preceded by a biographical introduction. While some of the authors' names may be at least vaguely familiar to readers of English (Manuel Peyrou, Rodolfo J. Walsh, Antonio Helu) and at least one world-famous (Jorge Luis Borges), the obscurity of most of the names points up the unfortunate paucity of foreign detective fiction in English translation.

8
NEW EDITIONS AND SUPPLEMENTS

542. **Adey, Robert.** *Locked Room Murders and Other Impossible Crimes: A Comprehensive Bibliography.* Revised and expanded edition. Minneapolis: Crossover, 1991. xliii, 411p.

First published in 1979 (see WAM #8), this invaluable specialized reference has grown from 1280 to 2019 numbered entries, adding not only the surprisingly healthy amount of new material that has appeared since the original publication date but newly discovered earlier works as well. Though no compiler could possibly turn up every locked room or impossible crime story through the whole history of detective fiction, Adey's net has been cast widely enough, even including a couple of comic book tales about Mike W. Barr's "The Maze Agency," to justify the newly-minted subtitle. Entries repeated from the earlier edition have been renumbered. The inclusion of check marks to identify the new entries is helpful to users of the earlier book.

To capture the critical and sometimes humorous flavor of the numbered solution guide, separated from the main listing to prevent undesired giveaways, I'll quote #1282 in full (without, of course, revealing what book it goes with): "The villain had on a parachute, crawled out of the rear platform of the last car and allowed the onward rush of the train to fill the parachute, drag him off the platform, and be saved from certain death by the effect of the parachute itself. The detective describes the escape as 'daring.' I'm sure that we can all think of other descriptive phrases."

543. **Barnes, Melvyn.** *Murder in Print: A Guide to Two Centuries of Crime Fiction.* London: Barn Owl, 1986. xii, 244p. Bibl., index.

Despite the new title, this is a much expanded and improved revised edition of *Best Detective Fiction* (WAM #9). According to the preface, coverage has increased from 122 authors to about 260 and from 220 titles to nearly 500. Thrillers and spy stories are still excluded. Separate chapters have been added on police procedurals and historical mysteries. Also new are a three-page secondary bibliography and an index to authors, titles, and series characters.

Barnes has obviously made an effort to address the limitations of the first edition. Some errors have been corrected; there is a greater recognition of trans-Atlantic title changes; and two authors I noted as surprising omissions from the first edition (Helen McCloy and P.D. James) have been added. The British bias is much less pronounced, with welcome tributes to long-time veteran American writers Aaron Marc Stein and Hugh Pentecost and the addition of several Americans in the expanded hardboiled chapter. (Some, however, are rather strained to fit—Henry Slesar? Donald E. Westlake of the comic novels?—and the female private eye series of Grafton, Muller, and Paretsky don't get in.)

While most of the additions are writers who have come to prominence in the decade since the first edition, oldtimers like Hake Talbot, Arthur W. Upfield, Charlotte Armstrong, and Vera Caspary have been added, and additional titles have been annotated for some included in the original volume, e.g. John Dickson Carr, Ellery Queen, Gladys Mitchell. Once again coverage is given to some less well-known names, usually British, e.g., J.F. Straker, Roger Busby, Emma Page, Gwen Moffat, Martin Russell, Roy Lewis.

In sum, this is a vast improvement on what was already a useful reference work.

544. Barzun, Jacques, and Wendell Hertig Taylor. *A Catalogue of Crime*. Revised and enlarged edition. New York: Harper and Row, 1989. xxxvi, 952p. Index.

One of the most wide-ranging, enjoyable, useful, and controversial references in the mystery fiction field (see WAM #10) reappears in a long-promised revision, completed by Barzun after the death in 1985 of Taylor. The total number of annotated entries has gone from 3476 to 5045, with the largest section, on novels, increasing from 2304 to 3549. The section on ghost stories has been omitted, and most biographical information on the authors has been dropped along with the "see also" references.

The latter had little point to begin with, and even less following the work of Hubin (see WAM #18 and present volume #548) and Reilly (see WAM #29 and present volume #556).

Barzun and Taylor's British and classical bias remains. Writers who have debuted since the first edition receiving substantial and favorable coverage include John R.L. Anderson, Robert Barnard, Simon Brett, and Dorothy Simpson. Among newer writers less well received are Sue Grafton, Tony Hillerman, and Herbert Resnicow. Oddities of selection and emphasis still exist. Why do the authors give virtually complete coverage to Joe L. Hensley when they find practically nothing to like in his novels? (Elmore Leonard, by contrast, is dismissed in two lines.)

The new edition seems generally less mistake-ridden than its predecessor. Many of the miscues from the first edition have been corrected, though the Frank Gruber entry is still confused as to Simon Lash and Johnny Fletcher titles. There are new errors. *Scrolls of Lysis*, a 1962 historical signed by Barnaby Ross, is credited to the Ellery Queen team—though they used the Ross pseudonym in the thirties on the Drury Lane novels, they had nothing to do with this one. William F. Buckley, Jr.'s *Who's on First* (1980) is miscalled the first Blackford Oakes novel.

545. Bryce, Ivar. *You Only Live Once: Memories of Ian Fleming.* Revised edition. London: Weidenfeld and Nicolson, 1984. 142p. Ill.

Not examined. The extent of revision of WAM #155 is not known.

546. Cook, Michael L. *Murder by Mail: Inside the Mystery Book Clubs with Complete Checklist.* Bowling Green, OH: Popular, 1983. Revised, expanded, and updated edition. 222p. Index.

The updated edition of WAM #13 extends the coverage of Detective Book Club through October 1983 and the Mystery Guild through September 1983. The following newer and less long-lived clubs have been added to the coverage: Ellery Queen's Mystery Club, Masterpieces of Mystery Library (Davis Publications), The Mystery Library (University of California, San Diego, extension), and Raven House Mystery Book Club.

547. **Francis, Dick.** *Sport of Queens.* Fourth edition. London: Joseph, 1988. 254p. Ill.

Not examined. To my knowledge, this is the most recent edition of WAM #165, surely the most frequently updated of mystery-writer biographies or autobiographies.

548. **Hubin, Allen J.** *1981-1985 Supplement to Crime Fiction, 1749-1980.* New York: Garland, 1988. xxi, 260p. Index.

Besides extending the coverage of his admirable bibliography of English-language crime fiction to the end of 1985, Hubin has added a valuable new feature. He identifies film adaptations of printed works in the main listing with "movie title, producing studio, year of first release, screenwriter(s) and director(s)." Additional indexes are provided by film title, screenwriter, and director.

The updating reflects Hubin's usual meticulous job. Among the especially commendable inclusions, he sorts out the authorship of the long series of Hank Janson novels, gives a name to the mysterious K.C. Constantine, and provides identification of the true identities of Domini Taylor and Francis Selwyn.

549. **Marsh, Ngaio.** *Black Beech and Honeydew: An Autobiography.* Revised and enlarged edition. Aukland, NZ: Collins, 1981. London: Collins, 1982. 310p. Illus.

Not examined. According to several sources, this revision of WAM #195 devotes much more space to discussion of the author's detective fiction than the first edition.

550. **Parish, James Robert, and Michael R. Pitts.** *The Great Spy Pictures II.* Metuchen, NJ: Scarecrow, 1986. xii, 432p. Illus., bibl.

The follow-up to WAM #24 adds over 400 more titles, again divided between the recent and ancient, the good and the bad, with considerable information on credits, plots, critical reception, and various sidelights. Vincent Terrace adds to the list of radio and TV spy shows, and T. Allan

Taylor's bibliography of spy novels and series has been revised and updated in 66 pages.

551. Pitts, Michael R. *Famous Movie Detectives II*. Metuchen, NJ: Scarecrow, 1991. viii, 349p. Illus., bibl., index.

The continuation of WAM #25 follows the same format, with 14 chapters devoted to individual detective series, including Sherlock Holmes (at 64 pages the longest chapter) and Philip Marlowe, both omitted from the first volume because they duplicated other Scarecrow books then in print; plus such figures as Hercule Poirot, Inspector Maigret, Mike Hammer, Miss Marple, and Perry Mason. A catch-all chapter covers shorter series more briefly, among them notable literary sleuths like Dupin, Duncan MacLain, Father Brown, Lew Archer, Lord Peter Wimsey, Thatcher Colt, and Travis McGee. The 16-page bibliography provides a checklist of the characters' literary appearances. There are also nineteen pages of additions and corrections to the parent volume.

As before there's a wealth of information presented in an undistinguished style. Pitts produces better prose in collaboration with James Robert Parish in *The Great Detective Pictures* (see #51), a volume that overlaps the coverage of this one to a considerable extent but treats the material differently, going film by film rather than series by series.

552. Riley, Dick, and Pam McAllister, eds. *The New Bedside, Bathtub, and Armchair Companion to Agatha Christie*. Foreword by Julian Symons. Second edition, with new material edited by McAlister and Bruce Cassiday. New York: Ungar, 1986. xviii, 362p. Illus., bibl., index.

Through page 315, this is a straight reprint with smaller page-size of WAM #135. That *Poirot Investigates* and *The Tuesday Club Murders* are still identified (in the book's system of visual symbols) as novels rather than short-story collections suggests no effort has been made to correct errors. The 34 pages of new material, mostly unremarkable, includes a supplement by Michael Tennenbaum to the Christie filmography, through the 1986 TV movie of *Dead Man's Folly;* articles by Bruce Cassiday (on Tuppence and Tommy and on serving as a victim at a Mystery Weekend), Edward D. Hoch (a welcome sorting out of the best of Christie's many short stories), Tennenbaum (on the film version of Kathleen Tynan's

Agatha and the B.B.C.'s recent Christie adaptations), editor McAllister (on recent Christie paperback covers, among other topics), Ann Romeo (on the Detection Club's various collaborative works), and Emma Lathen (on the *Murder, She Wrote* TV series, contrasting Jessica Fletcher with Miss Marple); plus an updated secondary bibliography and a list of Christie adaptations available on video.

553. **Robinson, Kenneth.** *Wilkie Collins: A Biography.* London: Davis-Poynter, 1974. 348p. Illus., bibl., index.

Not examined. Most sources show this as a reprint of WAM #144, but at least one Collins source indicates there has been some revision.

554. **Smith, Myron J., Jr.** *Cloak and Dagger Fiction: An Annotated Guide to Spy Thrillers.* Second edition. Santa Barbara: ABC-Clio, 1982. xxvi, 431p. Bibl., index.

Cloak-and-Dagger Bibliography (WAM #30) is revised and much expanded under a slightly different title. The number of entries has grown from 1675 to 3435, now divided into two separately introduced sections: Early Spy Thrillers, to 1940 (very selectively, comprising only the first 318 entries) and Golden Age and Beyond, 1940 to the Present. Annotations to the entries provide biographical information and plot summary, and indications of humor, low sex quotient, and suitability for young adults are continued. Appendices provide guides to pseudonyms, series characters, and intelligence and terrorist organizations. There are separate author and title indices.

Though this work is full of useful information, it continues to be error-prone. References to Michael "Avallon" and Patricia "McGeer" are uncorrected from the first edition. There is a double miscue in the reference to Poe's *Case of the Purloined Letter*—the title prefix is wrong, and the italics imply a novel rather than a short story. Smith mistakenly implies that Van Wyck Mason sometimes wrote about Hugh North under his Geoffrey Coffin pseudonym; Arthur S. "Wade" (should be Ward) is given as the real name of Sax Rohmer; and the house name Will B. Aarons is naively assumed to be Edward S. Aarons's son.

The volume begins with a foreword by Clive Cussler and a preface by James C. Stam.

555. **Symons, Julian.** *Bloody Murder.* Revised edition. New York: Viking, 1985. 262p. Index.

In a new edition of his 1972 history (WAM #5), first published in the United States as *Mortal Consequences,* Symons has maintained the original structure of his work but revised and updated every chapter, most extensively those about the current scene. It's still an impressive piece of work, strong on style and agonizingly tough critical standards, though not quite as successful in reflecting the current state of the art as might have been hoped. Among the writers added are P.D. James, Ruth Rendell, Ross Thomas, Charles McCarry, George V. Higgins, Reginald Hill, Edward D. Hoch, and Janwillem van de Wetering. Symons has not considered every important new name: Elmore Leonard, James Crumley, K.C. Constantine, Robert Barnard, Simon Brett, and Colin Dexter are a few of the well-established newer writers not discussed.

There are still careless errors in the book, including some near-miss dates (the first Perry Mason novel, Erle Stanley Gardner's death, S.S. Van Dine's birth) and a statement, unchanged from the first edition, that the Ellery Queen team also wrote under the name Drury Lane. (Again: Lane was the detective, Barnaby Ross the byline.) Curiously, Symons still does not note that the mystery novels signed by Gypsy Rose Lee were actually the work of Craig Rice.

In his final chapter, "The Crystal Ball Revisited," Symons looks at the predictions he made in the original edition and remarks on how nearly they have come true. He claims his forecast of the continued decline of the old-fashioned detective story was one of the winners. Am I dreaming or was there a considerable renaissance of the formal detective story in the decade before 1985?

Mysterious Press has announced a third (and final) edition for publication early in 1993.

556. *Twentieth-Century Crime and Mystery Writers.*
   Second edition. Ed. John M. Reilly. New York: St. Martin's, 1985. xx, 1094p. Bibl., index.
   Third edition. Ed. Lesley Henderson. Chicago and London: St. James, 1991. xxxi, 1294p. Bibl., index.

The second edition of WAM #29 is a considerable improvement over what was already one of the best and most indispensable reference volumes in the field. The smaller number of pages is misleading—the format is now double-column and the total number of writers covered has risen to over 640 according to St. Martin's publicity, including 109 new entries, 23 completely rewritten critical summaries, and many updated entries on active writers. Many of the prominent omissions I noted in the first edition (David Alexander, Howard Browne, Victoria Holt) have been rectified. Among other additions are old-timers like Peter Rabe, Stewart Sterling, Jonathan Craig, C.W. Grafton, Clifford Knight, Kurt Steel, and Clyde B. Clason, and such contemporaries as Dean R. Koontz, Marcia Muller, Robert Barnard, Richard Neely, K.C. Constantine, James Crumley, Elmore Leonard, William McIlvanney, Ralph McInerny, William Marshall, Richard B. Sapir and Warren Murphy, Gerald Seymour, and Jonathan Valin. There are good new essays on John Ball and H.R.F. Keating, whose works were treated too narrowly in the first edition, and on Jack Webb, who is now firmly separated from his TV-star namesake. A title index to novels and collections, but not individual short stories, has been added.

For the third edition, a new editor takes over, and the total number of authors covered is now around 700 according to Kathleen Gregory Klein's preface. Among the new names added are Harold Adams, Linda Barnes, James Lee Burke, Robert Campbell, George C. Chesbro, Tom Clancy, Bill Crider, Susan Dunlap, Aaron J. Elkins, Ed Gorman, Sue Grafton, Thomas Harris, Carolyn G. Hart, Jeremiah Healy, Robert Irvine, Faye Kellerman, Jonathan Kellerman, Joe R. Lansdale, Sara Paretsky, Anne Perry, Herbert Resnicow, Julie Smith, Scott Turow, and Andrew Vachss. Lillian Jackson Braun is perhaps unique in having appeared in the first edition, been dropped from the second, and (with her 1980s comeback) resurrected in the third. Fewer old-timers have been added than in the second edition, but one, the amazingly prolific plagiarist Gerald Verner, discussed by Jack Adrian, is especially interesting to read about, though it didn't send me rushing to find his novels. Among other desirable new features: larger type for easier reading, a list of writers not included here who appeared in earlier editions, and the addition of some Japanese authors (Seicho Matsumoto, Shizuko Natsuki, and Masako Togawa) to the section of foreign-language writers.

There are some new or intensified problems in the third edition. Typographical errors seem to be more frequent. More seriously, the separation of an author's "Crime" and "Other" publications is sometimes shaky. Some books clearly in the crime fiction genre are listed under "other" in the entries on Chesbro, Frank Parrish (the novels written as

Domini Taylor), E.X. Giroux (her books as Doris Shannon), Gorman, Stephen Greenleaf, Faye Kellerman, and Dean R. Koontz. (In fairness to the new editor, similar examples I noted in the entries on Basil Copper, Jack Finney and Ron Goulart were carried over from the previous edition.) There is an unfortunate multiple error in the Fredric Brown bibliography: the individual titles in Dennis McMillan's Fredric Brown in the Detective Pulps series are listed under "uncollected short stories" instead of with his collections.

Unevenness of treatment in the critical essays has always been a problem in this series, one impossible to overcome completely with so many different contributors. While most of the critical comments are evenhanded on their subjects' strengths and weaknesses, some (e.g. Wayne Dundee on Robert J. Randisi) are pure puffery. And while William Malloy's essays on Harold Adams, Jerome Charyn, Chesbro, and James Ellroy are excellent appreciations, it seems dubious to assign the assessment of these authors to an editor for their publisher, Mysterious Press. (It's only fair to add that since this volume was published, at least two of the four have moved to other publishers.)

Many of the entries include a comment by the subject. When these were written for earlier editions by authors now deceased, the date of the comment has been included. Possibly this should be done for all comments unchanged from earlier editions, certainly for those (e.g. by Max Allan Collins, John Gardner, William Campbell Gault) whose comments are clearly outdated by evidence in the bibliography. For at least one living writer, Koontz, this has been done. In at least one case, a statement in the critical essay is outdated: there are now three collections of Jack Ritchie's short stories, duly listed in the bibliography, not one as stated in Edward D. Hoch's essay.

Some missing information that should be noted in future editions: Thomas Gifford's pseudonymous work as Thomas Maxwell and Donald E. Westlake's as Samuel Holt; Henry Slesar's short-story collection *Murders Most Macabre* (Avon, 1986); and Ray B. Browne's critical study of Arthur W. Upfield, *The Spirit of Australia* (1988, see #340). Of course, there is always a temptation to second-guess the selection of authors treated. As one of the advisers to the project, I have had my say on the subject before the fact, and there have been so many estimable writers to debut or gain prominence since the second edition, it would be impossible to have a perfect score of choosing the most worthy ones. Thus, I'll confine myself to one double-barreled gripe: while I am happy to see the attention to feminist and/or lesbian mystery writers published outside the mainstream (e.g. Katharine V. Forrest and Barbara Wilson), two of the inclusions (the authors thus far of two mysteries each) gave me pause: Hannah Wakefield, whose Dee Street is wrongly credited in Linda Semple's essay as "the only female solicitor/detective" in British mysteries (what about Michael Underwood's Rosa Epton?); and, even more surprising given the largely negative tone of Roz Kaveney's essay, Mary Wings. It is no denigration of these writers to suggest that they are questionable inclusions compared to some of the accomplished practitioners left out (e.g. Sharyn McCrumb, Michael Nava, Parnell Hall, Sandra Scoppettone, Margaret Maron, P.M. Carlson, James Yaffe—but I said I wasn't going to do this).

Given the amount of new material in each edition, as well as the material rewritten or dropped, libraries and private collectors will want to retain all three editions if possible.

557. Tuska, Jon. *In Manors and Alleys: A Casebook of the American Detective Film.* Westport, CT: Greenwood, 1988. xxi, 462p. Illus., bibl., index.

You have to read the introduction to discover that this is a revised version of Tuska's *The Detective in Film* (Doubleday, 1978; see WAM #59). It's certainly a thorough one, though, drawing on many sources published since 1978, and a much better and more tightly written book than its predecessor. Enough has been dropped from the first edition to make it advisable to keep both. Though the new edition adds notes and a bibliography, the illustrations are fewer and confined to one section rather than being scattered throughout the text.

The chapter on S.S. Van Dine, kept short in the earlier edition according to Tuska because his editor at Doubleday disliked the works of Philo Vance's creator, is the most thorough bio-critical account of the author to appear in print prior to John Loughery's 1992 biography (see #341). (Much of it originally appeared in Tuska's pamphlet *Philo Vance: The Life and Times of S.S. Van Dine;* see WAM #225.)

Tuska makes some odd and inaccurate statements at times. I would like to know what sources "attempt a critique of every detective story every written" (page xvii)—certainly none that I've ever run across. Though it's a matter of opinion rather than fact, I don't believe he convincingly defends his statement that "Van Dine was scrupulously honest in laying before the reader the vital clues necessary to solve the mystery; Ellery Queen was not" (page 91). Actually, the opposite was the case, and finding a few plot flaws in the Queen novels is not enough to make me think otherwise. Finally, Raymond Chandler was never "viciously denigrated" (page 353) by Anthony Boucher, who generally admired his work.

558. Winn, Dilys. *Murder Ink.* Revised edition. New York: Workman, 1984. xv, 398p. Illus., bibl., index.

In a way, this is more than a new edition of the handsome mystery miscellany first published in 1977 (see WAM #107). Though many items are repeated, enough are new to make one wonder why the compiler didn't come up with all original material and make this *Murder Ink II*. Among the new features, balanced as before between the serious and the frivolous, the factual and the fictional: a playlet by K.C. Constantine that rather unfairly lampoons librarians; an article on the Canadian mystery scene by Eric Wright; a solid piece by Joseph Hansen on the image of the homosexual in mystery fiction; Julian Symons's account of his abandoned series sleuth Bland (a police detective not to be confused with Mignon G. Eberhart's butler of the same name), and why he has usually shunned recurring detectives in his novel since; a lively annotated guide to mystery bookshops by the obviously pseudonymous Desdemona Brannigan; a nice tribute to Fred Dannay by Eleanor Sullivan; Baird Searles on s.f.-mystery hybrids; Clark Howard on the career of J. Edgar Hoover; Treasury agent Gerald Petievich on counterfeiting; and John R. Feegel on "Forensic Protocol" (chattily written: "While we're in the water, let's drown"). Other new contributors include such major names as Robert Barnard, Simon Brett, Dorothy Salisbury Davis, Edward Gorey, Martha Grimes, Tim Heald, Ed McBain, Warren Murphy, Thomas Perry, and Martha G. Webb. Among the more memorable contributing noms-de-plume: Iphegenia Burton-Mall, Naomi Buttermilk, Ebeneezer Nizer, and Ahab Pepys. Also new is *Murder Ink's* own illustrated whodunit, called "The Tainted Tea Mystery" and running throughout the book.

In the parent volume of *What About Murder?*, I managed to misspell the last name of this book's compiler as "Wynn," an egregious error no one ever pointed out to me. Is it premeditated revenge or merely poetic justice that my first name is misspelled "John" here on two out of three opportunities?

ADDENDUM

3 SPECIAL SUBJECTS

559. Hilfer, Tony. *The Crime Novel: A Deviant Genre.* Austin: U. of Texas P., 1990. xiv, 180p. Illus., bibl., index.

In a challenging and readable study, Hilfer takes off from Julian Symons's distinction between detective story and crime novel but goes even further, taking a narrower definition of crime novel and attributing to it a whole different set of rules. Novels substantially discussed in the early chapters include Cameron McCabe's *The Face on the Cutting Room Floor*, Horace McCoy's *Kiss Tomorrow Goodbye*, Marc Behm's *The Eye of the Beholder*, Patrick Hamilton's *Hangover Square*, John Franklin Bardin's *Devil Take the Blue-Tail Fly*, Ann Chamberlain's *The Tall Dark Man*, Kenneth Fearing's *The Big Clock*, James Ross's *They Don't Dance Much*, Richard Hallas's *You Play the Black and the Red Come Up*, Flann O'Brien's *The Third Policeman*, Fredric Brown's *The Screaming Mimi*, Shelley Smith's *The Crooked Man*, Oliver Onions's *In Accordance with the Evidence*, Ernest Raymond's *We the Accused*, F. Tennyson Jesse's *A Pin to See the Peepshow*, Marie Belloc Lowndes's *The Lodger*, and Richard Hull's *The Murder of My Aunt*, along with Dennis Potter's TV script *The Singing Detective* and novels of Raymond Chandler, Cornell Woolrich, James M. Cain, Julian Symons, and Francis Iles. He compares the book and film versions of Cain's *Double Indemnity* and Vera Caspary's *Laura*. His final chapter discusses two books each by four writers of particular importance to the development of the crime novel: Simenon (of the non-Maigret novels), Margaret Millar, Patricia Highsmith, and Jim Thompson.

A discussion of terminology in the note on page 155 seems somewhat dubious. He rejects the term suspense novel because it "can be another name for spy novel" and states "inverted detective novel is used almost exclusively to describe English rather than American crime novels." On the contrary, an inverted detective story is a very specific (and somewhat rare) variety of detective fiction of which the American TV show *Columbo* is one of the best examples. Some of the recent torrent of cop-vs.-psycho books, most American rather than British, qualify as inverted detection and may be the most prominent examples today. At any rate, Hilfer is right that this is not what he's talking about when he talks about the crime novel.

560. Morris, Virginia B. *Double Jeopardy: Women Who Kill in Victorian Fiction.* Lexington: U.P. of Kentucky, 1990. ix, 182p. Illus., bibl., index.

Morris's well-demonstrated theme is that most women murderers in Victorian fiction had justification and most of their authors sympathized with them. Crime-fiction writers covered are Dickens (of *Bleak House* and others), Braddon (especially *Lady Audley's Secret*), Collins, and Doyle. Subjects of other chapters are George Eliot and Thomas Hardy. The period illustrations are well-chosen, and the author includes a fine bibliographic essay on both literary and factual sources.

561. Sampson, Amelia S. *Detective Fiction from Latin America.* Rutherford, NJ: Fairleigh Dickinson U.P., 1990. 218p. Illus., bibl., index.

Not examined. Per the subject headings, it is a general history of 19th and 20th century Latin American detective fiction.

4 COLLECTED ESSAYS AND REVIEWS

562. Tuska, Jon. *A Variable Harvest: Essays and Reviews of Film and Literature.* Jefferson, NC: McFarland, 1990. xi, 371p. Illus., index.

Most of the revised essays collected here are on western fiction and film, but two directly concern detective fiction: "Rex Stout and the

Detective Story," which appears in an earlier version in the author's *The Detective in Film* (see WAM #59), and "It's Murder, My Sweet," a 1979 roundup review article from *The West Coast Review of Books*. The latter article celebrates Dorothy B. Hughes's fiction but finds fault with her Erle Stanley Gardner biography (see WAM #168). The discussion of Gardner's novels makes some good points about his strengths and weaknesses. In typically provocative style, Tuska considers two 1976 essay collections, disliking *The Mystery Story* (see WAM 63) but appreciating *Dimensions of Detective Fiction* (see WAM #72). Along the way he denigrates John Ball and *The Armchair Detective* and confuses Bouchercon with the UC San Diego Mystery Library series. Of related interest are a piece on serial director Spencer Gordon Bennet, one of whose projects was *The House Without a Key* (1926), not, he insisted, a Charlie Chan movie, and an interview with director Dick Richards that includes discussion of his 1975 film of *Farewell, My Lovely*.

6 WORKS ON INDIVIDUAL AUTHORS

CHRISTIE, Agatha

563. Shaw, Marion, and Sabine Vanacker. *Reflecting on Miss Marple*. (Heroines? series) London and New York: Routledge, 1991. xiii, 111p. Bibl.

An opening note to this intelligent and well-written study states, "Agatha Christie Ltd. expressly forbids the use of any material in a publication that would reveal the identities of the murderers in the Christie novels and, furthermore, makes it quite clear that such identification would invite legal action on their part" (page vi). Thus, the authors, who quote rather extensively from Christie's texts, dutifully tiptoe around in their *Roger Ackroyd* discussion.

Following a biographical chronology are chapters putting Christie in context with Golden Age detective fiction, characterizing Miss Marple (including a comparison to Patricia Wentworth's slightly earlier Miss Silver, most unfavorably to the latter), and describing her detective methods, with refreshing appreciation of Christie's subtle brand of feminism. The final chapter, "Miss Marple's Afterlife," discusses her depiction on stage and screen (up on Joan Hickson, down on Margaret Rutherford), finding the BBC TV versions in some respects more effective than the novels! In one of the book's best features, the authors discuss several latter-day women mystery writers in relation to the Christie tradition, among them P.D. James, Antonia Fraser, Amanda Cross, Valerie Miner, Joan Smith, Barbara Wilson, Eve Zaremba, Mary Wings, and Ellen Dearon, the latter the author of a short story casting Gertrude Stein and Alice B. Toklas in the Holmes/Watson roles. A bibliography of mentioned novels by these writers is included, along with a secondary bibliography.

Shaw and Vanacker get plenty of content into a few pages, and it's good to see Christie and Marple getting credit from contemporary feminists.

Quibbles: the authors describe Poirot, Wimsey, and Campion as "effeminate" (page 30)—Poirot, maybe, but not the other two. And is it true that only Sherlock Holmes, among fictional detectives, is more famous than Miss Marple (page 89)? What about Maigret or Perry Mason or, for that matter, Poirot?

7 ANTHOLOGIES

564. **Breen, Jon L., and John Ball, eds.** *Murder California Style: A Collection of Short Stories by the Southern California Chapter of Mystery Writers of America.* New York: St. Martin's, 1987. x, 292p.

It's either incredible modesty or (more likely) fallible memory that caused me to forget this anthology's sterling qualities until it was almost too late. The biographical notes are substantial, and some of the contributors (Elizabeth McCoy, Maxine O'Callaghan, John Stevenson, Nan Hamilton, Raymond Obstfeld, Helene Juarez Phipps, Harry Prince, Lois DuLac, R.R. Irvine, Gary Brandner) are relatively little written about in other sources. Stevenson, chapter VP at the time the anthology was compiled, provides a brief introduction.

565. **Haining, Peter, ed.** *Murder on the Menu: Cordon Bleu Stories of Crime and Mystery.* London: Souvenir, 1991. New York: Carroll & Graf, 1992. 415p.

This unoriginally-titled but nonetheless welcome collection of culinary crime stories has an entertaining three-page introduction and substantial story notes on the authors and their subjects. The volume shares something in common with Raymond T. Bond's *Handbook for Poisoners* (see #375), though not all the stories deal with poisoning. Bookending the collection are the two most famous criminous food tales, Stanley Ellin's "The Specialty of the House" and Roald Dahl's "Lamb to the Slaughter," with most of the intervening entries far less familiar. Contributors range from expected crime specialists like Simenon, Stout, and Rendell to general literary figures like Alphonse Daudet, Alexander Pushkin, L.P. Hartley, and Washington Irving.

INDEX

Index references are to entry numbers. The index includes authors, titles, and series in the headings plus subject and author-title references in the annotations. References to authors, titles of entries, and other names appearing in the headings, as well as authors who are subjects of entire titles in Part VI, have been italicized and appear first.

Generally, the following have been omitted: most non-genre-related names, references to misprints and other errors or omissions, cross-references to other works listed in *What About Murder?*, names of newspapers, chapter titles, and references to a character name merely as a means of identifying the author. Cross references to other works that are not *WAM* entries have usually been included. References to mystery organizations and awards, periodical titles, and well-known essay titles have been included. Book, film, play, and television series titles appear in all capitals; story, essay, and individual episode titles appear in quotes. For indexing purposes, no differentiation has been made between actual persons and fictional characters. Where authors of reviews or bibliographies have been quoted on unexamined titles, their names appear in the index followed by (quoted).

I

J

ABOUT THE AUTHOR

JON L. BREEN (B.A., Pepperdine University; M.L.S., University of Southern California) is the author of six mystery novels, most recently *Hot Air* (Simon and Schuster, 1991), and over fifty short stories in various publications. Two of his previous Scarecrow Press volumes, the original *What About Murder?* (1981) and *Novel Verdicts: A Guide to Courtroom Fiction* (1984), won Edgar Allan Poe Awards from the Mystery Writers of America, while *Synod of Sleuths: Essays on Judeo-Christian Detective Fiction* (1991), coedited with Martin H. Greenberg, won an Anthony Award from the Bouchercon (Anthony Boucher Memorial Mystery Convention). Breen contributes "The Jury Box" book review column to *Ellery Queen's Mystery Magazine*. He is Professor/Librarian at Rio Hondo College, Whittier, California.